Three Eyes for the Journey

To Dr. Cone

Thanks so much for providing
a context for me to claim my
voice, passion, and heritage

Ancestral Blessings,

Dianne 5/24/06

Three Eyes for the Journey

African Dimensions of the Jamaican Religious Experience

DIANNE M. STEWART

OXFORD

UNIVERSITY PRESS

2005

OXFORD
UNIVERSITY PRESS

Oxford University Press, Inc., publishes works that further
Oxford University's objective of excellence
in research, scholarship, and education.

Oxford   New York
Auckland   Cape Town   Dar es Salaam   Hong Kong   Karachi
Kuala Lumpur   Madrid   Melbourne   Mexico City   Nairobi
New Delhi   Shanghai   Taipei   Toronto

With offices in
Argentina   Austria   Brazil   Chile   Czech Republic   France   Greece
Guatemala   Hungary   Italy   Japan   Poland   Portugal   Singapore
South Korea   Switzerland   Thailand   Turkey   Ukraine   Vietnam

Published by Oxford University Press, Inc.
198 Madison Avenue, New York, New York 10016
www.oup.com

Oxford is a registered trademark of Oxford University Press

Library of Congress Cataloging-in-Publication Data
Stewart, Dianne M.
Three eyes for the journey: African dimensions of the Jamaican
religious experience / Dianne M. Stewart.
      p.   cm.
Includes bibliographical references and index.
ISBN-13 978-0-19-515415-3; 978-0-19-517557-8 (pbk.)
ISBN 0-19-515415-0; 0-19-517557-3 (pbk.)
1. Afro-Caribbean cults—Jamaican.   2. Jamaica—Religion.
3. Womanist theology.   I. Title.
BL2566.J25 S574 2004
299.6'897292—dc22   2003025902

9 8 7 6 5 4 3 2 1

Printed in the United States of America
on acid-free paper

the coconut has three eyes
it sees you
before you
see it

To my mother, Ruby Burrowes Stewart, and my father, Roydel Alandro Stewart: You transmitted humanity to me, and for your vision, sacrifice, and protection I honor you always.

Preface

In African diasporic religious traditions, persons with extraordinary spiritual talents—gifts of perceiving the realm of the invisible, reading undisclosed phenomena (past, present, and future), communicating with spirits, and negotiating mystical power—are often referred to as "seers" possessing more than two eyes. The third eye, in ancient Egyptian and Eastern religions, represents the spiritual eye, connecting the mundane with the transcendent and the individual with mystical experience. In the African diaspora, seers have also been dubbed "four-eyed" or "two-headed men and women, believed to have two anterior and two posterior eyes or a pair of eyes in each head. For centuries, these gifted women and men have gone unnoticed and unrecorded in the annals of academia as carriers of valid knowledge and civilization. Monographs and publications have appeared, but the knowledge such seers inherit and transmit is customarily characterized as folk culture and folk religion—labels that convey considerable assumptions of inferiority, pedestrian unsophistication, and exotic but nonetheless primitive superstition.

In the hills of the Jamaican parish of St. Thomas, the descendants of BaKongo laborers shared with me the uses of the coconut in their tradition, including the relevancy of its three eyes for permitting contact with mystical power and the spirits of the departed. The coconut, which is known worldwide for its uses in human consumption, is simultaneously a vehicle for the transportation of messages and provides just one of many paths to the Divine Community. Given the hard blows African culture received as the result of slavery and colonialism, it is significant that at the close of the twentieth century (1995–1996), when I carried out my research among African practitioners in Jamaica, they were still invested in the responsibilities associated with the preservation of their heritage and were actively engaged in the processes of transmitting to posterity a culture and spiritual outlook that imbued human existence with meaning and gave purpose to a people's collective consciousness. In spite of exile, enslavement, and the psychosocial disorientation they cause, oppressed Blacks in contemporary Jamaica are still able to "journey" to Africa for empowering and sustaining resources to resist annihilation.

My roots are Jamaican. My parents are from parishes that boast the Maroon territory of Accompong (St. Elizabeth) and the "navelstrings" of Marcus Garvey and Robert "Bob" Nesta Marley (St. Ann). These metonyms of Africa's indelible imprint on Jamaica's collective memory are only some of the many traditions expressing the dynamism of Africa in the Jamaican and, for that matter, the Caribbean experience. The persistence of the African dynamic in Jamaican culture is a testament to centuries-long Black struggles for emancipation from European dominance.

After spending most of my life on the North American continent, in the urban northeastern region of the United States, where many Caribbean immigrants have forged new communities away from the islands they call home, I have come to appreciate the value of my passages through place, race, and class from Jamaica to America and from urban working-class Black communities to White middle- and upper-class academic environments. These migrations across multiple boundaries[1] stimulate internal reflection upon the communities indigenous to each location and the role each has played in shaping my theological consciousness and priorities as a woman of African-Caribbean descent (my indigenous heritage and primary culture) who bears the influence of an equally compelling cultural ethos of urban African North America (my secondary yet pronounced culture).

Having grown up in the 1970s and 1980s, I was a recipient of the "gains" of the civil rights movement—a product of integrated schools and busing, when integration meant 99 percent White and 1 percent Black. I was bused out of my urban (inner city) community to attend White schools between the ages of five and eighteen. In the small suburban Catholic primary school I attended, I encountered a subtle yet fierce racism, provoking within me a self-conscious defense of my humanity as a person of African descent. Had I attended one of the Black public schools in my local community, racism and anti-African attitudes would not have been as pronounced, and I would not have been intentional about developing positive feelings about Africa.

I used Black culture to defend the beauty, dignity, and ingenuity of being human via Africa, Jamaica, and North America. With childhood intelligence I chose to validate myself by clinging to the things that my peers and teachers could not understand about me. Since they were unfamiliar with my hybrid Caribbean and African-American culture, they could not define or signify me from an informed or authentic position; they could not degrade what they did not know or understand. Thus, I was intentional about wearing cornrows with pretty beads so that the Whites would marvel at the tiny braids woven into checkerboards on one day and a beehive on the next. The beautiful assortment of hairstyles defied their comprehension. They could only smile and pass compliments. I was Other to them and somehow untouchable. This was a decent compromise for me at the time. At recess, I played double Dutch with the two other Black girls in my class; we sang polyrhythmic songs to complex patterns of hand clapping and foot stomping, while White girls stood in amazement and begged us to teach them how to jump and move with the type of ancestral rhythms our bodies remembered.

These were the small measures I took to sustain myself in that hostile environment. I used culture instead of religion to affirm and defend my humanity because I was taught that I shared the same religion with the Whites who scorned me daily. No one ever told me that my religion was different—that the White Christian experience and the Black Christian experience were rooted in contradictory ideas about God and humanity.

It was not until I read the works of James Cone as an undergraduate student that I was able to locate my questions about God and humanity within the larger tradition of Black religion. Before I read Cone's *Black Theology and Black Power* and *A Black Theology of Liberation*, I did not know that Black people actually had a distinct Black theology of liberation that reflected our historical collective social experience of suffering, persecution, exile, and dislocation. I had always been taught that all Christians, regardless of color, ethnicity, or social location, adhere to a common orthodoxy as institutionalized within particular denominational traditions.

The validation that I felt after reading James Cone's works empowered me to pursue an even more steadfast search within Black Christianity for answers to my questions about God and humanity, but a lot of damage had already been done. In the furthest reaches of my spirit, I realized that Cone's books could not erase the ubiquitous *Whiteness* of Jesus Christ, which was deeply embedded in my consciousness and subconsciousness. My intellect was loyal to the Black Christ but nothing in my social reality, including my Black church community, reinforced Cone's Black Christ proclamation. I *knew* the Black Christ was the true Christ, but I did not *believe* it.

Not long after I read about the Black Christ, I was introduced to the writings of nineteenth- and twentieth-century Black nationalists and Pan-Africanists and discovered that anti-Blackness and anti-Africanness, while related, are not identical. During the nineteenth century, African Methodist Episcopalian bishop Daniel Alexander Payne was not anti-Black but anti-African (Eurocentric) when he expressed grave concern about the "heathen" practices of newly emancipated Africans in the nineteenth-century Black church.[2] In the same vein, Alexander Crummell was indisputably pro-Black but anti-African (Eurocentric) when he set out to "Christianize" and "civilize" African populations in Liberia. His disdain for their indigenous languages, which he believed were inferior to the "Anglo-Saxon tongue," indicates the extent to which he embraced anti-African beliefs and attitudes.[3] Another celebrated Pan-Africanist, Martin Delany, summarized nineteenth-century Black bourgeois anti-Africanness well with the proclamation "Africa for the African race and black men to rule them."[4]

Much of the twentieth-century Afrocentric and Black nationalist literature has attempted to address anti-Africanness, and thus it stimulated my growing interest in African religions and cultures. Although in retrospect I believe it is virtually impossible for outsiders to understand the significance of African religiosity without witnessing it in indigenous contexts, my intellectual exploration of classical African religions helped me to understand my own Caribbean religious heritage in ways that both my White *and* Black Christs could not.

The theological and sociopolitical discourses in the Black intellectual tradition have contributed significantly to my particular interdisciplinary concentration on the African heritage in African diasporic religions. African-centered postcolonial thought has been indispensable to my scholarly formation because it critically scrutinizes the Eurocentric cultural bias through its deconstruction of colonialist legacies of anti-Africanness and Afrophobia. Black theology is invaluable to my theological work because its insistence on liberation hermeneutics allows it to identify the hegemonic assumptions in White theology and White religion.

Because my introduction to Black nationalist and Afrocentric thought occurred through male authors from the United States, I am keenly aware of the sexist and Eurocentric ideologies implicit in the reigning androcentric constructions of Black nationalism. Black feminist and womanist scholars have provided me with the analytical frameworks to critique sexism and androcentrism in the Black intellectual tradition and within the Christian tradition, where Blackness and femaleness are often interpreted as obstacles to authentic communion with God. Alice Walker's womanist return to the culture, daily habits, and experiences of her mother and other well-known and anonymous Black foremothers has encouraged many womanist theologians to follow suit in our fashioning of an intellectual tradition in religious studies. My mother, the source of my religious grounding and trust in the power of the Divine, was never orthodox enough to promote my captivity to racist, anti-African, and sexist Eurocentric doctrines about God, humanity, and the religious life. She was more theocentric and pneumatocentric than christocentric, and she never once told me that I was sinful or that I needed to repent for anything. Nor did she remotely imply that my Blackness and femaleness were shameful things from which I needed redemption.

My mother valued her mother's spiritual intelligence and thus trained me to accept knowledge acquired through psychic and spiritual experiences as a credible epistemological source. My mother believes that psychic powers are evinced through dreams and intuition in part because her own intuitive sense is potent and, when coupled with her rational powers, it engenders a certain sensibility within that enables her to think and act with confidence. She always tried to help me cultivate my own intuition and often spoke—and continues to speak—of "seeing" and "feeling" things in her spirit.

The Ancestors are important to my mother insofar as she recognizes her deceased parents as disembodied elders with vital links to their descendants. Through a type of informal veneration and familial narratives, she kept the memory of her father (who died when I was two) and her mother alive although we emigrated to the United States, hundreds of miles away from Jamaica, where my grandmother lived until she died in 1993. I felt my destiny tied to their strivings here in the visible space of the living and in the invisible domain of the Ancestors, because of my mother's steady devotion to their legacies as outstanding parents and exemplary community leaders.

My mother's spirituality and my migratory experiences of crossing the boundaries of place, race, and class also inspired me to learn about the continental African religious traditions that comprise the foundation for a range of African-derived religions in the Caribbean and the Americas. Indeed, my mother's religiosity and cultural heritage are the most significant factors influencing my intellectual study of African-derived religions in the diaspora.

In my studies, I discovered profound cosmologies and an alternative anthropology and epistemology in the religions of African practitioners in the diaspora which yield indispensable sources for liberation theological discourse. For example, the case of Jamaica presents a Eurocentric metanarrative that suppresses the authentic struggles of Africans to free themselves from slavery, colonialism, and their toxic and seemingly permanent implications. Thus, when we dig deeply into the dynamics of what has been a perilous and antagonistic encounter between Europeans and Africans in the modern period, we approach an African counternarrative from which to tease out what womanist theologian Kelly Brown Douglas calls "a spirituality of resistance"[5] that is coherent with the imperatives of the liberation theological tradition.

My aim in writing this text is to uncover the nuances in the processes of religious formation among Africans in Jamaica by examining the dialectical nature of their personal and social existence, namely, their wrestlings with oppression and liberation in both colonial and postcolonial social milieux. Thus, I explore the encounter between African religious traditions and European missionary Christianity in eighteenth- and nineteenth-century Jamaica and its impact upon the practice of religion in twentieth-century Jamaica. My underlying thesis argues for a new paradigm in Caribbean theology that transcends the normative parameters for traditional theological reflection. Using Jamaica as an important local context for Caribbean theological construction, this text moves beyond exclusive studies of Christianity to analyze the broader Black religious experience, from the early manifestations of Obeah and Myal during the eighteenth century to Rastafari in the twentieth century. Paying particular attention to patterns of repression, censorship, resistance, and liberation in the African-Jamaican religious experience, this volume also rethinks the standard theoretical categories for describing the nature and function of African-derived religions in Jamaica.

To date, studies on the African religious traditions of the Caribbean and the Americas have been conducted primarily under the influence of disciplines such as anthropology, sociology, and history. Across these and other related disciplines, the works of scholars such as Leonard Barrett, Michel Laguerre, George Brandon, Monica Schuler, and others bear witness to a legacy of documentation on the role of African-derived religions in the formation of Black culture and Black consciousness.[6] One of the chief interpretive strategies in African-American and Caribbean studies has been to interrogate the extant sources on the African religious heritage in the shadow of the polemic between sociologist E. Franklin Frazier and anthropologist Melville Herskovits.[7] Herskovits attempted to prove that, in spite of the Middle Passage and slavery, diasporic Africans maintained direct ethnic cultural linkages with their classical African backgrounds. Frazier strongly contested Herskovits's theory on the grounds that virtually all North American cultural residues of Africa were destroyed by the deplorable conditions to which Africans were subjected during the Middle Passage and slavery.

There is a general agreement among scholars in African-American and Caribbean studies that African religiocultural retentions are more potent and consistent throughout the Caribbean and parts of Central and South America than they are in North America. The legacies of Yoruba, Dahomean, Asante, Congolese, and other African religious traditions in places like Cuba, Haiti, Jamaica, Brazil, and Suriname offer conspicuous evidence of linkages between Africa and the African diaspora. Nevertheless, Caribbean theologians have largely neglected to explore African-based religious traditions as sources for theological reflection.

The development of Caribbean theology follows the theological reformation inaugurated in the 1970s by Black liberation theologians. Through the methods and criteria of Black theology, pioneer Black theologian James Cone exposed the dominant European and Euro-American bias in Western academic theology, which had long been presented as veritable objective commentary on universal human experience. Using African-American history, culture, social context, and religious experience as sources for theological construction, Black liberation theologians have introduced new standards into the discipline of academic theology, arguing that the authentic message of Black faith is the sociopolitical liberation of the poor and oppressed in history.

Although Cone and other Black theologians identified the starting point of reference for Black liberation theology as the slave period, their theological reflections have distinguished Christianity as the generative tradition of liberative[8] theological ideas and praxes in African-American religious history. Because Black North American religious traditions demonstrating explicit connections to classical African cultures appear to be limited to regions such as Louisiana (Vodun or "Voodoo") and the Sea Islands, they have not been explored as sources for Black theological construction.

Since the 1980s, Caribbean theologians have developed a similar methodological pattern of arguing for the liberative potential in Caribbean Christian traditions while ignoring the liberation motif of the African religious traditions in Caribbean history and culture. In the following chapters, I use historical data to critique this methodological tendency in Black and Caribbean theologies as anachronistic and erroneous, thereby challenging the undimensional emphasis upon Christianity in Black liberation theology in general and in Caribbean theology in particular. I specifically argue that, prior to any extensive exposure to the Christian faith, enslaved Africans in Jamaica organized both personal and social acts of resistance against slavery and White supremacy within the structures of African-derived religions.

In addition to exploring what the historical evidence tells us about religious formation among African Jamaicans, this volume will provide a theological consideration of Christian attitudes toward African religious and cultural traditions. In so doing, I will demonstrate that there is a relationship between the marginalization of African-derived religious traditions in Caribbean academic theology and the censoring of those traditions in popular culture. While Black and Caribbean theologians have identified the slave era as the native context for liberationist ideas and praxes in Black religion, the slave period is also the context for the propagation of popular anti-African cultural beliefs and attitudes in the Caribbean. More specifically, the confrontation between African-derived religions and European missionary Christianity across the Caribbean is one of the most fertile historical moments for investigating how and why African religious traditions were officially criminalized and continue to be anathematized as morally corrupt and uncivilized.

Through such a study of a people's religious journey, one determines indigenous markers of comprehensive wellness in human experience and the place of religiosity in sustaining wellness and a hospitable environment for the transmission of ancestral wisdom. Indeed each of the world's religions has its particular "sacraments," which are ritually performed toward the end of wellness: reconciliation, equilibrium, commemoration, redemption, transcendence, prosperity, and transformation. Humans do not only have religion in common but common features can be determined across the world's religious traditions despite classifications such as primitive, historical, revealed or natural, which erroneously suggest ethical and developmental disparities among the world's religions.

The sacraments of divination, libation, incantation, offering, visitation, and communion are common features of African and African-derived religions. They are simultaneously revelation, prayer, incarnation, transformation, blessing, and thanksgiving. Each sacrament is administered for the purpose of establishing and sustaining conditions conducive for human thriving and the wellness of community and of all creation. At a fundamental and pragmatic level, individuals engage in these sacraments to address problems and crises that impede wellness and abundant life. Divination reveals the source(s) of affliction and misfortune in a person's life through a systematic process of deciphering coded knowledge so that prescriptions for enhancing wellness can be deduced. Libation gives honor to and summons the company and assistance of the Divine Community (divinities, spirits, and Ancestors). Incantations are utterances that activate the powers within creation toward the end of producing the desired outcome. Offerings are the sacrifices that the person makes (personal, substitutive, and symbolic) to restate her prayers and wishes and to effectively translate them to the Divine Community, which works to bring the desired outcome to fruition. Visitations are communications from the Divine Community to the human community through possession trance and mediumship. During visitations, the divinities, Ancestors, and spirits confirm, correct, or establish ethical standards, ritual obligations, and remedies against disease and oppressive forces. Finally, communion is the collective thanksgiving for the blessings brought about by the Divine Community's response to human agency, often concretized by the sharing of a communal meal prepared from the edible items ritually offered to the Divine Community. These sacraments are components of ritual processes that yield answers to human dilemmas.

I have elected to characterize each chapter thematically by invoking the sacramental meaning of these six ritual practices that together comprise the skeletal frame of African spirituality, as expressed in so many diasporic traditions. I do this for two reasons: first, to suggest the need for indigenous sacraments and ritual processes in African diasporic attempts to commemorate and preserve multiple African heritages and, second, to reinforce the potency of ritual as a tangible gateway to miraculous transformations from disease and oppression to wellness and liberation. The metaphoric meanings and the progression from diagnosis of a dilemma to the celebration of release from a dilemma will become more transparent as the reader moves through the chapters from the introduction to the conclusion.

Finally, I must say something about hermeneutics and the study of Black religion in the African diaspora. The religiosity of Blacks in the African diaspora suggests a typology of three major trajectories[9] that have influenced and cross-fertilized each other over the past five centuries of Black presence in the Caribbean and the Americas: (1) the persistence of African-derived religions and religious practices, inclusive of traditions such as Vodun, Yoruba/Orisha, Kumina, Candomblé, Obeah, Hoodoo, and Conjure; (2) the widespread Christianization of Black communities via independent Black Christian denominations (Baptist, Methodist, and Pentecostal) as well as Black Christian membership in the denominations established by White missionaries and evangelists (Wesleyan, Presbyterian, Catholic, and so on); and (3) Black nationalist approaches to religious formation, especially post-Christian religious movements such as the Nation of Islam, Rastafari, Black Judaism, and African-derived religious communities like Oyotunji Village.

Each of these trajectories has unfolded within the shadow of hegemonic Eurocentric Christian institutions, one of the results being the formation of coded Black religious institutions with ambiguous identities and practices yielding a surplus of seemingly contradictory complex meanings in their ritual uses of material from both African-based and Euro-Christian traditions. In Jamaica, these religious institutions have appeared as Native Baptist, Revival (Pocomania), and Zion. The latter two have become merged within various social contexts in contemporary Jamaica and will commonly be referenced as one tradition (Revival Zion) in this text.

What is the most fitting religious classification for these institutions? In both social scientific and theological scholarship, they are conventionally termed unorthodox Christian traditions or Afro-Christian traditions, titles similar to that used to describe the phenomenon of colonial and postcolonial African Christian religious movements—"African independent churches"—on the African continent. With regard to Jamaica, I am less inclined to endorse this classification, which privileges Christianity as the definitive religious identity of Native Baptist and Revival Zion devotees, because it belies the creative power of the African spirituality of resistance among the oppressed Jamaicans who forged the Native Baptist and Revival Zion traditions. These institutions were established in the Afrophobic context of Euro-Christian dominance and repression of African religiosity. If we ignore this struggle against the extermination of culture, heritage, and spirituality, we trivialize and negate the significance of the liberation praxis among Blacks in Jamaica. The very fact that these institutions are operative today is evidence that their nineteenth-century devotees were successful in thwarting European Christianity and its toxic consequences for people of African descent within their communal religious formation. Religiocultural censoring of African practices and traditions is the most important factor in interpreting these and other African-derived traditions in the Caribbean and the Americas. Thus I hold firmly to an African-centered interpretation of these institutions and admit my reluctance to concede this interpretation to those opting to expand the boundaries for identifying varying expressions of Christianity in the Black Jamaican context.

I maintain that, with little exception, Black Christianity in Jamaica is Eurocentric Christianity—the acceptance and preservation of Euro-missionary Christianity by Black converts who joined the Anglican, Methodist, Presbyterian, Catholic, and in some cases Baptist denominations as well as others established by European and White American missionaries. Black Christianity is also represented by Blacks who have joined African-American (Eurocentric in missiology, piety, structure, and doctrine) Christian denominations established in Jamaica by missionaries from the African Methodist Episcopal church and other similar, independent Black church traditions in the United States. The Native Baptist and Revival Zion traditions constitute a wholly different phenomenon in the Jamaican experience, which has been as significant as the other African-derived traditions (Obeah, Myal, and Kumina) in the chain of remembering and linking African traditions from the past to the struggle for liberation.

In the end, religious experience is what truly matters, not the labels we assign to particular modes of religious expression. Perhaps this is the ultimate lesson we should learn from complex and coded religions like the Native Baptist and Revival Zion traditions. However, we are far from the end of the abhorrent oppression that engulfs us and thus equally distant from the comprehensive liberation we seek for the African diaspora. In this regard, the politics of dehumanization and African cultural annihilation render the act of *naming* a powerful tool in our attempts to unearth the African ingredients of our people's spirituality of resistance and the theologies we discern from their energetic movements toward the wisdom of their Ancestors in their collective endeavor to transmit humanity[10] (as opposed to inhumanity) to posterity. My hope is that this text, which explicitly and sympathetically privileges the African counternarrative of religious presence in Jamaica, contributes in some small way to our understanding of Black religion in the African diaspora, to our rethinking of Black theology in the African diaspora, and to our appreciation of the spiritual intelligence of those foremothers and forefathers who, like Cuffy in Zora Neale Hurston's *Jonah's Gourd Vine,* hid the drum in their skins, under their skull bones, bequeathing to us imperishable resources for sustainable empowerment and life-enhancing transformation.

Acknowledgments

I am indebted to many persons who supported me during the writing of this book, in both the dissertation and postdissertation stages. I am grateful to Dr. Josiah Young, my undergraduate teacher and mentor who inspired me to pursue doctoral studies at Union Theological Seminary. I am also grateful to Dr. Harvey Sindima, Dr. Eleni Tedla, and the Reverend Charles Rice who, along with Dr. Young, encouraged me to pursue my interest in African religions and their legacies in the Caribbean and the Americas.

I am most grateful to the members of my dissertation committee, James Cone, Delores Williams, Christopher Morse, Chung Hyun Kyung, and Noel Erskine, for their critical readings of the dissertation and for mentoring me throughout my period of doctoral work at Union. I acknowledge with deep gratitude the late Dr. James Washington for introducing me to some of the most significant historical documents pertaining to the research for this book and for his support in all of my academic endeavors at Union. Dr. Cheryl Townsend Gilkes also read the manuscript in its entirety in earlier stages and has been a continual source of support over the years.

The following persons provided indispensable support for this project, especially during the dissertation phase: John Spencer, Joy Bostic, Pauline Muchina, Elizabeth During, Betty Bolden, Sylvester Johnson, Carla Beckford, David Asomaning, Adam Clark, Raphael Warnock, Maelinda Turner, and Mark Kellar. I thank them for helping me to realize my dreams. I am especially indebted to Mxolisi Mavi, Pulane Nathane, and Thamsanqa Mavi for opening their home to me and providing a supportive environment where I could think and write freely during the first phase of this project.

Major grants from the Fund for Theological Education, the

United Methodist Women of Color Doctoral Fellowship Program, and the Roothbert Fund subsidized my international research and education while I was a student at Union.

It has been said that every woman needs a room of her own, and I must add—and a table to write on. I am deeply indebted to Stephanie Sears-Louder, who made from scratch the table upon which I hammered out the final revisions for this book. Rondul Sears-Louder also provided constant support during my period of settlement in a new city and a new home. My adopted brother, Timothy Parker; my cousins twice over, Horace, Lance, and Gary Stewart; my beloved sister-cousins, Camile Byfield, Karlene Spence, and Alisa Stewart; and brother-cousins, Adrian and Jason Barret, all reminded me of the value of community and extended family bonds throughout the entire process.

Encouraging words and inspiring conversations on Black religious pluralism and the African heritage with Burton Sankeralli and with graduate students at Emory University especially reinforced my commitment to this project. Claudette Anderson's willingness to engage in exchanges about African Jamaican religious traditions from her informed location within the Jamaican cultural landscape and Thabiti (John) Willis's meticulous archival research skills were invaluable to me. LeRhonda Manigault worked tirelessly on preparing the final draft of the bibliography while Chika Okeke pushed my thinking toward deeper innovation. I am also grateful to Ndeye Adama Samba for the administrative assistance she provided over the past two years, and to Elana Jefferson for carrying the load in compiling materials and for working diligently with me to address other technical and administrative matters pertaining to the book. Emory librarians; Dr. Douglas Gragg, Head of Public Services at Pitts Theology Library; and Marie Hansen at the Robert W. Woodruff Library were instrumental in assisting me with rare documents and other pertinent research questions related to this book.

Several of my colleagues and friends in the academy have expressed enduring confidence in my scholarship, especially Shahzad Bashir, Randolph Potts, Carol Conoway, Ambroise Kom, Rhonda Brown, and Tracy Rone. My priceless conversations with a number of scholars influenced my writing of this book. Dr. Leonard Barrett, playmate to my grandmother, inspired me to focus on Jamaican religious experience and to remain committed to theological questions in researching African-derived religions in Jamaica. Drs. Fu Kiau Bunseki and Kalala Ngalamulume especially helped me to clarify and confirm my thinking about Kongo antecedents of the African-Jamaican religious complex. Dr. Wande Abimbola and his son Dr. Kola Abimbola have been wonderful priests and teachers in my life. Our dialogues on Yoruba religion and philosophy have changed the way I think about the study of African religions. I am fortunate to be in their circle of communication as the exchanges have encouraged me and enhanced my thinking about Africa and the African diaspora. Tracey Hucks was with me from the very beginning. We share the same narrative and we leave our offerings at the same crossroads.

Nuff love to the many Jamaican keepers of the culture who shared resources, insights, and information which contributed to this project. The late

Imogene Kennedy (Miss Queenie), Miss Bernice Henry, and countless others have kept the Kumina culture alive by "taking many journeys in the African world." Homer Lobban, Hazel Ramsay at the African-Caribbean Institute of Jamaica, and Joyce Wallen at Jamaica Library Services extended themselves to me in the most invaluable ways during the research phase of this project. I extend the most heartfelt appreciation to my aunt Janet Smith and uncle Ernie Smith, who nurtured and supported me in so many ways while I conducted research in Jamaica. I also thank my uncle Harold Stewart for lending tremendous support to me during my stay in Jamaica. I could not have completed the first phase of this project without the assistance and guidance of my family in Jamaica. I acknowledge with gratitude the Reverend Anthony Trufant, pastor of Emmanuel Baptist Church in Brooklyn, New York, who subsidized my related research in Cuba in 1993.

Words cannot express the love and thanksgiving I feel for my siblings, Richild Stewart, Rudolph Stewart, Adrian Stewart, and Roydel Stewart, Jr., for their understanding, confidence, undying support, and encouragement. I am equally thankful for the unwavering support and encouragement that my advisor, James Cone, has shown me over the years. He has been a model of excellence, passion, and compassion as a teacher, scholar, and mentor. I feel privileged to have worked so closely with him as I have only come to treasure and embrace more enthusiastically the vocation to which I have committed myself.

I also treasure Ismaila Ngom for the many gifts he brought to this book and for the sanctuary offered through his presence in my life. *Jock a n'jaa-al; in wey ngueed mangue.*

My parents, Ruby Burrowes Stewart and Roydel Alandro Stewart, taught me the value of critical thinking and academic achievement. They believe in me and my dreams. I owe all that I have become to them.

Contents

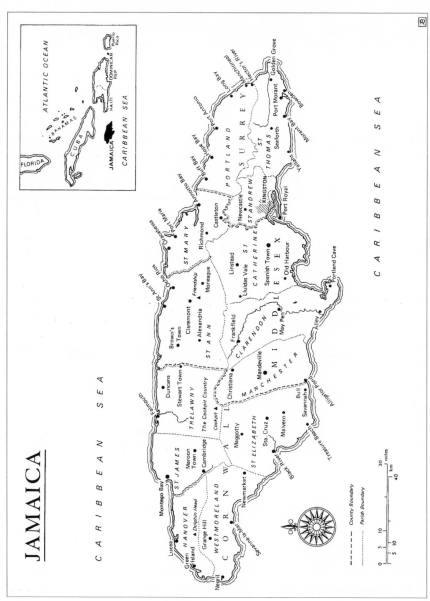

JAMAICA

From *Jamaica*, by George Hunt (B. T. Batsford, 1976). Reprinted by permission of Chrysalis Book Group.

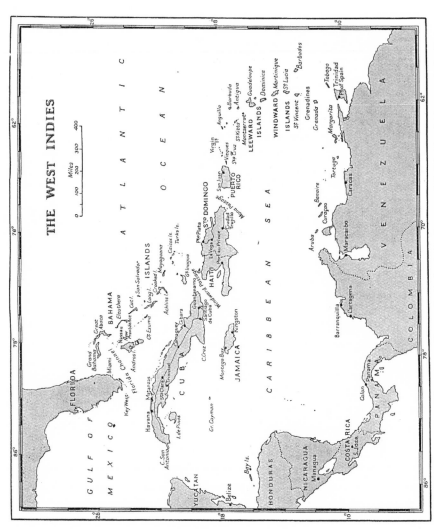

THE WEST INDIES

From A Short History of the West Indies, 2nd ed., by J. H. Parry and P. M. Sherlock, copyright ©
1968 by Beford/St. Martin's. Reprinted by permission of Beford/St. Martin's.

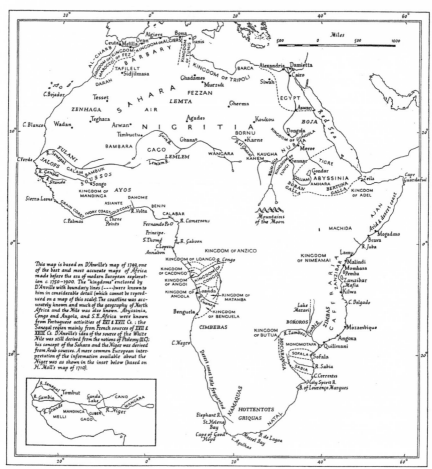

Africa as Known to Europeans in the Mid-Eighteenth Century. From *An Atlas of African History*, by J. D. Fage (E. Arnold, 1958). Reproduced by permission of Hodder Arnold.

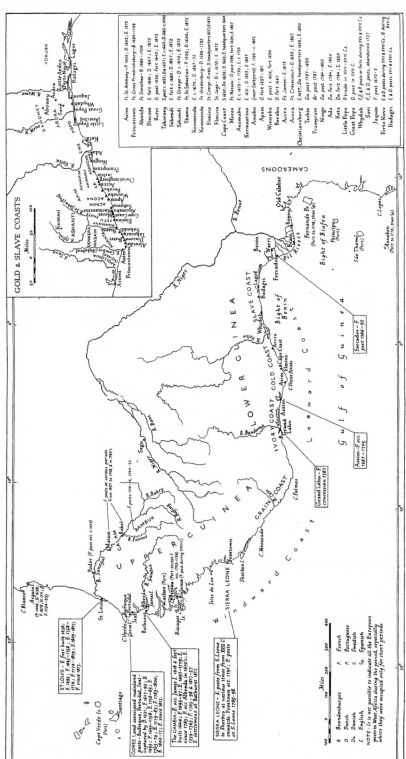

Europeans in West Africa, Seventeenth to Eighteenth Centuries. From *An Atlas of African History*, by J. D. Fage (E. Arnold, 1958). Reproduced by permission of Hodder Arnold.

Three Eyes for the Journey

Divination

Introduction

In the chapters that follow, I seek to address multiple issues regarding the discipline of theology as it relates to the religions of Africans[1] in the Caribbean island of Jamaica. As a discipline, theology has primarily been the property of the Western Christian tradition, a discourse that seeks to standardize the Christian faith by explaining its orthodox beliefs and practices and by proclaiming its significance for humankind. For the past 1,500 years, theology has distinguished itself as an elitist enterprise piloted by the formal reflections of clerics, monks, and scholars.

Disclosing the biases and prejudices of its exponents, Christian theology has also functioned as an agent of Western religiocultural, geopolitical, and socioeconomic dominance in the world. Simply put, when the Europeans came, they had the Bible and the Africans/Asians/Amerindians/Islanders had the land; now the Africans/Asians/Amerindians/Islanders have the Bible and the Europeans have the land.[2] While land possession ensures entitlement in terms of political sovereignty, as well as the resources and space for the development and expansion of civilizations, the Bible might provide those who adhere to its principles with sustaining spiritual power to survive land dispossession and colonization. Most important, the Bible does not offer the dispossessed and colonized direct access to the type of technological and military, socioeconomic and geopolitical power needed to resist, conquer, and punish the land takers.

There is an imperialistic trait in Christian theology, which is most audaciously portrayed in its missionary approach to Christian faith confession. In every period of Christian theological reflection, from the second-century literature of the apostolic fathers to the twentieth-century liberation and contextual approaches, theologians have—although to different degrees and, at times, endorsing contrasting meth-ods—embraced the missionary impulse of the Christian faith and its biblical foundations. This, I would surmise, is because, first, they actually believe that Jesus' death is universally redemptive, and, second, they hold this belief to be the sine qua non of Christian identity. Moreover, the confidence with which theologians proclaim this belief is bolstered by the repeated assertion that Je-sus' redemptive death distinguishes Christian faith and practice from all other religions. The uniqueness of the Christian passion-death-resurrection narrative becomes a justification for its validity as the supreme religious expression, that is, revelation.

In the minds of its orthodox exponents, Christian revelation is "true reli-gion,"[3] and its professed monotheism qualifies it as antithetical to the ancient African religious traditions that were transported to Jamaica, other parts of the Caribbean, and the Americas during the era of the slave trade and indentured servitude. Needless to say, the historic encounter between Western European missionary Christianity and African-derived religions in Jamaica was an ad-versarial one that led to the destabilization and underdevelopment of the latter. On the scale of global encounters between Western European and other relig-ions of the world, the pattern of the former's domination, censorship, and persecution of the latter is standard.

But to speak of a historic human-divine sacrifice as universally redemptive for human beings is to grant a place of authority to Christian anthropology, Christology, and eschatology. The idea that all human beings are in need of Christ's "redemption" is just that—an idea. Nevertheless, it is a potent one that has had far-reaching consequences for those dispossessed Africans/Asians/Amerindians/Islanders who now have the Bible. One such conse-quence has already been elaborated by the late African theologian Englebert Mveng. Mveng, a Camerounian scholar, wrote passionately about the demor-alizing impact of Western Christian culture on African peoples. In the follow-ing excerpt, he identifies the problem comprehensively as "anthropological poverty":

> First of all, the basic problem remains the foundations of Western
> anthropology, which would impose themselves upon the world. The
> concept of the human being that the West seeks to export to us is
> based on domination, power, death struggle, and so on—the tri-
> umph of death over life. There has never been a way to avoid an
> impasse. It is not easy to see how all this can be reconciled with the
> gospel. We hear of the church of the poor, and we are directed to the
> Beatitudes. But poverty is defined first of all in function of one's
> conception of the human being—and here we are back with anthro-
> pology again . . . for us Africans, the world's institutionalized poverty
> has other roots as well, and it is perhaps these other roots that are
> more serious, more important, and more relevant to the present mo-
> ment: slavery, colonialism, neocolonialism, racism, apartheid, and
> the universal derision that has always accompanied the "civilized"

world's discourse upon and encounter with Africa—and still accompanies it today. Strange, is it not, that in the immense literature that we have on the poor today, Africa is always looked down upon and derided? There is a type of poverty that I call, "anthropological poverty." It consists in despoiling human beings not only of what they have, but of everything that constitutes their being and essence—their identity, history, ethnic roots, language, culture, faith, creativity, dignity, pride, ambitions, right to speak . . . we could go on indefinitely.[4]

It is, as Mveng articulates, the manifestation of anthropological poverty in Jamaican religious experience that I attempt to expose and to which I respond in this work. I proceed with this task by engaging the norms, methodological insights, and hermeneutical principles of liberation theology, which argues that the Christian faith is a historically grounded witness to a Supreme Deity who opts preferentially for the poor, marginalized, and oppressed. But in so doing I immediately confront perplexing conceptual challenges and moral problems on several fronts. This is because my investigation of Jamaican religious experience is laden with the intentions and moral concerns with which the liberation theologians most passionately approach the study of religious experience. Yet, uncannily, this study is not particularly concerned with the relationship between oppressive (Western European and North American, male, heterosexist) Christians and oppressed (Third World, Third World diaspora, female, gay and lesbian) Christians. Unlike the liberation theologians, who, in the main, are committed to the truth of the gospel as good news for the oppressed and who seek to reorient the norms of Christian doctrine, faith, and practice toward a mission of sociopolitical justice-doing, this study, by the very nature of its inquiry as a Caribbean or African diasporic theology, indicts Western European Christianity and its Jamaican derivative. In this work, a "hermeneutics of suspicion"[5] is employed against all cultural manifestations of orthodox Christianity in Jamaica: Christianities are the oppressors and African-derived religions are the oppressed and anthropologically impoverished.

On another level, one might argue that the academic social location of this study is the "irruption within the irruption,"[6] for its main discourse is directed internally, toward African-Jamaican Christians and theologians. The Third World feminist, womanist, and *mujerista*/Latina theologians created this venue for internal conversation when they challenged their male counterparts to critique and respond to the oppressive factors of patriarchy and sexism in their culturally specific Christian traditions and theologies. The primary audience for this study, then, is Jamaican, other Caribbean, and Black theologians of North, Central, and South America as well as scholars of religion.

Since my starting viewpoint of Christianities is a pessimistic one—one that understands the imperialistic impulses within all forms of Christianity as uniform, omnipresent, and therefore a constitutive oppressive factor which is most vehemently expressed in Christianities' fixation upon "converting heathens" by any necessary means—I am faced with a conceptual problem in affiliating this study with the discipline of theology. If theology is, in essence, an apologetic discourse for the Christian faith, how is this work—which seeks to expose an intrinsic moral flaw in the essential propositions and practices of Christianities—an exercise of theological reflection?

Another obvious factor which complicates this problem is that theologians of the African diaspora do not consider African-derived religious traditions to be an appropriate point of departure for theological reflection.[7] To be fair, African North American and Caribbean theologians have repeatedly discussed the significance of the African religious heritage for Africans in the diaspora during the slave period—but mostly as it relates to Black and Caribbean Christianities. In this regard the historical theological projects of people like Gayraud Wilmore are more inclusive of the non-Christian manifestations of African diasporic religiosity than the systematic theological projects of people like James Cone, despite his emphasis on Malcolm X in one of his most celebrated texts.[8]

What is absent in these and other theological projects are developed reflections that leave the reader with a comprehensive presentation of African-derived religions as systems of thought, ritual, and social ethics. It is impossible to learn anything substantive about Vodun in Haiti and New Orleans; Yoruba in Cuba, Trinidad, New York, and Brazil; Kumina in Jamaica; and so on from the works of any theologian of the African diaspora, for their unsystematic reflections upon these traditions are abridged[9] and, at best, ancillary to their chief scholarly preoccupation, Christianity.

Indeed, calling attention to all of this only demonstrates that theologians of the African diaspora (Black, Caribbean, and Latin American men and women) concur with my initial point about theology as a discourse which explains, clarifies, and seeks to reinterpret the meaning of the Christian faith for Christians and potential Christians in every generation. This means, though, that Christian theology is not static in terms of its priorities, authoritative sources, norms, rhetorical strategies, hermeneutical principles, or methodological approaches as culturally specific experiences have accounted for the changing shifts in theological perspectives throughout the history of Christian thought.

In what follows, then, the engagement with anthropological poverty in Jamaican religious experience is not consistent with what has come before. This work departs from others in that it does not aim to show how African religions became Christian per se but to consider how they survived the anti-Africanness in Christianities from slavery up to the current time.

One development in Christian theology which, on the surface, appears a more promising social location for a project such as this is comparative theology. The contribution of comparative theology is that it is broader and inclusive of a number of non-Christian religions. Yet it is still exclusive in terms of its posture toward classical African religions.[10] Perhaps this is because theologians in this camp generally endorse the history of religions/comparative religion classification of religions into historical versus traditional; civilized versus savage; literate versus preliterate; and so on. As such, classical African religions and their diasporic derivatives are deemed to be products of tribal cultures and static traditions in primitive societies and thus not worthy of engagement.

The limitations of the comparative religion/history of religions approaches are evident in the tensions that arose between the European and North American schools of thought during the latter half of the twentieth century. With the launching of *History of Religions* in 1961, University of Chicago scholars suggested a new paradigm for the comprehensive study of religions. The European scholars held tenaciously to the descriptive approach in studying religions from historical and philological perspectives. Their aim was to maintain "integrity" within the scientific study of religions. Thus, they endorsed the "objective" standards of research associated with historical, philological, archaeological, and other studies. Theological approaches which aim toward the subjective engagement of and reflection on religious experience were dubbed unscholarly by most in this camp and, in the end, substandard. These and other methodological issues found a particular venue for debate in the International Association for the History of Religions (IAHR) and in the journals *Revue d'histoire des religions* and *Numen*, especially after 1960.

Mercea Eliade was one of the most ardent proponents of the new hermeneutical approach to the study of religion. In *The Quest: History and Meaning in Religion*, he remarked:

> [T]he scholar has not finished his work when he has reconstructed the history of a religious form or brought out its sociological, economic, or political contexts. In addition, he must understand its meaning—that is, identify and elucidate the situations and positions that have induced or made possible its appearance or its triumph at a particular historical moment.[11]

According to Eric Sharpe, the impact of Eliade's research, and that of the larger Chicago school, in terms of their emphasis on hermeneutics,

> widened the scope of the historian of religion, considerably. Most important, it acknowledged that the historian of religions might find himself playing an active role in the world's cultural dialogue, rather than merely sitting on the sidelines as a disinterested observer; also it committed the scholar to a search for the inner meaning of religion, and not only to a quest for historical fact and circumstance. The "objective" historian of religions was in danger, one feels, of being acknowledged as a skilled craftsman whose work might be admirable in itself, but who would have to learn new concerns and new techniques if he were to be of real significance in the new world.[12]

Theologically trained scholars such as Hans Küng, Wilfred Cantwell Smith, and Paul Knitter have claimed that hermeneutical task, which is one of the major distinctions between comparative theology and comparative religion.

Moreover, as theologians, they engage the comparative study of religions with the intention of raising and responding to the moral problems and grave sociopolitical consequences that attend the religious ignorance, arrogance, and exclusivism of the so-called world religions.[13] Because of their interest in exploring common motifs in some of the religions of the world, Smith, Küng, Knitter, and others have defined the task of theology more broadly than systematic theologians have traditionally and contemporarily, including liberation theologians. Smith believes that "the task of theology is to make rationally intelligible the meaning of human life in faith, and of the world in which that faith is lived."[14] Hans Küng adds:

> More and more theologians nowadays consider it a disaster that as a result of the theological revolution after World War II and of the influence of Karl Barth, Christian theology on one side and the history of religion, the phenomenology of religion, and religious studies in general have gone their separate and often mutually hostile ways. Theology can go along with Barth's legitimate grand design without closing its door on the scientific study of religion or encapsulating itself within the prickly defenses of Christian "faith"—as opposed to mere "religions." Splendid isolation is no longer possible for any religion. Conversely, however, more and more scholars of religion, with the Americans in the lead, are acknowledging that in the long run they mustn't dodge the normative questions of truth and values.[15]

Smith summarizes the goals of this approach well in his book *Towards a World Theology: Faith and the Comparative History of Religion*. He describes his task as "considering . . . whether the diverse religious communities of the world too have something in common at the transcendent level, despite their conspicuously disparate formulations."[16] And Knitter tackles the problem of Christian exclusivism in his book *No Other Name? A Critical Survey of Christian Attitudes toward the World Religions*.

Despite their attempts to address Christian intolerance of other religions, they uniformly make no mention of any classical African religion in their works. It is not possible to determine with certainty why they neglect to include the classical religions of Africa in their critical evaluations of Christianity's pejorative response to non-Christian religions, apart from what has been put forth above.[17] Needless to say, this theological camp of "inclusive exclusivists" cannot be a home for the type of theology attempted here. While these and other theologians in this camp help to frame general questions and issues related to this study, we still find unaddressed a host of specific questions about African religions, their legacies in the African diaspora, and their confrontations with Christianities and, for that matter, with Islam.

A common methodological strategy for both systematic and comparative scholarly approaches to theology is that the researchers primarily base their reflections upon literal texts and decreed teachings, even when such official documents of Christian, Buddhist, Islamic, Hindu, Jewish, and other faiths may represent only a fraction of the truth of the religious lives and spiritual experiences of faith communities. Are we to feel more assured as theologians that we are grappling with the "revelation of God" because these religions have sustained recorded testimony regarding what they believe and assume about the visible and invisible worlds? Why should people invest a sacred trust in the written texts of religious communities as opposed to the religious contexts where beliefs, assumptions, and traditions are exercised? Michel Foucault's theoretical reflections on what he terms "disqualified" or "subjugated" knowledges are useful in framing my approach toward fashioning a response to these questions through the authority I give to the religious ideas and practices embraced by members of "subjugated" non-Christian religions in the African diaspora. Foucault writes:

> [I]t seems to me that our critical discourses of the last fifteen years have in effect discovered their essential force in this association between the buried knowledges of erudition and those disqualified from the hierarchy of knowledges and sciences. In the two cases— in the case of the erudite as in that of the disqualified knowledges— with what in fact were these buried, subjugated knowledges really concerned? They were concerned with a *historical knowledge of struggles.* In the specialized areas of erudition as in the disqualified, popular knowledge there lay the memory of hostile encounters which even up to this day have been confined to the margins of knowledge. What emerges out of this is something one might call a genealogy, or rather a multiplicity of genealogical researches, a painstaking rediscovery of struggles together with the rude memory of their conflicts. Let us give the term *genealogy* to the union of erudite knowledge and local memories which allows us to establish a historical knowledge of struggles and to make use of this knowledge tactically today.[18]

In terms of the historical and contemporary relationship between African diasporic Christianities and African-derived religions in the diaspora, each cultural expression of Christianity has some place of privilege, authority, and public "permission" for expression and elaboration; for serving as a legitimate foundational narrative informing historical consciousness; and for being credited as the ultimate source of redemptive knowledge. Moreover, throughout their tenure in African diasporic cultures and histories, Christianities have antagonized African-derived religions with censorship, stigmatization, and persecution whether in North, Central, or South America or in the Caribbean. While it is the responsibility of the Christian theologian to engage in critical self-conscious reflection regarding Christian social ethics and praxis, no theologian of the African diaspora has reflected upon this tragic dimension of African diasporic religious history.

In the chapters that follow, I scrutinize the Christian faith, especially its metanarrative expressions of missionary theology and practice. My point of departure is the "local awareness" of constructed suffering,[19] that is, human suffering which is generated by human design and prolonged due to powerful ideological constructs and their influence upon cultural and social institutions that shape and regulate human relationships. Anthropological poverty, as described earlier by Mveng, is an example of constructed suffering which can affect both individuals and entire groups of people. Local awareness is a moral imperative that consequently demands a theological and ethical response. When local awareness of constructed suffering exists within an individual theologian or within a theological community, but is not reflected in the discourse of that theologian or theological community, the moral integrity of theological inquiry is in serious jeopardy. This is especially true of the discourse emerging from the liberation theological community because it self-consciously identifies with the suffering and the oppressed; claims to critique theologies and Christian practices that legitimize social systems of oppression and constructed suffering; and argues prophetically for praxis-oriented theologies that challenge the status quo.

On the subject of Christianities' unrelenting persecution and censorship of African-derived religions in the Caribbean and the Americas, Black, womanist, Latin American, Latin American feminist, and Caribbean theologians have not said much. In this regard, they implicate themselves when they assert:

> We favor ongoing dialogue between Christians and the members of other religions. But this dialogue cannot remain only on an intellectual level about God, salvation, human fulfillment, or other such concepts. Beyond dialogue, there must be collaborative action for the integral liberation of the oppressed, not only action to change unjust and oppressive social structures but also attempts to regain our lost identity and life-giving values. Our common praxis with the people of other faiths is a valid source of theology in the Third World.[20]

The purpose of this study, in the end, is to argue for a new paradigm in Caribbean theology, which will reflect the prophetic insights and liberative traditions in the African-derived religions of the region. The specific context for this study is the island of Jamaica. However, I make relevant comparisons between Jamaica and other islands in the Caribbean. Jamaica was one of the most productive European slave colonies. By the mid–eighteenth century, Jamaica had produced more sugar than all other British islands in the entire West Indies combined. Jamaica was Britain's largest and most treasured slave territory in the Caribbean and therefore became an important point of contact between Africans and Europeans.

In the context of Jamaica, Obeah and Myalism surfaced as the two major African-derived religious traditions during the slave period. These two traditions have been understood by scholars of religion, sociology, and anthropology as antagonistic traditions representing "bad magic" in the case of Obeah and "good magic" in the case of Myalism. A specific aim of this text is to utilize multidisciplinary strategies to present what Foucault would call a reconstructed "genealogy" of these traditions and their buried knowledges,[21] both esoteric and exoteric, during slavery and along the continuum of religious expression in post-Emancipation Jamaica.

In considering the African-Jamaican religious experience, this study problematizes the discipline of theology as uncritical of Christian norms—from liberationist to comparativist approaches—and emphasizes (1) the practical functions of African-derived religions in the context of slavery; (2) how the European missionary enterprise affected the religious life of enslaved Africans; (3) the dynamic religiopolitical responses of enslaved Africans to missionary Christianity; (4) the theological currents and emphases that can be identified as essential to African-derived religious traditions in the Jamaican experience, (5) why and how African-derived religious traditions were marginalized from the cultural capital they needed for unrestrained development; and (6) how that marginalization introduced other consequences of pauperization and stigmatization, which continue to threaten and undermine the legacy of African-derived religious traditions in contemporary Jamaica.

Chapter 1 explores the historical contexts of the encounter between Europeans and Africans during four centuries of European expansion (1492–1838), interrogating the historical legacy of African-derived religions in Jamaica during the slave period and its theological potential for contemporary Jamaicans. By examining Obeah and Myal within the sociohistorical setting of pre-Emancipation Jamaica, I refute the bad-versus-good classification of the two traditions as a product of absolutist reasoning in Western Christian thought. Instead, I posit that the idea of *moral neutrality* is most compatible with the metaphysical assumptions and ethical principles embraced by practitioners of both traditions.

Chapter 2 analyzes European cultural attitudes toward African people and African religions, especially during the eighteenth and nineteenth centuries. Here, I assess in greater depth the standard European planter and missionary responses to Obeah and Myal. I preface this assessment by considering the Afrophobic motif as the most essential ingredient in colonial scripts of European expansion and encounter with the African Other.

Chapter 3 examines two chief African responses to the European missionary enterprise from slavery to the twentieth century. One response was to incorporate aspects of the Christian faith into the African religious heritage. Native Baptist (c. 1830s–c. 1860s), Revival Zion (1860s–), and Rastafari (1930s–) traditions represent this type of religious formation. The Native Baptists were associated with the African-American evangelist George Liele, who began his missionary work in Jamaica during the late eighteenth century. Repudiated by White missionaries, Native Baptists were labeled heretics and quickly suppressed. The Revival Zion tradition represents a resurgence of Native Baptist religion. Appearing in the context of a major islandwide Christian religious awakening, Revival Zion has spanned a century and a half of social and religious formation in colonial and postcolonial Jamaica. Rastafari too is a resilient, dynamic phenomenon in the Jamaican experience. With a Pan-African orientation and deep sociopolitical convictions, Rastafari, more than any other

African-oriented tradition on the island, has shaped the postmodern, post-Christian African personality in Jamaica. Another African-Jamaican response to European missionary Christianity considered in this chapter is African loyalty to Christian orthodoxy as it was taught and reinforced by generations of missionary groups, especially after the last quarter of the nineteenth century.

Chapter 4 discusses the ambiguity, contradictions, and controversy surrounding the conspicuous legacy of African-derived religions in Jamaica, especially with regard to Kumina, a Kongo/Koongo-derived Jamaican tradition.[22] I note specifically the dualistic approach to African religions in Black Jamaican culture, especially during the nineteenth and twentieth centuries. On the one hand, African-derived religions and the people who sustain them have been and continue to be stigmatized as dangerous and pathological in Jamaican popular culture. Yet, on the other hand, practitioners of African-derived religions are consulted regularly for healing and crisis resolution. This factor is significant insofar as personal and social crises are chronic in a Third World country beset by geopolitical marginalization, economic deprivation, and social instability. In examining the value of the Kumina tradition to the wider Jamaican society, I develop an African-centered womanist "theology of the cross" which shows that Obeah, Myal, Revival Zion, Kumina, Rastafari, and other African diasporic religions share common religious foci that appear to be African-derived and that emphasize healing, well-being, and the integration and affirmation of purposeful life experience.

The concluding chapter considers the implications of the study of African-Jamaican religiosity for the discipline of theology and for the study of African-derived religions. I suggest new directions for Caribbean theology that are consonant with the historical manifestations of Jamaica's African-derived religions and with the spiritual insights and ethical imperatives of broader African-Caribbean religions. I ultimately argue that African-derived religions are critical in the shaping of liberative perspectives in Caribbean theology. In so doing I explore some methodological insights and limitations of contemporary Caribbean, Black, Pan-African, womanist, and Latin American theologies. I especially critique liberation theological approaches to indigenous religions, which seek to bring credibility to aspects of indigenous traditions as they have been incorporated into localized expressions of Christianity. This new turn in the discussion places my work face to face with standard theories of syncretism, which I argue do not provide the best framework for explaining the nuances and dynamics of religious interaction and exchange specific to the Jamaican context. Instead, I submit that the African-Jamaican religious experience lends itself to a theory of masquerading, which accounts for various types of African religious expressions that have been unfolding in Jamaica for the past three centuries.

All this brings me to a final point about my approach to the subject. This volume emerges from my interest in theology and religion. However, I want to make the point that the Africans who came to Jamaica during and after slavery erected recognizable African-derived religious institutions very early in their collective history. They also modified those institutions or created new institutions of resistance in response to their experiences of colonial Christianity and its legacy in Jamaica. Their statement of resistance through religious formation is just one of the many versions that we might find in the Caribbean and Americas. My reason for approaching the study of religion and theology in this way is to convey to Third World theologians, especially those from the African diaspora, that these disregarded narratives matter. They hold tremendous antidotes for our ruptured souls and defeated spirits.

In undertaking this task, I could not begin with doctrinal categories, search for relevant data, and weave them together into a coherent systematic treatise. Instead I had to examine historical documents and engage in ethnographic research in order to have some access to the lived religion of the people of Jamaica with a focus upon their expressions of African religious cultures in the Jamaican landscape. With this imperative in mind, I deliberately foreground primary source material, especially in the first three chapters. This was done to make the case for a contextual theology that addresses the theme of liberation through the narrative accounts of the various historical actors in and witnesses to the shaping of African Jamaican religiosity across several centuries. Since it is not customary for theologians to engage in documentary approaches to the framing of experience and context, I want to state here that my extensive citation of missionary records, plantation diaries, legislative acts, and other primary sources is nothing less than a desire for a richer engagement and interrogation of the data. I ask the reader to listen to the words of persons who were present during the formation of this religious tapestry and to weigh the merits and demerits of my argument against their testimonies. Using the material in this way thoroughly convinces me that the time for such an approach to theological studies in the African diaspora is long overdue.

I

Libation

Four Centuries of Encounter and Transition

I was playing by the sea-coast, when a white man offered me sugar-plums, and told me to go with him. I went with him, first into a boat, and then to a ship. Everything seemed strange to me, and I asked him to let me go back, but he would not hear me; and when I went to look for the place where he found me, I could see nothing of land, and I began to cry. There I was for a long time, with a great many more of my own colour, till the ship came to Kingston.[1]

The Coming of the Europeans, the Exile of the Africans

African people in the Caribbean island of Jamaica[2] have survived two types of European sovereignty: European enslavement of their ancestors and colonialism under British rule. The history of European occupation of Jamaica begins with the Spanish and specifically with Christobal Colón in 1494.[3] Shortly after Colón's voyage to Jamaica and neighboring islands of the Caribbean, other European voyagers went in quest of new trade routes and territories upon which to plant their home countries' flags. It was the age of European expansion, an age marked by competition and monopoly.

The struggle for sovereignty in the Caribbean crystallized early between Portugal and Spain after Colón's first voyage to the Caribbean in 1492. Pope Alexander VI attempted to satisfy each side by granting Portugal sovereignty over the eastern hemisphere and Spain sovereignty over the western hemisphere. In 1494, Portugal and Spain reached a separate agreement with the Luso-Hispanic Treaty of Tordesillas, which guaranteed an unsatisfied Portugal sovereignty over Brazil.[4] Other European nations scurried for territories as well and, between battles, negotiations continued. What was certain, even before the mid–sixteenth century, was that Europe found its diaspora to be one that could ensure prosperous market economies, technological advancement, and political and religiocultural dominance.

The crucial ingredient that provided such assurance was a consistent, reliable, African slave-labor pool. Europeans discovered that, on the whole, Africans survived the horrors of their transportation and resettlement from the continent to the Caribbean and the Americas. Many were skilled farmers and familiar with a variety of metallurgical technologies. Finally, Europeans encountered a population in Africa untutored by Christian religion and culture.[5] The absence of Christianity as an enculturating social factor in African societies fueled Europe's judgment of Africa as inferior and exploitable. Consequently, evangelizing Africans, although ambiguously and ambivalently affirmed, was a frequently adduced rationale for the enslavement and cultural domination of African people in the Caribbean and the Americas.[6]

In Jamaica, settler communities appeared in 1510, during the governorship of Juan de Esquivel, the first in the island.[7] Shortly after, in the year 1517, a limited number of private traders received import licenses (the *asiento*) from King Charles V to begin transporting 4,000 Africans annually to Jamaica, Puerto Rico, and Cuba.[8] By 1540, 10,000 Africans were being imported annually to labor as slaves in the Caribbean region. Nevertheless Jamaica remained a region of localized pastoral farming during its Spanish occupation. The Spanish at this time were preoccupied with gold, of which Jamaica had none. The number of Africans imported into Cuba and other Spanish territories where gold could be mined was much higher than that imported into Jamaica during the late sixteenth and early seventeenth centuries.[9]

Between 1517 and the British invasion of Jamaica in 1655, Jamaica experienced a series of conflicts as a number of European nations scrambled for possession of the island.[10] The competition for what we now know as the Caribbean and American territories was matched in the transatlantic slave trade. The transatlantic slave trade might be called a Pan-European enterprise, for virtually all of Europe participated in the transportation of Africans between 1518 and 1865. As noted by Daniel Mannix:

> Almost every European nation was . . . engaged in [the transatlantic slave trade] except the Italians, the Austrians, the Poles, and the Russians, none of whom had colonies—and each nation excused itself by depicting the Africans as hopeless savages, while blaming every other nation for treating them badly. The Dutch asserted that French slavers were devious and cruel. The Portuguese were not only brutal but incompetent. The English laughed at the French for being excitable, and at the Portuguese for baptizing whole shiploads of slaves before taking them to Brazil.[11]

The European demand for profit-making products such as sugar, tobacco, and cotton necessitated gang labor, and slave labor was most lucrative. Initially settlers in the Caribbean engaged in local small-scale farming. But, eventually, the Caribbean and select regions in the Americas became centers for massive cash-crop farming of sugar cane, tobacco, and cotton.

The British plantation system appeared first in 1640 on the island of Barbados. Twenty-four years later, Jamaica was earning its title as Britain's—and, for that matter, the world's—largest producer of sugar. A century after its institutionalization in Barbados, plantation sugar production in Jamaica claimed 430 estates.[12] By way of comparison, Eric Williams portrays the significant role of the Caribbean colonies in bolstering Britain's economy. "The amazing value of these West Indian colonies," writes Williams,

> can more graphically be presented by comparing individual West Indian islands with individual mainland colonies. In 1697 British imports from Barbados were five times the combined imports from the bread colonies; the exports to Barbados were slightly larger. Little Barbados, with its 166 square miles, was worth more to British capitalism than New England, New York and Pennsylvania combined. In 1773 British imports from Jamaica were more than five times the combined imports from the bread colonies; British exports to Jamaica were nearly one-third larger than those to New England and only slightly less than those to New York and Pennsylvania combined. . . . For the years 1714–1773 British imports from Montserrat were three times the imports from Pennsylvania, imports from Nevis were almost double those from New York, imports from Antigua were over three times those from New England. Imports from Barbados were more than twice as large as those from the bread colonies, imports from Jamaica nearly six times as large. For the same years Jamaica as an export market was as valuable as New England.[13]

Sugar production in the British Caribbean, then, yielded not only economic prosperity but a regional culture that would be characterized in large part by the Pan-African heritage of the enslaved populations, which exceeded that of the White planters almost immediately. In Jamaica, Africans numbered 9,500 in 1673 while Whites numbered 7,700. According to Parry and Sherlock, "The white population remained almost constant for fifty years, but the number of negro slaves in the same period rose to 74,000."[14] In total, Philip Curtin estimates that 747,500 Africans were transported to Jamaica throughout the period of the transatlantic slave trade.[15]

The Spanish, French, Dutch, and British were the main adversaries for political control of Jamaica, but it was the British who won sovereignty in the late seventeenth century,[16] and they managed to protect their economic and political interests against attacks from European adversaries in the region.[17] Another group of adversaries was the enslaved Africans, whose resistance strategies produced both desired and undesired results[18] throughout their troubled history with British expansionists (merchants, traders, settlers, and missionaries). Rebellions and uprisings were frequent in the islands. While most were unsuccessful, more than a few were victorious. One such mutiny occurred in St. John in 1733. There, rebels murdered all of the European residents save a few who took refuge in St. Thomas. Retaliation ensued, and the rebels were hunted and killed, leaving the Danish island basically unpopulated for centuries.[19]

British authorities and the Jamaican settlers had to contend with Maroon resistance and other African slave revolts.[20] Resistance and nonconformity characterized every stage of African-European relations in Jamaican slave history.[21] Africans resisted slavery in a number of ways. Orlando Patterson's study of slavery in Jamaica specifies that refusing to work, satire, running away, suicide, and individual or collective violence were standard African responses to enslavement.[22] Over several centuries, Jamaica registered more rebellions and uprisings than any other British colony. In *The Sociology of Slavery*, Patterson provides a cursory review of African rebellions against enslavement between 1655 and 1832. He also discusses the terror with which Jamaican Whites lived in the midst of chronic rebellion. "The average number of slaves in the Jamaica revolts of the seventeenth and eighteenth centuries," writes Patterson, "was approximately four hundred, and the three most serious revolts of the island—the first Maroon War (1729–1739); the 1760 [Tacky's] rebellion; and the 1832 [Sam Sharpe] rebellion—each involved over a thousand slaves."[23]

Patterson identifies some of the most obvious reasons for the excessive number of Jamaican rebellions. First, for three centuries, the ratio of enslaved Africans to Europeans in Jamaica was significantly higher than that in other British colonies.[24] Second, a large contingent of the enslaved population was African born (roughly half during the mid–eighteenth century and slightly less than 25 percent during the last ten years of slavery). The continental African presence was unmistakable as "almost every one of the serious rebellions during the seventeenth and eighteenth centuries was instigated and carried out mainly by Akan slaves."[25] According to Patterson, other factors that encouraged revolts in Jamaica were White Jamaicans' relaxed social attitudes regarding slavery; the prevalence of absenteeism;[26] the geographical terrain of the island; the sociopolitical climate of neighboring revolutions (United States and Haiti); and abolitionist protest.[27]

It might be obvious, but for our purposes it is important to add that Africans revolted against enslavement because they would not accept bondage and oppression as a way of life. African bondage entailed not only physical but psychological and cultural exile from the familiar institutions that signified what it meant to be human and provided occasions for Africans to create and recreate extended meaning out of being human. In classical African cultures, religiousness and a sense of the sacred permeated all dimensions of culture and human behavior. It was from this sensibility, that of religiousness, that Africans derived the mandate and resources to revolt against enslavement. Their protests were inspired by religious consciousness and were cultivated within contexts of sacred communion. Jamaican sociologist of religion Leonard Barrett describes this African sensibility most cogently with the term "soul force." His extended application of the term is worth citing as a working explication of the African religious impulse to, at the very least, survive enslavement and its aftermath and, where possible, attain freedom and control of destiny:

> "Soul-force" in "Black talk" describes that quality of life that has en-
> abled Black people to survive the horrors of their "diaspora." The ex-
> perience of slavery, and its later repercussions still remain to be
> dealt with; and "Soul" signifies the moral and emotional fiber of
> Black [people] that enables [them] to see [their] dilemmas clearly and
> at the same time encourages and sustains [them] in [their] struggles.
> "Force" connotes strength, power, intense effort and a will to live.
> The combined words—"soul-force"—describe the racial inheritance
> of the New World African; it is that which characterizes [their] life
> style, [their] world view and [their] endurance under conflict. It is
> [their] frame of reference *vis-à-vis* the wider world and [their] blue-
> print for the struggle from bondage to freedom.[28]

Religious studies as well as Black and Caribbean studies scholars have emphasized this soul force as the connecting thread between African religions and African protests against enslavement in the Americas and the Caribbean.[29] The legislative documents, travel logs, and contemporary histories of the slave period in the Caribbean and the Americas illustrate that there was an indisputable relationship between African religions and African revolts against enslavement. The fear of being poisoned by "Obeah" practitioners is a dominant motif in the European documents of the slave period,[30] which further indicate the fortification and perpetuation of Obeah within the cultures and "superstitions"[31] of African-born captives. Planters were suspicious of African gatherings and they learned to associate African drumming and dancing with rebellious intentions. Their suspicions were all too often confirmed during inquests of detained Africans after unsuccessful revolts.

It is this sociopolitical public dimension of classical African religiosity that emerges most potently in the literature of the slave period, because it was most threatening and offensive to the European ruling class. This being so as we attempt to explore the religious life of enslaved Africans and the theological import of classical African religiosity, we turn our attention, in what remains of this chapter, to this phenomenon—the force of the African soul's response to captivity.

The Rearticulation of Classical African Religions in Jamaica: The African Ethnic Roots of Jamaica

Scholars have committed years of research to the task of deciphering records pertaining to the transatlantic slave trade. Two questions provoking the attention of scholars to the extant records of this era linger after decades of unsatisfying answers and estimated generalizations, based upon misleading or inconclusive data. The first is, how many Africans were transported to work as slaves in the Caribbean and the Americas during the entire tenure of the trans-atlantic slave trade and African enslavement in the West?[32] The second is, what were the ethnic and cultural identities of the Africans who were exiled and enslaved in the Caribbean and the Americas?

Philip Curtin has been credited as the most prolific researcher on the demographics of the Atlantic slave trade. His comprehensive study, *The Atlantic Slave Trade: A Census* (1969), remains an authoritative source on the enter-prise.[33] Other influential studies include Basil Davidson, *Black Mother* (1961); Daniel Mannix and Malcolm Cowley, *Black Cargoes: A History of the Atlantic Slave Trade, 1518–1865* (1965); J. E. Inkori, *Forced Migration: The Impact of the Export Slave Trade on African Societies* (1982); Orlando Patterson, *Slavery and Social Death* (1982); and David Eltis and G. Ugo Nwokeji, *The Trans-Atlantic Slave Trade: A Database on CD-ROM* (1999).[34]

Due to the inconsistency that always exists between official records and their referenced events, it is difficult to ascertain what actually transpired be-tween Europeans and Africans on the shores, in the commercial ships, and in the Caribbean and the Americas from the simple review of official documents. For example, in the case of African transportation to the Spanish colonies, European companies vied for possession of the *asiento* which guaranteed the possessor commercial access to specific African markets as an accredited sup-plier of slaves. However, many commercial sailors used the *asiento* as an entry ticket, not to purchase human cargo but to purchase and distribute other prod-ucts indiscriminately on the triangular trade route.[35]

Another tendency has been that of confusing the names of slave-holding ports and their geographic locations with the ethnocultural origins of the Af-ricans who were transported from those ports to the Americas and the Carib-bean. Historically, some interpreters have assumed that the "Coromantee" ("Coromanti") Africans, known for their fierce resistance against enslavement in Jamaica, constitute an ethnic group.[36] In actuality, "Coromantee" refers to the slave-holding station on the Gold Coast[37] where Africans from sundry ethnocultural societies were detained and exported to Jamaica and other regions.

Modifications in importation patterns from the beginning to the close of the slave trade are also significant for understanding the impact of continental African cultures on the emerging diasporic cultures of the Caribbean and the Americas. Orlando Patterson has conducted a thorough study of enslaved Af-rican importation patterns pertaining to Jamaica and notes chronologically shifting patterns from region to region. Table 1.1., based upon Patterson's find-ings, summarizes his conclusions regarding the regional and ethnic prove-nience of Africans imported into Jamaica during the period of British rule.[38]

One explanation for the modifications in importation patterns is shifting prices in the market at different times during the trade. Africans from the most southern regions of the West Coast were generally cheaper. This might explain the provenience of Africans from the Congo and southwestern African regions during the later years of the slave trade. Additionally, as the eighteenth century

TABLE I.I. Synopsis of Importation Patterns and Demographic Data Pertaining to African Enslavement in Jamaica, 1655–1807

DATE	REGION	PERCENTAGE	ETHNICITY	ADDITIONAL INFORMATION
1655–1700	Coastal strip of Ghana	majority (percentage unknown)	Akan/Ga-Andangme	earlier years
	Angola	40%	Unspecified	1675–1700
	Dahomey	30%	Fon/Other Ewe-speaking people	
1700–1730	Slave Coast	no specified percentages	Akan/Ga-Andangme hinterland (unknown)	Ghana: 50% (Akan), 50% (hinterland) of Africans transported from Slave Coast
	Senegambia	"	Unspecified	
	Windward Coast	"	"	
	Niger and Cross deltas	"	"	remainder: equal proportions from each region
1730–1790	Ghana	40%	Fante (Akan) 1/3 of 40% Dagomba, Tallensi, Mamprusi, Mossi, Wala, Nandeba 2/3 of 40%	increasingly larger proportions from Nigeria and fewer from Ghana during the later years of this period; during last decade of 18th century, Nigeria: 40%, Ghana: 30%
	Niger and Cross deltas	30%	Igbo 3/4 of 30% Ibibios, Chambas, Okrika 1/4 of 30%	
	Slave Coast	12%	Andoni, Edoes 1/4 of 12%	
	Windward Coast	18% (approx.)	Kra-speaking people	
1790–1807	Southwestern Africa	40%	BaKongo provenience	especially Congo region
	Niger and Cross deltas	30%	"	
	Gold Coast	20%	"	
	Windward Coast	5%	"	
	Other areas in Africa	5%	"	

unfolded, Africans were most likely captured from regions incrementally farther from the coast. The supply of coastal Africans was dwindling because "the coastal tribes could not meet the demand for slaves from their own population, or by warring on their neighbors, and the result was that more coffles began moving toward the coast from the deep interior,"[39] which explains the variety of "hinterland" groups that were imported from Ghana during the entire eighteenth century.

We must consider also that, in the case of Jamaica, with the rise of the plantation slave system, the earliest importation of Africans forming significant labor units was from the island of Barbados. Barbados was the first British settlement in the Caribbean and emerged as Britain's most profitable colony in the seventeenth century.[40] Barbados contributed one-third of the African-Jamaican population between 1655 and 1674 and one-fourth between 1675 and 1688.[41] Consequently, to know something about the earliest population of enslaved African Jamaicans, who had to have established some of the dominant cultural patterns that later-arriving Africans adopted, studies of the ethnocultural origins of Barbadian Africans are in order.

One of the most plausible suggestions is that many of the enslaved Barbadian-Jamaican Africans were imported by the Dutch from their El Mina fortress on the Gold Coast (present-day Ghana). Mervyn Allyene explains:

> Though many authors are cautious about drawing firm conclusions, much evidence suggests that the Gold Coast was the main source of Jamaica-bound Africans in the formative period (1660–1700). By 1640 the Dutch had broken the Portuguese monopoly on the West African Coast and had become chief suppliers of slaves to the New World colonies of other nations (they themselves had as yet no colonies). They set up their headquarters at El Mina, on the Gold Coast. The Dutch became the principal supplier of slaves to the British Windward and Leeward colonies (and to Suriname), whence quite a few settlers migrated to Jamaica at the beginning of the British period. They also supplied Jamaica directly through the slave depots at Curaçao and St. Eustatius.[42]

Moreover, records indicate that, when the British entered and aggressively monopolized the trade, they too acquired most of their captives from the Gold Coast, specifically the holding factories at Coromantin and Cape Coast.[43] Another factor to consider in the search for Jamaica's African ethnic roots is the activity of "interlopers" throughout the slave-trading era. These individuals were free traders who defied commercial monopolies by ignoring the legal rights of larger companies to supply the colonies with African slave labor. In the case of Britain, the Royal African Company[44] had to contend with interlopers throughout its involvement in the slave-trading enterprise. Eric Williams notes, "The Royal African Company was powerless against [the] competition of the free traders. It soon went bankrupt and had to depend on parliamentary subsidy. In 1731 it abandoned the slave trade and confined itself to the trade in ivory and gold dust."[45] Interlopers were granted the right to trade freely in 1698 and continued to strangle the commercial position of the Royal African Company, which lost its monopoly on trade in the same year. The important point is that interlopers procured captives from the most convenient and accessible regions in Africa, for they did not establish factories or holding ports in specific geographical areas. Alleyne assesses their participation in the slave trade and attempts to discern their impact upon cultural consolidation among Africans in Jamaica:

> The interlopers acquired slaves from wherever they could: not only the Gold Coast but also the East Coast and Madagascar. But most agree that Angola [referring to the entire Central African region] was their main area of supply. . . . slaves shipped from Angola were acquired far into the hinterland, and were nowhere near as homogeneous as Gold Coast slaves. This suggests that Gold Coast Africans who came to Jamaica in this period [1670–1808] had a stronger group identity than Africans of other ethnic affiliations and more cultural resources, even if we cannot be sure of their exact numbers.[46]

Alleyne's historicization of African migration to Jamaica, which he divides into three periods, is even more helpful in understanding why particular African ethnocultural traditions now predominate in Jamaican culture. The first is 1498–1655 (the period of Spanish colonization); the second is 1670–1808 (the period inaugurated by British colonization and the institutionalization of a plantation slave-labor economy and terminated by British abolition of the transatlantic slave trade); and the third is 1841–1865 (the post-Emancipation period when Africans were transported to Jamaica to work as indentured laborers).[47]

As already noted, the first period was most insignificant because the Spanish did not sustain a large slave-labor pool. The data regarding the second period, as examined above, suggest a strong Gold Coast contingent among the Africans transported to Jamaica. The third period introduced distinguishable African features onto the face of Jamaican culture, especially Kongo-Kwango and Yoruba (Nago).[48]

On the surface, the ethnic origin of African-Jamaican culture during the slave period was conspicuously Akan, that is, Asante, Fante, Nziani, Agni, and Brong.[49] It is possible, however, to find a great deal of cross-cultural consistency among Jamaican, Akan, and many other West/Central African cultural regions, especially with regard to metaphysical orientation and religious logic, expression, and function. While broad generalizations about classical African religions conflate and distort important distinctions about the peoples who claim allegiance to them, scholars of African religions have identified consistent patterns of thought, organization, purpose, and practice in the religiocultural traditions among diverse peoples in sub-Saharan Africa.[50] The Gikuyu in Kenya, the Fante in Ghana, and the Shona in Zimbabwe adhere to diverse classical religiocultural traditions. Yet they resemble each other more closely than they do the religiocultural Christianity of England or the religiocultural Hinduism of India.

My aim in this chapter is not to meticuously affiliate African-Jamaican religions with parent sources on the African continent. Indeed, I presuppose such connections based on the breadth of scholarship already devoted to this task.[51] What I aim to explore here is the dynamic religiosity of the Africans who comprised the enslaved population of Jamaica. What characterized the religiosity of enslaved Africans in Jamaica? What role did religion play, if any, in the formation of group identity and in individual and collective resistance against enslavement? How might the options for religious expression and the modes of expression that were available to enslaved Africans be understood? Finally, are there any ethical or spiritual motifs or religious norms that lend themselves to theological reflection on African-derived religions during the period of bondage in Jamaica?

African Religions in Pre-Emancipation Jamaica

Across diverse patterns of religious differentiation, six foundational character-istics of continental African religions can be observed in the religious traditions of Caribbean Africans up to the present day: (1) a communotheistic (as opposed to a monotheistic or polytheistic) understanding of the Divine, which corre-sponds with a community of venerated deities and invisible beings;[52] (2) an-cestral veneration; (3) possession trance and mediumship; (4) food offerings and animal sacrifice; (5) divination and herbalism; and (6) an entrenched belief in neutral mystical power. Each of these institutions portrays fundamental Af-rican ideas about theism, cosmology, anthropology, and ethics, what Josiah Young calls "the 'grammar' of existence that imbues the human body and soul with religious meaning."[53] They are pivotal focal points for understanding Af-rican forms of logic and spirituality, especially with regard to experiences of fortune and misfortune, well-being and disease, life and death. These features are present in the religious traditions of Haitian, Dominican, and Louisianan Vodun as well as Cuban, Brazilian, Trinidadian, Puerto Rican, and U.S. Orisha communities.

The inherent problem of essentializing or overgeneralizing haunts any system of classification. And so, in naming these features of African-derived religions, I self-consciously attempt a balance between, on the one hand, in-terpretations of African religions as primitive, capricious, presystematic prac-tices that yielded nothing among the religious cultures of enslaved African communities besides pathetic superstition and magical beliefs and, on the other, apologetic attempts to tidy up and package African-derived religions as a presentable religious tradition in the study of world religions, the latter iron-ically fueled by "the old theological and imperialistic impulses toward totali-zation, unification, and integration."[54]

Additionally, in positing these six foundational features of African-derived religions, I in no way preclude their appearance in other ancient and contemporary global religions and I fully resist what Jonathan Z. Smith calls "the temptation to reduce phenomena to 'essences.' "[55] I specifically want to argue that Africans in the Caribbean have generally held to these six theological and ritual patterns as a direct result of their African religiocultural heritages. The record of testimony from the slave period actually supports this thesis as a number of documents, mostly written by Whites, identify certain religious beliefs and practices as culturally derived from Africa (the "Guiney" or "salt water" Negroes). Indeed, numerous witnesses, as we will later see, are adamant about distinguishing Guiney or salt water Negro "superstitions" from their "legitimate" Christian religious beliefs and practices. But to take a most befitting example, the earliest written document (Charles Leslie, 1740) describing the religiosity of enslaved Africans in Jamaica, introduces the topic with the following:

> Most of these Slaves [speaking generally about enslaved Africans island-wide] are brought from the Coast of *Guiney*. . . . Their Notions of Religion are very inconsistent and vary according to the different Countries they come from: But they have a kind of occasional Conformity, and join without Distinction in their solemn Sacrifices and Gambols.[56]

Beyond the religious defense for scripting African Otherness, often conspicuous in White descriptions of African religious cultures, is the observation of nascent panethnic *African* religious formation in pre-emancipation Jamaica. Their ability to "occasionally conform" and "join without distinction" this early in African-Jamaican history suggests an African intercultural predisposition which was only further enhanced by the exigencies of slave life in colonial Jamaica.

Keeping this observation in mind, coupled with those that take great pains to describe, label, and distinguish African religious cultures as Other than Euro-Christian, I was led to consider the actual types of practices, beliefs, and assumptions that provided such meaty material for White writers to ponder. Even with clear differentiation, which must be taken for granted in any religious culture, I could still identify continuity and conformity across several centuries of African-Jamaican religious formation, spanning five major African-derived religious traditions. These sites of continuity and conformity were loci where Africans from diverse backgrounds could "join without distinction" in common beliefs and practices grounded upon communotheism, ancestor veneration, divination and herbalism, ritual food offerings and animal sacrifice, and mystical power.

Of course, the White observer's habit of dichotomizing African religious cultures and Euro-Christianity is fueled by much more than mere innocent observation. David Hall's compelling historical approach to the "lived religion" of seventeenth-century Puritans in the North American colonies, Robert Orsi's works on popular/lived religion across a number of historical and sociocultural American landscapes, and Charles Long's deconstruction of the savage/civilized dichotomy as a mechanism for operationalizing imperialism, racisim, and Eurocentricism at the theoretical heart of the field of comparative religion,[57] together serve as a cautionary note to this colonial binary construction in the theological language and thinking of the Whites of this period. We cannot divorce the binary construction of African religion as "Christianity's" detractor from the colonizing impact of Christendom on pagan Europe, especially the resultant classification of Europe's pre-Christian and at times popular Christian lived religion as blasphemous magic and a threat to Christian orthodoxy. So, while any number of Whites in pre-emancipation Jamaica may have been familiar with a popular Christianity that accommodated "pagan" beliefs and practices of Europe, I begin from the premise that these forms of lived religion among Whites in Jamaica were not essential constitutive features of African-derived Jamaican religions.[58]

This is not to say that people of African descent in the Caribbean, and in Jamaica in particular, have not identified comparable rubrics within European Christian, pre-Christian, Asian, and Amerindian religious cultures that complement or, as we will later discuss, mask their kaleidescopic expressions of African religiosity.[59] It is to say, however, that the starting point and paradigmatic religious framework for what we now identify as African-derived religions in the Caribbean and Americas is grounded upon an identifiable religious orientation, as expressed through the rituals and practices of African existence and essentially shaped within the horizon of continental and diasporic Africa.

In Jamaica, and most of the islands colonized longest under British Protestant rule, the six foundational characteristics delineated above abound with one exception. There is little evidence that Africans in Jamaica, across the centuries, have recognized a community of independent though interrelated deities, a prominent feature among African populations in the Caribbean islands that received Catholic Christian instruction. What cannot be denied, though, is the widespread notion that the invisible world-domain is populated with spirits and ancestors, a central feature of several African-derived religions in Jamaica, where practitioners acknowledge and relate with a community of invisible beings.[60] It bears reiteration that intercourse with invisible beings, ancestral veneration, possession trance and mediumship, food offerings and animal sacrifice, divination and herbalism, and reliance upon mystical power have been salient in the religious culture of Jamaicans from enslavement to the present day on both micro and macro levels.

In some cases, these six religious elements are aspects of a single religious tradition.[61] In other religious traditions we observe a limited combination of these elements. In any number of instances, all six constituents appear in unsystematized configurations within "secular" culture. One example from Jamaica is the contemporary practice of killing (sacrificing) chickens or pigeons and pouring the blood on the earthen perimeter of a building foundation prior to construction. This procedure is customarily followed in both rural and urban areas in preparation for constructing any edifice—a personal home, office, church, or commercial skyscraper. And it is done to ensure success, protection, and "blessing."[62]

One of the most important yet unemphasized details about the religiosity of enslaved Africans, especially in the British Caribbean, is the fact that it was distinctively African-derived. In large part, there was no sustained encounter between classical African religions and Christianity until the later decades of the slave era.[63] In Jamaica, between 1655 and the early 1800s, religious exchange occurred primarily among the sundry religious traditions of classical Africa, as the enslaved populations struggled to create coherent institutions in an exilic and highly pluralistic cultural context. The end products of African people's encounters with each other were Pan-African syntheses of religious and cultural practices that could serve the needs of individuals and communities at large.

Leonard Barrett maintains that the Pan-African religiosity of the slave period was and continues to be the most salient ingredient in Caribbean culture. "It would be a formidable task," says Barrett,

> for one to provide a detailed study of the various African traditional religions which have come down to the present day. But it cannot be denied that these religious systems, which are usually called cults in our day, were so well established that, despite the onslaught of the European ruling class with their numerous laws aimed at eradicating them, and despite the onslaught of the Christian missionaries who spent their lives and their financial resources in an attempt to convert the slaves to Christianity, these New World African religions have remained to this day as the psychic monitors of the vast majority of New World Blacks. And although their confessed devotees may be few, in some areas of the Caribbean and Brazil, these cults still dominate the consciousness of the majority of the inhabitants, both peasant and elite.[64]

There is a significant body of literature from the slave era that renders obvious reasons for the well-established status of classical African religious traditions. White missionaries, residents, and visitors to the Caribbean were prone to comment upon the religiosity or nonreligiosity of enslaved Africans. We learn three specific things about African religions (and Christianity) during the slave period from contemporary Caribbean literature: (1) Whites viewed African religions with irreverence and antipathy; (2) African religiosity was firmly established in the cultural and social fabric of African life throughout the period of enslavement; and (3) Christianity was not a prominent factor in African religiosity for most of the period of enslavement. These points are attested to in the following account from the Society for the Propagation of the Gospel in Foreign Parts's history of enslaved Africans in the Caribbean and the Americas:

> The negro had left his idols behind him in Africa, and all he had brought with him in the way of religion was a vague belief in spirits, good and bad, but mostly bad, and a firm belief in charms and talismans to avert the powers of evil that lurked around him. He had

practically no moral code, though he was capable of an honest faithful, though somewhat dog-like attachment to his master. In addition
he was very hard worked, and had very little time for any form of
instruction and was of course completely illiterate. These facts in
themselves would have made the task of the missionary sufficiently
difficult, but when to them was added the active opposition, or cal-
lous indifference of the owners, the difficulties were increased a
hundredfold.[65]

The nineteenth-century Anglican church historian Alfred Caldecott also submitted his reflections on the prevalence of African "heathenism" in the British
Caribbean islands. In *The Church in the West Indies*, Caldecott penned his assessment as follows:

Colonial opinion and practice being such as is above described, and
such being the atmosphere in which a scanty and scattered and un-
guided clergy lived, we are not able to seek to minimize the failure
of the Church in the Slavery period. West Indians themselves
[meaning Whites], looking back upon the past, do not scruple to
speak of "Slavery with its inhuman and anti-Christian spirit," as
"neutralizing all efforts for good." We cannot deny that for one hundred and fifty years the vast majority of our fellow-subjects in the
West Indies lived in unrelieved heathenism amid the so-called "parishes" of Jamaica, Barbados, and the Leeward Islands. . . . During
the first century of Slavery nothing [in terms of missionary work
among enslaved Africans] was done.[66]

Caldecott discloses that, even when missionaries became active in the British
Caribbean, they faced tremendous opposition from the planters. It is safe to
say that, during the slave era in the British Caribbean, most White planters did
not view Christianity as a pacifying doctrine that would encourage compliance
and docility within the enslaved African population. And, of the portion who
held such views, many were not willing to sacrifice labor time for religious
instruction, no matter the outcome. Caldecott is decisive about this issue when
he writes, "What was the character of the reception given to these Noncon-
formist Missions? The attitude of the Whites was generally that of decided
opposition. The honourable exceptions are rare."[67]

Moravian missionary documents lend support to Caldecott's reflections.
Walter Hark's *The Breaking of the Dawn* summarizes the activity of the Moravians in Jamaica from the mission's inception in 1754 to 1904. The document
discusses in detail the planters' hostile response to missionary work among
enslaved Africans and the conditions that prevented optimum success in converting Africans to Christianity.[68] Under the leadership of Zacharias George
Caries in 1754, the missionaries struggled for acceptance among the enslaved
African population on estates in St. Elizabeth and Westmoreland and for tolerance among the planters. Although Caries and his two assistants gained the
allegiance of some Africans on three estates in the parish of St. Elizabeth:

On the Lancaster plantation [missionary work] remained fruitless. There the Negroes clung to their African superstitions with a pertinacity that could never be overcome. They had little intercourse with the slaves of other estates, and with sullen indifference turned a deaf ear to the entreaties of the missionaries.[69]

Almost twenty years later the Moravian missionaries reported that "very few" of the enslaved Africans working on their 700-acre estate, Old Carmel,

> could be persuaded at any time, of their own accord, to attend the services. Most of them would only come when they were commanded to do so. . . . "We have ventured, in the name of the Lord, to command our slaves to attend the meetings; for a period of four years, not more than four or five would attend, and we think we have a right to command them to come in."[70]

African "indifference" coupled with planter opposition posed one obstacle after another for the missionaries to tackle. In fact it was not until 1815 that the right of enslaved Africans to receive Christian instruction was legally acknowledged in the British Caribbean.[71]

The non-Christian character of African religiosity became a cause for serious concern among the missionaries and other Whites especially during the last three decades of enslavement (1800–1832). Invested parties even cited statistical data to bolster their arguments for African Christianization. For example, in 1823 a British member of Parliament, G. H. Rose, wrote *A Letter on the Means and Importance of Converting the Slaves in the West Indies to Christianity* in which he presented a summary of the missionary activity in the British Caribbean. Rose concluded from his study:

> The number of slaves in the British West Indian settlements, including those on the main land of Demerara and Berbice [the Guianas in South America], is about seven hundred and thirty thousand. In looking to the quantum of Christianity existing among them, I put out of the calculation the mere circumstance of baptism, where it has not been followed up by Christian instruction, and by the amendment of the neophyte. I would speak only of those, who having been baptized live in general conformity to their belief; [and] of their progeny, either actually under religious instruction, or who will of course receive it when of a suitable age, and of other children receiving such instruction in schools. Their number then may be taken at about one hundred thousand, or at nearly a seventh part of the whole.[72]

Regarding actual figures, missionary records reveal that few Africans converted to Christianity. The Moravian documents note, "At the close of the first 50 years of work, in 1804, the missionary baptisms in Jamaica numbered only 938, less than a rate of 20 per year."[73] Like the Moravians, the Methodists also had a difficult time winning African converts to Christianity. Their Jamaican missionary work began in 1789, and they were most effective among the White and "free" African population.[74]

Scholars speculate that the relatively high percentage of continental African-born captives, even at the close of the slave era, had a significant impact upon the various expressions of African-derived religions in Jamaica. Unfortunately, the institution of slavery required censorship, destabilization, and dehumanization of Africans and their cultures in order to flourish. Enslaved Africans had limited clandestine space to produce and institutionalize social customs, not to mention religious rituals. Thus Europeans glimpsed a fraction of African culture and religion in what they observed as antipathetic outsiders.

The European gaze was intrusive and untrustworthy, and Africans knew it. Much of what Africans thought and did as religious beings was safeguarded within the boundaries of African communal life. Whatever they displayed publicly before Whites, it must be assumed, was coded with the intent of generating if not tolerance, then indifference from the planters and missionaries. That which the Whites witnessed or heard about was culturally unfamiliar to them, and many of their reports and interpretations of African culture and religion lack hermeneutical integrity and must be examined with this awareness in mind.[75]

In examining the record of testimony about African religious traditions in Jamaica, we see the unmistakable signature of classical West and Central African religions in the descriptions of two widely reported religious traditions, Obeah and Myal, as well as internment rituals and other unspecified African-derived practices. Unsatisfied with the limitations of scholarly interpretations of Obeah and Myal, I contest established meanings and assumptions associated with each tradition and thus reassess the cultural, theological, and historical rubrics for conceptualizing Obeah and Myal as dynamic and symbiotic paradigms of African religiosity in the Jamaican experience. The remaining sections of this chapter consider these three major dimensions of African religious life among enslaved populations in Jamaica: burial rituals, Obeah and Myal, as well as other unlabeled religious practices of African derivation.

Funerals and Burial Rituals

The public nature of funerals allowed the White ruling class some access to African religious behavior associated with burial rituals. Of the documentation regarding specific religious practices of enslaved Africans in Jamaica—and, for that matter, the entire Caribbean—funeral narratives appear to be most popular. Detailed accounts of "Negro" funerals illustrate that enslaved Africans viewed death as a sacred occasion. Within the context of slavery, death invited a particular response, no matter the cause: Africans ritualized the alleviation of suffering—that is, release from the danger and misfortune that attended chattel enslavement—and reunification with the African homeland. Such ritualization was concretized in the funerary rites and the religious obligations to the Ancestors. Referring generally to funeral practices of enslaved Africans throughout the Caribbean, the Religious Tract Society reported:

> Their practices were unnatural, and revolting in a very high degree. No sooner did the spirit depart from the body of a relative or friend, than the most wild and frantic gesticulations were manifested, accompanied by the beating of drums and the singing of songs. When conveying the corpse to the place of internment the most strange and ridiculous practices were often exhibited by the bearers. They would sometimes make a sudden halt, put their ears in a listening attitude against the coffin, pretending that the corpse was endued [sic] with the gift of speech, and was determined not to proceed to burial until some debts due to him were paid, some slanderous imputation on his character removed, some theft confessed, . . . they would pretend to answer the questions of the deceased, echo his requirements, and run back with the coffin upon the procession. Frequently, on the most trivial pretences, they would leave the corpse at the door, or even in the house of a neighbour, from which they would not remove it until the demands were satisfied. The last sad offices were usually closed by sacrifices of fowls, copious libations upon the grave, (customs which were annually repeated,) and a few violent signs of sorrow. No sooner did they return to the house of the deceased, than every sign of regret and sadness vanished. With drums and songs, the whole night was spent in riot and debauchery; death being considered by them as a welcome release from the calamities of life, and a passport to the never-to-be-forgotten scenes of their nativity.[76]

Another passage describes specific funerary traditions of enslaved Africans in Jamaica:

> But, though much good was done, many of the negroes were still the slaves of ignorance and superstition. One sabbath, in the month of January, 1820, after Mr. Ratcliffe had been preaching in one of the chapels at Kingston, his attention was excited by a rumbling noise, like that of distant cannon, and looking out of the window of his apartment he saw a heathen funeral advancing, very numerously attended. "It moved forward," says he, "with a solemn pace; a flag was waved on a pole in front of the corpse, which was carried on the heads of two strong negroes; at every ten or twelve steps there was a sudden rattling of the drums called tom-toms; and then the poor devotees set up their hideous shouts, which might have been heard to the extremities of the city. The Africans in this colony retain many superstitious funeral rites, such as dancing round the grave, sacrificing poultry, pouring out libations, and affecting to hold conversation with the spirit of the deceased."[77]

Charles Leslie provided one of the more precise descriptions of the funerals of enslaved Africans (c. 1740) offering insight into their conception of the afterlife:

> When a Negro is about to expire, his Fellow-slaves kiss him, wish him a good Journey, and send their hearty recommendations to their Relations in Guiney [generic reference to Africa]. . . . When one is carried out to his Grave, he is attended with a vast Multitude, who conduct his Corpse in something of a ludicrous manner. They sing all the way, and they who bear it on their Shoulders, make a Feint of stopping at every Door they pass, pretending that if the deceased Person had received any Injury the Corpse moves towards that House and that they can't avoid letting it fall to the Ground, when before the Door. When they come to the Grave, which is generally made in some Savannah or Plain, they lay down the Coffin, or whatever the Body happens to be wrapt up in: and if he be one whose circumstances could allow it, or if he be generally beloved, the Negroes sacrifice a Hog, in honour of him; which they contribute to the expenses of among themselves. The manner of the sacrifice is this: The nearest Relation kills it, the entrails are buried, the four Quarters are divided, and a kind of Soup made, which is brought in a calabash or Gourd, and after waving it Three times, it is set down; the Body is put in the Ground; all the while they are covering it with Earth, the Attendants scream out in a terrible manner, which is not the Effect of Grief, but of Joy; they beat on their wooden Drums, and the women with their Rattles make a hideous Noise: After the grave is filled up, they place the Soup which they had prepared at the Head and a bottle of rum at the Feet. In the meantime cool Drink (which is made of the Lignum Vitae Bark or whatever else they can afford) is distributed amongst those who are present; one half of the Hog is burned while they are drinking, and the other is left to any Person who pleases to take it; they return to Town or to the Plantation, singing after their manner and so the ceremony ends.[78]

These passages indicate that Africans believed reincarnation was an anticipated privilege obtained in the afterlife. Leslie specifically remarks that "they look on death as a blessing . . . are quite transported to think their slavery is near an end, and that they shall revisit their . . . old Friends and Acquaintances,"[79] suggesting an eschatology of repatriation.

Reports from a number of other chroniclers acknowledge that repatriation was an expectation enslaved Africans believed would be fulfilled after death. Writing during the seventeenth century (though published in the eighteenth century), Hans Sloane documented that some Africans, believing that they would return to Africa following death, were inspired to "cut their own throats," "imagining that they could change their condition by that means, from servile to free."[80] According to Patterson, "A planter writing about the same time [as

Leslie] also makes the same observation, adding that to prevent suicide as a result of this belief 'they are often hanged up' by the planters to demonstrate to the living that the dead remained in Jamaica."[81] This evidence, coupled with the fact that they looked forward to reestablishing relationships with "old friends and acquaintances," suggests that, in the context of Caribbean exile and slavery, Africans in Jamaica and elsewhere believed in the regeneration of the soul, the resurrection of the body, and the reconstitution of personhood, essentially conceiving of the afterlife through the lens of repatriation.

We also ascertain from the references above that death was an occasion for reconciliation and resolution of problems within enslaved communities, specifically, the communities of the living *and* the dead (ancestors). Offending parties were publicly indicted as a means of bringing closure to the departed person's earthly conflicts. It would appear then that the accused had the opportunity to express remorse and compensate for their offenses if so moved. The theological implications of these ideas and practices will be discussed later in this chapter, following an examination of the three broader and more complicated categories of African religious behavior in pre-emancipation Jamaica.

Pre-emancipation Manifestations of Obeah, Myal, and Other African-Derived Practices

In order to understand Obeah and Myal, as what I would describe as institutional paradigms of African-Jamaican religiosity as well as their history of interpretation in Jamaican society and in scholarly research, it bears repeating that African religious traditions have been the subjects of ongoing hermeneutical controversy since Europeans began to shape the discourses that explain their content and significance, and not without moral assessment. This is especially true of diasporic African-derived religions because Africans were often barred from practicing and transmitting accessible transgenerational records of their authentic heritages, whether orally or literally. In European literature, African ideas about the invisible and visible worlds are constantly belittled and discredited. The following passage is a classic example of this pattern in missionary reports concerning enslaved Africans in the Caribbean:

> If one ray of light gleamed amidst this universal gloom, it was only sufficient to make darkness more visible; only enough to render it (if so it may be said) still more offensive to the eye of Deity. Hence it appears as if all the vices and abominations of the world had been collected and united here. Their ideas of the deity were few, and those few confused and unbecoming. Some were papists, some professedly belonging to the coptic or abyssinian churches, some mohammedans, most of them idolaters, paying an uncertain reverence to the sun and moon, to the ocean, to the rocks, to the fountains of rivers, and to images of various kinds. Serpents and other reptiles were also classed with their divinities. Many worshipped the devil himself.[82]

As noted above in our discussion of African burial practices in Jamaica, the evaluations of White outsiders are always suspect in ascertaining the ethical and social significance of African-derived religions to practitioners, especially during the slave period. At the same time, their recorded observations of specific rituals and practices, however limited, provide a clear view into the complex and nuanced religiosity of enslaved Africans in Jamaica during a period characterized by severe censorship and suppression of African culture and self-representation.

Three centuries of observations and current Jamaican traditions portray African-derived religions as vibrant and widespread from the eighteenth century (if not before) to the present day. The majority of these observations can be classified accordingly: (1) unscholarly observations of White settlers and tourists, (2) unscholarly observations of missionaries, (3) official court records and legislative documents, (4) newspaper accounts, and (5) scholarly research and documentation. In each corpus the narration, publication, and dissemination of ideas and experiences pertaining to African-derived religions reflect the White colonialist and neocolonialist control of discourse, history, and representation of the Other. This is even apparent when White observers record the words and thoughts of enslaved Africans as relayed to them in discussions and in court and newspaper interviews. Notwithstanding all of this, the commentary on African-derived religions, which also includes citations of songs, prayers, phrases, proverbs, and other sayings often heard by White residents and visitors who were witnesses to a variety of African-based ceremonies on the island, discloses something of the religiosity of African descendants in Jamaica that can be interrogated.

Attention to the biased interpretations of African-derived religions in the literatures produced by Whites does not discount the fact that Black missionaries and scholars have also contributed to the discussion. However, Black missionaries, primarily from North America, were fewer in number and left insufficient written records of their activities when compared with the detailed volumes authored by White missionaries. In addition, Black missionaries either abstained from describing the African religious practices of the enslaved or, similar to their White counterparts, expressed disdain toward them.

From a different social-historical location, twentieth-century Black scholars, many of them native Caribbeans, began to publish on the subject of African-Jamaican religion. Their insights, along with the research of other scholars, have deepened our knowledge about the African religious heritage in many areas, especially as conveyed in diverse postemancipation traditions. The scholarly community, however, has largely neglected to scrutinize the apparent contradictions in the established characterizations of Obeah and Myal. This slippage in the scholarly representation of Obeah and Myal amounts to inadequate and at times faulty analysis of the extant data from the eighteenth and nineteenth centuries, the result being that the ideological biases and superficial judgments in the conclusions and interpretations of earlier unscholarly observers remain fixed in the scholarly record of research on African-derived religions in Jamaica.

Across the Caribbean, legal records suggest that African religious practices flourished clandestinely within slave quarters during the seventeenth century. One can only speculate about the religious premise for the gatherings, dances, drumming, and noise disturbances often cited in the legislative acts governing slave life in the early colonial period. In the Jamaican context, speculation yields to specification with the 1740 publication of Charles Leslie's *A New History of Jamaica.*[83]

Although a number of seventeenth-century publications chronicle the experiences of tourists and colonial officials in Jamaica and offer descriptions of the island, I have not come across any direct reference to African religiosity in the literature of that century. Official legislative acts passed by the Jamaica Assembly of 1689 make no mention of Obeah, Myal, or any African religious practice. In fact, there is more attention to stipulations regarding "White servant" labor than "Negro" slave labor. Richard Blome's *Description of the Island of Jamaica* (1672 and reprinted in 1678) makes a passing reference to a "Negro revolt" and indicates that "[white] servants and Negro-slaves" are "vendible" in Jamaica. Fr. Clark's *The Present State of Jamaica* (1683) briefly mentions "Runaway Negroes" in recounting the political history of Jamaica.[84] Even Leslie's 1739 publication, *A New and Exact Account of Jamaica,* refrains from any discussion of African religiocultural life.

Published on the heels of *A New and Exact Account, A New History of Jamaica* appears to be the first text that provides colorful details not only of burial ceremonies as delineated above but also of the theistic beliefs of enslaved Africans in Jamaica. Leslie specifically comments upon the religious behaviors and inclinations of the enslaved Africans he observed. In one passage, he attempts to cite specific names of deities, the earlier of two references I have seen in my research thus far to communotheistic belief among the enslaved population:

> They generally believe there are Two Gods, a good and a bad one;
> the First they call Naskew in the Papaw [Dahomean] Language and
> the other Timnew; the good God they tell you, lives in the Clouds; is
> very kind, and favours Men; 'twas he that taught their Fathers to till
> the Ground, and to hunt for their Subsistence. The evil God sends
> Storms, Earthquakes, and all kind of Mischief. They love the one
> dearly, and fear the other as much.[85]

Following Leslie's commentary on African religious life, in 1774, Edward Long appears to have written the first nonlegislative text that attributes the names Obeah and Myal to the religious practices of Africans in Jamaica. In that same text, volume two of *The History of Jamaica,* Long describes the two institutions as formally connected. After naming the practices of "Obeah-men" he goes on to relay:

> Not long since, some of these execrable wretches [Obeah-men] in Ja-
> maica introduced what they called the *myal dance,* and established a
> kind of society into which they invited all they could. The lure hung

out was, that every Negroe, initiated into the myal society would be invulnerable by the white men; and, although they might in appearance be slain, the obeah-man could, at his pleasure restore the body to life.[86]

Long's observations about Obeah's institutional connection to Myal is substantiated in the historical record by subsequent observers throughout the eighteenth and nineteenth centuries. The many references to Obeah, Myal, and other African religious practices in the extant documents illuminate the multilayered meanings we must attribute to these trajectories of African religiosity in Jamaica. These meanings are polyvalent, that is, simultaneously dissonant and harmonious, contesting any unidimensional interpretations scholars and observers may have given to them in the past. A systematic cataloguing of the descriptions of Obeah, Myal, and other African-derived religious practices facilitates a more thorough and reliable interpretation of African-Jamaican religiosity over the centuries. The three tables below, chronicle pre-emancipation descriptions of African religious traditions, beginning with Leslie's 1740 observations and ending with the Baptist missionary James Phillippo's 1843 observations. Although Phillippo published his narrative in 1843, he took up residency in the island in 1823, eleven years before emancipation and fifteen years before the eradication of the indentured labor system. Table 1.2 contains descriptions of Obeah, Table 1.3 catalogues descriptions that note a relationship between Obeah and Myal, and Table 1.4 includes descriptions of alternative African-derived religious practices. When perused and arranged in this way, the data are striking as we note the conspicuous absence of any pre-emancipation descriptions of Myal as a tradition independent of Obeah.[87]

Pre-Emancipation Descriptions of Obeah

Table 1.2 provides descriptions of Obeah practices and rituals as presented in court cases, missionary and plantation diaries, and other primary records.

Across the wide range of descriptions we can deduce several independent and overlapping conceptions of Obeah:

1. Obeah as poison
2. Obeah as evil magic/witchcraft
3. Obeah as actual neutral mystical power
4. Obeah as ritual negotiation of invisible and visible forces (oath-taking, physical invulnerability)
5. Obeah as pharmacology and energy (empowered religious objects/ charm work, root work/mystical technology)
6. Obeah as divination (detection, revelation)
7. Obeah as specialized religious knowledge reserved for the priesthood
8. Obeah as a religious institution with a foundational cosmology or several cosmologies, ritual life, philosophy and theology, iconography, ritual language, and text.

TABLE I.2.

DATE	OBSERVER/ SOURCE	DESCRIPTION OF PRACTICES/RITUALS	LOCATION	CLASSIFICATION
1760	Jamaica Code Noir (Laws affecting Negroe and other Slaves)	Negroes found with blood, feathers, parrots beaks, dog's teeth, alligator's teeth, broken bottles, grave dirt, rum, egg shells will be declared guilty of Obeah	Island-wide	Obeah
	Code Noir, summary provided by Edward Long, (1774)	Obeiah-men pretended conjurors, or priests, upon conviction before two justices and three freeholders of their practising as such, to suffer death, or transportation, at the discretion of the court		Obeah
1773	Criminal Record-Book (cited by Richard Madden)	Sarah tried "for having in her possession cats' teeth, cats' claws, cats' jaws, hair beads, knotted cords, and other materials, relative to the practice of obeah."	Cases tried in St. Andrews parish	Obeah
1782		Neptune tried "for making use of rum, hair, chalk, stones, and other materials, relative to the practice of obeah, or witchcraft		Obeah
1775	Reported by Bryan Edwards in 1793 publication	An elderly Popo/Papaw [Dahomean] woman is accused of using Obeah to cause deaths on her plantation; fellow slaves testify that the woman "had carried on her business ever since her arrival from Africa." Obeah contents found in her house include: rags, feathers, cat bones, an earthen jar kept under her bed with many round balls of earth or clay of various sizes, whitened on the outside and variously compounded, some with hair and rags, or feathers of all sorts, and strongly bound with twine; others blended with the upper section of the skulls of cats, or stuck round with cats' teeth and claws, or with human or dogs' teeth, and some glass beads of different colours, egg-shells filled with a viscous or gummy substance and many little bags stuffed with articles	Unspecified	Obeah

(continued)

TABLE I.2. *(continued)*

DATE	OBSERVER/ SOURCE	DESCRIPTION OF PRACTICES/RITUALS	LOCATION	CLASSIFICATION
1780	Descriptions from Frederic Cassidy and R. B. Le Page	Obi of Three Finger'd Jack described as consisting of a goat's horn, filled with a compound of grave dirt, ashes, the blood of a black cat, and human fat, all mixed into a paste: also in Obian bag were a cat's foot, a dried toad, a pig's tail, a slip of virginal parchment, of did-skin, with characters marked with blood on it	Called the "terror of Jamaica"	Obeah
c. 1800		Amalkir hung an obi horn about his neck, rare for its supposed virtues	Unspecified	
1788	Peter Marsden	Negroes name poisons used to cause mischief Obea	Unspecified	Obeah
1793P	Bryan Edwards	All professors of "Obi" are native Africans; they brought the science to Jamaica "where it is universally practised"	Island-wide	Obeah
1823P	Author Unknown *Koromantyn*	"The trade of an Obeah man or woman was not a little lucrative, as they manufactured and sold their obies or spells, or preservatives, adapting them to different cases, and changing them accordingly. . . . They generally possess some skill in plants of the medicinal and poisonous species."	Unspecified	Obeah
1824	Cited in Richard Hart "Mack": African rebel informant	Regarding conspirators in botched revolt: The conspirators took a solemn oath. "they had a large Basin standing in the middle. Henry Oliver Cut his finger and put the Blood into the Basin. The Obeah Man then threw a quart of Rum into it, and something else but could not tell whether grave dirt or Gun powder, he saw the prisoners there drink of it and swear to one another, they then proceeded to the low pen to learn Exercise, they had all [their] different Stations."	Parish of St. George (present-day St. Mary and Portland)	Obeah/oaths

TABLE 1.2. (*continued*)

DATE	OBSERVER/ SOURCE	DESCRIPTION OF PRACTICES/RITUALS	LOCATION	CLASSIFICATION
	"Jack": African rebel informant	Described as "a Guinea negro" who "understood how to do everything and knew every sort of bush." He was accused, in addition to the charge of conspiracy, of practising obeah and using his pretended supernatural powers to bolster the courage of his fellow conspirators. He did this, it was alleged: "by rubbing the said Negroes and other Slaves with certain Bushes at the same time saying that such rubbing . . . would give them Strength and cause them to be invulnerable."	Parish of St. George (present-day St. Mary and Portland)	Obeah
1825P	De la Beche	Contents seized from a man tried for having "materials in his possession notoriously used in the practice of Obeah": small pieces of chalk, broken pieces of wood of different lengths, roots of grass, pieces of eel skin, bat wings, two or three pieces of old leather, also a round piece of leather, painted different colours with small bags of different sizes attached to the rim, an English sixpence, a gilt button, the gilt handle of a small drawer, with a string of beads, small bags with mixtures, including one with a human tooth, enveloped in a mixture of a brown soapy substance	Unspecified	Obeah
1826P	Alexander Barclay	At Obeahman's trial, slave witness calls the accused a shadow-catcher who uses Obeah to catch people's shadows in a little coffin, which results in the victim's death	St. David's Parish (present-day St. Thomas in the East and Port Royal)	Obeah Theological anthropology/ shadows (soul complex)
1833 1835P	Richard Madden	Madden recounts incidents of Negroes accusing other Negroes of Obeah for the following purposes: smoking a pipe so that fumes of a particular bush when burned will be inhaled by	Pipe smoker committed to the Spanish Town prison	Obeah

(*continued*)

TABLE I.2. (*continued*)

DATE	OBSERVER/ SOURCE	DESCRIPTION OF PRACTICES/RITUALS	LOCATION	CLASSIFICATION
		another person and cause illness; provoking barrenness; disrupting romantic attachments		
		Madden describes Obeah ceremony performed by coloured man, during which the initiated person's vesture was dispensed with; an iron pot was placed in the center of the room around which the dancing occurred; the pot contained a cock's head, serpent's eggs, blood and grave dirt. Perfectly white cock carries the highest value for obeah rites; the snake, snake's head and tooth are also highly valued for such rites.	Case tried in Spanish Town	Obeah
		Madden describes prevalence and seriousness of obeah oath	Unspecified	Obeah/oath
1843 P / 1970 P Resident of Spanish Town since 1823	James Phillippo	Obeism consisted in placing a spell or charm near home of intended victim or conspicuously displayed to prevent the depredations of thieves; it was signified by a calabash or gourd containing among other ingredients: combination of different coloured rags, cat's teeth, parrot's feathers, toad's feet, eggshells, fish-bones, snake's teeth, and lizards' tails	Island-wide: A few years since [between 1823 and 1843] there was scarcely an estate which did not contain a priest or priestess of this deadly art [Myalism/ Obeah] nor did there appear to be a single negro escaping under its influence	Obeah
		Fetish oath: (consistent part of Obeism) pledge of inviolable secrecy was usually administered before insurrections or individual murders. Blood drawn from each individual present was mixed with grave-dirt and gunpowder in a bowl and was partaken of by each individual as a ratification of his sincerity		Obeah/oaths

Considered within their broader narrative contexts, the descriptions suggest that at some point in the communal formation of African Jamaicans, they exhibited a collective consciousness of malicious uses of mystical power (what Europeans had deemed black/evil magic, sorcery, or witchcraft), which they called "Obeah."[88] This truncated and narrow reading of mystical power as conceived by African Jamaicans is the most popular one advanced by contemporary White observers and by scholars, even though it is evident that Obeah, as mystical power, could be accessed and asserted to achieve communitarian and life-affirming aims, such as political and social solidarity (Obeah oath); divination/revelation (connecting with Ancestors at grave sites, detecting agents of social and cosmic disruption); healing (shadow catching/restoration, removing spells and curses); and protection (charms, medicine bags, spiritually "charged" religious objects/mystical technology).

Although African Jamaicans held widespread beliefs in the notion of evil, the categorical definition of Obeah as evil magic is erroneous and untenable. African cosmologies and theologies account for malicious agents and harmful or disruptive agency with pronounced emphasis upon neutrality and potentiality in terms of theistic, ancestral, and cosmic capacity.[89] With this in mind, a more sophisticated analysis of the data is required to counter the construction of Obeah as evil magic, especially as conceived by Africans themselves. Deriving its meaning from continental African notions of power, in the African-Jamaican imagination, Obeah is capacity and encompasses unlimited operative meanings. It is the capacity to use energy dynamically,[90] which requires specialized knowledge acquired naturally or through training. In the pre-emancipation period, Obeah encompassed then a priesthood of sorts, religious offices such as mediums, diviners, and other gifted or trained spiritualists.

My suspicion is that the manifold and sometimes contradictory descriptions of Obeah across the centuries are snapshots of the multiple (Obeah) practices that comprise larger and differentiated institutions of African religion. In the slaveholding context of Jamaica, where ethnic African identities intermittently and ultimately yielded to the acculturating influence of Pan-Africanization, these religious practices were thus collapsed under the generic category of "Obeah."

A simple comparison with Western Christianity might be useful at this juncture. On the one hand, we can identify Christianity as a religious institution. In the same breath, we can also identify discernible practices such as prayer, administering sacraments, reading the Bible, singing hymns, and ecstatic behavior as Christian, that is, as manifestations of Christianity. Obeah is religious practice: oath taking, divination, healing, and so on. However, as the sum of its parts, Obeah is simultaneously a religious institution reflecting not one particular continental ethnic African religion but the synthetic institutionalization of Pan-African religious institutions on Jamaican soil. This characterization of Obeah is most compatible with the pre-emancipation Obeah narratives. I would still leave room, however, for the reality that, at any given period in pre-emancipation Jamaica, some manifestations of African religiosity (which came to be called Obeah in Jamaica) may have been ethnically based or predominantly shaped by one ethnic group of which the enslaved would have been well aware. Monica Schuler's research on Afro-American slave culture presents compelling data from various regions in the Americas and the Caribbean in support of "ethnicity or the microcosm [existing] within the context of a pan-African macrocosm." She also aims to show "how ethnic solidarity can eventually give way to pan-African solidarity within the context of slavery," referencing the Jamaican Myal tradition as a "more universalistic religion" which "constituted a pan-African, universal . . . religious movement in Jamaica which addressed itself to the entire slave society."[91]

Purged of the older paradigm of Obeah amounting to evil magic, my hope is that scholars will take the lead in expanding interpretive discourses on Obeah in academic and popular imaginations to at least include competing construals of the Obeah phenomenon in the Caribbean. My work in this chapter is just the beginning of my entry into this expanded conversation, allowing me then to reframe Obeah as a protean institutional structure encompassing ethnic and Pan-African religious cultures, which co-author an African-derived understanding of mystical power as the capacity to use energy dynamically. This definition in the making is at least a new starting point in the scholarship on Obeah in Jamaica and in the broader Caribbean and is pivotal to the interpretive logic I employ in characterizing postemancipation African-derived religions throughout the remainder of this text.

The legacy of testimony about Obeah indicates that enslaved Africans relied upon Obeah for a variety of individual, collective, personal, and social reasons. Obeah permitted powerless enslaved Africans access to forces that could and often did help them regain control and authority over their lives. It also allowed them to exercise control over other people and invisible forces, functioning thus as a form of social control and as a system for checking and balancing power and authority in enslaved African communities, where personal disputes were censored. To injure or kill an enslaved African was to trespass upon and destroy a White person's property, and Africans were punished for public demonstrations of violence against one another.[92] Obeah, then, served as a mask behind which enslaved Africans could unleash vengeance or retribution against each other and, for that matter, against anyone in the larger society.[93]

Accordingly, as a weapon against the slave regime, Obeah was notably offensive and hazardous to the colonial success of the White ruling class. Throughout the Caribbean, Whites lived in constant fear of being poisoned and marked for death via Obeah practices. They learned that the Obeah practitioner was a professional herbalist. Obeah practitioners knew how to combine natural bushes to bring their enemies to horrible deaths. Evidently, on the plantations where Obeah practitioners were enslaved and Whites were enslavers, Whites were perpetual enemies and targets for annihilation.[94]

Richard Hart's study of Jamaican revolts confirms pre-emancipation reports that enslaved Africans relied upon Obeah to ensure physical invulnerability and loyalty among rebel comrades. For example, he examines the testimonies of rebels who were captured during an 1824 revolt in the parish of St. George (current-day Portland and St. Mary):

> The conspirators took a solemn oath. How this was administered was described by the informer Mack: "they had a large Basin standing in the middle. Henry Oliver Cut his finger and put the Blood into the Basin. The Obeah Man then threw a quart of Rum into it, and something else but could not tell whether grave dirt or Gun powder, he saw the prisoners there drink of it and swear to one another, they then proceeded to the low pen to learn Exercise, they had all [their] different Stations."[95]

The Obeah oath was a standard practice in preparation for revolt. According to Caribbean historian Gordon Lewis, the "Obeah oath" was "a practice mentioned by all the extant accounts of the uprisings."[96]

Describing the Obeah expertise of another participant in the 1824 St. George revolt, Hart emphasizes the Obeah practitioner's specialization as a skilled herbalist, who engaged in tactile applications of protective medicine to shield conspirators' bodies from harm in battle:

> Confirmation of the fact that the conspirators had received some guns was, however, provided by one of the last of their number to be arrested. This man answered to the name of Jack and Corberand described him as "a Guinea negro" who "understood how to do everything and knew every sort of bush." He was accused, in addition to the charge of conspiracy, of practising obeah and using his pretended supernatural powers to bolster the courage of his fellow conspirators. He did this, it was alleged: "by rubbing the said Negroes and other Slaves with certain Bushes at the same time saying that such rubbing . . . would give them Strength and cause them to be invulnerable."[97]

This passage also supports the broader narrative on Obeah as an institution entailing much more than expert knowledge of botanic therapeutic properties. Jamaican Obeah has always included the exercise of spiritual and mystical power.[98] Whites were aware of these aspects of Obeah, as they compared them with some of Europe's pre-Christian traditions, which they classified as sorcery and witchcraft. To say the least, this Afrophobic signification has distorted African people's perception of ancient African religious cultures. Both on the continent and in the diaspora, far too many Africans have adopted and identified these condemnatory Eurocentric labels with their indigenous religions.

I define Afrophobia as the hatred and fear of that which is African and of being associated with things and peoples African.[99] Afrophobia is Euro-derived and is arguably one of the greatest obstacles to overcoming anthropological poverty in Africa and across African diasporas, as so many people of African descent have internalized the symbols and ideas of the White oppressive imagination. Countless Blacks harbor Afrophobic sentiments that inform African diasporic religiocultural languages, symbols, and attitudes. For example, in contemporary Jamaica an Afrophobic characterization of "Obeah" signifies any practice related to or believed to be related to African-derived religions, in part because Europeans applied the term, with its negative signification, to virtually any African religious practice they observed or heard about.[100] Thus, the popular demonization of Obeah in Jamaica, a protracted European practice of "shadow-thieving,"[101] is ultimately the categorical demonization of African religiosity. African religion as ethnic or pan-ethnic practice and institution *is* Obeah's shadow, and it is within Obeah's shadow that African practitioners in Jamaica move and have their being.[102] The same can be said of Myal, the other paradigmatic institution of African religiosity in the Jamaican experience.

Pre-Emancipation Descriptions of Myal-Obeah

To my knowledge, the pre-emancipation literature offers no independent descriptions of Myal. In each of the five pre-emancipation references to Myal that I have been able to examine, the observer describes Myal as a component of Obeah practice, as noted below in Table 1.3.

These accounts offer a common description of Myal as a ritual dance often enacted to conduct initiations. It is also described as something Obeah men introduced or as a "class" of specialists within the institutional framework of Obeah. The title of "doctor" reportedly reserved for Myal leaders among devotees, and the frequent external notations of their use of "poisonus drugs," "medicinal herbs," and specifically "calalue and rum" to induce alternate states of being,[103] further indicate their priestly specialization as diviners and herbalists. Frederic Cassidy and R. B. LePage draw a connection between Edward Long's eighteenth-century discussion of Myal herbalism and the popular designation of the *Eryngium foetidum* plant as the "Myal weed" in the wider Jamaican culture. In the *Dictionary of Jamaican English*, they offer the following definition of the Myal weed. "The common weed *Eryngium foetidum*, which has a powerful aromatic odour and is used to revive people in a faint or a fit. (This may be the weed unknown to Long, 1774—with which the [Myal] dancer, supposedly dead was resuscitated.)"[104]

Contemporary expressions of Myalism in Jamaica particularly suggest that the "Myal dance" mentioned in the pre-emancipation literature is a reference to ecstatic ritual performance required to invoke manifestations of invisible, revelatory, and transformative powers, deities, and Ancestors. To derive a more comprehensive portrait of the "Myal dance," it may be worthwhile to cite the three most thickly detailed accounts from the pre-emancipation literature of Edward Long, Bryan Edwards, and Matthew Lewis:

> Not long since, some of these execrable wretches [obeah-men] in Jamaica introduced what they called the *myal dance*, and established a kind of society, into which they invited all they could. The lure hung

TABLE 1.3.

DATE	OBSERVER/ SOURCE	DESCRIPTION OF PRACTICES/RITUALS	LOCATION	CLASSIFICATION
1774P	Edward Long	The most sensible among them fear the supernatural powers of the African obeah-men or pretended conjurers; often ascribing those mortal effects to magic. Obeahmen introduced Myal dance as central practice for initiating into "Myal society"; promised invulnerability to harm by Whites and especially bodily resurrection if slain Myal infusion renders body impenetrable to bullets Calalue and rum ingested to induce sleep state/lifelessness Rubbed with another "infusion" terminates sleep state and awakens initiate The dexterity of these priests, or conjurers, in preparation of poisons, has been mentioned by many authors.	Island-wide	Myal/Obeah
1793P	Bryan Edwards	Obia-men or women is currently a general term to denote Africans who practise witchcraft or sorcery comprehending also the class of what are called Myalmen, who employ narcotic potions, made with the juice of a herb (Calalue or species of Solanum) to induce trance or profound sleep of a certain duration, as they attempt to convince the deluded spectators of their power to re-animate dead bodies.	Island-wide	Myal/Obeah
1815–1817 1834P	Matthew Lewis	The Obeah ceremonies always commence with what is called by the negroes "the Myal dance" where the chief Obeah-man sprinkles powders over "devoted victim," blows upon him, dances round him, obliges him to drink a special liquor, seizes him and whirls him rapidly round and round until unconscious; chief Myal-man then retreats to woods for several hours and returns with large bundle of herbs, applying them to the dead person's mouth, eyes and fingertips while assistants hand in hand dance slowly around them in a circle, stamping the ground loudly with their feet to keep time with the chant	Savannah la Mar, Westmoreland (30 miles from Montego Bay)	Myal/Obeah

(continued)

TABLE 1.3. (*continued*)

DATE	OBSERVER/ SOURCE	DESCRIPTION OF PRACTICES/RITUALS	LOCATION	CLASSIFICATION
		An accused Obeah-man Adam was in possession of "a string of beads of various sizes, shapes and colours, arranged in a form peculiar to the performance of the Obeah-man in the Myal dance; the beads are commonly known as Obeah paraphernalia"		
1833/1835P	Richard Madden	Two types of Obeah : (1) practiced by means of incantations, (2) practiced by administering of medicated potions—in former times, it is said of poisons, and these practitioners were called Myal men		Myal/Obeah
1843P/1970P Resident of Jamaica (Spanish Town) since 1823	James Phillippo	Myalism and Fetishism were constituent parts of Obeism . . . Myalism is a secret fraternity whose rituals are not fully disclosed to the uninitiated; they actively recruit initiates with promise of exemption from pain and premature death, from death especially as designed by white men, or recovery from its influence when life was actually extinct; Myalism also understood to counteract the effect of Obeism; at rituals, master of ceremonies is called "Doctor" and engages in violent and excessive dancing and uses poisonous drugs to deprive "victims" of sensibility and apparently of life and subsequently uses medicinal herb to restore victims to former condition, proof of which is the Obeah ingredients extracted from victims' bodies such as pieces of glass bottle and snakes	Island-wide A few years since [following 1823 but before 1843] there was scarcely an estate which did not contain a priest or priestess of this deadly art [Myalism/Obeah] nor did there appear to be a single negro escaping under its influence	Myal/Obeah/ rituals

out was, that every Negroe, initiated into the myal society, would be invulnerable by the white men; and, although they might in appearance be slain, the obeah-man could, at his pleasure, restore the body to life. The method, by which this trick was carried on, was by a cold infusion of the herb *branched colalue* . . . which, after the agitation of dancing, threw the party into a profound sleep. In this state he continued, to all appearance lifeless, no pulse, nor motion of the heart, being perceptible; till, on being rubbed with another infusion (as yet unknown to the Whites), the effects of the colalue gradually went off, the body resumed its motions and the party, on whom the experiment had been tried, awoke as from a trance, entirely ignorant of any thing that had passed since he left off dancing. [Long, 1774][105]

"*Obia*-men or women" . . . is now become in Jamaica the general term to denote those Africans who in that island practise witchcraft or sorcery, comprehending also the class of what are called Myal-men, or those who, by means of a narcotick potion . . . which occasions a trance or profound sleep of a certain duration, endeavour to convince the deluded spectators of their power to re-animate dead bodies. [Edwards, 1793][106]

The Obeah ceremonies always commence with what is called, by the negroes, "the Myal dance." This is intended to remove any doubt of the chief Obeah-man's supernatural powers; and in the course of it, he undertakes to show his art by killing one of the persons present, whom he pitches upon for that purpose. He sprinkles various powders over the devoted victim, blows upon him and dances round him, obliges him to drink a liquor prepared for the occasion, and finally the sorcerer and his assistants seize him and whirl him rapidly round and round till the man loses his senses, and falls on the ground to all appearance and the belief of the spectators a perfect corpse. The chief Myal-man then utters loud shrieks, rushes out of the house with wild and frantic gestures, and conceals himself in some neighbouring wood. At the end of two or three hours he returns with a large bundle of herbs, from some of which he squeezes the juice into the mouth of the dead person; with others he anoints his eyes and stains the tips of his fingers, accompanying the ceremony with a great variety of grotesque actions, and chanting all the while something between a song and a howl, while the assistants hand in hand dance slowly round them in a circle, stamping the ground loudly with their feet to keep time with his chant. A considerable time elapses before the desired effect is produced, but at length the corpse gradually recovers animation, rises from the ground perfectly recovered, and the Myal dance concludes. [Lewis, 1817][107]

These characterizations of Myal indicate that Myal and Obeah were not antagonistic traditions during the slave period, as scholars have conventionally portrayed them. From Long's, Edwards's, and Lewis's descriptions, Myal is characterized as a distinguishable class of Obeah religious leaders with a particular specialization called "Myal," or at the very least Myal is one of the chief components of the Obeah religious practice.

If we treat the data from another angle, we might consider that Myal was a freestanding institution of African derivation with its specialized language and rituals unknown to White observers, whose proclivity was to stamp a generic "Obeah" label on diverse African religious cultures in Jamaica. Still, Myalists and Obeah practitioners appeared to have many things in common. They were both skilled herbalists and skilled in the uses of empowered religious objects and spiritually "charged" substances, and they both appealed to invisible forces for guidance in their ministries. George Blyth, a Presbyterian missionary, published memoirs of his Jamaican experience in 1851. He spent some time reflecting on Obeah and Myal, especially as they appeared after slavery.[108] Blyth is careful to acknowledge the differences between Obeah and Myal that were most publicly displayed in the anti-Obeah Myal movement of the 1840s. However, in comparing his account with those presented above, one discovers any number of similarities between Obeah and Myal with regard to their content and socioreligious significance. According to Blyth:

> The superstitions which prevail in Western and Central Africa have been brought to the West Indies and may be comprehended under the two systems of Obeahism and Myalism; the first of which is entirely mischievous, and the other professes to counteract it. The principal actors in the former are old men, generally Africans. These pretend to have power over others, even at a distance. . . . One of the plans which the overseers adopted during slavery for breaking the spell of Obeahism . . . was to procure baptism for the negroes. . . . Latterly, however, baptism or as they call it, christening, has become so common, that it seems to have lost its charm, and the doctor, or Myal-man, is resorted to, that he may neutralise the power of the Obeah-man. Sometimes his remedies are of a very simple character, particularly if his object be to cure some local disease. . . . Sometimes the Myalists meet in large companies, generally at night, and dance in rings, till they become excited and frenzied, singing Myal songs accusing others of being Myal-men, and pretending to discover enchantments which have been made by them. . . . These Myal men also pretend to catch the shadow or spirit of persons who may have lost their lives by lightning or accident. When the spirit is caught, it is put into a small coffin and buried, by which the ghost, as the superstitious of this country would call it, is laid to rest. The Myal men are resorted to in a great variety of cases, when disease is obstinate, or the nature of it not understood: if a man's wife has forsaken him; if he thinks there is danger of losing the favour of his employers; if he supposes his horse has been bewitched; in all such cases the Myal men are consulted.[109]

Reading Blyth's account with earlier descriptions of Myal-Obeah in mind, we see similar skills and practices attributed to both Obeah practitioners and Myalists, namely, negotiating mystical power, shadow catching, divination, overcoming misfortune, curing diseases, restoring health and wellness, and so on. Thus, the weight of testimony contests characterizations of Obeah as evil and Myal as good and suggests that the most striking distinction between Obeah and Myal is not moral but possibly structural. While Obeah is often described as a practice for individuals as well as groups, Myal is *only* described as a religious ceremony, an association based upon corporate duty, which featured charismatic leaders with identifiable groups of adherents.[110] Cassidy and LePage's attempt to summarize the complexities of Myal affirms the theological and religiocultural connections between Myal and Obeah and is quite compelling in the face of the evidence considered here. In their *Dictionary of Jamaican English* they define Myal as:

> A form of witchcraft not clearly distinguished from Obeah: though some myalists sought to represent themselves as the undoers of the evil done by Obeah . . . , this distinction is neither early nor consistent and may be no more than a defence made against the whites' opposition to Obeah. The practices of obeahman and myalman were much the same, though the early Myal Dance offered itself as a rite of resurrection, hence as curative.[111]

Although it is undeniable that Myal was an established institution in Jamaican slave culture, witnesses to their rituals clearly state that many of their esoteric rites and religious meanings were never divulged to the uninitiated, White or Black. For an exhaustive understanding of the Myal institution, it may be helpful then to move back and forward in time to consider any possible African connections as well as postemancipation data that may offer clues into its meaning in the Jamaican context. To a lesser degree, the same can be said about Obeah and so we will examine linkages to Africa with both traditions in mind.

Continental African Antecedents of Obeah and Myal

The terms "Obeah" and "Myal" and the concepts they signify have been linked to a number of plausible cultural orientations in West and Central Africa. Some of the earlier researchers such as Joseph Williams and Leonard Barrett suggested that Obeah is a derivative of the Twi word *obayifo* or *bayi* which means "witch" in Asante and Fante cultures. Cassidy and Le Page also link Obeah to an Efik (Nigeria) term *ubio*, defined as "a thing or mixture of things, put in the ground, as a charm to cause sickness or death." Many of the later scholars substantiated their definitions of Obeah by citing one or all of these earlier scholars. Orlando Patterson, however, contends that the word *obeye*, also a Twi word, is a more fitting cognate in that it signifies the concept of "moral neutrality" in its original usage and because it is closer in terms of pronunciation to the Jamaican term "Obeah" than *obayifo*.[112]

Fewer scholars have speculated about the etymology of the term "Myal." Cassidy and Le Page postulate a Hausa antecedent *maye*, which can mean "sorcerer," "wizard," or "intoxication." It has also been suggested that Myal is Akan[113] or Central African[114] in origin. In earlier publications, I was less inclined to support the standard assumption that the term "Myal" is of Central African derivation primarily because the Central African Kumina community in Jamaica observes a ritual practice of Myal. Because the Myal institution was established in Jamaica since at least the 1770s, and the Kumina community was established in eastern Jamaica only through the settlement of post-emancipation African immigrant indentured laborers, I suspected that Myal, both the term and the institution, may have been influenced by another ethnic African culture or by several other ethnic African cultures, including Central African traditions.[115]

After consulting more recent studies on Central African religious traditions in Africa and the diaspora and conducting personal interviews with Congolese scholar Dr. Fu-Kiau Bunseki, I find the Kikongo etymology thesis, as argued by Maureen Warner-Lewis, especially tenable.[116] Warner-Lewis, a Caribbean linguistic scholar who has studied the Jamaican cultural and religious landscape for several decades, has published a formidable volume on Central African cultural influences upon Caribbean cultural formation. Her location of Jamaican Myal traditions within a Central African Kongo cultural continuum is consistent with the text of my conversations with Dr. Bunseki, the first scholar to compile a Kikongo lexicon of Kumina terms.[117] Dr. Bunseki believes the term *myal* is derived from the Kikongo term *mayâla* (the one who leads/rules). Other related terms include *yâla* (to rule, lead, govern), *kimyâla* (one's authority as ruler), and *luyâlu* (rulership). According to Bunseki, the "*mayâla* can rule because he has *mwela*, a breathing power, within him." And so, *myal*, is particularly derived from the Kikongo term *miela*, the plural form of the term *mwela*, which literally means "breath," that is, the "energy coming from human beings but . . . also a living breath coming from planetary living energy as well as cosmic living energy." Bunseki elaborates:

> It is a breath that comes from a source which is a living source; the Kongo sees that breath can only come from a living thing—the planetary living energy, the cosmos living energy, and from humans and living plants, but spiritually when we speak of *mwela*, we are referring here first to the elders in the community and second, to the ancestors. If you have misfortune, you need a spiritual ritual, energy, and you go to the community to seek for *miela*. . . . The village will congregate to hear your problem. You will sit in the circle to explain your problem and to ask if you have wronged the community and if your behavior is out of the cosmic balance.[118]

Bunseki's specific identification of *mwela* (myal) as the breath and energy of plant life provides some insight into why Myal/Obeah rituals were reportedly enacted around trees or involved trees (for example, dancing under or around trees and nailing shadows to trees). Bunseki notes how the Kongo-based Cuban religion of Palo (Mayombe) demonstrates a precise connection with the religious significance of trees for BaKongo people. "Palo," he says, "is the Portuguese term for Tree and Mayombe is the Central African region with the deepest forest area." In Cuba, trees are central to Paleros and their rituals. I spent a day with a Cuban Palero in her Havana home in November 1999. At the center of her ritual courtyard was a massive tree around which were placed numerous ritual offerings and symbolic items. Bunseki explains further:

In Kongo all judgments, all courts are held under trees, any debate, marriage, initiation, is done under a tree. The tree is seen as the symbol, the pipe through which the *miela* comes to us. Any plant is a pipe through which substances, the *miela*, all the medicine from the earth, comes to us.[119]

The spiritual and ritual significance of trees in Central and West African religions would not have been lost among enslaved African communities in an island dubbed the land of wood and water.[120] Over the past century, scholars have documented the particular focus on accessing ancestral sources of *miela* as a definitive feature of Myal religion in Jamaica. For example, Maureen Warner-Lewis's extended analysis of Myal links the ancestral ritual emphasis in Jamaican Myal traditions to Central African religious cultures. Echoing Bunseki's comments, she proposes:

> . . . the Jamaican term mayaal (generally spelled myal) derives from *mayaala*, the physical representations of power. In a secular context *mayaala* are agents of a paramount chief's authority. The abstract power *mayaala* wield is called *kiyaazi*, a Yombe cognate of the term *nkisi*. Thus Laman, writing out of his early-twentieth-century experiences, averred that "Nkisi, and nkisi nsi do not correspond to what is now connoted by nkisi [the physical talismans], but to what higher up-country [in the hinterland] is called kiyaazi (from yaala, to rule), thus a power of religious character that is needed to strengthen the authority of the regent." *Mayaal* [myal], so seminal a concept in Jamaican religious culture, may thus be said to refer to spiritual power and/or a person possessing spiritual power on behalf of another: a *mayaal* man or woman exercised the power of the Creator God, or of powerful spirits or of ancestral presences.[121]

In the early 1990s, Kenneth Bilby conducted research in the Jamaican parishes of St. Elizabeth, Manchester, Portland, and St. Mary and confirmed what Martha Beckwith had documented as Myal practices in St. Elizabeth in the 1920s. Bilby's recent study is an important contribution to the current scholarly discourse on Myal, for the trend among scholars throughout the twentieth century has been to identify Myal as a direct offspring of Kumina culture in modern eastern Jamaica. Interrupted by six decades, Beckwith's and Bilby's fieldwork studies, however, independently document Myal as a product of the Jonkunnu (John Canoe) masquerading institution and its *gumbay* drumming rituals in modern southwestern Jamaica. Bilby summarizes best the significance of this discovery:

> In Jamaica today, there are, to my knowledge, only five communities in which the rectangular, bench-like frame drum called gumbay is still used: 1) Lacovia, in St Elizabeth; 2) Nassau, in St Elizabeth; 3) the Maroon town of Accompong, in St Elizabeth; 4) the Maroon town of Charles Town, in Portland parish; and 5) the Maroon town

of Scotts Hall, in St Mary parish. Whereas the first three communities are clustered together in the western parish of St Elizabeth, the last two are located far to the east, on the opposite side of the island. In all five of these communities, the gumbay drum is intimately tied to local ancestral religions in which spirit possession plays a central role, and in all five, this form of spiritual possession is still known as *myal*. Indeed, these communities, whose locations span a substantial geographic spread, appear to be the only places in Jamaica (other than locales in which Kumina is found) where the term myal, so common among slaves in the eighteenth and nineteenth centuries, remains current.[122]

To be sure, Martha Beckwith provided vivid accounts of the connections between Myal and Jonkunnu. In her 1928 publication, *Christmas Mummings*, she writes:

> The man Ewan [Jonkonnu dancer from Lacovia] (and very likely Swabe [of Prospect] as well) was a notorious *myal* man in Lacovia, that is, a man who held communication with the spirits of the dead. He was believed to be able to summon the spirits of the dead to work mischief upon an enemy. Mary Campbell, his leading singing girl at that time, told me that he always took the cap [i.e., the Jonkonnu house headdress] out into the graveyard on the night before it was to be brought out upon the road, and performed the songs and dances there among the dead.[123]

When Bilby conducted research in Prospect, Manchester, seventy years later, he found that "[s]everal older residents remembered the gumbay tradition well, and they assured me that it had indeed been connected with both Jonkonnu and myal." Encouraged to continue west into the parish of St. Elizabeth, Bilby soon discovered a thriving Jonkunnu culture in Nassau, St. Elizabeth, where he was informed that he had arrived just in time, for that very night was "the night the Jangkunu will be destroyed, when we dance myal."[124]

Bilby noticed that Myal was the common denominator of two independent but related traditions known as Gumbay Play and Jonkunnu among local residents, and he specifically describes the Myal specialist as a male or female who "is an expert dancer and spirit medium." He goes on to describe how "[w]hen spiritual assistance is needed the *myal-man* [or woman] calls a Gumbay Play ceremony, which is announced by the blowing of a conch shell, or *conk*; the notes blown on the shell invite both the living and the spirits of local ancestors to the ceremony. Although a wide range of problems can be handled by the myal-man, ceremonies are most often held for the purpose of healing." Bilby also notes that a class of songs called *myal sing* are "used to invoke ancestral spirits, who, if things are done properly, will eventually come and take possession of the myal-man."[125] He distinguishes Gumbay Play from Jangkunnu, by describing the former as a need-based ad hoc ritual practice and the latter as an annual Christmas tradition, and offers detailed evidence of the role of ancestral veneration in family lineages as the essential feature of all the Myal rituals he encountered throughout the region. Describing Myal possession in Gumbay Play, he writes:

> Once the myal-man achieves the desired state of myal, or spirit possession, he is usually directed by the spirit to make his way down to one of the family cemeteries, in Rhoden Town or Brown Town, where he is expected to dance in the presence of the ancestors, and to receive additional spiritual counsel from them. Located alongside each of these cemeteries is a small clearing called the "healing ground," where the myal-man carries out some of his operations while in possession. He may also be sent by the spirit into the woods to collect herbs that will eventually be brought back up to Big Yard, where they will be used on the person receiving treatment.[126]

Bilby, a scholar with a long research trajectory in Jamaica, had conducted fieldwork among Kumina practitioners in eastern Jamaica during the 1970s and was fully aware of the Myal rituals in Kumina religious culture, as noted above. After doing research in southwestern Jamaica twenty years later, he concluded in a 1999 article:

> Gumbay Play is one of the most African of Jamaica's indigenous religions. . . . in contrast to the attenuated version of Gumbay Play that has survived in Lacovia, that of Nassau remains relatively robust, although it has been seriously challenged in recent years by a variety of evangelical Christian churches based in the same area. This local community religion is probably closer than any other in Jamaica to the forms of slave religion described by European writers during the eighteenth century (before missionary Christianity had made major inroads) as "myal" or the "Myal Dance." Even today, Gumbay Play shows virtually no evidence of Christian influence.[127]

While scholars may never exhaust the search for Myal's continental African antecedents, the Myal stamp on Jamaican religiosity is unmistakable and warrants continued investigations into its connections to Central African Kongo culture and other African religious cultures.[128] Myal emerges from the written and experiential records as an imperishable force in diverse expressions of African-Jamaican religiosity from slavery to the present moment. In the words of Joseph Williams, who wrote in the 1930s:

> Myalism . . . was of so potent a religious force, that it has survived a century and a half of legal proscription . . . and still is able to vitalize each recurrent upheaval against formal Christianity, even as it inspired the futile efforts to break the chains of slavery and cast off the white man's rule, before constitutional methods had found a way to right the crying wrong of humanity.[129]

General/Unspecified Descriptions of African-Derived Religiosity

Within the historical records, there is yet another category of general or un-specified descriptions of African religious practices emerging from enslaved populations in pre-emancipation Jamaica. Five of the six entries in Table 1.4 are not connected to any commentary on Obeah or Myal in the sources. The sixth entry, details from an 1826 court case, describes shadow catching as an Obeah ritual, a common association also made by a number of post-emancipation observers. It is specified here though because the descriptions of shadow-catching rituals indicate something particular about the theological anthropology of any number of Africans who came to Jamaica. Scholarly re-search has shown that the multiple soul or soul complex concept is widespread in West and Central Africa[130] and it was apparently influential in the religious consciousness and ritual life of enslaved Africans in Jamaica. Indeed, beliefs about the shadow as an essential component of the soul complex are still ger-mane to popular Jamaican ideas about spiritual, psychological, and physical fortitude and vulnerability.

What is evident from the six descriptions is that Africans in Jamaica es-tablished religious observances, utilizing the theological, philosophical, and wider cultural resources of the societies from which they came. These included practices associated with the following categories of ritual and religious culture: (1) offerings and sacrifices to invisible powers; (2) communotheistic under-standings of the divine; (3) ritual obligations to spirits and ancestors (duppies) and ancestor veneration rituals through masquerading traditions of Jonkunnu; (4) a complex African-based theological understanding of medicine, power, and agency conveyed through the uses of quotidian charms and medicine bags, all local New World adaptations of West and Central African therapeutic devices and empowered religious objects such as the bocio (Dahomean) and minkisi (Kongo); and (5) a practice of self-mastery intrinsic to African understandings of the soul complex, a theological anthropology that encompasses sophisticated ideas about personhood, knowledge, destiny, and power.

While these descriptions of African religious practices are not identified with specific labels, several observers attribute sets of beliefs or practices to specific African ethnic cultures or religious cultures, establishing that the as-sociation of specified religious practices with particular ethnic groups is not unfounded in the pre-emancipation literature. Leslie identifies the names of what he perceives to be deities (Naskew and Timnew) with the Popo/Papaw, and Long attributes Obeah practices to the Marabouts, carriers of indigenous African and Islamic traditions to Jamaica. He also describes religious practices among the enslaved Mandingo and provides common African names given to children, noting the West African tendency, especially among the Gold Coast captives, to name their progeny after the day of the week on which they were born.[131] Bearing in mind Schuler's argument, these references suggest that any number of African religious traditions during the slave period bore the ethnic autographs of recognizable cultures in Africa, even as Pan-Africanization, so essential to African Jamaican social and religious formation,

TABLE I.4.

DATE	OBSERVER/ SOURCE	DESCRIPTION OF PRACTICES/RITUALS	LOCATION	CLASSIFICATION
1740P	Charles Leslie	Belief in two Gods: good God "Naskew" and bad God "Timnew"	Unspecified	African theism
		To detect thieves, eldest Negro administers very sacred solemn Oath where participants consume a little grave dirt and the guilty party is detected because his/her stomach swells causing death		Oaths
1774P	Edward Long	Negroes firmly believe in the apparition of spectres. Those of deceased friends are duppies; others, of more hostile and tremendous aspect . . . are called bugaboos	Island-wide	Ancestors/ spirits
		Long attributes the origin of John Canoe to an honourable memorial of John Conny, a celebrated cabocero at Tres Puntas, in Axim, on the Guiney coast; who flourished about the year 1720. He bore great authority among the Negroes of that district. . . . In 1769, several new masks appeared; the Ebos, the Papaws, &c. having their respective Connús, male and female		Jonkunnu/ masquerading traditions
		The Negroes wear the teeth of wild cats, and eat their flesh, as a charm for long life; for they hold the vulgar opinion that a cat has nine lives. Thus by assimilation of the cat's flesh and juices into their own, they imagine they can ensure longevity, and a power of sustaining great fatigues. Bits of red rag, cats teeth, parrots feathers, egg-shells, and fish-bones are frequently stuck up at the doors of their houses when they go from home leaving any thing of value within to deter thieves. These are also hung on fruit-trees and in corn-fields. Upon conversing with some of the Creoles upon this custom, they laughed at the supposed virtue of the charm and said they practiced it only to frighten away the salt-water Negroes		Neutral mystical power/ protective charms

(continued)

TABLE 1.4. (*continued*)

DATE	OBSERVER/ SOURCE	DESCRIPTION OF PRACTICES/RITUALS	LOCATION	CLASSIFICATION
1793P	Bryan Edwards Copied in Author Unknown, *Koromantyn*	"Koromantyn" [Gold Coast] Africans believe in: (1) a creator God called "Accompong" to whom they offer only praises and thanksgivings but no sacrifices; (2) an earth god, "Assarci," to whom they offer first fruits of the ground and pour libations of the liquors they drink; (3) "Ipboa," god of the sea, to whom they sacrifice a hog; (4) "Obboney," who pervades heaven, earth and sea and can send cosmic and social calamities if displeased; human sacrifice is required to propitiate Obboney; (5) individualized familial tutelary deities	Island-wide	African theism
		Kormantyns administer "oath of secrecy" by mingling human blood or ancestral grave dirt with water for consumption; the consequences for violating oath are also named, usually death or severe illness leading to death		Oaths
		Eboes [Igbos] described as holding the "guana," a species of lizard, in the highest estimation		African theism/ totems
1815–1816 1834P	Matthew Lewis	Negroes afraid of ghosts/duppies but choose to bury their dead in their personal gardens with the explanation that they only fear the duppies of their enemies and have nothing to fear from their deceased loved ones	Savannah La Mar, Westmoreland (30 miles from Montego Bay)	Ancestors/ spirits
		Neptune requests to change his son's name from Oscar to Julius, the name of his father, believing that the child's ill health was the result of his deceased grandfather's displeasure at his original choice of name for the child		
		Lewis suspects that many Africans are unwilling to be christened because they conceive that the ghosts of their ancestors will be offended if they replace their familial names with Christian names		

DATE	OBSERVER/ SOURCE	DESCRIPTION OF PRACTICES/RITUALS	LOCATION	CLASSIFICATION
1825P	H. T. De la Beche	"Negroes still continue to place 'watchmen' in their provision grounds, commonly composed of:" pieces of the wood-ant's nest; roots of a particular grass, grave dirt; bunches of feathers; some people make small coffins, line them with black or white cloth and fill them with earth, most often grave-dirt	Unspecified	Empowered religious objects, protective devices/charms
1826P	Alexander Barclay	At Obeahman's trial, slave witness calls accused a shadow-catcher [in this case thief] who uses Obeah to catch people's shadows in a little coffin which results in the victim's death	St. David's Parish (present-day St. Thomas in the East and Port Royal)	Obeah Theological anthropology/ shadows (soul complex)

necessarily entailed the evisceration of some of those ethnic signatures in African-Jamaican religious culture.

In connection with this, it is quite significant that Patterson, relying on the research of Melville Herskovits, locates precise African ethnic antecedents for the names of the gods mentioned in Charles Leslie's text. He identifies "Naskew" as the Dahomean *Nesuxwe* and "Timnew" with another Dahomean term "Tovodu," citing Herskovits's explanation that "Just as when, in speaking of the ancestors, the word *Tovodo* was applied to them so in speaking of the ancestral dances, the term *nesuxwe* was heard."[132] Herskovits elucidates the complex meanings attached to the *nesuxwe*, rituals associated with the elite class of ancestors, the deceased royalty, and so both terms concern religious practices related to ancestors.[133] As scholars continue to study the history of African-derived religions in Jamaica, attention to specific data that intersect multiple cultural locations across the Caribbean and Africa will perhaps expand current and generate new theses on African-Jamaican religious formation over the past five centuries.

Another point of relevance is the rather early acknowledgment of an African-oriented "creole" religious consciousness in pre-emancipation Jamaica. When discussing with Creoles the common practice of displaying protective charms to guard their homes and fields, Edward Long says "they laughed at the supposed virtue of the charm, and said they practised it only to frighten away the salt-water Negroes, of whose depredations they are most apprehensive."[134] This eighteenth-century detail is intriguing because it documents that "Creoles" (African descendants) identified charms, medicine bags, and other empowered religious objects with continental African religious systems of thought. It also indicates that those same Creoles, eager to publicly disassociate with such "unvirtuous depredations," actually did engage in the same African-derived religious practices as their fellow "salt-water Negro" bondspersons.

There is no escaping the overwhelming evidence for the dynamic presence of African religious institutions, African religious specialists, and African religious cultures in pre-emancipation Jamaica. With pre-emancipation Obeah and Myal as foundational institutional frameworks, African Jamaicans have been able to restate the meaning of ethnic and Pan-African configurations of religion in the African-Jamaican psyche. And they have done so within the shadow of colonial Christian Afrophobic culture and its lethal shadow-thieving trajectory of bondage and anthropological impoverishment. A theological analysis of pre-emancipation African-Jamaican religious formation accents the spiritual intelligence and dexterity of the Africans, who navigated multiple worlds, cultural locations, and permutations in creating stable African-oriented religious mechanisms for self-preservation and self-representation.

Theological Dimensions of African-Jamaican Religions during the Slave Period

It is a lamentable consequence of history that Africans were prohibited from uncensored expression and preservation of their cultural heritages during the era of their enslavement. The case of the Caribbean is especially grave when compared with North America. Unlike the North American Africans, Caribbean Africans have no corpus of slave narratives, nor do they have on record any extensive survey of African testimonies about their experiences with enslavement.[135] One would expect that there is yet a wealth of credible information to tease out of history's annals about the sociocultural lifestyles of enslaved Africans. However, it might require interdisciplinary collaboration to arrive at creative methods for accessing and analyzing that information. This will certainly be the case for projects that aim at reconstructing a well-grounded theological interpretation of African religions during the period of enslavement.

In suggesting continuities between continental and diasporic African religions, I identified six general components of classical African religions that consistently appear in most, if not all, traditions. Those tenets are: (1) a community of deities or invisible beings (communotheism); (2) ancestral veneration; (3) possession trance and mediumship; (4) food offerings and animal sacrifice; (5) divination and herbalism; and (6) a strong belief in neutral mystical power. From our examination of both primary and secondary literature, these characteristics are authenticated within the religious institutions of enslaved Africans in Jamaica. Obeah practitioners and Myalists are both described as priests, diviners, mediums, and herbalists. Possession trance or the "Myal dance" is attested to in a number of sources. Ancestral veneration and animal sacrifice are also discussed in the literature pertaining to "African superstition," "duppies," and burial rituals. Ancestral work was a ritual responsibility of the Myalist as well as the secret masquerading societies such as Jonkunnu, apparently one of the last standing Myal preserves in Jamaica today.

While most of his predecessors and contemporaries were satisfied with simply documenting and describing Myal as an episodic phenomenon in the Jamaican experience, Joseph Williams, a Catholic priest who lived and worked in Jamaica during the early twentieth century, was one of the earliest writers to provide a complicated reading of Myal in its variety of expressions in Jamaican culture. In his 1932 publication, *Voodoos and Obeahs: Phases of West India Witchcraft*, he described Myal as:

> the old tribal religion of the Ashanti . . . with some modifications
> due to conditions and circumstances. It drew its name from the
> Myal dance that featured it, particularly in the veneration of the mi
> nor deities who were subordinate to Accompong, and in the com
> memoration or intercession of ancestors.[136]

Although we can infer that Myalists were communicating with ancestral spirits, other invisible spirits, and African deities, given the number of reports of their "dance" and "shadow-catching" rituals, Williams does not provide any specific firsthand accounts of Myalists venerating specified or unspecified deities nor, for that matter, the Ancestors. His interpretation of Myal as an Ashanti tradition predates the rich data now, suggesting salient Kongo antecedents of Myal religiosity. Just as observers and scholars have been persuaded to collapse generic African traditions under the Obeah framework, Williams interpreted references to spiritual dance or ecstatic behavior as expressions of Myal tradition.

Considered as a whole, the varied accounts of African-derived religious traditions in pre-emancipation Jamaica demonstrate that Myalists, Obeah practitioners, and enslaved Africans, in general, did not relinquish their belief in the world as comprised of both visible and invisible domains with corresponding beings: humans occupying the visible space and the Ancestors, spirits, divinities, and a Supreme or remote Deity occupying the invisible. In this cosmological outlook, well-being and fulfillment are contingent upon constant communication among all beings in the visible and invisible world domains. And this communication is enhanced by matter, the natural environment: animals, plants, minerals, elements, vibrant colors, and other material which become vehicles for revelation, power, energy, and capacity.

The testimonies about Obeah, Myal, and funerary rituals suggest that in Jamaica African religiosity of the slave period was dynamically conveyed in the fertile use of terrestrial material. These material elements, ranging from grave-dirt to colored beads, were instruments of divine revelation, the media for divine communication, with the quintessential medium being the human subject. As such, all material entities were fluid receptacles for spiritual forces. Even spirit possession unfolded as a narrative made possible through the material resource of the human body. This ritual practice and others were enriched by the flora and fauna of the earth and by the colors and elements of the natural environment.

The ritual process of spirit possession was most conspicuously observed in the ecstatic behavior of Myal leaders. While under possession, they reportedly prophesied, resurrected, uncovered evil, healed, and impeded misfortune. Moreover, as we shall see, African Jamaicans have continued to view spirit possession as the pivotal indication that God is with them, present in their experiences and efforts to overcome adversity.

In the light of the foregoing, how might we understand the religious ideas and attitudes as they have been presented above? Moreover, what relevance might they have for theological reflection on the religiosity of enslaved Africans in Jamaica? In Jamaica, the anthropological poverty caused by exile, enslavement, and nonpersonhood led to a construction of the ideal and undisturbed homeland. This construction, however, was not unique to African Jamaicans, for it emerged within multiple religiocultural heritages of the African Americas and Caribbean, and it has shaped the intellectual, psychological, and spiritual outlook of peoples and traditions across the entire African diaspora.

Afterlife Ideas: Repatriation and Reconciliation

It is significant that White chroniclers commonly record that Africans believed they would return to their specific homelands after death. Repatriation to what is considered home is one of the most powerful religious motifs from the period of African exile and enslavement in Jamaica. And repatriation, or re-connection with Africa, has a sustained legacy in the theological material of the religious traditions that appear later in Jamaican history, namely, Revival Zion, Kumina, and Rastafari. Repatriation has never been solely a political idea for Africans in Jamaica. No matter the context today, repatriation emerged as a spiritual desire, a yearning, an appetite and need for home, freedom, and fulfillment, and it was institutionalized in the funerary rituals during slavery. Charles Long's reflections upon the religiosity of African North Americans lends theoretical support to my interpretation of repatriation as an essentially religious concept in African-Jamaican culture. Writing about the religiosity of African Americans, Long argues:

> they came to a knowledge and experienced *another reality*, a reality
> not created or given by the Man. This otherness is expressed in the
> spirituals as God, or as a mode of perception that is not under the
> judgment of the oppressors. It is equally expressed in the practical
> and concrete proposals that speak of *another space*, whether Africa or
> another geographical location, or heaven.[137]

Theologically speaking, then, enslaved Africans believed in the resurrection of human beings: body, soul, and person. They placed ultimate trust in the afterlife as "another space" and time where exile, enslavement, and non-personhood would be abolished and replaced by repatriation, freedom, and rekindled relationships. This is why Africans packed in burial coffins items which they believed would assist deceased travelers on their journeys home.

This is also why they asked these deceased persons-in-transition, to deliver messages and greet friends upon returning to their homelands in Africa.

Funerary rituals were also manifestations of covenantal arrangements between the living and the Ancestors. Enslaved Africans were careful to ensure that the departed would journey in peace and contentment. It was the duty of the living then to prepare the departed for the journey home. An important part of that preparation was the subtle yet public indictment of those who may have inflicted injury upon the departed.[138] Obviously, the slave master was the most ruthless debtor, slanderer, and thief. Yet to demand the "confession" of offenses from the one who controlled the whip would only cause more injury and abuse. Because of his social location, the White enslaver stood beyond the reach of public African indictment.

The reconciliation ritual might also be understood heuristically for African Jamaicans of any religious persuasion today in that it encourages each generation to remember and honor Ancestors by demanding justice on their behalf.[139] There is, in the African-Jamaican heritage, a blueprint of sorts for developing traditions that honor and respect African Ancestors. If seriously considered, contemporary African Jamaicans might be inclined to establish meaningful connections to the ancestral legacy they have Afrophobically been conditioned to disregard.

Obeah and Myal: Avenues to Neutral Mystical Power

The above examination of Obeah and Myal during the slave period in Jamaica also presents us with a number of theological issues for consideration. As stated above, the history of scholarship on Obeah and Myal is basically consistent in defining these traditions as innately antagonistic and morally antithetic. Both Jamaican and non-Jamaican scholars have perpetuated this view of Obeah and Myal as true not only of Jamaica today but also of the slave period. This is due to vivid accounts of a particular emphasis in the Myal tradition, which were written in the postemancipation period during the Myal "revival" of the 1840s. It was during this period that Myal practitioners emerged with a public anti-Obeah campaign.[140]

Across the board, scholarly commentary on Obeah and Myal presupposes that the public projection of Myal as anti-Obeah practice in the 1840s was a consistent characteristic of the Myal tradition throughout the slave period. This reading of Obeah and Myal, however, is an anachronistic interpretation which neglects to account for the evidence of collaboration between Obeah practitioners and Myalists during slavery, as substantiated by nearly a century of observations and documentation.

The tendency to characterize Obeah as "bad magic" and Myal as "good magic" or as Obeah's nemesis might well be founded upon Western Christian moral theology, which conceives good and evil as contradistinctive forces. Because Obeah was officially condemned as sorcery early in Jamaican history and because Whites were determined to portray Obeah as a menace to all of Jamaican society (including enslaved Africans), scholars, writing with this Western Christian bias in mind, assume that a dichotomy always existed between Obeah and Myal. After reviewing relevant seventeenth-, eighteenth-, and nineteenth-century documents, it is apparent that the interpretation of Myal as good magic was only firmly established with the 1842 anti-Obeah Myal campaign. This movement necessarily reinforced long-held interpretations of Obeah as pure evil.[141]

In reconsidering the records on Obeah and African religious cultures in pre-emancipation Jamaica, we established that the "Obeah" of the slave period signified a wide number of diverse ethnic African and Pan-African practices and institutions. In this sense, Obeah was multilayered and came to be associated with manifestations of elaborate African-derived systems of communal belief and practice as well as solo practitioners' assertions of power via the exercise of specialized knowledge of forces and spirits. We also determined that Obeah was capacity, strategy, as well as weapon (for defensive protection against White aggression and for offensive attack on White aggression). Obeah was the ultimate antidote to colonial African enslavement since Obeah played a social and public role in militant resistance and revolts. We also identified Myal as a religious association with a leader and adherents. It was informed by a spiritual orientation most potently manifest in possession trance; spiritual insight into the invisible world of ideas and ancient African lore; healing, cleansing, exposing, and eradicating evil and negativity; and other subversive traditions which undermined the slave regime. In pre-emancipation Jamaica then, Myalists and Obeah practitioners cooperated in both covert and overt protests against slavery and forged a distinct religiocultural orientation of political praxis around the goal of liberation.

This interpretation invites elaboration on the concepts of moral neutrality, moral accountability, and moral responsibility in African-Jamaican religious consciousness. The social performances of both Obeah practitioners and Myalists do not render one specialist evil and the other good. Both can use power in constructive or destructive ways, depending upon the context and circumstances involved. Research has shown that across African religious cultures morality is rarely absolutized. What we find are neutral notions of morality and moral agency, and the emphasis on capacity as a religiously and philosophically rich concept and practice, despite the theoretical distinctions scholars make between persons who illegitimately practice "sorcery" and those who legitimately practice divination and healing. This was especially true it appears to me within the context of slavery, where White enslavers constituted an evil force to be eliminated, by any available means. White slave masters were the true sorcerers and soul thieves, for they did everything they could to destroy African community: The White enslaver brought sheer misfortune and the depreciation of African life. "Those who practise witchcraft, evil magic and sorcery are the very incarnation of moral evil. They are, by their very nature set to destroy relationships, to undermine the moral integrity of society."[142] To many captive Africans in Jamaican slave society, White slave masters were the very "incarnation of moral evil," which Obeah practitioners and Myalists had a moral responsibility to contest. Monica Schuler further explains:

[Wrenched away] from their kin, the experience of the middle passage, and people's reduction to units of labour in the New World—all accompanied by excessively high death rates—were cataclysmic misfortunes that could only be accounted for by the actions of the most viciously anti-social creatures, i.e., sorcerers. No wonder slaves en route to the Americas thought Europeans were going to eat them, a common pastime of witches [and] no wonder the Myal society in eighteenth century Jamaica offered protection against "death caused by Europeans."[143]

The vast lists of Obeah paraphernalia noted in the colonial literature indicate that Obeah practitioners and Myalists attempted to counteract slavery and its promoters through any number of approaches to mystical power. John Mbiti offers a view into what this concept most likely suggested in slaveholding Jamaica. Describing mystical powers as neither good nor bad, Mbiti explains how African peoples access such powers for protection, detection, prosperity, success, revenge, control, and so on. Mbiti writes:

There is mystical power which causes people to walk on fire, to lie on thorns or nails, to send curses or harm, including death, from a distance, to change into animals (lycanthropy), to spit on snakes and cause them to split open and die; power to stupefy thieves so that they can be caught red-handed; power to make inanimate objects turn into biologically living creatures; there is power that enables experts to see into secrets, hidden information or the future, or to detect thieves and other culprits. African peoples know this and try to apply it in these and many other ways. For that reason, they wear charms, eat "medicines" or get them rubbed into their bodies; they consult experts, especially the diviners and medicine-men to counteract the evil effects of this power or to obtain powerfully "charged" objects containing the same power. The majority, if not all fear it, and many of them have encountered it in their normal life. This mystical power is not fiction: whatever it is, it is a reality, and one with which African peoples have to reckon. . . . African peoples are aware of a mystical power in the universe. This power is ultimately from God, but in practice it is inherent in, or comes from or through physical objects and spiritual beings. That means that the universe is not static or "dead": it is a dynamic, "living" and powerful universe.[144]

Both Obeah and Myal allowed enslaved Africans access to this type of mystical power. Obeah and Myal traditions emphasize the relativity of good and evil and the potential for good and evil in every person under variable circumstances. Because African religious cultures often adhere to some principle of moral neutrality, they hold persons accountable for how they access and use mystical power. Free will is a responsibility in African religious consciousness and when it is used to exercise evil or to destabilize social or cosmic harmony, the perpetrator is indicted, punished, and at times ritually cleansed or expelled from the community.[145]

Situating this understanding of Obeah within classical African approaches to morality, where neutrality is emphasized, then the most plausible interpretation of its significance as an African-derived institution and as a system for accessing mystical power is the one forwarded by Orlando Patterson in *The Sociology of Slavery*. As mentioned earlier, Patterson posits that the term *obeah* best approximates the linguistic composition of the Twi word *obeye*, which conveys the idea of moral neutrality. Patterson makes comparisons with other West African cultures to explain the theory of moral neutrality. For example, among the Ga of present-day Ghana, the word for mystical (medicinal) power is *won*. "A *won*," says Patterson, "is morally neutral and can be employed for evil or good."[146] Among the neighboring Dahomeans, Herskovits's findings support the theory that Africans conceive of mystical power as morally neutral. He asserts that in the Dahomean theory of *gbo*, "good and bad magic are merely reflections of two aspects of the same principle."[147] Simon Bockie also explains the concept of *kindoki* as neutral mystical power among BaKongo groups in Central Africa.[148]

These examples are relevant to the case of Obeah because the data specify that Africans from these religious cultures had tremendous influence over the shaping of African-Jamaican religiosity in both ethnic and pan-ethnic configurations. I wish not to overstate the case for Central African continuities, but the parallelisms between the types of items colonial observers describe as Obeah paraphernalia, as well as the carrying cases and pots used to hold or bind such items as a unit (charm), are far too conspicuous when compared with Wyatt MacGaffey's illustrated explanations of 45 out of the 100 Kongolese *minkisi* (medicine bundles) and *mpiya* (ancestrally charged revelatory instruments) collected by the Swedish missionary Karl Laman in the early twentieth century.[149] The Kongo, Dahomean, Ga, and Akan are examined here as representative samples of the many African thought systems where good or evil moral agency is associated with the person, his or her intentions, and his or her actions as agents of injury or well-being via *obeye*, *won*, or *kindoki*. For example, the Twi term for "sorcerer" (the person who utilizes *obeye* maliciously) is *obayifo*, but for the priest (diviner/healer) it is *obirifo*. The Ga term for the person who utilizes *won* maliciously is *wontfulo (wonchulo)*, while the one who employs *won* beneficently is called *wontfe (wonche)*.

The unfixed nature of moral potential (capacity) is an important tenet of classical African religious thought, which was and continues to be embraced by African Jamaicans in spite of the absolutist Christian notion that evil and good are diametrically opposed and ultimately personified by Satan and God. This African understanding of good and evil as contingent, although not exhausting, has significant potential for an African-centered theological anthropology that responsibly discredits absolutism in Western Christian theology, especially the idea that White people are innately good and Black people innately evil,[150] and perhaps in more promising ways than the dualistic anthropology embraced by the Nation of Islam and other post-Christian Black religious cultures in the New World.[151]

Obeah-Myal: African Religion as Resistance Culture and Liberating Theopraxis

It is difficult to read primary and secondary literature on Caribbean slave societies without paying attention to the significance of African-derived religions to Black resistance movements. The religious pursuit of freedom, which theologians call liberation praxis, is conspicuous in the social formation of enslaved Africans in Jamaica, as noted by scholars in their treatments of diverse topics from missionary studies to Caribbean slave economies. The idea that human beings are created for freedom, freedom to participate fully in personal and communal destiny, could not be dispelled by the realness of slavery or by its ideology of African inferiority.

The record of testimony about African religiosity in Jamaica discloses the extent to which European outsiders reacted with fear and brutality to militant Obeah and Myal insurrectionists.[152] History the world over presents us with a complex portrait of the interplay between religion and politics and the social implications of their collaboration. The ancient nature of the African religious traditions, which were rearticulated in variegated Jamaican forms during the slave period, qualified them as holistically interwoven throughout all dimensions of African life. The extant commentary on slave life and behavior in Jamaica indicates the triadic union of religion, healing/medicine, and divination/prophecy. To speak of one necessarily implicates the other two. They are distinct but inseparable aspects of African people's approach to understanding and responding to the changing world in which they find themselves.[153] It should not be surprising then that one type of African religious response to enslavement was individual and collective overt resistance.[154] In Jamaica, African resistance and African religiosity were asserted in distinct but often cooperative and at times overlapping practices that contemporary writers routinely attribute to the institutional frameworks of Obeah-Myal.

Although "Myal" is not specifically mentioned as a factor in African uprisings during slavery, it can be taken for granted that Myal, like Obeah, was necessarily at the root of many rebellions. First, we must remember that Obeah was employed as a generic term to refer to any form of "African superstition." Second, the literature on the two traditions does not support the thesis that they were antagonistic during the slave period. Third, Myal was centered upon possession trance, which was achieved through dance or ecstatic worship. In both continental African religions and their diasporic derivatives, divine and ancestral spirit possession is desired for the practical purpose of helping a person or community to solve problems. That Africans sought out Myalists for resolutions to problems is inferred in the literature presented above. Whether Whites were aware of it or not, it is unlikely that enslaved Africans would *not* then seek assistance in their plots against their most insufferable problem, the slave regime. The commentary of a nineteenth-century White Grenadian writer punctuates the point:

> In former years, when African slaves were still being imported into these islands, the negroes used to indulge in a great variety of dances, some of which were, unfortunately, so indecent and voluptuous that laws were enacted to forbid their practice. The Government of the colonies repressed these dances, no doubt as much on account of the danger consequent on the gathering together of so many slaves in one place, as for the moral damage it did the negroes. During the time of slavery, if the owner of a plantation did not allow his slaves to dance on his estate, they would think nothing of walking eight or ten miles on Saturday nights to some place where a dance was to be given, and many of the outbreaks and rebellions of the slaves were no doubt concocted under cover of these gatherings.[155]

The mere assumption that dances were used as a "cover" for sociopolitical acts of resistance reveals a great deal about the European worldview and the European's psychological and cultural distance from the African-oriented worldview which the writer Hesketh Bell sought to interpret. Bell presupposes a dichotomous worldview where dance belongs to the cultural arena and rebellion to the sociopolitical. Bell and many of his contemporaries, who were confused by the role of dance in the lives and well-being of enslaved Africans, did not have the hermeneutical tools to interpret the significance of dance as a religious action metaphysically uniting Africans with the Ancestors and deities. The psychological, physical, ethical, and sociopolitical manifestations of such communication and coexistence with the Ancestors and deities necessarily involved "outbreaks and rebellions" within the context of slavery, for slavery represented everything that deprived Africans of a life of continuity with the Ancestors, ancestral traditions, and the life force that gave meaning and purpose to all creation.

To say this is not to deny that enslaved Africans did dance for the purpose of entertainment and celebration. But it is also to say that the White authorities were absolutely correct in linking dance with not only cultural rejection of Eurocentric Christian "virtues" but with sociopolitical resistance as well. What they did not understand, nor would they accept, were the links among dance, African religion, and rebellion. We will turn to the example of the religiously inspired Haitian Revolution to underscore this point.

On August 14, 1791, an enslaved African (Jamaican born) Vodun priest, Boukman, organized a major Vodun ceremony. During a possession trance he told the community that the spirits of Vodun wanted their assistance in emancipating the enslaved Africans and in banishing the French from the entire island. This experience was the impetus for a slave rebellion that was led by several Vodun priests and Maroons. It was reported that, when under possession, Boukman had a vision of a woman waving a machete over her head while commanding the community to engage in forceful resistance against the regime.[156]

According to Michel Laguerre, Boukman offered the following prayer to the God of his Ancestors during the ceremony that preceded the rebellion:

> The God who created the sun which gives us light,
> Who rouses the waves and rules the storm,
> Though hidden in the clouds, he watches us.
> He sees all that the white man does.
> The God of the white man inspires him with crime,
> But our God calls upon us to do good works.
> Our God who is good to us orders us to revenge our wrongs.
> He will direct our arms and aid us.
> Throw away the symbol[157] of the God of the whites
> Who has so often caused us to weep,
> And listen to the voice of liberty,
> Which speaks in the hearts of us all.[158]

In addition, the following song was ritually intoned during Vodun initiation rites:

> We swear to destroy the whites
> And all that they possess;
> Let us die
> Rather than fail to keep this vow.[159]

Boukman's revolutionary group even sent the governor, De Blanchelande, a letter saying "It is too late. God that struggles for the innocent is our guide. He will never abandon us. So here is our motto: to vanquish or to perish."[160]

Boukman's Jamaican identity may or may not have had significance for his praxis as a Haitian revolutionary.[161] The point is that his African religious identity, as a practitioner of Vodun, had significant consequences for his understanding of sociopolitical resistance as a religious and moral responsibility. This relationship between theology and praxis[162] was authenticated in Jamaica and other Caribbean islands where rebellions and social solidarity were undeniably inspired and nurtured within contexts of African religious fellowship.[163]

African religions, like all other religions, are esoteric in some aspects. Yet religious resources are accessible to nonspecialists in very practical ways. African religious cultures value temporal harmony and material well-being and convey that these blessings are meant to be experienced on earth, as are punishments for offenses. Moreover, religious action (not confession of belief) is required to maintain harmony and well-being. As Mbiti notes, "The majority of African peoples believe that God punishes in this life. Thus [God] is concerned with the moral life of [humankind], and therefore upholds the moral law. With a few exceptions, there is no belief that a person is punished in the hereafter for what he does wrong in this life."[164]

Enslavement tested the practical value of African religious institutions for addressing the social predicament of oppression. And the data examined in this chapter suggest that African religious institutions passed the test, not necessarily because the deities, Ancestors, and mystical powers saw them through in periodically defeating White oppressors but because, time and time again, they inspired Africans to refuse dehumanization and oppression and to pursue freedom, control of destiny, and well-being as signs of the life to be experienced on earth.

This African religious response to anthropological poverty, exile, enslavement, and the negation of African personhood is the foundation and organizing principle for any liberation theology which claims to (1) evolve from the religious history of African-Jamaican protest against oppression and (2) speak for the poorest and most oppressed in contemporary Jamaican society. To further examine this legacy of spiritual intelligence and subversive resistance, we turn to critical moments and religious trajectories in the African-Jamaican experience to note some specific implications of colonial anti-African and Afrophobic ideologies and practices for the African-Jamaican personality and to probe some of the African-Jamaican responses to the totalizing discourses and institutions of the colonial enterprise.

2

Incantation

European Attitudes toward Africanness in Jamaica

But how deficient are we in authenticating information respecting this country! We barely know its coasts; and are in many parts acquainted with these people no further than our cannons reach. No modern European has traversed the interior of Africa, which the Arabian caravans frequently do . . . and what we know of it is either from tales of blacks, [or] pretty ancient accounts of lucky or unfortunate adventures.[1]

A Survey of Afrophobic Ideas in the European Imagination

By the time Europeans began to encounter Africans in Jamaica, there was in European culture a long-standing tradition of myths, tales, and recorded accounts depicting Africans as savage, intellectually inferior, physically grotesque, sexually promiscuous, and morally depraved. How and when did such a disparaging narrative of the Other come into being? Three significant cultural settings in history have produced a body of literature on European perceptions of Africans, especially regarding their physical characteristics, religiocultural traditions, and moral attributes. Anti-African ideas emerged from the cultures of ancient Greece and Rome, early Jewish and Christian literatures, and the European medieval period, all of which predate the inauguration of the transatlantic slave trade.

Alvin Thompson's condensed study of European depictions of Africans makes this point. After examining an extensive body of literature from the three mentioned periods, Thompson argues that, although

[t]he history of European race and colour prejudices against Africans has been seen commonly as being largely a function of slavery in the Americas . . . many of these prejudices had their origins in the period before 1600, and in some instances as early as the Graeco-Roman period. By 1600 blacks were being criticised for what was considered by many whites to be their moral, social, intellectual, and economic inferiority, compared with themselves. When the trans-atlantic slave trade really got underway, from around the mid-seventeenth century, there was already a solid body of prejudicial lit-erature in Europe, which could be exploited to "justify" this trade.[2]

It is tempting to consider the sociocultural and perhaps even psychological factors that may have engendered anti-Africanness/Afrophobia in the Euro-pean consciousness and consequently in the records that Europeans left about their encounters with Africans. However, I do not aim here to speculate *why* Europeans viewed Africans and Africanness pejoratively.[3] What I aim to expose is the fact that anti-Africanness was an identifiable sentiment—if not an ide-ology—in European culture long before the establishment of the transatlantic slave trade. And since the period of Europe's modern encounter with Africa, anti-Africanness has emerged as a unifying ideology, enabling European na-tionalism and imperialism as well as White supremacist ideology and its geo-political influence. Alvin Thompson's and Winthrop Jordan's scholarship on anti-Africanness in European thought provide a wide (chronological) range of disparaging commentary on Africans and Africanness. The classical period alone furnished a body of degrading depictions of Africans in well-known texts. For example, the Latin writer Diodorus of Sicily characterized African popu-lations within and close to the region of modern Libya as " 'entirely savage . . . display[ing] the nature of a wild beast . . . in their ways of living.' " " 'Squalid all over their bodies,' " they wore long nails "like wild beasts, and were as far as possible removed from human kindness to one another; they spoke with a shrill voice and cultivated 'none of the practices of civilized life.' "[4]

During this period, the subhuman characterization of Africans was accom-plished through two descriptive motifs. On the one hand, the animalization of Africans allowed for slippages in cross-cultural comparison, as Africans instead were compared with dogs and other wild beasts. On the other hand, the equa-tion of Africans with the dreaded monsters one would expect to encounter in one of Homer's epic journeys framed the African Other as authentic man's quintessential antagonist, an abominable opponent with the potential to de-stroy his legacy of civilization and to extinguish his heroic destiny. "For some classical writers," explains Thompson,

black Africa produced several *"animal and human monstrosities."*
Pliny . . . lists a number of these "human monstrosities:" some
tribes without noses; others without tongues; yet others with a part
of the mouth closed up, and with a single orifice instead of regular
nostrils; some others who communicated by nods and gestures,
since they had no speech; then those who had a dog as their king,

commanding them by his movements. These belonged to certain "uncivilized" groups of southern Ethiopians. The western Ethiopians, whom he termed "*Nigroi*" and who seemed to have been West Africans, were regarded as being no less monstrous. Some had a king who had only one eye in his forehead; others, such as the *Artabatitae*, had four legs and roved about like wild animals; others had dogs' heads, and drank dogs' milk; there were likewise those who lived chiefly on human flesh.[5]

Establishing a link between Pliny's comments and the published views of his predecessor Herodotus (fifth century B.C.E.), Thompson remarks: "In regard to those people, of whom Pliny said that they had no language, these are believed to have been Troglodytes, perhaps the early inhabitants of northern Chad, to whom Herodotus referred as people living in holes (i.e. caves), and not using ordinary language, but screeching like bats."[6] In this classical corpus the ancient roots of pseudoscientific modern racism are discernible in Ptolemy's eagerness to ponder the physiological effects of the sun upon the phenotype and cultural disposition of Ethiopians. Ptolemy opines that "[t]hose [Ethiopians] from the equator to the summer tropic, since they have the sun over their heads are burned by it, have black skins and thick, woolly hair, are contracted in form and shrunken in stature, are sanguine of nature, and in habits are for the most part savage because their homes are continually oppressed by heat.[7]

Winthrop Jordan's scrutiny of Judaic literature confirms that this type of Afrophobia was known in the ancient Mediterranean and Middle East:

Talmudic and Midrashic sources contained such suggestions as that "Ham was smitten in his skin," that Noah told Ham "your seed will be ugly and dark-skinned," and that Ham was the father "of Canaan who brought curses into the world, of Canaan who was cursed, of Canaan who darkened the faces of mankind," of Canaan "the notorious world-darkener. . . ." The Hebraic literature of *ca.* 200–600 A.D. which saw the posterity of Ham and Canaan as smitten in the skin speculated as to whether Ham's offense was (variously) castrating his father Noah (described in the Midrash Rabbah as Noah's saying "You have prevented me from doing something in the dark"), and (in the same source) as copulating "in the Ark," and (again) copulating "with a dog . . . therefore Ham came forth black-skinned while the dog publicly exposes its copulation." The depth and diffuse pervasiveness of these explosive associations are dramatized in the mystic Zohar of the thirteenth century, where Ham, it was said, "represents the refuse and dross of the gold, the stirring and rousing of the unclean spirit of the ancient serpent."[8]

Overtime ideas and descriptions such as these survived in European consciousness as reliable data, information so credible as to render Africans (as a whole) inferior to Europeans (as a whole). Additionally, blackness has denoted negative feelings, danger, evil, ill health, and death in European culture and in Western society and intellectual traditions for centuries. Westerners associated African people and Africanness with the demeaning signification of blackness and darkness in their language symbol system. This is unequivocally shown in the commentary of even a (Westernized) African church father, Origen (c. 185–c. 254), who wrote the following about Solomon's bride: "it seems to me that he is said to be *beyond the rivers of Ethiopia* who has been darkened with exceeding great and many sins and, having been stained with the inky dye of wickedness, has been rendered black and dark."[9] Origen also remarks that Abdimelech, an Ethiopian mentioned in the Hebrew Testament, was from a "dark and ignoble race."[10]

Other Christian writers, influenced by the European perspective that Blackness has ontological significance, contributed to the derogative commentaries on Africans and Africanness in Christian theology. Robert Hood identifies Jerome (342–420) as "the first Christian theologian to link blackness with carnal knowledge[,] . . . carnal lust and sexual prowess." Hood also cites Jerome's anti-African commentaries about Ethiopians. For example, Jerome translates the word *Chus* from the Hebrew Testament to mean "Ethiopian—one who is 'black and dark, one who has a soul as black as his body.' "[11]

During what is known as the European "Dark" Ages (455–1000) and even in the broader Middle Ages (476–1492), brutally insulting depictions of Africans continued to appear in print. In *Etymologies*, one of the most popular seventh-century encyclopedias in Europe, Isidore of Seville described Ethiopians as follows: "The race of the Sciopodes is said to live in Ethiopia. They have one leg apiece, and are of a marvelous swiftness, and the Greeks call them Sciopodes from this, that in the summertime they lie on the ground on their backs and are shaded by the greatness of their feet."[12]

Europeans were equally, if not more, brutal in their comments about West Africans. Alvin Thompson notes that "little was known about [West Africa] until the early Portuguese voyages of exploration in the 15th century. No medieval travellers are known to have travelled southwards beyond Cape Bojador, on what is now the northern coast of the Western Sahara." Nonetheless, Thompson discloses:

> According to the myths current up to that time, the region beyond that point was one of impenetrable mist, where all was blackness. It was the undiscovered bourne from which no traveller would return. Should whites manage to survive the liquid fire that was waiting to consume them, they would nevertheless be turned from white to black. They were also likely to be eaten by the Africans. They had no right going there, since the region was intended by God to be the denizen of wild beasts.[13]

Thompson further observes, "The writers of the 'Age of Reconnaissance' [1450–1650] were much more prejudiced against blacks than their predecessors."[14] The English writer George Best, for example, endorsed the racist mythology of the congenital Hamitic African curse, ensuring that "all his posterite after him should bee so blacke and lothsome, that it might remaine a spectacle of disobedience to all the worlde." He persisted in describing Africa as a "cursed, dry, sandy, and unfruitful ground, fit for such a generation to inhabit."[15]

Apart from Best's 1578 remarks, other European writers during this period customarily compared Africans to beasts. Thompson summarizes:

> We find quite commonly the use of such terms, in describing blacks, as "a beastly Savage People," (by Baker, 1563); "brutish," (Azurara c. 1453); "monstrous," (Pacheco c. 1506); "beasts" (Azurara and López c. 1591); and "beastly" (Lok, c. 1554). They were also compared in their traits to dogs (Pacheco); hogs (anon. Dutch writer, c. 1600); and goats (Towerson c. 1555). . . . Pacheco, writing about the Wangara peoples of the area of modern Guinea, about whom he had heard, declared that they were "monstrous folk," with faces, teeth and tails like dogs. . . . According to Cadamosto the Wangarawa were a people whose lower lip was usually very red, and sometimes blood dripped from it. They also had great teeth in the corners of their mouths and large black eyes. In short, "they made a terrible Figure. . . ." He ended his account by stating that "It is believed, that their lips began to putrify . . . through the excessive Heat of the climate," and so they had to use salt to preserve their lips![16]

Thompson additionally credits Azurara (c. 1453) with describing Africans as living "like wild beasts, without any of the customs of rational creatures . . . and worse still was their ignorance, which deprived them of all knowledge of good." He also notes Pacheco's claim (1495) that "some 35 Flemish soldiers were captured by the inhabitants of Praya dos Escravos (Sinu Bay) and eaten"[17] and cites comparisons made between West Africans and tailless apes. "European writers," says Thompson, "were uncertain whether these were man-like apes or ape-like men."[18] Another degrading depiction was forwarded by the French political theorist Jean Bodin, who in 1566 wrote that "promiscuous coition of men and animals took place, wherefore the regions of Africa produce for us so many monsters."[19]

It is important to acknowledge that, apart from missionaries, European explorers and secular writers described African religions as immoral. According to Thompson:

> Religious differences between Africans and Europeans were also the basis for critical comment. Europeans generally divided West Africans along religious lines into Muslims, and heathens. . . . Adherents [of African religions] were deemed to be "*idolaters,*" "*sorcerers,*" practicers of "witchcraft," worshippers of "*devils,*" etc. One writer thought that their "*uncivill*" nature was reflected in the fact that they had "*neither Scripture nor Bookes, nor any notable Lawes. . . .*" Another inferred that the absence of Christianity among them "*deprived them of all knowledge of good.*"[20]

These beliefs about Africans represent an anti-African trajectory in European thought that gained currency as European encounters with Africans evolved within plantation slave-labor societies in the Caribbean and the Americas.

Although Africans in Jamaica were exposed to Spanish and British settlers, and therefore to different styles and approaches to the formation of Jamaican society, by the time the Spanish began to claim sovereignty over the island in the late fifteenth century, the reality of Europe and European culture had already been more than five centuries in the making. James Muldoon describes the cultural components that came to comprise a discernible European identity by the eleventh century, namely, "the classical tradition of late Mediterranean antiquity, the barbarian or Germanic tradition, and the Christian tradition, which, in the changing institution of the Christian Church, blended these different traditions into a single culture."[21] Spain, Britain, and other European nations no doubt embraced Eurocentric ideas about Africans which were predicated upon religiocultural ethnocentrism. Most of all, antipaganism and aversion to African people's physical features were predominant motifs in what became "European culture."

From the foregoing we may conclude that anti-Africanness was an established idea in European culture prior to the slave trade. Indeed, a culture of anti-Africanness provided ammunition for proslavery advocates who vehemently defended the enterprise in the face of the abolitionist movement. The following example, a passage from a proslavery pamphlet titled *Slavery No Oppression* describes Africans by using similar parlance as did Europeans from earlier periods. Even more significant is the universalization that takes place in the discourse as the writer describes, not specific ethnic groups, but all (African) peoples dwelling on the "eastern and western coasts":

> It is well known that the eastern and western coasts of Africa are inhabited by stupid and unenlightened hordes; immersed in the most gross and impenetrable gloom of barbarism, dark in the mind as in the body, prodigiously populous, impatient of all control, unteachably lazy, ferocious as their own tigers, nor in any respect superior to these rapacious beasts in intellectual advancement, but distinguished only by a rude and imperfect organ of speech, which is abusively employed in the utterance of dissonant and inarticulate jargon. Such a people must be often involved in predatory battles to obtain a cruel and precarious subsistence by the robbery and destruction of one another. The traffic (the Slave Trade) has proved a fortunate event for their miserable captives.[22]

To say the least, British anti–slave trade and abolitionist propaganda invited a concerted response from proslavery advocates. In their defenses of African enslavement, eighteenth-century Jamaican historians such as Bryan Edwards and Edward Long embraced long-held Eurocentric notions about African moral, cultural, and biological inferiority. For example Long likened Africans to orangutans in terms of intellectual capabilities and physical characteristics. He further opined that Africans appear distinguished from the rest of mankind, not in person only, but in possessing, in abstract, every species of inherent turpitude that is to be found dispersed at large among the rest of the human creation with scarce a single virtue to extenuate this shade of character, differing in this particular from all other men. We cannot pronounce them insusceptible of civilization, since even apes have been taught to eat, drink, repose and dress, like men.[23]

Like his compatriot, Bryan Edwards maintained that Africans were "of a distrustful and cowardly disposition, a liar, prone to theft, a remorseless tyrant, addicted to wanton cruelty, promiscuous to the point that life to him was mere animal desire."[24]

Perhaps the most egregious example of European racism toward Africans is the nineteenth-century phenomenon of exhibiting the African. In one of the most deplorable cases, the British and French publicly displayed a Khoi (South African) woman called Saartjie Baartman as a spectacle for viewing. Between 1810 and 1815 patrons paid to see Baartman's naked body at public exhibitions. Of especial interest were her buttocks and vagina, which after her death were pickled, along with her brain, and remained in a French museum until her remains were finally returned to South Africa in 2002. Baartman's genitals were compared with that of European women and deemed to be outrageous and "beastly" due to their size. Many cartoons ridiculing Baartman as subhuman and subwoman appeared in British and French literature.[25]

Building upon its past, nineteenth-century Europe produced some of the most vulgar ideas about African inferiority, as a cadre of intellectuals sought to explain African inferiority upon what they put forth as objective research and scientific grounds. Arthur de Gobineau, famous for his notion of the Aryan master race, was one of the chief architects of the intellectual racism tradition. Although published after African-Jamaican emancipation, his *Essai sur l'inégalité des races humaines* (1854) was as much a promotion of White supremacy as it was a denigration of African humanity.

> Such is the lesson of history. It shows us that all civilizations derive from the white race, that none can exist without its help, and that a society is great and brilliant only so far as it preserves the blood of the noble group that created it, provided that this group itself belongs to the most illustrious branch of our species. . . . Of the first seven civilizations, which are those of the Old World, six belong, at least in part, to the Aryan race, and the seventh, that of Assyria, owes to this race the Iranian Renaissance, which is, historically, its best title to fame. Almost the whole of the Continent of Europe is inhabited at the present time by groups of which the basis is white. . . . There is no true civilization, among the European peoples, where the Aryan branch is not predominant. In the above list no negro race is seen as the initiator of a civilization. Only when it is mixed with some other can it even be initiated into one. Similarly,

no spontaneous civilization is to be found among the yellow races; and when the Aryan blood is exhausted stagnation supervenes.[26]

With these precedents in mind, it is safe to say that anti-Africanness was present in European thought long before, during, and after African enslavement in Jamaica. This is not to say that everything written about Africans by Europeans was negative. However, negative images of Africa and Africans were more prominent and publicized than were positive images.[27] An exception was the abolitionist camp in Britain, which produced a body of apologetic literature depicting Africans as human beings with defensible rights. Overshadowing sympathetic treatments of Africa and African people in the literary and experiential record is the protracted institution of modern racial slavery. For centuries, Europeans enslaved Africans in the Caribbean and the Americas. Slavery was brutal and correlated suitably with the established history of anti-African ideas in European culture. The same might be said about European efforts to Christianize Africans. In the following sections we will examine how the planters and missionaries expressed anti-Africanness with regard to African religiosity in Jamaica.

The Planter-Class Campaign against African Religions

But in the year 1760, when a very formidable insurrection of the Koromantin or Gold Coast Negroes broke out in the parish of St. Mary, and spread through almost every other district of the Island; an old Koromantin Negro, the chief instigator and oracle of the insurgents in that Parish, who had administered the fetish or solemn oath to the conspirators, and furnished them with a magical preparation which was to render them invulnerable, was fortunately apprehended, convicted, and hung up with all his feathers and trumperies about him; and this execution struck the insurgents with a general panic, from which they never afterwards recovered. The examinations which were taken at that period first opened the eyes of the public to the very dangerous tendency of the Obiah practices, and gave birth to the law which was then enacted for their suppression and punishment. But neither the terror of the Law, the strict investigation which has ever since been made after the professors of Obi, nor the many examples of those who from time to time have been hanged or transported hitherto produced this desired effect. We conclude, therefore, that either this sect, like others in the world, has flourished under persecution, or that fresh supplies are annually introduced from the African seminaries.[28]

In England and in Jamaica, among various factions of White society (the planters, government officials, and missionaries), the period between 1760 and

1838 could rightly be seen as nearly a century of conflict over the question of African enslavement. It was during this period that a series of military revolutionary activities caused the Jamaican planters tremendous concern regarding their invested security in slavery as a guaranteed labor-profit system. The British colonies in North America won independence and became a sovereign nation in 1783; the Napoleonic Wars (1803–1815) were bubbling in Europe. But of primary concern were African slave rebellions across the Caribbean.

The Haitian Revolution of 1791 (which resulted in the expulsion of French settlers from the island)[29] followed the Jamaican rebellion of 1760 and intensified the sense of panic about African insurrections among the White Jamaican planters. The 1760 slave rebellion was in fact a pivotal event in identifying African religion as the source of African resistance to slavery. When the leaders of the rebellion confessed their reliance upon Obeah rituals in plotting and carrying out their revolutionary goals, the Jamaica House of Assembly ratified a series of legislation against the practice of African religious traditions. Obeah was indicted as the criminal practice of sorcery, punishable by death.

The 1760 rebellion was not, however, the first occasion for legal injunctions against the practice of African religious traditions in Jamaica. Joseph Williams cites legal codes against the use of poisons (1684), against the beating of drums and the congregating of enslaved Africans for "feast" or "revel" (1699), and against the beating of drums, barrels, gourds, and boards, the blowing of horns, and other noisy instruments (1717). Williams notes, however, that the 1760 rebellion forced Jamaican planters to equate Obeah, that is, African religion, with political activity, which threatened their social and economic order. Prior to 1760, Obeah "was looked upon with amused toleration as foolish superstition and nothing more."[30]

More acts against African gatherings, drumming, music of all kinds, and Obeah were passed in 1781 and 1784. In 1788 prohibitions against Obeah were restated with the specification "In order to affect the health of lives of others, or promote the purposes of rebellion."[31] In 1808 and 1816 acts were passed to ensure better material provisions for enslaved Africans. The 1816 act allowed for "amusements on the properties 'so as they do not make use of military drums, horns and shells . . . [and] are put an end to by ten o'clock at night.' " This same act includes prohibitions against "poisoning" and possession of poisons, pounded glass, and other paraphernalia associated with Obeah practices.[32] Still other legislation that prohibited the practice of Obeah, Africans from teaching and preaching to one another, and private meetings among Africans followed in 1826 and 1827. Obeah was perceived as a threat to civil society, for it incited enslaved Africans toward insurgent activities[33] which had grave economic and political consequences for the planter class.

The Jamaican planters' concern for preserving their opportunities to acquire and amass wealth and their personal interest in fortifying their social and political dominance over enslaved Africans especially influenced their development of anti-African legislation and social norms. While they went to great lengths to describe Obeah as a threat to human safety and prosperity within the entire Jamaican society, including the enslaved African community, a careful review of eighteenth- and nineteenth-century legislative documents and other contemporary literature reveals that the planters' genuine preoccupation was with the potential within Obeah to destroy the slave economy and, ultimately, to destroy White control of the society by motivating rebellions, acts of sabotage, and the systematic killing of the planter class.

Their protracted characterization of Obeah as the malicious use of poison discloses their greatest fears that they (not the enslaved) were the most targeted group for the lethal potions of Obeah practitioners. In spite of how Obeah was used as a method for social control by enslaved Africans among themselves, and regardless of how it was perceived by Africans who used it to effect certain goals and desires within the reaches of their communities, Obeah was consistently deployed to challenge, destroy, or rebel against the social order, which often included the local or mass murdering of slave masters. Obeah, in the eyes of the planters, was a public enemy of the state. Thus, especially after the 1760 rebellion, the planters began to criminalize Obeah as reflected in the official decrees and rulings of legislative and judiciary authorities.

Citing William Wilberforce's reflection on Obeah in Jamaica, Joseph Williams concludes that he "was not far astray in his estimates . . . of the . . . toleration with which Obeah was usually regarded by the planters of the island, until the rebellion of 1760 opened the eyes of all to the connection between Obeah and poisonings, and led the Assembly to legislate directly against the practice of this black art."[34] Wilberforce noted, "The Jamaica planters long imputed the most injurious effects on the health and even lives of their slaves, to the African practice of Obeah, or witchcraft. The Agents for Jamaica declared to the Privy Council in 1788, that they 'ascribed a very considerable portion of the annual mortality among the Negroes in that island to that fascinating mischief.' "[35] Yet Williams finds evidence that contradicts the assertion that Obeah was a perpetual cause of disease and death among the enslaved population and cites Dr. Patrick Browne as noting "the presence of poisonous plants" in the island. "However he ascribes the high death rate among the slaves not to poison but rather to the poor medical attendance on the island."[36]

As slaveholders, their entire economic and social privilege was contingent upon their exclusive control of enslaved Africans and slave production; the planters could not afford to interpret or depict Obeah and other African religious praxes as political activity against the slave regime. Rather, to defend their nefarious practice of slavery, they had to signify Obeah as an innately evil transgenerational tradition serving the exact same function of poisoning and killing in ancient Africa and among the enslaved Africans in Jamaica.

The planters' primary concern was maintaining efficiency within the slave system. They waged war against anything that attracted the attention of enslaved Africans away from their assigned tasks. Furthermore, the laws governing the treatment of enslaved Africans were designed to ensure the system's social and economic success. The brutality of the planters was backed by the brutality of the law, which sanctioned corporal punishment by burning, starving, amputation, flogging, and the like.[37] From his study of nearly two centuries of Jamaican legislation on the institution of slavery, Orlando Patterson concludes:

> The laws . . . gave the master absolute power over his slave.[38] Until about the middle of the eighteenth century this power was greatly abused; after this there was some mitigation in the treatment of the slave (although the extent varied with the personality of the master) culminating in the period of the first phase of the abolition movement; then, with the growing certainty of emancipation, a return to the excessive brutality of the pre–mid-eighteenth century period took place.[39]

Religious affiliations, which for Africans necessarily involved drumming, singing, and possession trance (dance), were prohibited not only because they created contexts for inciting rebellion but also because they promoted relationships, intimacy, and loyalty within a labor-intensive structure that thrived upon maintaining division, suspicion, and isolation among Africans. Above all this, the labor system was structured by time shifts. Time, production, and profit were one and the same, especially on the sugar plantations where freshly cut cane had to be juiced and boiled immediately to prevent spoilage. On the sugar plantations the average workday began at about 4:00 A.M. and ended at about 7:00–8:00 P.M. Thirty minutes and two hours were allotted for breakfast and lunch, respectively. However, most Africans used their lunchtime to attend to their own provision grounds and animals.[40]

Enslaved Africans grew and marketed their own food in Jamaica because it was the most cost-effective way of maintaining the food supply for laborers within a mono-crop plantation system. Personal farming, marketing, and the limited time allotted for festivals during Christmas permitted Africans to exercise some control over an informal economy and the promotion of cultural institutions steeped in the rhythms, sounds, and styles of Africa.[41] Nonetheless, controls were tightly enforced, and African religions suffered. Under the whip and scrutiny of the plantation managers, African deities were forgotten, religious rites and dances were secularized, and whatever remained was tested by the legitimate religious authority accorded to missionary Christianity.

The European Missionary Campaign against African Religions

From the beginning, Caribbean peoples experienced the European enterprises of voyaging and evangelization in virtually the same breath. While it cannot always be assumed that European voyagers and settlers gave deliberate thought to the evangelization of the indigenous and enslaved African populations in the Caribbean, it is certainly the case that Cristóbal Colón (the initiator of Europe's political, economic, and cultural relationship with the Caribbean) did. On November 6, 1492, Colón recorded these feelings about the inhabitants of Cuba in his log:

I hold for certain . . . that as soon as some missionaries are able to speak their language, they will all become Christians. I hope to God that Your Highnesses [Ferdinand and Isabella of Spain] will promptly decide to send them some missionaries, so that this multitude of people may come into the Church.[42]

Colón's sentiments were shared enthusiastically by King Ferdinand and Queen Isabella of Spain, who arranged for the appointment of Fray Bernardo Boil[43] as the first vicar apostolic in the Caribbean as early as 1493. The Papal Bull of Alexander VI (June 25, 1493) authorizing Boil's post in the Caribbean unambivalently declared the Catholic church's official sanction of the Christian evangelization of non-Christians. It states:

We willingly accede to the pious wishes of the faithful, particularly those of Catholic kings and princes, when such wishes have reference to the spread of Religion, the exaltation of the Catholic Faith, and the salvation of souls. We honour such wishes with fitting favours as best we can, with God's help. Now, the illustrious personages, our most dear son in Christ, King Ferdinand, and our most dear daughter in Christ, Queen Isabella, rulers of Castille, Leon, Aragon and Granada, recently informed us as follows. In the fervour of their devotion, they desire that the Catholic Faith should flourish and be exalted in the lands and islands out in the West in the Atlantic Ocean, which have been discovered through their agency. . . . They have decreed, therefore, to send you out to those regions, so that the word of God may be preached and sown there, by yourself and by other priests, secular or religious, suitable for that task, whom you may depute to it. So too, that the natives and inhabitants of the aforesaid islands and lands (people who have no knowledge of our Faith) may be brought to the True Faith and the Christian Religion, and be taught and trained to walk in the Commandments of God, by you and your collaborators. . . . Furthermore, in order to encourage Christians to go out to the said lands and islands more readily, through a sense of devotion, with a view to saving their souls, by the aforesaid authority, and by special favour, we grant the following privileges to each and every one of the said faithful, of either sex, who may personally go to the said lands and islands, by the order, however, and will of the aforesaid King and Queen.[44]

Even though Boil's missionary appointment was short-lived, wrought with strife, and therefore unsuccessful,[45] missionaries were repeatedly sent to convert "African heathens" to "civilized" religion and culture.

Although Christianity's impact upon African Jamaicans was minimal until the nineteenth century, missionaries arrived with the agenda of demolishing African culture and religion. We owe much of what we know about the religious traditions of enslaved Africans to missionary diaries, for they consistently registered complaints against the two main obstacles preventing successful conversions among Africans: one was entrenched planter opposition and the other was African religion and culture. John Lang, a celebrated Moravian missionary of the early nineteenth century, said it this way:

> The whole island is against us all; who will defend us? But Thou, O
> Friend of the friendless, pity Jamaica! pity the poor slaves whom
> Thou hast redeemed with Thy precious blood, not from servitude in
> body, but from serving sin and Satan. Oh, my dear Saviour, help and
> let us prevail in Thy cause against all the malice of Satan and the
> power of darkness! Amen![46]

While the 1760 rebellion set the context for a uniform, islandwide demonization of African religious traditions (Obeah) within Jamaican society, the introduction of missionary Christianity only intensified this process as African religious traditions were marked for annihilation. The European missionaries were convinced that enslaved Africans were destined for eternal damnation if left alone to perpetuate the "heathen" and "barbaric" practices of their native lands. Whereas the planters' anti-African values emerged primarily from their economic and political interests in preserving slavery, the missionaries' anti-African values stemmed from an ethnocentric evangelical conviction that Christianity was the "true religion," essential for eternal salvation. They viewed African religion and culture as demonic and aimed to replace what they perceived to be African polytheism, witchcraft, and fetish practices with initiation by baptism into the Christian faith. They were constantly on guard, prepared to denounce and punish converts who demonstrated any attachment to Obeah or Myal as admitted by George Blyth in the following narrative:

> While those who have recourse to such expedients [Myal and Obeah]
> are generally ignorant, and make no profession of religion, these su-
> perstitious practices are not unfrequently the cause of much disquie-
> tude to churches, by members being detected in them. The black of-
> fice bearers are as decidedly opposed to such superstitions as the
> ministers can be. They look upon them as evidences of a heart to-
> tally estranged from the fear of God, and utterly unfit for church
> membership; and there is no doubt but that those who betake them-
> selves to such expedients show a decided trust in God's providence,
> as well as a lamentable ignorance of the laws of nature. When I had
> occasion to discuss this subject in the pulpit, I treated it as a system
> of idolatry, injurious to those who practised it, and most dishonour-
> ing to God. . . . The well-disposed and religious portion of the com-
> munity detested these Myal people.[47]

The missionaries assumed that Africans came to the Caribbean in a state of moral depravity and cultural barbarism. While many of them deplored slavery and believed the institution to be in contradiction with the gospel,[48] they assumed cultural and religious superiority over Africans and saw themselves as endowed with the highest religious and cultural knowledges, which could save their inferior African brethren from sin and eternal damnation. Francis Cox's account of Baptist missionary activities in Jamaica offers ample evidence of their religious chauvinism and cultural ethnocentrism. Describing the religious[49] practices of enslaved Africans in Jamaica, Cox resolutely affirms the missionary enterprise:

> They retain many funeral rites of a superstitious nature; such as dancing round the grave, sacrificing poultry, pouring out libations, and affecting to hold conversation with the spirit of the deceased. Other practices similar in principle might easily be adduced; but these are sufficient to show the general character of the African people, and the necessity that existed for christian efforts to raise them from their mental and moral degradation.[50]

In defense of the Baptist missionaries who were specifically identified and penalized as sowers of sedition among the rebellious Africans of 1831, Cox appends the supportive remarks of a parliamentary official. Viscount Goderich's commentary demonstrates the deep assumptions of moral superiority that prevailed among the missionaries and their European sponsors in their quest to redeem lost souls from "the darkness of heathen idolatry." Like many of the evangelists, he also saw the spread of Christianity among the enslaved Africans as having the eventual effect of upsetting and rendering impossible the master-slave relationship, reinforcing at the same time the European caste consciousness of associating idolatry and heathenism with enslavement and the right and duty of Christians to enslave the pagan idolater.

> I could not, therefore, acknowledge that the slaves in Jamaica could be permitted to live and die amidst the darkness of heathen idolatry, whatever effect the advancing light of christianity might ultimately have upon the relation of master and slave. Nor am I anxious to conceal my opinion, that a change in this relation is the natural tendency, and must be the ultimate result, of the diffusion of religious knowledge amongst them. . . . It is also well worthwhile to reflect upon the inevitable tendencies of the laws for the abolition of the slave trade. So long as the islands were peopled by the importation of native Africans, who lived and died in heathenism, the relation of master and slave might be expected to be permanent. But now that an indigenous race of men has grown up, speaking our own language, and instructed in our own religion, all the more harsh rights of the owner, and the blind submission of the slave, will inevitably, at some period more or less remote, come to an end.[51]

Although the missionaries sympathized to some degree with enslaved Africans, before leaving England they were specifically trained to separate their political views from their evangelical theology. Already suspicious of African religion as a source of insurrection, the Jamaican planters carefully monitored the religious activities of the missionaries and insisted that they preach a Chris-

tian doctrine that could in no way be adduced to endorse the abolitionist political ideology which was circulating among religious and secular liberal circles
in Britain. Indeed, some missionaries were emphatically critical of slavery, not
solely because they understood it to be unethical, but because—in defense of
slavery—the planters exhibited significant control over the missionary enterprise and often disrupted or sabotaged religious services. The missionaries
opposed anything that interfered with their religious duty of saving "heathen"
souls.

Because the missionaries took extra pains to ensure that their message of
spiritual salvation through Christ would not be interpreted by slaves to support
their desires for temporal social freedom, they specifically instructed enslaved
Africans to hold in abeyance any such hopes. Instead they could anticipate a
delayed compensation in heaven for the daily suffering they endured in the
present life. The missionaries accomplished this by propagating ethical teachings from select biblical texts that supported the bipolarization of human experience—texts that emphasized spiritual salvation in spite of physical captivity. This theology of suffering was reinforced through devotional instruction,
where the missionaries firmly preached compliance and willing cooperation
with the social norms and regulations of the slave system. Social subordination
based on race had to be reinforced among enslaved Africans. Missionary Christianity, with its attending doctrines of sin, repentance, salvation, a providential
Deity, and so on,[52] functioned ideologically as an important form of social
control and cultural hegemony.

The 1831 rebellion is a suitable occasion for examining missionary theology
as a form of social control. On the eve of the rebellion, Cox notes, many of the
enslaved Africans in the province of Cornwall had determined not to work after
Christmas. The missionary response was an immediate attempt to suppress
any insurgent plans among the enslaved Africans who had been attending their
services. One such missionary, William Knibb, told his congregation that "God
commands you to be obedient to your master; if you do as he commands you
may expect his blessing; but if you do not, he will call you to an account for it
at the judgment day. If you refuse to work, and are punished, you will suffer
justly; and every friend you have, must and will turn his back upon you."[53] Cox
goes further in insisting that the missionaries could not be implicated in the
1831 rebellion when he writes:

> What then, it will be naturally inquired were the real causes of the
> Jamaica insurrection? Whatever they might have been, it is plain
> that religion and missionaries were free from all just imputation. It
> was no part of their scheme to promote revolt: their entire purpose
> was to diffuse the knowledge of Christ and salvation. It does not ap-
> pear that they ever deviated from their avowed object, or violated
> their compact, in this respect, with the Society by whom they were
> sent forth as agents. The insurrectionary movement was as great a
> surprise to them, as to any part of the community, and they were
> the first to aim at its suppression.[54]

Gordon Lewis succinctly summarizes the sociopolitical implications of missionary Christianity in his assertion: "What the Christian mission seeks to do in the West Indian society is not abolish slavery but rather, by inculcating the general lesson of obedience to divine law, to help stabilize it."[55] As the 1831–1832 revolt unfolded during the Christmas season, the Presbyterian missionary George Blyth "counted sixteen incendiary fires around my house" and was "incessantly employed in urging upon the consciences of my people [enslaved Africans] the duty of abstaining from acts of wrong and violence. With, two exceptions," writes Blyth, "all promised to act on my advice."[56] Recounting the experiences of the Moravians in Jamaica at the time of Tacky's 1760 Rebellion, the Religious Tract Society reports, "It was . . . encouraging to the missionaries to find, that none of the slaves belonging to the five plantations in which they laboured were implicated in a rebellion of the negroes in 1760. On the contrary, they were often in danger of being surprised by the rebels, till the latter were driven to seek an asylum in the woods and mountains."[57] Moreover, "The progress of the [Moravian] mission was still further impeded, in 1797, by a rebellion of the maroons or runaway slaves, who occupy several villages in the mountains."[58]

The missionaries who traversed seas to save the souls of enslaved Africans in Jamaica were part of a larger evangelical movement of religious enthusiasm and voluntarism. In Britain, evangelicalism, with its revivalist flavor, managed to "uplift the moral consciousness of the laboring classes."[59] In the North American colonies during the mid-1740s, evangelical Presbyterian ministers spawned a series of revivals in which the Baptists and Methodists later participated across the South. These revival cycles continued into the nineteenth century. John Boles identifies "a feeling of crisis" as a significant factor in motivating evangelical activity. During the last decade of the eighteenth century, evangelicals felt the threat of deism and universalism, which in their minds jeopardized the propagation of "true religion" throughout the newly independent nation.[60] According to Boles, the resultant revivals were attempts to revitalize the culture and preserve their religious values and ideals, "attempts to 'create a more satisfying culture' by purposely reviving real or idealized conditions of the past, especially those traditional customs that appear[ed] near extinction."[61]

Oddly enough, while a perceived threat of religious extinction or religious failure may have had motivational impact upon the missionaries who committed themselves to the charge of Christianizing Jamaica's enslaved Africans, this same threat of extinction was the order of the day for enslaved Africans. Isolation from ethnic community, anonymity within a stratified labor pool, and cycles of premature mortality[62] made the possibility of extinction an omnipresent reality for enslaved Africans throughout the Caribbean. The missionary enterprise, with its tenacious attack on African religion and culture, only intensified this problem for enslaved Africans. Mary Turner describes the missionary struggle to convert enslaved Africans in Jamaica as "a battle with the slaves' traditional religion."[63] Turner goes on to say:

The morality demanded by the road to salvation also included a total ban on drumming and dancing. European and African dancing were indicted, though the latter was instinctively recognized as the greater enemy; it was connected with the slaves' traditional religion. . . . The three-day Christmas holiday was a testing time even for settled congregations. While rowdy heathenish processions with "revolting attitudes in their dances," filled the slave villages and the streets outside the chapels, the missionaries tried to encourage their congregations by contrasting their clean, dignified appearance with the "half-mad, half-naked" goombah dancers. . . . Even so, the festivities usually took their toll on converts; at best, Christian and African celebrations were juxtaposed and if the drums were silent on one estate, they were busy nearby. The missionary was fortunate if, drummed to sleep on Christmas Eve, he was roused by carol singing on Christmas morning.[64]

The Religious Tract Society's publication *Missionary Records: West Indies* celebrated as a great evangelical achievement that:

[w]ith many, the love of rioting, in violence and iniquity, has been superseded by an earnest desire after [Christian] instruction, and a diligent and industrious pursuit of that knowledge which is able to make wise unto salvation. Instead of their former heathenish songs and obscenity, the voice of prayer and praise to the true God may often be heard from the negro's hut. The dreadful power of obeism and sorcery has, in numberless instances, given place to confidence and hope in the promises of Scripture, and the faithfulness of the Most High. . . . Many, also, have received that liberty wherewith Christ makes his people free. Instead of the fond but delusive hopes which they formerly cherished that death would not only end their oppressions, but transport them to the sunny hills, sparkling streams, grassy valleys, and majestic forests of their native land; numbers have passed the dark valley with enlightened faith and Divine support and have left the world with a well-grounded hope, full of immortality, even of departing to be with Christ.[65]

In order to accomplish their goal of converting Africans to the doctrine of personal salvation through Jesus, the missionaries insisted that Africans acknowledge and "repent of their sins." William Knibb, well known for his sympathy and support toward enslaved Africans, was intent on stressing personal sinfulness to one of his converts, Mary, on her deathbed:

When I was requested to visit her, she was in the last stage of consumption. On entering her lowly hut, I found her lying on a mat. . . . She looked at me with much affection and said . . . "Minister, me wish to tell you how good God is; Him is too good, Him is too good, minister." After speaking with her for some time, I said, "Well you are about to die, my sister; are you afraid to die!" "No, minister me is not afraid to die." "Do you not know that you have been a great sinner?" "Yes, me *feel* that; but, minister, Jesus; Him die for sinner, and me is not afraid to die. Me shall soon be with Jesus and me shall sing with Jesus for ever and ever."[66]

Missionary preoccupation with salvation after death is punctuated in accounts of African sickbed testimonies. In the following narrative, a Baptist missionary identified as Mr. Coultart speaks of the fulfillment he experienced upon hearing an African confess Christ on his deathbed:

Minister, bless you; I am safe; Jesus Christ has not forgotten a poor, wicked, worthless sinner. No, I am a dying man; but thank thee, O Saviour, for the gospel, for thyself; come, and take poor me. . . . My heart leaped for joy to see this poor *black* brand plucked out of the fire. I never saw such ecstasy in death before. . . . I thank God I crossed the Atlantic to see this, to receive the blessing and the delightful testimony of this poor descendant of Canaan, going where there is no more curse.[67]

The biblical "curse of Ham" and his African progeny, as it was construed and propagated, especially by White proslavery advocates, was also part of missionary catechisms. The Ham narrative from Genesis 9–10 was the foundational source of missionary theological anthropology, justifying the anthropological privilege of Whites and the anthropological impoverishment of Africans.[68] In the above report, Coultart suggests that anathematization can only be removed when one returns to the Judeo-Christian God who inflicted it—the implication being that Africans had no power to change their destiny as enslaved people. African "emancipation" would come temporally only by God's act of mercy or eternally by God's pardon in the afterlife.[69]

One of the most offensive and "immoral" components of African religion and culture to the missionaries was the pervasiveness of dance. The missionaries detested the embodied spirituality and sensuality of enslaved Africans and required that they refrain from participating in any such gatherings as a prerequisite for baptism and acceptance into the Christian community. Africans, in the company of the missionaries, were required to choose one or the other: African dance and spirituality or Christian instruction; African expressions of sensuality via dance or Christian ecstasy via fixation upon Christ and the Holy Spirit. In essence the missionaries presented this choice as one between damnation and salvation, eternal death and everlasting life. The moral incompatibility (insisted upon by the missionaries) between (African) dance and (Christian) religion is conveyed in the following narrative about enslaved Africans in Antigua:

Richard, one of the native assistants, closed his earthly pilgrimage in his ninety-ninth year. Even at that advanced age he was very active,

and much respected by his proprietor. A rather singular circum-
stance led to his conversion. He and another slave once endeavored
to promote a dance, in order to keep the negroes from going to
church. But this scheme was defeated, for all the rest declared they
"preferred going to church." This irritated Richard and his comrade.
They however resolved to go to the meeting, to see and hear for
themselves; when the Lord opened their hearts, so that they both seriously attended to the things which were spoken by the missionary.[70]

The same pattern of depicting dance as un-Christian is illustrated in the
following missionary narrative about enslaved Africans in Barbados:

Sunday dancing is promoted as a matter of gainful speculation, by
the individual who makes the necessary preparation for it; the dancing commences at an early hour in the afternoon, with flags flying,
drums beating, and such a savage uproar, that a stranger would
think himself anywhere rather than in a christian land. Nothing can
be a more glaring violation of the Divine commandment; nothing
can be more injurious to the morals of the younger slaves, especially
the females; nothing can present more temptations to fraud, stealing, and every other vice, than Sunday dancing, as it has been going
on during the year 1829, among the slave population.[71]

Wesleyan missionary Thomas Coke submitted a similar report of disdain, not
only for what he understood to be African dance in Tortolla but for the expression of African religiosity (ancestral veneration) through spirit possession
rituals:

Among other branches of iniquity to which the negroes were addicted, there was a filthy luxurious dance called the *Camson*, originally imported from Africa, which at once gratified their sensual ap-
petites, and indulged their native superstitions. In the delirium of
their passions, when abandoned by all restraint, they pretended to
hold intercourse with their departed relatives, and to receive from
them instructions, which they considered themselves religiously
bound to obey. . . . This diabolical custom, however, is now totally
abandoned, through the preaching of the gospel; and many of the
slaves who have received the truth in sincerity, relate with feelings of
horror, the part which they formerly took in these detestable transac-
tions.[72]

In Jamaica, missionaries were contented by "the effects of the gospel on the
slaves," as another Wesleyan missionary reported:

During the last Christmas there was not a drum heard, nor any of
the old heathenish sports carried on; but all spent the holidays in a
rational manner, in the worship of God. It is also worthy of observa-

tion that, instead of singing their old negro songs in the field, the slaves now sing our hymns; and I was much pleased, one night, when passing the negro houses, to hear them engaged fervently in prayer.[73]

On the face of it, one might suppose that the missionaries were more sincere in their encounters with Africans than the planters and slave traders. However missionary altruism stood alongside that of slave traders and planters. Slave trading was a lucrative commercial business and, as Eric Williams notes, "[T]he slave traders were among the leading humanitarians of their age." Williams documents some of the humanitarian contributions of prominent British slave traders to the poor and needy in their communities. They supported charity schools, hospitals, and institutions for aiding the poor. They were also counted among the gentry in Parliament, the House of Lords, learned societies, and elite clubs.[74] Furthermore, missionaries accommodated and participated in the institution of slavery.[75] They expressed feelings of disapproval about the institution itself and about the specific brutality meted out to Africans by planters and overseers. Yet they uniformly condemned African attempts to resist social control and enslavement, especially through strikes or rebellions. The connection between African dances and rebellions particularly challenged Eurocentric missionary theology and planter interests. African dances were anathema to both the planters and the missionaries because they provided occasions for Africans to organize against European domination.

The planters and the missionaries were adversaries over the issue of converting enslaved Africans to Christianity. However, they were united in their campaigns against Obeah and other African religious traditions—one group for sociopolitical reasons, the other for "moral" or theological reasons. The former's categorical dehumanization of Africans and the latter's conviction that they were ordained by God to bring true religion to depraved heathens were pronounced demonstrations that Eurocentric anti-African values inspired the reigning ideology, customs, and practices of the colonial slave society.

As human beings, Africans and Europeans shared much more in common than the planters and missionaries were willing to admit. But as human beings brought together through relationships of inequality, European planters and missionaries signified Africans as ontological Others,[76] as the embodiment of evil, polluted with every undesirable human quality they imagined. Africans' attempts to free themselves from dehumanizing social arrangements necessarily involved killing White planters and resisting White missionary theological values. In this sense, Africans were quintessentially opposed to Europeans and their culture of domination. In pre-emancipation Jamaica, to be pro-African was to be anti-European. Ironically, the master class did not belie Obeah (African religion) with the appellations of "black magic" and "black art." African religion was "Black" because it aimed to destroy White supremacy; such Blackness was evil in the eyes of Europeans, but it was good and divinely inspired in the eyes of countless Africans.

The planters tried to suppress "black magic" with legislated brutality; the missionaries tried to suppress it with Christian conversion. Some Africans resisted anti-Africanness by continuing to be who they were as drummers and dancers and by adapting Christianity to their moral concerns, to the dismay of their missionary teachers. As one nineteenth-century missionary in Jamaica complained, "Very few turn to God. . . . [This truth] often hangs like a dead weight on all my exertions and, after a week of incessant toil, causes me to sit down and mourn over the unproductiveness of all my labours."[77]

Missionary insistence upon a Eurocentric appropriation of Christianity made Christian conversion unappealing to many enslaved Africans. It likewise made those who claimed to be transformed by Christ (but not by the Eurocentric interpretation and expression of Christianity) unacceptable to the missionaries. The missionaries were mistaken in their estimation that "very few turn[ed] to God," for the Africans already knew the power of the Divine, and they expressed their communion with the Divine through autochthonous traditions, which the missionaries stigmatized as "barbaric," "heathenish," "licentious," and "demonic."[78]

Invariably, some Africans surrendered their Black values and loyally defended the interests of White enslavers and missionary teachers.[79] Yet a great number of Africans managed to subvert European attempts to exterminate Black values. They authenticated themselves within a context of censorship by identifying their illicit African religious imperatives with legitimate Christian religious imperatives and formed independently led congregations, which came to be known as "Native Baptist sects." But even on the continent, African religions were dynamically innovative and interpenetrable, symbolically and theologically open to universalisms.[80] When faced with cultural confrontation, African incorporations of Christian ritualistic elements, doctrinal formulations, and theological tenets attest to the authentic spirit of universalism intrinsic to African systems of thought.

Conversely, European missionary Christianity paraded behind a doctrine of universalism but actually presented itself imperialistically, demanding total allegiance from enslaved Africans to Euro-religion, Euro-culture, and Euro-authority through religious conversion and social control. The planters and the missionaries did not see that there was an authentic organic connection between the religious imperative of the Africans to seek social freedom and the moral imperatives of the Christian Bible. Any attempt to link the Christian message with African emancipation was interpreted by Whites as a corruption of the gospel.

What sort of "corruption" did Africans introduce to missionary Christianity? And how were they able to sustain their convictions in such repressive contexts of censorship? Moreover, what patterns emerged in the religious expressions of enslaved Africans after their consistent encounters with the missionaries? These questions are addressed in the subsequent chapters.

3

Offering

Trajectories of African-Jamaican Religiosity

By the Rivers of Babylon, there we sat down
And there we wept, when we remembered Zion[1]

The Triumph of Eurocentric Christian Authority: Religious Conversion and the Disintegration of African Religious Memory

Missionaries were always suspicious that beneath the polished Christian demeanor of African converts lay a "heathen" in remission. They constantly demanded that Africans prove disdain for their heritage and ancestral traditions. For example, a Baptist minister in Jamaica reported: "On asking another [enslaved African] if he loved the Saviour, he took off his hat, and showing me his gray woolly head 'Ah! Jesus,' said he, 'take care of me long time, when I was taken from Africa, and bring me to the gospel, and take care of me till now: me must love him.' "[2]

Despite the low rates of Christian conversion among enslaved Africans during the eighteenth and early nineteenth centuries, European Christian doctrines began to gain legitimacy among some Africans during the slave era. As discussed in chapter 2, the question of how to be African and Christian was not up for debate in missionary circles. The decision was made before the missionaries ever heard the sound of the *abeng* and the *goombah* drums:[3] the African instruments were the devil's instruments. That Africans embraced the notion that Jesus took them from Africa and brought them to the gospel was only the beginning of the problem. The heart of the matter was anthropological poverty, for European Christianity was not neutral in its response to African religion and culture.

The missionaries insisted that Western Christian culture was the antidote for African spirituality, religion, and culture. Africans had to equate all of their inherited traditions with a sinful past if they were to convince the missionaries of their authentic conversion to Christ. European Christianity forced African religion underground (away from public view and influence) and there it remains even today.

Enslaved Africans who considered the missionary prescription for salvation also had to withstand missionary condemnation for "sinful behavior" which they had no power to change. How could enslaved Africans maintain stable, monogamous relationships in a system that prohibited marriage, separated families, and enabled enslavers to habitually abuse African girls and women as sexual objects? African females had to recover from the effects of physical and psychological violation. And Christian missionary teaching on sexuality only intensified their predicament as they were made to feel ashamed of their bodies and were taught to disassociate pleasure and fulfillment from sexual encounters. For example, a Mrs. Brooks recounted how the formerly enslaved African (North American) missionary George Liele rebuked her for "living with my master":

> [T]his man took me to a fine house, and there I saw a white gentle-
> man, who was to be my master; and he took me to live with him.
> . . . Then I had a dear little baby. But I heard that a black man (Liele)
> was preaching, and I went to hear him; and he said that the great
> God in heaven was angry with me for living with my master, and I
> went home, and cried to myself many days: then I told my master
> that God was angry with me, and would send me to hell-fire, and
> that I could not live with him any more. Then he was vexed and
> rough to me and told me that I should work like another neger then:
> so I went out to work.[4]

In the temporal secular domain the punishment for resisting White male sexual aggression was increased brutality. The punishment for accommodating it was, according to the missionaries, a life after death of "hell-fire."

It appears that some Africans embraced the anthropological impoverishment that attended membership in the missionary churches because affiliation with White Christian traditions provided the best options for religious freedom, social privilege, and cultural legitimacy as a non-White. By nature, Africans did not possess the right color, they could not erase their Blackness or "Negroness"; it was there for everybody to see. ("Can Ethiopians change their skin or leopards their spots?")[5] But they could choose Christ and reject African religion and culture. They could throw away their Ancestors' garb and put on Western garb.

Though a number of Africans found the anti-African (Eurocentric) interpretation of Christianity to be illegitimate, the missionaries, nonetheless, introduced a religion that was legitimate among the Whites. Embracing Christianity provided African captives with opportunities for leadership, education, travel, and social mobility, which were unavailable to them as adherents of African religious traditions.[6] Becoming a Christian, in many cases, meant having the opportunity to learn how to read and write along with the opportunity to receive standard theological training. This offered converts more potential for upward mobility than the ancestral religions of Africa. For example, in honor of African emancipation from enslavement, the Bible Society of England granted "a copy of the Testament and Psalter, to those of the emancipated who possessed the ability to read on the first of August 1834." In addition the British Parliament "voted . . . for the erection of school-houses in the West Indies, which is divided among the respective missionary societies."[7]

The missionaries uniformly understood that their contribution to the African "heathens" was providing them with the opportunity to participate in spiritual redemption and civilized culture. Furthermore, they were eager to document their contributions in letters and reports to their sponsors and religious societies. In 1837, two missionaries had this to say about their work in the West Indies:

> Representation . . . cannot picture the happy result of these efforts; description can convey no idea of their excellence and magnitude. A few years ago, the negroes were heathen and benighted; now they are to a great extent enlightened and christian. The sabbath, once desecrated, is now devoted to public prayer and thanksgiving, and to the enjoyment of christian communion. A few years ago, education was unknown; now it is making progress under many disadvantages, and waits but for freedom to become soon more generally diffused than in our own country.[8]

Even more revealing is the governor's notice to enslaved Africans announcing their full emancipation from slavery and apprenticed labor.[9] Here we have more information which is useful for discerning why Africans may have chosen to identify with the missionary enterprise as they endeavored to improve their social and economic conditions:

> In a few days more, you will all become free labourers,—the legislature of the island having relinquished the remaining two years of your apprenticeship. The first of August next is the happy day when you will become free—under the same laws as other freemen, whether white, black, or coloured. I, your governor, give you joy of this great blessing. Remember that in freedom you will have to depend on your own exertions for your livelihood, and to maintain and bring up your families. You will work for such wages as you can agree upon with your employers. It is [in] their interest to treat you fairly. It is [in] your interest to be civil, respectful, and industrious. Where you can agree and continue happy with your old masters, I strongly recommend you to remain on those properties on which you have been born, and where your parents are buried. But you

must not mistake in supposing that your present houses, gardens, or provision grounds, are your own property. They belong to the proprietors of the estates, and you will have to pay rent for them in money or labour, according as you and your employers may agree together. Idle people who will not take employment, but go wandering about the country, will be taken up as vagrants, and punished in the same manner as they are in England. The ministers of religion have been kind friends to you; listen to them,—they will keep you out of troubles and difficulties. Recollect what is expected of you by the people of England, who have paid such a large price for your liberty. They not only expect that you will behave yourselves as the queen's good subjects, by obeying the laws, as I am happy to say you always have done as apprentices; but that the prosperity of the island will be increased by your willing labour, greatly beyond what it ever was in slavery. Be honest toward all men; be kind to your wives and children; spare your wives from heavy field work, as much as you can; make them attend to their duties at home, in bringing up your children, and in taking care of your stock; above all make your children attend divine service and school. If you follow this advice, you will under God's blessing, be happy and prosperous.[10]

What other options for social upliftment were available to the Africans on the eve of Emancipation? The missionaries represented a strong institution which could offer them the tools they needed to realistically prepare for official and worthwhile entry into White society.

Although the opportunities for improved social status and economic privilege provided by missionary Christianity did not include transcending the burdensome badge of racial inferiority, even the slightest improvement had to be incredibly valuable to persons who labored under the status of movable property. The faith testimonies of enslaved African Christians also suggest that some of them had overwhelming existential and mystical encounters with the Christian God and Jesus Christ.

Despite the missionaries' biased exhortations, the story of Jesus convinced some Africans that he was a divine incarnation with whom they could identify. Furthermore, Jesus was both God and human, an unconditional universal God for all who would believe and a human being who suffered undeserved persecution and death. The experience of unjust suffering, persecution, and death was chronic, visceral, and immediate within the daily experience of the enslaved population. Accounts of the forms of corporal punishment Africans endured suggest that some of them had witnessed the persecution of their fellow bondsmen and bondswomen through an even cruder form of crucifixion than that of Jesus. In his memoirs, *A Voyage to the Islands*, Hans Sloane recalls:

The Punishments for Crimes of Slaves, are usually for Rebellions, burning them, by nailing them down on the ground with crooked

Sticks on every Limb, and then applying the Fire by degrees from
the Feet and Hands, burning them gradually up to the Head
whereby their pains are extravagant. For Crimes of a lesser nature
Gelding, or chopping off half of the Foot with an Ax. These Punishments are suffered by them with great Constancy.[11]

Jesus, the resurrected Christ, resolved the existential problems of defeat,
anonymity, and personal worthlessness for some enslaved Africans, who decided to come to terms with their oppressed condition in ways that were acceptable to the missionaries. The Christian God became the source of personal
value for Africans who were moved to conversion by their encounters with a
transcendent deity—all-just, all-powerful, and all-knowing. John Boles argues
that within the southern United States, the image of Jesus "as a loving son of
a caring and forgiving father" was palpable to audiences because the "emotive
content" of evangelical preaching was "evidenced when the deeply religious
ministers described the moving panorama of Jesus Christ's spiritual agony and
physical suffering. Such a momentously poignant story of suffering and love,
guilt and forgiveness, elicited the innermost feelings from the faithful."[12] The
same could be said for the Jamaican context where African converts encountered an impartial incarnated God in Christ, whom they believed authenticated
their worth as persons through the ultimate act of self-sacrifice. Cox recounts
one such experience:

> A Guinea negro, whose experience we lately heard, observed re-
> specting himself, that from the time he came from the Guinea
> coast, "him no able to take word; if any one offend him, me take
> knife, me take tick, me no satisfy till me drink him blood;—now me
> take twenty bad word: then me tief, me drink, me ebery bad ting.
> Somebody say me must pray: me say no,—what me pray for? rum
> best pray for me; give me something good for eat, dat better dan
> pray." "What made you change your mind then?" "Massa, me go to
> church one Sunday, and me hear massa parson say, Jesus Christ
> come an pill him blood for tinner. Ah something say, you heara dat,—
> him pill him blood! Ah so! den me de tinner, me de tief, me de
> drunkard! Him pill him blood for Guinea niger! Oh, oh! Jesus
> Christ die for poo niger before him know him!"[13]

Here, an African man found, in Jesus Christ, God's grace and mercy demonstrated through the redemptive act of "pilling blood." It is significant to note
that enslaved Africans—a substantial percentage of whom were native Africans—were familiar with the phenomenon of incarnation and thus the Christian doctrine of incarnation might have been appealing to some.[14] In African
religious cultures, deities frequent human communities by uniting with the
human form. Through incarnation, the deities visit with adherents, express
revelations, heal, and help to resolve personal and social problems.[15]

The convert experienced Christ as a merciful healer who entered into his
spirit and healed him from his "sinful" habits of destruction—drinking rum,

stealing, fighting, and so on. The exhortation to pray was useless to the convert. He scoffed at the idea of praying and perhaps believed that praying distracted Africans from focusing upon their oppressive predicament. "Give me something good for eat, dat better dan pray" was his response until he met Jesus Christ and found himself renewed.[16] The following dialogue between another African man with failing health and his pastor also attests to the enslaved convert's perception of the power of Jesus and the salvific blood that he shed for all humanity:

> [D]o you think your prayers will take you to heaven? No, no. But do you expect to go there, because you are not so wicked as before, but are become a member of the church? No, me no have one good ting to tink of nothing but Christ, him precious blood. Ah, massa! him no pill him precious blood? him no say, Come unto me? me know him true. What do you think of religion now? . . . Ah, massa, what become of poor neger if him no hear religion! What me tink!—me feel, me no able to tell what me feel: it good, it make neger happy to die.[17]

The speaker makes a similar distinction between "prayers" and "Christ's precious blood": Christ, not prayers, has ultimate redemptive power. His reference to "feeling" religion is also significant, for he dismisses his pastor's assumption that religion is an intellectual experience. "What me tink!—me feel," he retorts. His religious rationale is not heady. Rather, the locus of his knowledge of God is the somatic domain where the perceptive potential for receiving and responding to spirit is nurtured. Evangelical Christianity, then, was perhaps best prepared to receive the conspicuous involvement of the senses and the body in religious worship to which enslaved Africans were accustomed in their indigenous religious traditions.[18] Knowing God was an existential and sensational experience that informed the enslaved person's logic, enabling her to distinguish between the sensible and the unreasonable. Mrs. Brooks, an African-born captive, testified:

> After a time, she became afflicted; God told her mind, she said, she was a great sinner; she believed it, and felt that poignant distress which some convinced and hopeless sinners feel; went to hear Mr. Liele, and by him was told to go to Jesus Christ, which after some time she ventured to do. Her own words are "Massa, me feel me distress, me heart quite big wi grief, for God no do me no wrong; him do all good for me,—me do all bad to him. Ah massa! me heart too full an too hard; me eye no weep, but someting so gentle come through me heart, den me eye fill, and God make me feel dat him so good to notice poor me, dat me throw meself down, and weep quite a flood."[19]

For this convert, God becomes truly manifest upon affecting the senses and the emotions and upon convincing her that her personal pain is significant in

God's eyes. Furthermore, the testimony below suggests that enslaved Africans evaluated their feelings with critical consciousness. One African told a missionary that God came to her in a dream and told her how to recover from an illness. The following is an excerpt from their dialogue:

> "Mary take care; God is very good, but you must not think too much about dreams, for Satan sometimes puts on white clothes." "Yes, massa," she replied, "me know; but me no heed so much what me feel, as what dat me feel make me do." She added, "when me hear any body peak, me say, Well, me see what you do; and me watch quite close, for it no hard ting to peak christian, but it quite hard to maintain the christian."[20]

"Maintaining the Christian" meant being in right relationship with God. Mary's emphasis upon how one *acts*, rather than how one speaks, as a Christian is rooted in the belief that righteousness or moral correctness is real when it is lived. She took the Jewish (Old Testament) understanding of faith as something one "does" very seriously. But, once again, such an understanding of faith was not solely Jewish; it was and continues to be an underlying assumption in the practice of African traditional religions.[21]

The central place of righteousness in the Christian attitudes of enslaved Africans may account for the recurrent references in Cox's text to their undying appreciation for the missionaries. The sympathy that converts showed to the missionaries, who were falsely accused of inciting the 1831 rebellion, demonstrates that they did see integrity in the missionary contribution to Jamaican society. Moreover, when juxtaposed with the behavior of the White planters, the missionaries, as a whole, were less disrespectful to Africans. They assumed that African souls were important to a God of the universe who was "no respecter of persons." African souls had as much potential for salvation as European souls.[22] As such, they presented a theology that subverted and invalidated the planter-class ideology that Africans were ontologically unworthy of God's "redemption." Thus the words of condolence offered by an "imprisoned negro" to Thomas Burchell (an incarcerated missionary), in the wake of the rebellion, emerge, perhaps, from his awareness that, as Whites, missionaries did not have to renounce their personal privilege to work among poor enslaved Africans:

> Minister, what make me feel is to see minister in trouble; me can bear it myself; me willing to suffer what God see fit; but when me see my minister, him leave father and mother and country to come to teach me it be more than me can bear. Never mind, massa, bear up, keep good heart, you know we Saviour suffer more than we suffer.[23]

Burchell also wrote, "On his liberation [from incarceration], the negroes crowded around him, and his feelings were over powered by their sympathy. They said, in reference to their persecutors, 'We know they wicked, but we must pray for them.' "[24] Another showered him with appreciation, saying: "Now, massa, me know dat God him true—him hear for we prayer—but him take him own time—and him work him own way—but him do every ting quite good." Also, "Massa, me hear you come—and me hungry for see you—and me cry for see you—me take two day for walk for see you—and now me believe—God him too good—me now willing for die, for now me know God him true."[25]

It has already been established that the missionaries, though consistently anti-African in their moral theology, were often sympathizers with the plight of the enslaved. Africans welcomed missionary pity for whatever it was worth, especially when juxtaposed with the contempt and malice of their enslavers.[26] In addition, the missionaries introduced enslaved Africans to literacy and other welcomed social options that they could not enjoy within the plantation labor structure. The exuberance with which some enslaved Africans embraced Christianity was informed by these and other forenamed "blessings," which came their way as baptized members of the faith.

An equally contributing factor to the religious excitement and conviction expressed by the enslaved converts in Cox's narrative was their very specific social context as nearly emancipated or newly emancipated subjects. Most of the African testimonies presented by Cox were dated immediately after the 1831–1832 rebellion, after the 1834 modification of status from slave to apprentice, and after the 1838 August 1 celebration of full emancipation. The *Sitz im Leben* for African Jamaicans in the 1830s was not simply chattel slavery. Specifically, it was the heightened anticipation of freedom, ignited by the Native Baptists and kept ablaze by abolitionist and missionary efforts to ameliorate slave conditions or to advocate for emancipation.[27]

With the gradual legislative enactment of Emancipation—officially rendering all enslaved Africans indentured servants in 1834 and fully emancipated in 1838—African converts exhibited exuberance toward and conviction for the Christian God. Their Christian faith was emboldened by the entire context of freedom, the urgency which fed the debates and tensions over slavery, and the presupposition that a providential God ordered the thoughts and steps of those who dared to protest slavery and demand African emancipation. The prayers of newly emancipated Africans in Jamaica are the best illustrations of how their excitement for the Christian faith was undoubtedly bolstered by the event of Emancipation, which they understood as divine intervention:

> Oh Lord, our gracious Saviour, what we is meet togeder for dis mornin' when we don't usual do so on dis day of de week? We is come to bless and to magnify dy great and holy name dat dou has done of bondage dis day. O Lord, what is dis dat we eye see, and we ear hear? Dy word tell we dat king and prophet wish to see de tings dat we see, and to hear de tings dat we hear, and die without de sight. O Lord, if we desperate wicked and tubborn heart won't prais dee as dey ought, pluck dem up by de root! Here Lord, we give dem up unto dee; melt dem wid de fire of dy love, wash dem in de

pure fountain of dy blood, and make dem what dou would have dem to be.[28]

O dat we may love dee and dy gospel more; may we neber turn dy blessing into a curse, may we be diligent in our proper calling, fervent in spirit, serving the Lord. O Lord, now do dou make thine arm bare, and turn de heart of all de people unto dee. We bless dee dat dou has incline so many poor dyin' sinner to come up to dy house dis day. O Lord, teach deir heart, turn dem from deir own way, same as dou did de city of Nineveh. Now make them trow down deir rebellious weapon, fight against dee no more, for dou say, Who eber fight against dee and prosper? Our eye is up unto dee, we cannot let dee go, except dou bless us wid dy grace: dou only canst change de stubborn heart,—turn it like de river of water is turned, dat all may serve dee from de least even unto de greatest.[29]

But how credible are missionary records of African attitudes toward them and toward the Christian faith? While there is clear evidence of African appreciation for the missionaries,[30] it was in the missionaries' best interest to depict their converts as unanimously and unambivalently grateful for the efforts made to introduce them to Christ and "civilized" culture. European sponsors required assurance that their monies were being well spent on a worthy cause. Furthermore, one wonders how the missionaries were able to cite verbatim the prayers of enslaved Africans. Did they take copious notes while Africans were praying? Although it is probable that a number of enslaved Africans did appreciate and support the missionaries, the following account by Thomas Burchell appears to be contrived, especially in the light of a contradictory account given by his colleague William Knibb. Is it possible that Burchell conveniently described his congregation as uniformly opposed to the 1831–1832 rebellion in order to appease a European audience? From his Montego Bay Chapel Burchell claimed:

There were now . . . twenty-four churches in Jamaica; and the conduct of the negroes belonging to them, during the late disturbances, gave a testimony to the purity of their faith; for he never heard one of them, throughout the whole, use a harsh expression respecting their persecutors. Whenever they spoke of them, they did so in terms of compassion and pity, and they prayed heartily for the forgiveness of those who were hunting them to death. Their sympathy for their ministers was so intense, that they quite forgot themselves.[31]

On the other hand, Knibb, who, at this time had a mission station in the neighboring parish of Westmoreland, recalls a very different response from enslaved Christians when he implored those in his congregation to be obedient to their enslavers after Christmas 1831—as they had planned to abandon slave labor:

Much dissatisfaction was manifested by some of the slaves at this address, and many murmurs were heard. . . . They said that "parson Knibb had no business to meddle with the free paper—that white people had bribed Mr. Blyth to tell lie, and that Mr. Blyth had given Mr. Knibb half the money to keep free paper from them." So angry were they with Mr. Knibb, for this interference to frustrate their intentions, that they declared they would have maltreated him, had he not had so many ministers with him. . . . On that night the burning of the properties began.[32]

The accounts explored above challenge any monolithic interpretation of the feelings and attitudes Africans expressed toward the missionaries. We can infer though that, while some Africans ignored and perhaps resented the missionaries with their moralistic condemnation of African-derived religious and cultural traditions, others accepted their Afrophobic Christianity and were grateful for their contributions. Still a great number of Africans experienced aspects of the Christian tradition as consistent with their African spirituality and with their Black values.

The next section examines the enslaved Africans' religiosity as a source of social transformation. These Africans came to be known as the Native Baptists, and they exercised authority over Africans who were members of White missionary congregations. The impulse of the 1831 rebellion was nurtured within Native Baptist congregations but, once in bloom, it stimulated African Christians who worshiped in the White missionary churches to assert their latent Black values by participating in the strike for freedom. As William Knibb reports above, on the very night he exhorted the enslaved not to rebel, "the burning of the properties began."

Religious Improvisation and Struggles for Sociopolitical Freedom among Africans in Jamaica

It is important to consider the social dynamics that contributed to the development of certain theological currents in nineteenth-century African-Jamaican religiosity, bearing in mind the limits upon and options available to the enslaved populations through African religious traditions (namely, Obeah and Myalism), through their encounters with missionary Christianity, and through their stratified relationships with their enslavers within the social hierarchy. On one level, there existed a sturdy abolitionist movement which involved discussions and activities among liberals in Britain, missionaries, government officials, and the Jamaican planters. On another level, there were the religious and political activities of enslaved Africans, which were developed in secret, with conspiratorial flavor, within a culture of censorship. Finally, there was the encounter between enslaved Africans and the missionaries, which took place both within a context of suspicion and censorship and within a context of legitimacy and opportunity.

The most successful encounters between missionaries and enslaved Africans occurred with the work of the African-American Baptists beginning in 1784. After conflicts with the planters, which landed African-American missionaries George Liele and Moses Baker in prison, Baker wrote to the Baptist Missionary Society requesting support for their endeavors to convert enslaved Africans to Christianity in Jamaica.[33] In 1816 a cadre of European Baptist missionaries landed in Jamaica with the intention of continuing the work started by Liele and Baker among the enslaved populations. Their arrival marked the beginning of a sustained encounter between African-derived religions and missionary Christianity. Christianity provided African religiosity with a public face or, as I will argue in the final chapter, a public mask for both concealment and expression. But, even as self-identified Christians, adherents of African religions proved unacceptable to Whites—unacceptable because the focus of African religiosity was still the pursuit of temporal African liberation and its spiritual and ritual expressions were African-oriented rather than European-oriented.

The encounter between the African and Western Christian religions gave birth to African-centered religious movements and traditions that remain vibrant in Jamaican society even at the present moment. The following sections explore the historical contexts, religious and theological content, and sociopolitical significance of these traditions as they have affected each other and the wider Jamaican society. The emergence of the Native Baptists (c. 1830s), the emergence and legacy of Revival Zion (1860–1861), and Rastafari and its critical stages of development from the 1930s to the present day are considered chronologically.

Native Baptists

The late Robert "Bob" Nesta Marley, master reggae artist, expressed the tenuousness of Black freedom through his music and lyrics. Marley experienced firsthand the reality of Black impotence. Abandoned by his White British father, he grew up an "illegitimate" child of a poor, uneducated Black woman in colonial and neocolonial Jamaica. Marley warned his Jamaican comrades that their identification with British values, culture, and political habits invited unpredictable social consequences, especially for the most powerless people in the island—Jamaican Blacks. Furthermore, Marley saw that the benefits that accompanied assimilation into British culture were not available to the majority of Black Jamaicans. Thus, he sang from the center of "primordial Blackness"[34] and his prophetic declarations about the preacher's heaven and the Black person's hell are connected to a legacy of dissent espoused by African-based movements in the Jamaican religious landscape.[35] The development of the Native Baptist movement, I would argue, was motivated by the same critical "primordial" Black consciousness that Marley expressed in many of his songs. Although Black Christian acquiescence to missionary Afrophobic theology was a developing phenomenon in the nineteenth century, when some enslaved Christians experienced aspects of White religion and Euro-Christian values as a threat to their Black values and their commitment to be free—when they experienced missionary Christianity as an ideology from hell rather than heaven—they often resorted to critical forms of Black consciousness, which kept Black demands for social equity and autonomy alive and central in Black religion and culture.

From this standpoint, some enslaved Africans were attracted to Christ because his teachings could be cited to endorse their Black values, their thirst for the social freedoms denied to them as chattel property. Knowing that their Black values were repressed within the White missionary churches, they created their own religious institutions, authenticated them with the appellation "Baptist," initially derived from the tradition of African American Baptist missionaries in Jamaica, and developed a spiritual piety which was consonant with their Black values. Mary Turner is correct in her analysis of these Native Baptist congregations when she writes: "The slaves' political consciousness, though fed and watered by the mission churches, came to fruition outside them, in the religious groups they developed under the tuition of leaders recruited among themselves. It was in these groups that their political ideas took their most radical form."[36] That form was a Myal-inspired religious conviction that African liberation was ordained by God, an expression of Christian Myalism, shaped by Old and New World experiences and orientations.

Historical data pertaining to the Native Baptist movement can be gathered from contemporary missionary reports. Moravian mission documents note the impact of the Native Baptists on their own missionary efforts in the following citation:

> The work of grace continued, and it received a most helpful impulse through the influence of a number of black and coloured men— slaves who had been granted liberty by their owners, and who had undertaken some religious work among the former fellow-slaves in the island. They had been led to the knowledge of the Gospel by American Baptists [George Liele's contingent]. But, as their knowledge of religious truth was very imperfect, and they were unable to read and study the Scriptures, a curious mixture of superstition and truth was present in their teaching. Still, Christ was preached, and with striking effect; interest was roused among the slave population in the Christian religion, and a desire to acquire a fuller knowledge of the Gospel of Christ. [John] Lang became aware of the effects of these evangelizing efforts by the increase in the number of those who attended his ministry.[37]

The document further discusses the evangelical influence of one of the Native Baptists who encouraged a number of enslaved Africans to "seek further Christian instruction from the Moravian missionaries." Although George Lewis "never entered into fellowship with the Moravian Church . . . through his influence, people left off worshipping the cotton tree, forsook their house idols, lived better lives, and went in search of Christian instruction. 'Whether in pretence or in truth, Christ was preached.' "[38] If it is true that Native Baptists encouraged Africans to renounce rituals involving the silk cotton tree, we could infer that they rejected some of the African traditions associated with Myal religion. However, by 1873—sixty years after the above report—William Gardner wrote, "With few exceptions, native Baptist churches became associations of men and women who, in too many cases, mingled the belief and even the practice of Mialism with religious observances, and who perverted and corrupted what they retained of these: among them sensuality was almost entirely unrestrained."[39]

One of the striking differences between Native and missionary Baptist piety was the central role of visions or dreams to the former. According to the Baptist missionary James Phillippo:

> Dreams and visions constituted fundamental articles of their creed.
> Some supernatural revelations were regarded as indispensable to
> qualify for admission to the full privileges of their community. Can-
> didates were required indeed, to dream a certain number of dreams
> before they were received to membership, the subjects of which
> were given them by their teachers.[40]

The "superstition" and "pernicious follies"[41] in this emerging Christian Myalism confused and frustrated the missionaries. However, the pursuit of temporal sociopolitical liberation incensed them and invited their ardent protestations. The Native Baptists inspired and led the 1831–1832 rebellion, which had direct influence upon the abolition of slavery in 1834. Testimonies about the 1831–1832 rebellion substantiate Turner's claim that the revolutionary spirit of the Native Baptists was cultivated and nurtured within the African communities that spawned the movement. For example, Francis Cox recounted:

> Mr. Annand, the overseer, who was confined on the estate called
> Ginger Hill, attributes to the slaves the following language:—"that
> they were obliged to assist their brethren in the work of the Lord"—
> "that this was not the work of man alone, but that they had assis-
> tance from God." A slave named Samuel Sharp, who is designated
> as a "ruler of the sect of the Baptists," is described by the same wit-
> ness as having said, "that it was but lately that he had begun to
> know much of religion, but that now he knew, and I knew as well,
> that freedom was their right, and freedom they would have. He said
> a great deal more, all tending to show that from the religious no-
> tions he had imbibed, he conceived that the slaves had a right to be
> free."[42]

The assertion that the uprising was "the work of the Lord" and "assisted by God" is a subversive refutation of the White Christian assumption that African forms of social resistance could not be linked to "religion." When Africans exclusively used Obeah (and Myal) to inspire and achieve successful rebellions, Whites categorized African spirituality as superstitious and irreligious. But during the 1831 rebellion, Obeah and Myal were reasserted under the mask of Christianity. When modified in this way, White planters could not totally dismiss the religious foundation that obviously nurtured insurgent activity. The following account of how the rebellion was planned infers as much:

> On Christmas day, they [the implicated Africans] met Guthrie,
> Sharp, George Taylor, and others in the street as they left the chapel,
> who were talking on the subject. Taylor was advising Sharp not to
> refuse to work after Christmas, as it would bring disgrace upon the
> gospel; to which he replied, "What then is to become of the oath we
> have taken in the country?" He added, "I know we are *free*; I have
> read it in the English papers. I have taken an oath not to work after
> Christmas, without some satisfaction, and I *will not*." This statement
> was confirmed by [Sam] Sharp, the individual who planned the
> whole. He confessed that several weeks before Christmas, they met
> at a house at Retrieve, where the insurrection was determined; and
> he put every one to the oath not to work after Christmas. A Bible
> was brought and placed on the table, when he rose, and said, "If
> ever I witness any thing against my brother and sister concerning
> this matter, may hell be my portion!" They met again a fortnight be-
> fore Christmas, and resolved and swore, "that as we know we are
> free, we will not work for buckra, unless he pay us for it." These
> people, and some others, afterwards held a meeting at Cunningham
> Hill, where very violent language was used.[43]

The primacy of the oath (Black values)[44] over "disgracing the gospel" through rebellion (White values) surfaces in this testimony, demonstrating the clash between the two value systems with which Africans were forced to contend. Sam Sharpe, however, challenges the view that seeking liberation will scandalize the gospel, first by identifying his commitment to the plan with the religious act of taking an oath; and second, by reauthenticating the secret oath on what would have been viewed as the sacred credibility of the Bible.[45]

The planters could not implicate Obeah or Myal (superstition) as the true cause of the rebellion because they understood Obeah as "poison" and Myal as "heathen fetishism." They never conceived of Obeah as an entrenched African-derived religious framework that could sponsor social resistance with or without the use of poisons. Instead, they pointed the finger of suspicion at the persons who introduced Africans to Christianity ("religion")—the White missionaries. One sympathetic slaveholder, Samuel M. Barrett, wrote a letter to William Knibb expressing his disagreement with the widespread belief that "religion" (Christianity) stimulated the revolt:

> I deeply regret that the feelings of the country should have so
> strongly marked yourself, and the other Baptist missionaries, as ob-
> jects of persecution. My opinion, and opinion resulting from my
> own frequent and confidential intercourse, not only with my own
> negroes, but with the negroes of various other estates is, that reli-

gion had nothing to do with the late disturbances; but on the contrary, its absence was a chief cause of them.[46]

If "religion" meant European missionary Christianity, then "[Barrett's] negroes" were not telling a lie, for in actuality, the Native Baptists emerged as a
religious movement when enslaved Africans and free persons of color—who
were converted to Christianity by African-American Baptist missionaries—established congregations across the island over a forty-year period with little
opposition from White authorities. They were later joined by other African
Christians who had been converted by White missionaries, some of whom
maintained official membership in the White churches. In the months before
the rebellion, Sam Sharpe, a stellar and inspiring preacher, used the White
missionary meetings as a network for systematically communicating with fellow enslaved Africans. He and other freedom-seeking leaders frequented
White missionary services and stayed after with the aim of convincing as many
Africans as possible to commit to the impending protest against slavery. By
the time the Native Baptist war was waged, the biblical phrase " 'No man can
serve two masters,' persistently quoted by Shape, became a slogan among the
slaves."[47]

Sam Sharpe and the numerous Christian Myalists who participated in the
rebellion heard murmurs about abolitionist activities in England. Many of
them were counting on the "good" people of England, including the missionaries, for support in their freedom struggle.[48] But most of all, they were counting on the Divine Community,[49] which impressed upon them the thirst for
freedom. For this, the Native Baptists were discounted as a "sect" by White
contemporaries. Their Baptist piety was unorthodox by European Christian
missionary standards, for it was rooted in Myalism, where dreams and visions
(as opposed to repentance and confession of Christ) were the criteria for orthodox participation and official membership in the Native Baptist community.

No doubt, the shadow of history obscures the intricate patterns of indigenous African organization and practice during the period of Native Baptist
formation in Jamaica. While the written records suggest that George Liele,
Moses Baker, and to some extent George Lewis attempted to establish Baptist
congregations among the enslaved populations that would win the approval of
White authorities, the spread of the largely acephalous movement across the
estates yielded ritual and theological formation to localized expressions, which
probably varied from those assuming nearly orthodox Christian postures, as
established by the White missionaries, to those assuming nearly orthodox Myal
postures, which, one could argue, constituted the popular religion of the enslaved in the late eighteenth and early nineteenth centuries.[50]

What is certain is White contemporaries of the movement found it an
unacceptable localization of Christianity in terms of its pervasive religious culture, theological standpoint, and political orientation. At best, it provided an
ancillary stepping-stone toward authentic conversion and official membership
in God's true church,[51] and approximately forty years after the rebellion (1873),
White historian William Gardner attempted to set the record straight for any

confused interpreters: "The so-called 'Native Baptist Churches' are not to be confused with the regular Baptists. They had their origin, it is said, in groups expelled from the older organization for superstition and immorality. They carried with them the name of Baptist and little more."[52] In the eyes of most Whites, the Native Baptist movement was a new amalgamation of the old hazardous "black magic" and "black art," that is, Obeah oaths, Myal traditions, prophetic visionary insight, mystical power, and the pursuit of temporal freedom from the bondage of mental and chattel enslavement.

Revival Zion

Revival Zion has its origin in the Native Baptist religion (Christian Myalism), the older traditional African Myalism, and what came to be called the Great Revival of 1860–1861.[53] The Great Revival was a movement of religious enthusiasm that grew out of a North American revival in 1857. It spread among the Moravians in the southwestern region of Jamaica by October 1860 and eventually encompassed the entire island.[54] Eyewitness reports describe the movement, including its African overtones. For example, William Gardner, a contemporary of the movement, wrote:

> In many of the central districts of the island the hearts of thoughtful
> and good men were gladdened by what they witnessed in changed
> lives and characters of people for whom they long seemed to have
> laboured in vain; but in too many districts there was much of wild
> extravagance and almost blasphemous fanaticism. This was especially the case where the native Baptists had any considerable influence. Among these, the manifestations occasioned by the influence
> of the Myal-men . . . were very common. To the present time, what
> are called revival meetings are common among these people.[55]

Gardner's testimony provides evidence that the Revival Zion religion is a direct descendant of the Native Baptist faith. Of the Native Baptists, we know most about the theological foundations for their sociopolitical pursuit of African liberation. Not enough has been written about the structure and doctrines of the religion. In the case of its progeny, Revival Zion, we have the groundbreaking article of Edward Seaga, which presented the religion in the light of its sociohistorical background and its contemporary (1969) context. Other scholars, such as Chevannes and Wedenoja, continue to broaden our understanding of Revival Zion as a dynamic force in the social fabric of contemporary Jamaican life. The research of African studies scholars who are uncovering connections between Africa and the African diaspora with new detail must also be introduced into the conversation on Revival Zion origins. John Thornton's work on Kongo culture and the slave trade introduces the plausibility that any number of captives from the Kongo groups of Central Africa may have had tangential to significant exposure to some form of Christian theology and piety. Indeed, some may have been self-identified practicing Kongolese Christians.

In the future, scholars will have to interrogate this thesis more rigorously, but I want to give attention to it here because it corroborates the Revival Zion narrative I encountered when conducting research in Jamaica in 1996. The commonly held view of the origins of this religion was that their ancestors carried the tradition from Africa to Jamaica during slavery. Initially, I treated this datum as an important example of popular postcolonial subversive religious imagination, which only fortified my position that the religion is indeed African-derived. Since the practitioners are of the mind that their tradition is an inherited African Christianity, which the colonial European missionaries sought to counterfeit, I began to reconsider this myth of origin as a memory of origin when interpreting their claim in the light of current research on the Kongo and the Kongo diaspora. The Kongo kingdom's early promotion of and official conversion to Christianity during the late fifteenth century was more influential and infused with Kongo culture during the period of the transatlantic slave trade than many scholars in Caribbean and African American religious studies were previously aware. Kongolese captives (during the slave and indentured labor periods) may have been practicing a thoroughly indigenized Christianity, bearing the signature of Kongo culture, cosmology, and spirituality.

Descriptions of Kongo Christianity during this era speak to the common regard for the ritual of baptism/the baptizing priest among Central African Kongo Christians and Jamaican Revival Zionists. They also emphasize the importance of ancestors and the Divine Community, which is germane to the ritual life of the Revival Zion tradition. Thornton provides a portrait of sixteenth- and seventeenth-century Kongo Christian piety:

> Priests were mainly for performing sacraments, and the Capuchin missionaries, who came to Kongo in fair numbers after 1645, spent most of their time administering them, especially baptism. Many of the Capuchins would baptize tens of thousands of children during their seven-year terms in the country. Many regularly attended Mass when it was being said—often thousands would come to open air chapels or the rural crosses to hear mass or say the Rosary. They baptized their children, took Christian names, wore the cross, and described themselves as Christian. However, they also continued to visit their ancestors' graves and seek luck, health, and blessing. They respected the territorial deities that they sometimes came to identify also as Christian Saints, but sometimes worshipped separately. They sought out witches to destroy, and resisted attempts of missionaries to describe all these activities as witchcraft. Conversion to Christianity rarely involved any fundamental religious change.[56]

Although they are not always easy to detect, the beliefs and structure of Revival Zion are steeped in classical African ideas (perhaps with a Kongo influence) about the Divine Community, the Ancestors, and the relationship among forces, spirits, elements, and beings in the visible and invisible domains of the world. Given this focus, the question might be asked: What was being revived as Native Baptist religion gave birth to Revival Zion religion? To this question, Leonard Barrett has fashioned the most satisfying response. Of the Great Revival, Barrett writes:

> Was it really a revival of Christianity? The answer is no. There was no Christianity to revive among the slaves. What actually happened was a result of the confused state in which the Blacks found themselves after the Emancipation of 1838. Their expectation that Emancipation would result in freedom and self-betterment was disappointed and instead they found themselves disenfranchised, landless, homeless and without the means to support themselves. The missionaries, who played a great role in the liberation movement, had built up their expectations of a better life in a free Jamaica, but this proved to be nothing more than empty talk. The Great Revival is thus better understood as a rejection of Christianity and a revival of the African force-vital. . . . The behavior patterns of seizure, or spirit possession, stirring prayers and dancing were thus nothing more nor less than the surfacing of traditional African religion which had been suppressed for almost a century.[57]

In the nineteenth century, White evangelical piety, especially revivalist fervor, was the most accommodating uncensored locus for African religious expression. The chief characteristics uniting traditional Myalism, Native Baptist Christian Myalism, and Revival traditions remain prominent in contemporary Jamaican Revival Zion religion. The most significant are divination, visions, prophecy, and healing. Up until the recent past many Revival sites were elaborate balmyards or healing centers as well as places of religious worship. This was certainly true of the religion's two prominent centers: Blakes Penn in Manchester (bordering St. Elizabeth) and Watt Town in St. Ann. Blakes Penn flourished under the leadership of "Mammy" Rozanne Forbes and her daughter Rita for more than one hundred years. The two renowned healers were consulted by Jamaicans and Jamaican expatriates alike. Leonard Barrett, one of the first Jamaican sociologists of religion to conduct research on African-derived Jamaican religions, described a personal experience of being treated by one of "Mother" Rita's assistants. In his book *The Sun and the Drum*, Barrett recalls that he

> decided to take a[n] herbal bath. . . . An enamel tub filled with herbal mixture was in the centre of the enclosure, with a stone slab nearby on which the patient stands. The bath-man entered and asked that 50 cents in coin be thrown in the tub. This done, I was asked to assume a squatting position. With towel in hand, the balmer applied the mixture to my head, sponging down my back, and at the same time reciting the 23rd Psalm. This operation continued from my waist to my heels, and was then carried out from my face to my toes, while a new Psalm was recited. . . . After all parts of my body had been thoroughly sponged, the sign of the cross was made from

the nape of my neck to my waist crossing at the shoulders. This was repeated in front . . . while the balmer recited the benediction: "In the name of the Father, Son, and Holy Ghost, as it was in the beginning, now, and ever shall be, world without end, Amen." The incantation was timed to conclude with the words "world without end" at the toes. I was then asked to dress myself and refrain from taking a bath for twelve hours to allow the medicinal properties of the herbs to be absorbed into the pores. . . . I was able to spend some time persuading the balmer to divulge the names of the plants used in the bath. . . . he gave me the names of as many of the seventy-seven plants as he could remember. . . . Here are the few he remembered: yellow saunders bush, casha-marrior, sweetsop bush, sour-sop bush, willow bush, rosemarie weed, lakka bush, candle wood bush, leaf-of-life, High-John-the-Conqueror weed, soap bush, ballad weed, rickie-rocher bush, wild cinnamon, semen-contra, strong-back and dead-and-wake.[58]

Barrett's "bath narrative" describes the conventional procedure followed by most Revival Zionists in ritual bathing. Also typical of Revival Zion leaders is the expert knowledge of botanical properties.[59]

Other characteristics which can be found uniformly in traditional Myalism, Native Baptist Christian Myalism, and Revival Zion traditions include the beating of drums; a community of spirits, which are linked with the elements of nature; possession trance; animal sacrifice; ancestral veneration; and a strong belief in neutral mystical power. In short, the cosmology, metaphysics, rituals, and spirituality of Revival Zion religion are steeped in ancient African ideas about the world and human responsibility for preserving the continuity of life. In addition, Revival Zionists promote a self-conscious identification with Africa, and it is within this religious Pan-Africanism that they, like the Rastafari, view the Hebrew and Christian scriptures as sacred texts of African people.

Scholars customarily term Revival Zion an "Afro-Christian" religion. They tend to classify it as such by describing it as less African than Kumina and, therefore, more syncretized with Christianity. Although I have never seen any reference to Revival Zion as an African-derived religion, I argue that it is the African religiosity as opposed to the Christian belief system that gives the religion its structure and purpose. Revival Zion is the offspring of Myal's (African-centered) appropriation of Christian symbols and sources. As Barry Chevannes writes:

In Christian teaching, the central relationship is between Jesus Christ, the mediator with God and the Father, and [humankind]. Jesus brings [humankind] to his Father, and he does so through his Spirit. This complex theological doctrine was transformed by Myal: [a person's] primary relationship with God was sought not with the Father or with Jesus the Son but with the Holy Spirit. Myal at first placed even John the Baptist above Jesus because it was he who transformed Jesus through the power of Baptism, and not the other way around. Where Christianity is transfixed on Jesus as mediator Myal was transfixed on the Spirit as possessor and sought [the Spirit] in dreams and secluded retreat. Whereas Christianity placed its emphasis on transmitted *knowledge* (doctrine, Bible, catechism) for conversion, Myal placed its emphasis on the *experience* of the Spirit. When followers found [the Spirit] it was to be filled by [the Spirit], to be possessed. Possession by the Spirit thus became the quintessential experience of the myalized Christianity.[60]

While Christian elements and religious traditions have been incorporated into Revival Zion piety, they appear to be tangentially and perfunctorily observed within the context of diverse religious ceremonies for the reasons identified by Chevannes.

The academic study of Revival Zion presents a particular set of challenges in the interpretive history and future of the tradition. While the scholarship on Revival Zion is steadily increasing, we still confront substantial interpretive problems due to the lack of consistent and comprehensive research on a broad range of Revival Zion congregations in Jamaica. On the surface, it is tempting to compare Revival Zion with Kumina and conclude that Revival Zion is more Christian and therefore less African than Kumina. Revival Zion appears to be a tightly woven syncretized package of African and Christian religiosity. William Wedenoja's evaluation of Jamaican Revival Zion religion brings to the fore a number of unanswered questions about its origin, nature, and, I would even say, identity. He maintains:

The real importance of the Great Revival was that it redefined Creole religion—the Myalists and Native Baptists—as Christianity and led to a rather complete adoption of Christian beliefs and practices without abandoning the African foundation. Today, revivalists do not recognize that much of their faith is derived from Africa or the syncretic cults of slavery. They think they are true Christians, in fact better Christians than the members of denominations, which they refer to derisively as "nominal" churches.[61]

Two significant questions emerge for me in the light of my encounters with Revival Zion practitioners.[62] First, on what basis can we assert that Revival Zion is a "complete adoption of Christian beliefs and practices without abandoning the African foundation"? Second, is it in fact the case that "revivalists do not recognize that much of their faith is derived from Africa or the syncretic cults of slavery"?

The claim that Revival Zion is a "complete adoption of Christian beliefs" might be tolerated, but the question must first be asked: What is meant by "Christian beliefs"? Revival Zionists accept that Jesus Christ is the redeemer, but they have a very low Christology. Jesus is deemphasized while the spirit messengers are emphasized. Revival Zion worship and healing services include sermonic material, but trance experience and laboring in the spirit are punctuated throughout. Most Zionists claim to have a special relationship with a designated spirit messenger, who serves as their personal guide and protector. Some spirit messengers are biblical figures such as Miriam, Jeremiah, or Isaiah. Others appear to be extrabiblical, such as the Dove,[63] River Maid, Bell Ringer, and Hunter.

Like orthodox Christians, Revival Zionists read the Bible. However, in it, they find justification for African traditions such as animal sacrifice, veneration of ancestral and spirit messengers, erecting tables and altars (shrines), and other practices that might correspond with biblical traditions but would be considered heretical practices in orthodox Christian theology and piety. Furthermore, Revival Zionists approach the Bible with an African-based consciousness of moral neutrality. Like Obeah and Myal, the Bible offers Zionists access to neutral mystical power. Each person is responsible for how he accesses that mystical power. In her research, published in 1994, Emanuela Guano found:

> The Bible is both revered and feared, as it is also a dangerous inexplicable mystery that can be used for destructive purposes. "You can find answers to all your problems in the Bible," a pastor told me once, "but you can also destroy a person with the Bible. Somebody sends you a message with a special verse from the Bible, and when you read it, you are reading your death sentence." Everything is in the Bible: the rules for Christian moral conduct, the techniques of healing by manipulating spiritual power, the ways to approach the spirits. A simultaneously literal and creative approach to the Bible turns this book into the focus of [the] Revival Zion system of beliefs.[64]

Revival Zionists, then, are biblically focused but, in many respects, do not conform to the doctrines and piety of orthodox Christianity. Yet, because they find justification for what they believe and practice in the Bible—the professed source of Christian identity—they claim a legitimate space within the Christian community. It appears to me, however, that this approach to scriptural interpretation betrays a discreet agenda of African religiosity and spirituality lurking behind the biblical (Christian) mask of authority. In my encounters with Zionists, they were able to theologically authenticate seemingly non-Christian practices such as animal sacrifice, devotion to a community of spirits, and feasting altars or tables with reference to the Bible, especially the Old Testament and specific apocalyptic literature like the Book of Revelation.

The host of spirit messengers and the spreading of feasting tables and altars—whether biblically endorsed or not—are particular to Revival Zionist "Christians" in Jamaica. These beliefs and practices are not embraced by any other Christian denomination in Jamaica. In my research, the theological justification offered by some Revival Zionists for their devotion to many spirits is rooted in the metaphysical logic found in classical Trinitarian theology. Revival Zionists see no contradiction between the Holy Spirit attested to as the third person of the Trinity and the community of spirit messengers they venerate. In their theology, the spirit messengers are legitimate manifestations of the Holy Spirit, just as the Holy Spirit is a legitimate manifestation of the Creator God.

This component of Revival Zion spirituality accommodates not only Trinitarian logic but classical African communotheism as well. The spirit messengers are associated with the forces of nature, which, in many classical African religious cultures, are manifestations of a Creator or representative Supreme Divinity. For Revival Zionists and practitioners of classical African religions (Kongo, Asante, Fon, and so on), natural creation—such as the sun, moon, stars, mountains, and stones—and the specific elements of water, air, earth, and fire are sources of life, power, healing, cleansing, and harmony.[65] Revival Zionists demonstrate devotion to the spirit messengers by wearing their favorite colors and by decorating their tables and altars with items that symbolize the characteristics of the messenger(s) to whom they relate most. As observed by Emanuela Guano, "[o]ccasionally . . . pools[66] are decorated with silverware and dishes (the River Maid is supposed to eat), and with perfume and cosmetics: like her equivalents in other Afro-American religions, the Fish is concerned with her appearance."[67]

In an article published in 1955, George Simpson also describes the religious culture of the Revival communities he observed in West Kingston, providing a window into the religious significance of stones and other African-derived practices to Revivalists:

> Blood is not used extensively in revivalist rituals, at least not in West
> Kingston, although a blood sacrifice, pigeon or other fowl, or a
> blood bath, may be a part of the treatment of a sick person. One
> leader known to the writer sprinkles goat's blood on the ground and
> on healing stones at his annual sacrifice ceremony. Stones, similar
> in size and shape to polished stone celts, as well as round stones,
> and, occasionally, stones resembling the human figure or the heart,
> head, kidney, or other anatomical parts, and carved stones, are
> found in the homes, yards and churches of nearly all revivalist leaders.
> The most knowledgeable revivalists disagree on whether the ceremonial
> stones have spirits in them, but even those who say the
> stones do not contain spirits believe that a spirit rules all the stones.
> In any event, the stones "carry" power.
>
> These sacred stones grow either by finding food for themselves
> or through being fed. Some leaders "feed" their stones from time to
> time by leaving a saucer with crackers or a fried dumpling for the
> spirits to eat and by pouring aerated water or rum on the stones.
> One leader who does not feed his stones, prays over a head or figure
> carved by himself, sprinkles it with consecrated water, and anoints it
> with olive oil, King Solomon's oil, and oil of Moses before staring
> intently at the stone. "Concentration" on the stone makes him more
> receptive to messages from the spirits and deepens his understanding
> of spiritual matters. In dealing with a serious illness, a river
> stone may be placed in a jar or a pool of consecrated water to in-

crease the curative powers of the water. Some stones are used to invoke particular spirits, others guard a church against evil spirits, and still others are used in sympathetic magic.[68]

It is hard to say for sure how widespread these specific African-derived practices were or whether they have been transmitted from one generation to the next, although I have seen stones on some Revival altars and in some of their churches. That Revivalists understood stones as spiritually charged, and observed ritual obligations of feeding those stones, clearly indicates a divergence from the kind of orthodox Christian doctrines and culture with which they would have been familiar.

The organization of ritual space in Revival Zion churches also distinguishes the tradition from orthodox Christian denominations. In Revival Zion worship spaces, the tables are centrally located and the altars are peripherally stationed, usually on the back wall. Everything significant in the worship service occurs around the table or one of the external sacred stations. The congregation sings and prays; the leader speaks; the mediums go into trance; and the sick are healed around the table. The table is the locus for mystical encounters between the visible and the invisible, between humans and the Divine Community. The table, which is spread with curative plants, beautiful flowers, fruit, bread, and water, symbolizes the fulfillment that is sought and received during worship. The Revival Zionist concept and use of a table in worship is a very fitting way to welcome the Ancestors[69] and spirit messengers. Tables are used in everyday activities in very intimate ways. People eat, chat, work, and reinforce relationships around the table with family and friends, and at times even permit strangers to participate. The table invites intimacy, bonding, fellowship, and fulfillment. It is a place where the spirits, especially the Ancestors, can feel welcomed and united with the living in a comfortable and familiar setting.

In addition to Sunday worship, Revival Zionists hold a variety of services, including prayer meetings, healing services, street meetings, and thanksgiving services. They also erect altars, ritual feasting tables, or "duties" and officiate over clearings and ritual baths.[70] The leadership structure of the church and the roles and responsibilities of the members are extremely complex and have been modified as different Revival traditions merged and interfaced over time. Today, the Revival Zion churches are led by "pastors," "priests," or "mothers." The leadership structure often includes, however, bishops, leadresses, governesses, and shepherd boys.[71]

As noted above, the central focus of Revival Zion services is "working," "laboring," or "trumping" in the spirit. The services create the space for contact and communication between humans and spirit messengers. In Revival Zion cosmology, the invisible domain mirrors the natural terrain and societal structures of the visible domain: "It has rivers, lakes, forests, mountains, churches, cities and so on."[72] During the services, members are escorted into the invisible domain where, under states of trance, they sojourn through a host of experiences before returning to the visible domain to share insights with the congregation. While on their journeys, the tranced members dramatize their experiences. Thus the Bell Ringer will ring his bell at precise moments; the River Maid will swim across the river; and so forth. The entire scene is epic-like, for the travelers encounter obstacles and advantages during their journeys. Most of all, they tap into mystical powers that help them to detect and cure the sick, rebuke evil, make plans for the future (both personally and collectively), counsel and advise those in need, and so on. Guano adequately assesses the stages and purpose of possession trance when she writes:

> The most intense phase of possession is what Revivalists call "spirit work," or "laboring," or "groaning." When their possession is deep enough, Revivalists turn to a pattern of movements (a rhythmic bowing forward of the back, while swinging the arms and stepping in a circle) accompanied by loud inhalations and exhalations that sound like a percussion music. During this phase, those who are possessed (and hence have absorbed the spiritual power in them) "work" in order to bend this power to their will. They want to receive a message from the spirit, but they also want this spiritual power to help them achieve concrete goals and benefits in their everyday life.[73]

Bearing in mind that the relationship I have suggested between possession trance and achieving "concrete goals and benefits in . . . everyday life" is a recurring theme in African-Jamaican religiosity, comparisons can be made concerning the theological implications of possession trance for the Revival Zion, Native Baptist, and Obeah-Myal traditions of the slave period. Thus far, this study has emphasized the direct correlation between a theology that values African people in terms of their human and cultural dignity and the praxis of rebellion that was nurtured within the Obeah-Myal and Native Baptist traditions. Most scholars classify Revival Zion as thaumaturgical, that is, "magico-religious" in focus, having turned "to the powers of the supernatural to accomplish their ends, and . . . primarily concerned with the cure for illness, the placation of the spirits and the comforting of the aggrieved."[74] They have also classified Revival Zion as millenarian and "implicitly militant."[75]

It is true that these motifs characterize significant components of Revival Zion religion. Yet we might push Barrett's "implicit" a little further with reference to Alexander Bedward's influential leadership and theology early in the movement. Bedwardism is still remembered in Jamaica today as a distinguished Revival trajectory. Bedward, the son of emancipated Africans, launched his ministry as a prophet and healer in 1895. He was charged with sedition and arrested in 1921 "for preaching that Blacks should rise up and overthrow White domination."[76] Although Revival Zion does not appear to promote an explicit militarism, the practical focus upon alleviating concrete problems cannot be underestimated in a religious context where North American fundamentalist theology has come to symbolize the same threat that the planters and missionaries together posed to African religious cultures and grassroots political mobilization. Before turning to explore what might be termed the "explicit militarism" in Rastafari, some final remarks pertaining to Revival Zion's African and Christian identity are in order.

Midway into my field research with Revival Zion churches, I would have agreed wholeheartedly with Wedenoja's assertions that "[t]he real importance of the Great Revival was that it redefined Creole religion—the Myalists and Native Baptists—as Christianity and led to a rather *complete* adoption of Christian beliefs and practices without abandoning the African foundation" and in part with Joseph Murphy's assertion that Revival Zion is "a religious tradition of Jamaica which offers an African way of entry into the spiritual world of the Christian scripture."[77] This was because, up until that point, I had spent all of my time attending Sunday morning worship services at Revival Zion churches in St. Thomas and Kingston. Revival Zion piety perplexed me primarily because much of it appeared to be unique and so uncharacteristic of anything I had ever observed in continental African religions and in other African diasporic religions. The trumping, travailing, heavy breathing, incessant visions, and whirling were basically unrecognizable to me, as were the altars, tables, and specific ritual objects with their endless complex of meaning. Although I had read extensively about Revival Zion piety before attending my first service, it was not until I entered a Revival Zion church that I came to appreciate the dynamic character of Revival Zion faith and piety. Yet, even in its unfamiliarity, Revival Zion piety appeared to be very Christian, and I too was tempted to compare it with the religiosity I encountered in the Kumina communities, which was unmistakeably African-based.

What changed my perspective and shifted the focus in my research on Revival Zion was the comment of the most pious-appearing Zionist with whom I had worshiped on several occasions. On our way home from a Sunday morning worship service at Zion Sacred Heart of Christ Sabbath Church (Kingston), without any prompting from me, she most excitedly proclaimed, "The best Zion meetings are when we hold a Kumina!"[78] It was at that point that I came to understand the spiritual camaraderie and religious solidarity that exists between the two traditions. While I knew that Kumina practitioners attend Zion churches because Zionists are tolerant of Kumina as an African tradition, I did not know that many Zionists respect and regularly participate in Kumina activities. After further investigation, I learned that Revival Zion religiosity resembles that of Kumina in more than one way. First, most (if not all) Revival Zion pastors are diviners or healers; and second, Revival Zion practitioners are often called upon by fellow practitioners *and* nonpractitioners to heal, protect, restore harmony and prosperity, and so on during times of trouble and crisis.

I have come to see that it is in the extrachurch activities that Revival Zion religiosity is most vibrantly and authentically conveyed: during weekly healing services but especially in private divination sessions with clients. Sessions may take place at the church site in a special "message room" or at the client's home. The healing function of religion sustains the pervasive African core of Revival Zion. For example, during unrelated conversations and interviews, Zionists from different churches in Kingston and St. Thomas confessed that when a problem is very grave, they do not attempt a resolution but immediately organize a Kumina to take care of it. When asked why, one informant replied, "[T]he Kumina people work fast. . . . Their work is the fastest and everyone knows it. And they have the strongest power. Whoever says different is fooling themselves!"[79]

Unfortunately, this was the most I was able to glean from Zionists concerning why they would claim to be Christians yet practice or initiate Kuminas to alleviate their deepest problems. Nevertheless, this type of dual allegiance[80] to both traditions obfuscates any clear demarcations one might be tempted to draw between Kumina as an African-derived religion and Revival Zion as Afro-Christian. It appears that, within at least some Revival Zion churches today, the most public expressions of Christian piety occur during the most officially acceptable ceremony—Sunday morning worship.[81] On the other hand, the most conspicuous expressions of African religiosity—namely, animal sacrifice; feeding the earthbound, waterbound, and airbound spirits; spiritual cleansing baths; and so on—are to be observed in the practical extrachurch rituals called for by persons in need and crisis.[82]

The key to formulating a theoretical model for understanding how the dual allegiance to both African and Western Christian religiosity is tolerated in Revival Zion can be found in the Revival Zion church's historical and contemporary experience of being condemned and stigmatized by orthodox Christians. Revival Zion's tumultuous struggle to retain its core African identity under the mask of Christian piety exposes the moral problem of Afrophobia and anti-Africanness with which Africans in Jamaica have been wrestling since the days of enslavement. Revival Zion signifies how and why an imperialistic religion (Euro-Christian) is adduced to legitimize African spirituality in contexts of religiocultural genocide. This awareness should bring about new approaches to the interpretation of African-derived religions in Jamaica. Wedenoja's interpretation of the Great Revival as the context for "redefining Creole religion (the Myalists and Native Baptists) as Christianity" with an "African foundation" is dubious or at least points to a bias shared by many scholars of African-derived religion, who readily collapse the data on Revival Zion and other related traditions under the category of Afro-Christianity. Labels like Afro-Christian or Afro-Christian cults indicate the extent to which scholars are capable of understanding Christianity as dynamic, culturally located, and transcontextual in terms of rituals and symbols. Yet they are incapable of perceiving African religion as equally dynamic, culturally located within New World diasporic communities, and transcontextual in terms of rituals and symbols. The dominant research patterns would encourage one to conclude that if Revival Zion fails to exhibit conspicuous Africanisms with direct linkages to ethnic communities in Africa, then it absolutely cannot qualify as an African-derived religion. For example, some might conclude then that the possible interfacing of the two traditions, one Kongolese Christianity and the other Jamaican Revival Zion, weakens my theory that revival in the 1860–1861 Jamaican context signifies an awakening of Myal as opposed to the spread of (colonial) Christianity. My thinking on this though is that the seventeenth- and eighteenth-century expressions of Kongolese Christianity constitute an authentic localization of Christianity within Kongo culture. If this religious culture was in turn influential in the formation of Revival Zion in Jamaica, I would infer that, in that Afrophobic colonial space of contested religious meanings, it served to fortify the Myal (classical African) foundation of the tradition and functioned as a hermeneutical key for interpreting and appropriating Christian resources in ways consistent with that Kongolese Christian religious culture, where Kongo religiocultural life provided theological orientation for Christian converts.

It is here that I would argue that some of the most influential social science paradigms for studies of cross-cultural contact and religious formation, while yielding tremendous resources for a theological project such as this one, have serious limitations. There is an impoverishment of creative interpretation among these social scientists who pose narrow questions about *theological* content and meanings as they are reflected in the rituals, material culture, and the grammar of symbols connected with Revival Zion religiosity.[83] What makes a religious tradition what it is? For Christianity, the interplay among doctrines, beliefs, and ritual (liturgy) is a salient marker of religious identity. In the case of Jamaica, enslaved Africans were for the most part exposed to Western European–centered Christianity (as opposed to East African Christianity or Eastern Orthodox Christianity). My study of Revival Zion religion in Jamaica indicates that the orthodox beliefs, doctrines, and rituals of Western Christianity are either absent or superficially present in Revival Zionism, while the foundational features of African-derived religions are commanding, authoritative, and orthodox with regard to spiritual outlook, ritual processes, theological meaning, and, ultimately, religious identity. And before we continue along the conventional path of interpretation, which would label Revival Zion an Afro-Christian syncretic cult, it may be worthwhile to consider once again classical Kongo religious culture as a possible African ethnic antecedent for this complex tradition. My proclivity for this approach is strengthened by comparative data from earlier and more recent studies, as well as recent consultations with Kongolese scholar Fu Kiau Bunseki.

Bunseki believes that the term "poco" (a common designation for Revival groups in Jamaican folk parlance) is actually a derivative of the Kikongo term "mumpoko." Mumpoko, he explains, "is a plant and this plant is very powerful; it is used also in rituals and it has many properties for healing and blessing. So mumpoko is one of the most powerful healing plants in the Kongo. It is also used to chase away bad spirits. Mumpoko has the property to make people fall into trance." Bunseki also describes the ritual significance of mumpoko:

> When people are doing rituals, these mumpoko leaves are put in water and then the leaves will be used to spray the liquid on their bodies and mostly on their feet because it is believed that their energy, when someone is falling into trance, the current comes from the earth and rises in the person. The leaves can be picked up by those leading the ceremony, nganga lemba, [lemba priest] who may touch people with them (either to neutralize because the spirits can be very violent or to induce trance), especially their feet, and by do-

ing so, sooner or later you will see people rise into trance. Lemba means to neutralize, to cool, to restore balance, to heal. Sickness is energy that reaches a level that cannot be controlled, so to lemba is to push down the energy, to keep the balance.[84]

Several ritual congruences are striking when comparing Revival Zion's Myal-based religious culture with Kongo religious culture, which we already discussed as a likely antecedent for Myal rituals. Both use special plants in their ceremonies to heal and to expel evil spirits or to "cut and clear destruction," as I often heard declared by Revival Zion informants. The term *poco*, which many have come to assume was an abridgement of the label pocomania, may actually prove to be an original term belonging to Revival Zion vocabulary and, with further comparative studies, may serve to concretize the link between Revival Zion and Kongo religion. Indeed, one of the most pronounced features of Revival Zion is their use of specific plants, which they often soak in vases, jars, or basins of water in preparation for rituals. Spirit travel is also the dominant form of trance experience in Revival Zion and is a widespread practice among banganga (priests) in Kongo rituals, who often travel to the spirit world to acquire knowledge for purposes of divination and healing.[85]

Postemancipation literature describing Myal and early twentieth-century studies of Myal traditions, Revival Zion, and Pocomania or Pukkumina also document practices that appear comparable to Kongo religious practices. The most baffling to scholars has been the use of a powerfully charged religious object called "amber" or "amba" by observers and researchers' informants. Thomas Banbury (1894) described the "amber" as "a talisman by which they [Myalists] pretend to divine. Both the mial and obeahman use it. Anything through which they look at the obeah . . . is called an 'amber,' the name is not confined strictly to the substance so called."[86] During her research trip between 1920 and 1921, Martha Beckwith's informant Mary Cambell of St. Elizabeth described the "amba" as a "fetich secured from the spirits of the dead by means of the myal dance. 'The spirits carry you dancing all through the bush, then you come back to the grave and the amba comes rolling to you over the ground.' " Beckwith continues to note that "Ewan [a jonkunnu dancer and Myal man] had one of these fetiches in the shape of a transparent little ball with red lines about it and something blue inside. . . . He soaked it in rum and kept it in a little pouch."[87] In her later publication, *Black Roadways* (1929), Beckwith writes, "[a] Myal Man is called a 'fore-eyed man' because he alone has the power to see where the shadow is nailed or the obeah buried. He has this power through a talisman which he has received from the spirits or 'deaths,' during the course of the myal dance. Originally this talisman was in the form of an amber bead; it may today be represented by a glass marble." (This calls to mind pre-emancipation descriptions of Obeah practitioners in possession of glass beads.) According to one of Beckwith's informants with the surname White, "[w]hen you dance the Myal, if Death loves you and you deal with him, he will give you one [an amba] . . . you must keep it nice—keep it clean in a little thread bag." Beckwith further notes that another "talisman which Death presents in the dance is a bunch of herbs called 'jiggey.' "[88]

Although Beckwith discusses Myalists, Revivalists, and Pukkumerians as three distinct groups in Jamaica during the 1920s, which suggests that African-based Myal groups were still active in the twentieth century, within the context of the wider literature, we know that Myal is the parent source of the movements emerging from the Great Revival of 1860–1861. Consequently, any connection drawn between Myal and Africa is plausibly a connection between Revival Zion and Africa.

In her recent publication on Central African traditions in the Caribbean, Maureen Warner-Lewis confirms that there is a relationship between Myal and Revival and goes on to indicate parallels between their function in Jamaican society and that of the Lemba society in Kongo, as Bunseki supposes. She describes the Myal and Revival "recurrence of mass 'hysteria' as "particularly West Central African" and says "in *mayaal*, the charm or 'medicine' which could exert its force against the evil under attack earned the name *amba*, etymology unknown."[89] Bunseki's determination, however, is that the term *amba* is derived from two possible Kikongo terms, "mamaba," which literally means "medicinal water" or from "mpiya," "which was a very spiritual tool among Kongo priests; it is also a statuette, so *mpiya*, the statuette, is used to symbolize the *mpiya* force." *Mpiya* is represented by a red color and sometimes blue, black, and white. And "the Kongo believe that you can send *mpiya* (especially as a statuette) from one location to another." Bunseki explains in more detail:

> Mpiya can be a bundle with or without beads. In the Kongo they use three beads: red, white, and black. They use crystal beads and paint them red, white, and black and they can be put into a sash and wrapped inside the nkisi [empowered religious object/medicine]. Mpiya can also signify a statuette with those colors with feathers at the head of the statuette. It is made out of small wood and can be used as a spying device. Mpiya is a message, information, power that can be sent without material means; so mpiya is energy, a kind of bundle of energy, it is a spiritual bundle, a force that can be sent somewhere as a person to collect information. It can have a face at the handle, but where the feathers are attached, the part that is directed to make the motion does not have a head. Sometimes it is just a plain piece of wood. It can be sent to cause problems, to fight against enemies. In Congo it can be used negatively or positively. If they are inquiring about a disease, they will use the mpiya to discover the origin of psychosomatic diseases and know how to counteract it. There is a special nganga who uses mpiya, who is called nganga-mpiya.[90]

In light of the current scholarly interest in Central African cultural influences in the African diaspora, the emphasis on medicinal water, plants, glass containers, and other empowered religious objects in the Revival Zion Christian Myal tradition lends credence to the argument that Kongo-based religious culture is one of the most resilient African religious cultures influencing Black religious formation in Jamaica over the past four centuries. With this in mind, interpreting Revival Zion as an African-derived rearticulation of Myal and Native Baptist religions laced with christianisms might better reflect the process of religious formation among Revival Zion communities of the nineteenth and twentieth centuries. It will be left to time and expanded scientific research over the next decades to discover what Revival Zion is becoming in the twenty-first century.

Rastafari

Of all of the religious orientations in contemporary Jamaica, Rastafari has gained international attention and allegiance from people of African descent and, peculiarly, from some non-Africans as well. Given its humble beginnings in a small Third World island of the Caribbean Sea, Rastafari has made a larger-than-life contribution to the religion and culture of the Caribbean and the world. Rastafari is a religious response to anthropological poverty not just for Africans in Jamaica, but for Africans the world over. Rastafari, a twentieth-century religion, can be described as a movement with a specific philosophy, theology, and political ideology, the foundational commitment being Pan-Africanism.

One symbolic genesis of Rastafari was the crowning of Prince Tafari Makonnen as emperor of the Ethiopian (Abyssinian) kingdom in 1930. The significance of this event for diasporic Africans in a context where the White power structure associated Africa with every vile and despicable thing imaginable should not be underestimated. Horace Campbell describes this eventful time appropriately in the following passage:

> Between April and November, when the official coronation took
> place, Ras Tafari went to great lengths to let the world know that a
> black African leader was joining the international community of
> Kings and Princes. Arrays of princes and other powers attended the
> ceremony and the retinue of journalists recorded for history the
> pomp and colour as ras [nobleman] after ras in full regalia bowed in
> homage before the imperial throne. Colour pictures of the proceedings were reprinted in newspapers throughout the Western world
> and newsreels of the ceremonies for the first time gave many blacks
> a visual perception of Ethiopia. The pictures of this African King
> with an African army, along with the Duke of Gloucester—heir to
> the British throne—bowing before him sent a surge of pride
> through all Africans.[91]

Marcus Garvey's prophetic influence was felt by some Jamaicans in his exhortation that diasporic Africans must "look to Africa for the crowning of a king to know that your redemption is nigh."[92] Garvey's pronouncement was launched within a larger religiocultural milieu of Ethiopianism in the African diaspora,[93] which necessarily punctuated the urgency with which some Jamaicans began to associate their aspirations for genuine social upliftment with the promise of freedom guaranteed in icons, symbols, and events pertaining to the only sovereign African territory of historical prominence, the kingdom of Abyssinia, or Ethiopia. Three Jamaicans independently saw the "sign of the time" and made the connection between Garvey's mandate and the new Abyssinian emperor, Ras (Prince) Tafari. Leonard Howell (and his assistant Robert Hinds), Archibald Dunkley, and Joseph Hibbert were the chief shapers of the movement for two decades.

The central teachings of Rastafari at this early stage were (1) the notion that redemption was the impending repatriation of all (diasporic) Africans to Africa; and (2) Haile Selassie's divinity (the living Black messiah) and the divinity of the African race. As pictures of the full-bearded Black Christ, Haile Selassie, circulated, Rastas soon refrained from shaving their facial hair and justified the practice as a sacred biblical mandate.

The movement entered a second stage as those who joined during the 1940s instituted the wearing of locks, ganja (marijuana) smoking, a unique vocabulary known as "Rasta talk" or "I-talk," and the concept of "Jah" or "Jah-Jah" associated with Haile Selassie. By the 1960s, reggae music became the bullhorn for Rastafari philosophy and theology as urban youths such as Bob Marley, Peter Tosh, Dennis Brown, Bunny Wailer, and others began to embrace aspects of the Rastafari lifestyle.

Since the 1980s, the symbols and ideas of Rastafari have increasingly become the public property of the wider secular culture in Jamaica and in other parts of the world where the Rastafari ethos has wielded influence. However, in such contexts, the appeal of Rastafari symbols inspires superficial and tenuous sociocultural allegiance to "race pride" or "Jamaican identity" for many who attach no sacred value to them and make no commitments to "the livity."[94]

From its inception, the colonial Jamaican establishment recognized the movement's potential to politically mobilize Africans against European rule. Rastas like Leonard Howell advocated that Africans should recognize a new identity in the kingdom of Ethiopia and a new political leader in the person of Haile Selassie (Ras Tafari Makonnen). In 1933, the Jamaican *Daily Gleaner* denounced the Rasta meetings that Howell had been holding in St. Thomas when it reported that "devilish attacks are made at these meetings on government, both local and imperial, and the whole conduct of the meeting would tend to provoke an insurrection if taken seriously."[95] Howell was arrested on charges of sedition and was indicted for "intending to excite hatred and contempt for his majesty the King of England and of those responsible for the government of the island, and to create disaffection among the subjects of his majesty in this island and to disturb the public peace and tranquillity of the island."[96]

The pledge of allegiance to Haile Selassie is perhaps the most popular Pan-African idea espoused by Rastas. However, the attention given to continental African struggles against colonialism in the reggae songs of Bob Marley,

Peter Tosh, Burning Spear, and others cannot be disassociated from Rastafari *Nyabinghi* consciousness. The *Nyabinghi* anticolonial movement in Kigezi, Uganda, was inspired by classical African religion and called for "death to Black and White oppressors." The denouncement of Africans who cooperate with White oppressors is also a motif in Rasta-inspired reggae music. Today, *Nyabinghi* is the Rasta orientation claimed by most followers in Jamaica and abroad.

The early history of Rastafari is one of incessant attempts on the part of the White colonial regime to destabilize the movement. The most political Rasta leaders were incarcerated, stigmatized as insane, and quarantined in asylums.[97] Even after Jamaica gained independence from Britain in 1962, Rastas experienced harassment, repression, and condemnation from the establishment—"the babylon system"—and from the general public. And the Rasta musicians expressed their trials and tribulations, their quest for redemption from "sufferation"[98] in their reggae lyrics. For example, Bob Marley recounts the Rastafari struggle for human dignity in Jamaica and the Rastafari preoccupation with African people's liberation everywhere. His songs proclaim some of the theology of Rastafari—its theism, anthropology, Christology, eschatology, ethics, and piety.

Rastafari doctrines are simple enough to state, but Rastafari practice is ostensibly diverse, depending upon the community and specific sociohistorical context. This is because the movement is, in large part, acephalous. Most Rastas identify as members of the "House." Others belong to the only two organized communities: the Bobos and the Twelve Tribes of Israel. The Bobos believe in Black supremacy and have been officially recognized as an independent flag-bearing nation by the United Nations. They appear to be the only Rastafari commune on the island, and they view Jamaica and Jamaican identity the way Malcolm X viewed America and American identity.[99] Bobo Rastas claim with indignation that they are "Africans in exile" and that "Jamaica is the land of slavery and oppression." They despise the Jamaican identity and long for the African homeland. Bobo Rastas have proselytized and founded communities in Ghana and Nigeria. One of their major concerns is financing their permanent return to Africa.[100] The hope of repatriation and their unwavering religiopolitical commitment to Black liberation is expounded in their printed literature. For example, in a collection of speeches and reflections of their late founder, Prince Emmanuel Edwards, we find the following words:

> Righteousness in Black Supremacy. Let everyone turn back to the world of right. . . . Re-repatriation internationally, the mighty great I am who take us out of the land of Egypt-Jamaica, we must have no other God before him—Christ our Lord and King, the offspring of David and the root of Jesse, the alpha and omega that sit on the side of the north, Haile Selassie I. Black man see yourself and know yourself. Black woman see yourself and know yourself as God and Goddess of the earth. The black world is the highest people upon the face of the earth in flesh. . . . The Black Christ come with life

more abundantly, black Jerusalem is the first heaven for the black [people] when [they are] living, not when [they die]. So all captives to be set free says the I am: All black people must be free under the globe.[101]

The Bobo Rastas adhere to the most extreme formulation of Black nationalism within the religion. They comprise a simple, poor community of men and women, some apparently well into their sixties. They adhere to ascetic principles and observe a host of taboos, which they believe purify and cleanse the individual and the community. The teachings of Rastafari, however, also appeal to middle-class Jamaicans. According to Chevannes, the Twelve Tribes is an affiliation of "middle-class men and women, mulatto and Black."[102]

Of all of the postemancipation manifestations of African-Jamaican religion, Rastafari is the clearest rearticulation of African religious resistance to enslavement and captivity, as shown in the Obeah-Myal and Native Baptist traditions discussed above. Rastafari's political and cultural visions demand direct confrontation with White supremacy and its legacy of anti-Africanness that has crept into African diasporic cultures. Thus Rastas insist that African people embrace a natural appearance, natural food, and natural (ital) lifestyle. Rastafari doctrine is critical of the manufactured products of White supremacist culture— the processed foods, hair-straightening chemical compounds, cosmetics, and facial dyes. Adherents strive for purity, cleanliness, and righteousness, that is, being in right relationship with Jah and the natural environment. In Rastology, naturalness and purity are essential for conforming to the *livity*.

Communal *Nyabinghi* Rastafari piety is generally expressed at *Nyabinghi* (or *Binghi*) meetings where Rastas drum, dance, and "reason" through communal ganja[103] smoking. *Binghis* are held to commemorate events pertaining to the life and death of Haile Selassie, Marcus Garvey's birthday, African Emancipation from enslavement (August 1), and other important events. Chevannes notes that one chief difference between Rastafari and Revival is the "relative dearth of religious ritual" among the former when compared with the latter. Chevannes duly acknowledges, however, that Rastas compensate for this "dearth" individually in the private sphere:

Rastafari observe a number of personal ritual taboos and practices. The most significant of these govern food, nature and the environment, and Africa. Among foods, pork and crustaceans are universally avoided, but many Rastafari refrain from all meat and fish products. Salt is also taboo. Food cooked without salt is referred to as *ital*, that is, natural. Rastafari rejects, as much as possible, all artificial things and celebrates the use of the natural: manure instead of artificial fertilizers and sprays; herbs and barks instead of pharmaceuticals. Rastafari life is centered on Africa. Every Rasta home is adorned with photographs of Haile Selassie . . . , maps of Africa and posters with African themes and the Ethiopian colours. Every Rasta . . . possesses an array of decorative buttons, with replicas of Emperor Haile Selassie or some other African leader, which he proudly wears in public.[104]

Personal devotion to the principles and ideals of one's religious tradition is commendable and not always observable in the lifestyles of individuals in the established Christian churches. Nonetheless, Ras Leahcim Semaj, a professional psychological consultant, has argued that Rastas must develop the religion's institutional structures to suit their holistic needs. "It's ironic and objectionable that Rastas go to Christian churches to get married or christen their children. . . . We need our own rituals so that Rastas do not have to rely on the formal services of a religion they do not adhere to."[105]

Rastafari culture is patriarchally structured, and the male leadership in the religion continues to promote sexist ideas about women and women's nature. Rastafari culture is constructed with the expectation that women submit to male authority. In so doing, practitioners learn to ritualize female "inferiority."[106] Although some women have begun to challenge the sexist taboos and norms within the religion, the feminist critique of Rastology is categorically dismissed by Rastamen, who have ultimate authority over the taboos, norms, and values of the *livity*. Female vocalists like Judy Mowatt, a former "I-Three" (backup singer) in Bob Marley's band, have used the reggae genre to creatively express the Rastawoman's struggle for respect and dignity within the religion and within the wider Jamaican society. Mowatt speaks for all Jamaican women when she sings, "[T]hey treat us inhuman, just because we are woman!"[107]

Maureen Rowe and Imani Tafari-Ama, two practicing Rastawomen have done extensive research on the status of Rastawomen in the religion and their efforts to challenge sexism and patriarchy. Their published research examines the interplay among gender socialization, patriarchy, and female status as an extremely complex phenomenon in Rastafari, as the religion embodies sexist traditions from both Western and African cultures. Both Rowe and Tafari-Ama indicate that women have been resisting sexism and patriarchy in the movement since the 1970s, and according to Rowe:

> Daughters [Rastawomen] are speaking out more and more about
> their concerns and their hopes. Even more important, daughters
> have begun to articulate their own perception of Rastafari. More and
> more daughters were beginning to reason together and this created
> a solid base from which to approach the society in general and the
> Rastafari community in particular.[108]

To say the least, while a Rasta feminist consciousness is slowly emerging, it has not spawned an identifiable social movement powerful enough to eradicate normative traditions and taboos that prescribe inferior roles and status to Rastawomen and exclude them from access to ritual and social power as well as epistemological authority in defining the *livity*. Increasingly though, as documented by Rowe, Rastawomen are challenging women's anthropological impoverishment within the religion by defying oppressive ideology, ritual taboos,

and dress and household codes.[109] For example, in 1985, the *Rasta Voice* printed
what might be called a womanist statement, which claimed:

> *African women are in double jeopardy.*
>   My black brothers, your black sisters are not your enemy. Your
> black sisters are not a threat to your masculinity.
>   In this system she is in double jeopardy.
>   Just as the white man system provide[s] for the use, abuse and
> refuse of the black race, so too is the system of the black man on
> black woman. At this point-in-time black sisters are forced to recog-
> nise their role in the black brethren scheme of things to be one of
> inferiority. She now see herself at the mercy of black men who, un-
> fortunately have inherited much of the white man attitudes. Worst
> of which is now manifested in the use, abuse and refuse of black
> sisters. For black sisters who recognise themselves to be assets to
> our liberation struggle, the role of inferiority is unacceptable.
>   In the quest for the liberation and oneness of our people, the
> black man must discontinue the practice of subordination of black
> sisters, and come to grips with the facts; we are just as needed as
> the brothers in the struggle for liberation and continuous prosperity
> of the black race.[110]

Within the context of religion, the authority and agency of women in the
African-Jamaican pursuit of freedom and control of destiny are most conspicuously disclosed in the Kumina tradition. But before turning to Kumina, we
will conclude with some analysis of the Black religious complex as represented
by the three postemancipation trajectories explored above.

Three Trajectories of African-Jamaican Religious Experience

The first trajectory, represented by the African Jamaican's acceptance of Euro-
missionary Christianity and theology, is most pronounced in contemporary
displays of public religious life in Jamaica. This trajectory promoted the disintegration of African religious memory as Africans were conditioned to believe that Christianity and African religion are antithetical and to associate the
former with the true, good, and beautiful and the latter with chaos, barbarism,
and satanic powers. The missionaries presented Christianity as the prize of
exile from Africa packaged within the gift wrapping of slavery. And the Christian religion became a rite of passage justifying the Middle Passage as the
necessary event removing Africans from the source of their satanism and barbarism. Acceptance of the Christian faith, then, guaranteed a secure place for
African souls in heaven with God, Christ, and the saints.

By converting to Christianity, Africans were accepting the New World, modernity, civilization, and salvation—all components of European expansionism

and the Eurocentric ideologies of progress and White supremacy undergirding it.[111] Africa, the Old World, the ancient, uncivilized, and damned continent, the missionaries claimed, offered no cultural resources for their new life in Christ in the African diaspora. The missionaries even found African modes of singing to be repulsive and grotesque. They were not satisfied that their new African converts were pleasing to God until they adopted European hymns and vocal styles.

More than anything, proponents of the Eurocentric Christian worldview promoted a Manichaean anthropology that corresponded well with European enslavement of Africans. They began from the premise that Africans were the cursed descendants of the biblical figure Ham and were therefore destined to serve as slaves on plantations owned by Europeans (Whites) who, some even went as far as to claim, were the blessed descendants of Ham's brother Japheth.[112] Furthermore, their dark or "black" complexion indicated their moral and cultural inferiority when compared with the light- or "white-" complexioned ruling class. The missionaries maintained, nonetheless, that, although the African people's external features and physical and cultural traits invited slavery and an inferior existence "naturally" suitable for the cursed descendants of Ham, their interior souls were redeemable and no less so than the souls of their White rulers. They believed that the equality of souls across racial groups was of ultimate value and deserved more consideration than the inequality of bodies across racial groups. They complemented this dualistic anthropology with a stratification of human experience that was derived from their orthodox Christian doctrine,[113] which functioned in consort with White supremacist, anti-African values and practices in the context of slavery. The missionaries exhorted African converts to tolerate temporal corporeal experiences of physical, emotional, and psychological suffering with the anticipation that the afterlife guaranteed soul salvation and heavenly bliss as an eternal compensation for their earthly suffering. African converts often abandoned their fixation upon alleviating their suffering and improving their social condition and adopted a fixation upon the suffering Christ, who redeemed their souls from eternal damnation.

As discussed above, the missionaries sympathized with their converts and disapproved of the brutalities they endured in the plantation system. But, in the end, the missionaries accepted and cooperated with the plantation regulations. They also taught African converts that the Christian virtues of obedience, humility, docility, and dependency, when internalized, would equip them with the appropriate moral attitude and spiritual armor to withstand their oppressors. As the cited testimonies indicate, with this type of Christian consciousness, Africans would think less about their concrete social predicament as undernourished, underclothed, brutalized captives as they thought instead about the suffering, crucified Christ, who paid the price for their personal sins and made salvation possible for even the "poo Guinea niger."[114]

Comprehensively, the records indicate that the missionaries placed the greatest emphasis upon condemning personal offenses against White planters such as stealing from one's master, lying to one's master, running away from one's master, disobeying one's master, and so on. The Eurocentric missionary Christian conception of morality and suffering made Jesus Christ (who suffered unjustly) the paragon suffering servant for Africans to emulate by obediently withstanding; if not embracing, their own unjust suffering as enslaved exiles. Africans realized that Jesus suffered like they did, that is, he was tortured by means with which they were familiar. This realization undoubtedly facilitated an existential identification with the incarnate Christian divinity of the missionaries. The enslaved Africans simultaneously learned that Jesus suffered for them, for the absolution of their sins and the redemption of their souls if they would just accept Christ as their personal redeemer and discard heathenism and fetishism forever. Enslaved African converts, brutalized in their bodies and cleansed in their souls, became acceptable candidates for eternal life with the Christian God.

Africans following this religious trajectory appear to have experienced the assurance of salvation brought by the Christian God and Christ in sensory and mystical ways alien to the missionaries and more consistent with their African spiritual heritage and their suffering as enslaved exiles. Consequently, their acceptance of Euro-missionary Christianity meant that they too had come to internalize and perpetuate Afrophobic values and anti-African traditions in a religion that could no longer be viewed as completely Euro-colonial because Africans had begun to participate in its vision and mission.[115] Afrophobia and anti-Africanness, promoted by African Christians, elevated Eurocentric Christianity to a revered status among many Blacks in the Americas and the Caribbean as the standard against which all religious and theological claims are judged. When compared with Eurocentric Christianity, features of African religions—Divine Community (communotheism), ancestral veneration, divination and herbalism, food offerings and animal sacrifice, possession trance, and neutral mystical power—were deemed heathenish and incompatible with Christianity by missionaries and their African converts.

Within this trajectory of African conversion to Christianity, the encounter between Africans and European missionaries resulted in the disintegration of African cultural and religious memory as true memories about African ideals and values pertaining to wholeness, health, fulfillment, and liberation were replaced by false memories of African religiosity as evil, harmful, shameful, and retrogressive. Moreover, the incarnation of duplicity within the Black or Creole personality qualified human experience as innately riddled with tension, and menacing, paradoxes as converted Africans have never been able to reconcile the positive values they have been conditioned to assign to the painful human experiences of corporeal suffering, material poverty, and emotional and psychological abuse with the (ecstatic) joyful human experiences of grace and spiritual redemption.

At best, enslaved African converts embraced a Manichaean anthropology and consequently a docetic soteriology, thereby ignoring their actual bodies and the burdens they bore. This type of Creole, Negro, or Black Christian identity has contributed significantly to what the African-American philosopher Lucius Outlaw has called "the existential crisis of divided self-consciousness" and "the struggle to achieve cultural integrity." Outlaw identifies "symbolic reversal" and an unmitigated self-determination as "decisive features" of this struggle for wholeness.[116] The struggle for cultural integrity in Jamaican religious history is especially noticeable in the African-derived and African-centered religions. However, it can be seen in Black Christian circles across the African diaspora as contemporary Black Christians attempt to "Africanize" their liturgies and worship services. For example, the practice of decorating church sanctuaries and choir and ministerial robes with African textiles is currently popular in the United States across African and Caribbean American Christian congregations.

The second trajectory, represented by the incorporation of christianisms into the practice of African-derived religion, is characterized by the Native Baptist and Revival Zion religions. In assessing their impact upon the Jamaican religious experience, I hold that the Native Baptist and Revival Zion religions characterize one dimension of African-derived religious expression, which I call Christian Myalism. The Native Baptist and Revival Zion traditions might actually be interpreted as two components of Christian Myalism, as practitioners of the older eighteenth-century African traditional Myalism encountered Christianity, were attracted to aspects of the tradition, and simultaneously needed to conceal their devotion to African-derived religion in the form of Myal spirituality.

First, the Native Baptists, who became visible in Jamaica during the last decade of African enslavement (1830s), were described as a distinct sect with connections to the African North American missionaries such as George Liele, Moses Baker, George Gibb, and George Lewis, who first introduced the Baptist faith to Africans in Jamaica. Liele's ministry began in 1784, approximately thirty years before his cohort, Moses Baker, requested assistance from European missionaries in the Baptist Missionary Society of London and fifty years before White missionaries began complaining about the Native Baptists in their diaries.

Although the nature of Liele's ministry is shrouded by ambiguities, Liele's work among enslaved Africans was viewed as a threat by the planters and even landed him in prison on several occasions. It appears overall though that Liele and other African American Baptist missionaries were cautiously appropriate under the scrutinizing gaze of local White authorities, canceling many of their doubts or fears. The numbers of Black preachers trickling in from the United States, Cuba, the Bahamas, Santo Domingo, and the newly liberated Haitian Republic, however, were more than discomforting to colonial authorities and White residents across the island. They, along with the African Jamaicans who came under their influence, became a force so fluid, widespread, and decentralized that they more easily escaped the White gaze and were less monitored, if at all, by White officials.[117] In one sense then, we can envision the Native Baptists at one extreme, patterning themselves after White congregations, as much as cultural and experiential limitations allowed, and preaching basic Christian doctrines. At the other extreme, we see a flexible and open tradition, capable of absorbing the Myal-Obeah religious culture and its political aspirations.

It is possible that Liele and his assistants persuaded their Myal converts to abandon the practice of holding spiritual meetings around silk cotton trees[118] while other Native Baptist leaders may have invited their followers to hold services around cotton trees. It is difficult to know with certainty all that took place. What is certain is that the Native Baptist tradition was diverse across communities and penetrable with regard to Myal religious influence. Undoubtedly, Myal converts learned soul salvation through faith in Jesus Christ, yet, as Native Baptists, they uniformly attached more ritual significance to and displayed more reverence for the biblical figure John the Baptist, who baptized Jesus before he began his ministry.

Historical records indicate that the "Christian" identity of the Native Baptists was distinguishable from that of their comrades who embraced Euromissionary Christianity, especially given the former's pursuit of temporal social and political liberation. In her study of the Native Baptist rebellion, Monica Schuler argues that it was a Myal movement that "extracted and emphasized two central elements of the Baptist faith . . . the inspiration of the Holy Spirit; and Baptism, in the manner of John the Baptist."[119] Barry Chevannes too argues that the foundational religious structure of the Native Baptist movement was Myal. Drawing from their conclusions, I understand the Christian Myalism of the Native Baptists as a nineteenth-century expression of African-derived religion in Jamaica. Native Baptist religion exhibited at least three of the foundational features constituting classical African and African-derived religions. Adherents embraced communotheism (a community of divinities and invisible powers, including the Christian Trinity). They also practiced spirit possession, believed in neutral mystical power, and specifically enacted the Obeah ritual of oath taking as indicated by Samuel Sharpe's accomplices in the 1831–1832 revolt.

Although I have not uncovered any conclusive evidence that the Native Baptist (Christian Myalist) religion included practices of ancestral veneration, food offerings and animal sacrifice, and herbalism and divination, it is probable that at least some denominations did because these practices correspond with other features to promote fulfillment and well-being for adherents and they were also standard in popular African-Jamaican (Myal) religiosity at the time. In addition, because the Revival Zion religion remains a contemporary tradition in Jamaica, we can form two basic hypotheses about the Christian Myalist tradition (1830s–) from studying Revival Zion spirituality and religiosity.

Thirty years after the Native Baptist Christian Myalist movement emerged and twenty years after the Christian Myalist anti-Obeah campaign, groups of ecstatic Christian Myalists emerged from the Great Revival of 1860–1861 calling themselves Revivalists and Zionists and apparently manifesting every foundational feature of African-derived religion. If the contemporary practice of Revival Zion can be accepted as a credible approximation of the earliest Revival Zion expression during the latter nineteenth century, Leonard Barrett is absolutely correct when he maintains that the Great Revival among Africans was a revival of traditional African religion—and, I would add, especially as represented by its earliest identifiable Jamaican traditions of Obeah and Myal.

Revival Zion has no doubt adopted more christianisms during the latter half of the twentieth century as some adherents are now affiliating with ecstatic Christian traditions like the Pentecostals, and thus some contemporary communities cannot be used as a categorical benchmark for understanding and interpreting nineteenth- and early twentieth-century Revival Zion religiosity.[120] Drastic alterations in worship space, ritual, and liturgy are only some examples of the increasing Christian influence on the structure of Revival Zion that parallel modifications in gender roles and the authority of women in the religion. As discussed earlier in this chapter, traditional Revival Zion worship spaces were balmyards often managed by women. Since the 1970s, however, church buildings have replaced the balmyards, and male priests and pastors now officiate at worship services and maintain ultimate power and authority within the religion. If increasing Christian influences in the religion have not eradicated the six main features that characterize it as African-derived (communotheism, ancestral veneration, herbalism and divination, food offerings and animal sacrifice, spirit possession, and a belief in neutral mystical power),[121] I am inclined to believe that these features were even stronger and more visible characteristics of the religion during the time of its emergence in the 1860s. Furthermore, as the records indicate, it is possible, although not likely, that a significant number of Myal converts to the Native Baptist tradition abandoned several important traditional Myal religious practices. If indeed they had dispensed with significant features of African-derived religions such as ancestral veneration, herbalism and divination, and food offerings and animal sacrifice, the Revival Zionists have no doubt resurrected these practices by remaining faithful to traditional African Myalism and Obeah (divination, herbalism, and neutral mystical power), which were still operative alongside the Christian Myalism of the Native Baptists during the time of the Great Revival (1860–1861).

In the end, the Revival Zionists of today might have stronger ties to traditional features of African religions than the Native Baptists of yesterday, if we consider the full range of their religious activities within and outside of the context of church worship. In other words, I am suggesting that Revival Zionists of the 1860s may have been the architects of a Myal revitalization movement in response to a Native Baptist tradition that was perhaps undergoing rapid ritual and theological modification in the direction of Christian orthodoxy. What else would explain the conspicuous absence of actual Native Baptist congregations in contemporary Jamaica? If we consider along with this, the fact that more than a few Revival churches have the qualifier, "Baptist" incorporated into their congregational names, for example, Holy Mount Zion Baptist Church in St. Thomas, Barrett's theory, that the Great Revival of 1860–1861 was a Myal Revival among the Africans is quite convincing.

Zora Neale Hurston argued something similar in her interpretation of the formation and proliferation of the Black sanctified church in the United States during the early twentieth century. Hurston viewed the new religious movement as a protest against the "high-brow [Eurocentric] tendency in Negro Protestant congregations as the Negroes gain more education and wealth." To quote Hurston more thoroughly:

> The rise of the various groups of "saints" in America in the last twenty years is not the appearance of a new religion as has been reported. It is in fact the older forms of Negro religious expression asserting themselves against the new. . . . In fact, the Negro has not been christianized as extensively as is generally believed. The great masses are still standing before their pagan altars and calling old gods by a new name.[122]

Since the 1860s, the new name and new site for Native Baptist Christian Myalism has been Revival Zion religion, where many of the Christian elements (christianisms) of the tradition serve as a mask to conceal its identity as an African-derived religion and to give it legitimacy in an anti-African and Afrophobic Christian society.

Distinct from Eurocentric Christianity (which is simply Christianity to the Rastas) and the Christian Myalism of the Native Baptists and Revival Zionists, the third trajectory, representing the Rastafari religion, is not an African-derived religion but must be explored for its peculiar contribution to promoting the ideals and liberation norm of African-derived religions that were especially manifested in the pre-emancipation period through the activities of Obeah practitioners, traditional African Myalists, and Christian Myalists (Native Baptists). The Rastafari religion constitutes a third trajectory in postemancipation Jamaican religious experience; it expresses the African Jamaican's militant rejection of Eurocentric Christianity and thus directly responds to the loss of African religious memory represented by the first trajectory, that is, Africans who accepted Euro-Christian theology. Rastafari, currently a global phenomenon, is a distinctly Jamaican-derived religion. Yet, Rastafari's orientation toward Africa cannot be interpreted in isolation from the multiple expressions of African-derived religions in Jamaica. In fact the explicit memory of Africa and the conspicuous militarism characterizing Rastafari politics and theology positions the religion as a critical shaper of African-Jamaican consciousness in the twentieth and twenty-first centuries.

A century after the emergence of the Native Baptist Christian Myalism, Rastafari came to represent African communal memory while eschewing the explicit features of African-derived religion present in traditional African Myalism, Obeah, and Christian Myalism (Native Baptist and Revival Zion). The Rastafari religion maintains no community of divinities and supernatural powers and no practice of divination, although herbalism is crucial in its approach to disease prevention and curing. It has no practice of offering food and animal sacrifices to deities, and spirit possession and Obeah practices are taboo in Rastafari. While there are major traditions centered upon remembering and honoring the achievements of African-Jamaican Ancestors of national and international import for contributions to Black liberation and Pan-Africanism, Rastas do not practice ancestral veneration as it is sustained in African and

African-derived religions—that is, feeding the Ancestors, maintaining ancestral altars, and soliciting their direct intervention in human affairs.

The question might be raised as to why Rastafari does not incorporate any major features of African-derived religions while it promotes the liberation theological principle that Africans were created by God for freedom long held by generations of practitioners of African-based religions in Jamaica. The connections between Rastafari and other African-derived religious traditions in Jamaica, however, cannot be overlooked, not only because of its preoccupation with Black liberation, but because Rastafari most probably emerged as the result of a critical reformation of African-derived religions in Jamaica.

It is noteworthy that several of the earliest Rastafari leaders had connections to African-derived religions. Leonard Howell, who was a Garveyite, lived in the United States for some time and was known by many in New York as an Obeah man. Robert Hinds was both a Garveyite and a Bedwardite (Revival Zionist). He was arrested with Alexander Bedward and others during Bedward's 1921 anti-oppression protest and spiritual reform march.[123] According to Barry Chevannes, Hinds also spearheaded a group called the King of Kings Mission, which was "organized along the lines of a Revival group."[124]

In 1974, Chevannes attended a Rasta celebration of Ethiopian Christmas. During the ceremony, he was shocked to discover a ritual unfolding before his eyes that encompassed many Revival elements and ritual objects, including a table adorned with objects associated with Revival worship (a white tablecloth, an open Bible, glasses of water, a healing plant, and so on). Chevannes, a Jamaican authority on Rastafari, maintains, "The character of Rastafari has been shaped by Revivalism to a far greater degree than is thought."[125] Chevannes's conclusions are substantiated by Rupert Lewis, who notes that Garvey had serious reservations about the religiosity that characterized Rastafari during the 1920s and 1930s and "had been critical of revivalist practices, Obeah (not in modern Rastafari), and the smoking of Ganja."[126]

Because spirit possession is considered taboo in many Rastafari communities, the spiritual and ritual connections between Rastafari and earlier Myal-based traditions (Native Baptists, Revival Zion) are not so easily established. Yet in 1969, while visiting one of Claudius Henry's Rasta meetings, Chevannes recalls that a "woman experienced a fit of convulsions, and without any reproof, she was given assistance by two other women who succeeded in calming her."[127] In her discussion of gender socialization among the Rastas, Maureen Rowe reports that she had "been told of a female visitor to a Nyabinghi I-assembly in recent times who succumbed to the drums. She was chased away by irate brethren on the grounds that she was bringing devil business into the Bingi."[128]

It is worthwhile to read Barry Chevannes's comments about the evolution of Rastafari against Rowe's report. Chevannes sees uncontestable evidence in the ministries of Hinds and Howell demonstrating that Rastafari had specific connections to Revival Zion. More important, however, "as Rastafari underwent further development of [the] three aspects of Revivalism—fasting, baptism, and high female participation—only one, fasting, was retained."[129]

Rowe's report that "in recent times" a spirit-possessed woman was reprimanded, identified with evil ("devil business"), and banned from a *Binghi* gathering bears witness to Chevannes's theory of Rastafari evolution as a process distancing Rastafari from Revival and, by implication, from African-derived religion where women have been central, authoritative leaders.

What should one make of the linkages and severances between Rastafari and African-derived religion, especially Revival Zion, in Jamaica? As Rastafari became more routinized as a movement, it problematized the mystical spirituality associated with divination and spirit possession in favor of a mysticism associated with ganja smoking, "reasoning," and locked hair. Rastafari anthropology also points to linkages with and severances from African-derived religion. The proclamation that the Black person's nature is divine and the degree to which Rastas cooperate with nature and what is "natural" for Black people, including self-upliftment through the personalized divine power of Jah, are not just responses to Christian dualistic anthropology, which maligns Black humanity while affirming White humanity. Rastafari anthropology reinterprets aspects of African-derived religions pertaining to spirit possession or divine incarnation. In African-derived religions, members of the Divine Community are incarnated in the bodies of their devotees for the express purpose of assisting the individual and community in eradicating problems and pursuing freedom, whereas Rastas claim that each Rasta is a temple for divine indwelling. In this regard, Rastafari anthropology is deeply informed by biblical Christology. Just as Jesus shared in Jah's divinity, Rastas and, to be sure, all Africans share in Jah's divinity.

The chief distinction between Rastafari and African-derived religious anthropology is that of temporality. Divine incarnation is a permanent phenomenon in Rastafari, recurring in each individual. And despite dualistic popular beliefs about women's nature as both divine and evil, orthodox Rastology embraces universal divinity as African people's true nature. On the other hand, in African-derived religions, manifestations of divine incarnation occur randomly among devotees for a limited period of time. Rastafari anthropology, then, shares the belief with African-derived religions that divine incarnation is a recurring event in African communities. This is in direct opposition to the Christian proclamation that divine incarnation was contextualized historically in the first-century birth of a Palestinian itinerant preacher, Jesus of Nazareth.

Rastafari anthropology, while related to biblical Christology, contests Euro-Christian anthropology, which makes an ontological distinction between the essential natures of Jesus and other human beings. This is significant given the legacy of religious imperialism and persecution spawned by self-righteous missionaries who audaciously committed themselves to spreading the gospel message that Jesus Christ is God's unique and special revelation. As noted in the introduction in the context of the African diaspora of plantation slavery, the Christian doctrine of special revelation has produced devastating consequences for African religious cultures. Rastafari religiosity, despite its appropriation of the Bible as a primary source for theological construction, came into existence in Jamaica to dispute the classic claims of Euro-missionary

Christianity and to invalidate the pseudoconnections between African spirituality and the Euro-Christian faith that African Jamaicans had begun to make after experiencing sustained encounters with Euro-Christian missionaries. To be sure, Rastafari emerged as a bifocal (externally and internally) critical religiocultural tradition[130] in that it viewed Christianity with a hermeneutics of suspicion, identifying it as intrinsically Eurocentric and anti-African in doctrine and piety. Rastas have also employed a hermeneutics of suspicion to interpret and discredit the African-Jamaican acceptance of (Euro-)Christianity as expressed by increasing numbers of Africans, especially since the mid–nineteenth century. Rastology exposes the African-Jamaican Christian identity, represented by the testimonies examined in the first section of this chapter, as an oxymoron that promotes African enslavement, impotence, and anomie.

Returning to the puzzle of both the critical closeness and the distance between Rastafari and African-derived religions, the essential key is Revival Zion. I have already discussed above the findings of scholars who support the thesis that Rastafari is undeniably related to Revival Zion. However, I want to suggest that Rastafari arose in Jamaica as an African-centered, iconic[131] tradition that critically evaluated the characteristics and practices of the (Christian Myalist) Revival Zion religion, accepting and expanding upon some while rejecting others. For example, George Simpson recalls that, while he was conducting research on Rastafari in Kingston:

> [R]evivalists [during the 1950s] were engrossed mainly in the quest for personal salvation and the satisfaction to be gained from ritual observances, [and] Rastafarians were concerned and very vocal about economic hardships and racial discrimination. Although many Rastas in the 1950s had been involved earlier in some type of revivalism, most subsequently became hostile to these religious groups. Among Rasta groups I encountered, repatriation to Africa was preached as the solution to the hopeless hell of Jamaica.[132]

In preaching about a return to Africa, Rastas, nonetheless, retained the symbol of Zion most treasured by their Revival Zion compatriots.

Within the Revival Zion tradition, Africans appropriated the Old Testament biblical symbol and conceived of Zion much like the ancient Hebrews did. Zion came to represent another space,[133] both geographic and existential, where Africans were ensured freedom, dignity, the conditions for authentic self-repossession, and the eradication of European colonial authority. Revival Zionists assert that Zion, the place of freedom, is in Africa, and Rastas passionately concur. Yet, while affirming the religious significance of Zion for Africans, Rastology crystallized more than anything around a different symbol: a specific political and historical symbol of contemporary relevance that was and continues to be Ethiopia, or Abyssinia.[134] Rastafari's Ethiopianist Pan-Africanism was apparently inspired by the Bible, where among numerous references to Ethiopia is the prophetic utterance to "let Ethiopia hasten to stretch out its hand unto God."[135] Ethiopia was also meaningful because, by the 1930s, when Rastafari began to take shape in Jamaica, Ethiopia had emerged as the only African country to resist European colonialism, in spite of Italian invasions and temporary occupations. The political status of Ethiopia in the 1930s as a sovereign kingdom only reinforced what Rastas understood as God's providential will for Africans.

The Ethiopianism of Rastafari, though, must be examined as an integral component of the multiple expressions of African religiosity and spirituality in Jamaica, if we are to properly assess its critical contribution to African people's unceasing struggle for liberation and autonomy in the island. In chapter 1, I examined records pertaining to the burial rituals of enslaved Africans in the British West Indies and especially in Jamaica. I also explored primary and secondary sources that connected the motivations for suicide among enslaved Africans to the desire to be reincarnated in specific African continental communities, to reestablish familial ties and fulfilling social relationships of good will and well-being. The prevalence of this desire and the confidence that Africans placed in their beliefs about repatriation via reincarnation cannot be understated at a time in Jamaican history when a significant percentage of the enslaved population was native African.[136]

By the late nineteenth century, when Revival Zion was spreading its wings as a novel manifestation of Myal spirituality, African-Jamaican memories of the African continent were dissolving under the anti-African influence of Euromissionary Christianity, and what remained was naturally diluted by generational distance from Africa, loss of contact with Africa, and the loss of actual memories of Africa as formerly enslaved African-born Jamaicans aged and passed on. Jamaican-born Revival Zionists, then, appropriated Zion as a substitute for specific peoples, cultures, civilizations, and regions on the African continent that had given their African-born ancestors the courage to struggle to free themselves from dehumanizing relationships and social arrangements. Revival Zionists developed spiritual hymns celebrating Zion and its promise of freedom and abundant life for Africans. As they sang "don't trouble Zion," Rastas heard their cry and related the symbol of Zion to their Ethiopianism, bringing precise definition and geographic specificity to the African-Jamaican desire for freedom and autonomy. Like their African-born enslaved ancestors, Rastas related their liberation struggle to a specific place in Africa: a country or kingdom with a history of political sovereignty that African Jamaicans yearned for and viewed as the solution to their condition of deprivation and misery. Thus, Rastafari has embodied critical ancestral responses to the African-Jamaican predicament from slavery to colonialism. Moving toward the ideas of their enslaved Ancestors, Rastas embraced the view that repatriation to the continent of Africa is essential for authentic liberation. Their Ancestors had seen the possibility for eschatological repatriation through the afterlife experience of reincarnation because of the brutal limitations slavery placed upon spatial mobility in predeath lived experience. In postemancipation Jamaica, Rastafari came to assert that the African quest for freedom and political sovereignty must be expressed not only by references to symbolic biblical concepts and icons but through concrete concepts and icons that have temporal historical significance and thus offer Africans opportunities to pursue liberation in predeath lived experience.

Rastafari demonstrates how the African "soul force" so eloquently described by Leonard Barrett[137] has evolved holistically in the Jamaican religious consciousness. Retaining useful aspects of African expressions of liberation as the highest human ideal, Rastafari innovatively coordinated ancestral religious traditions of repatriation and Zionism[138] to conceive of a particular expression of Ethiopianism—a vision for African liberation that expanded at once upon the specificity of the repatriation-via-reincarnation liberation vision of their African-born enslaved Ancestors and the Revival Zionist application of biblical symbols to the African-Jamaican quest for liberation (Zion and Ethiopia).

Ultimately, Rastafari established the urgency of African peoples' struggle for liberation by constantly articulating a temporal vision of liberation in human history over and against Euro-missionary theology, which promoted temporal historical suffering for Africans and delayed eschatological relief. The Rastafari vision of temporal historical liberation also functioned as a critical protest against postdeath liberation visions expressed by Revival Zionists and, before them, "reincarnation repatriationists." Thus Rastas could accept Zion as a place of freedom, but they went beyond Revival Zionists to define freedom exclusively in noneschatological terms as a historical ambition. Rastas were intent on specifying that religious talk about freedom was only meaningful with reference to predeath experience. Committed to the religious imperatives of generations of freedom-seeking Africans, Rastas could audaciously modify a biblical verse about Zion and sing it with their hearts and minds focused upon their Zion: Ethiopia (Abyssinia):

> By the Rivers of Babylon, there we sat down
> And there we wept, when we remembered Zion
> For the wicked carried us away in captivity
> Required from us a song
> But how can we sing King Alpha's[139] song
> In a strange land.

Even with its shortcomings, the prophetic theological import of Rastafari as a critical reflection upon the legacy of African religious experience in Jamaica cannot be overlooked. It is left for Jamaican and other Caribbean theologians to recognize this and consider the hermeneutical implications of Rastology and the other African-Jamaican religious traditions examined in this chapter (Native Baptist and Revival Zion) for liberation theological construction. The implications, as I see them, will compel Jamaican theologians to raise serious questions about the compatibility between Christianity and the approximation of authentic liberation for the people of African heritage in Jamaica. But before exploring such questions in the final chapter, there is one more significant manifestation of African-derived religion in Jamaica. In the next chapter, then, the discussion of African-Jamaican religion shifts from the Rasta king-men to the Kumina queen-mothers, exploring the legacy of an African-derived religious tradition in Jamaica and the moral problems that attend Kumina's historical and contemporary encounter with Jamaican Christian culture. The chapter also reflects more broadly upon the shades of ambiguity and contradiction with which Jamaican theologians must wrestle if they care to respond to the church's unmistakeable sponsorship of anthropological poverty/anti-Africanness, especially at the expense of those who sustain and are sustained by African-derived religions in Jamaican society.

4

Visitation

The Legacy of African-Derived Religions in Jamaica

There are at the present time many herbalists in the Caribbean and
South America, and the evidence of their influence is found in the
United States wherever there is a heavy concentration of Afro-
Americans. Every island of the Caribbean is a veritable pharmacological garden in which there can be found every type of herb and root
sufficient for the healing of the nation. One only needs to spend a day
with an old woman to be impressed by the assortment of weeds necessary for each ailment liable to occur.[1]

An Ancient Remedy for a Postmodern Age

The sociopolitical focus in Rastafari theology might be well paired
with the healing focus in Kumina. Kumina is perhaps the most misunderstood African-Jamaican religious tradition, in part because Kumina practitioners produce no liturgical or theological literature pertaining to their beliefs and practices.[2] It is also misunderstood
because it is conspicuously African-oriented and therefore stereo-
typed by the dominant society. As attested to by Kumina devotees,
the weight of such social condemnation is felt via Christian anti-
African ideas.[3]

The scholarship on Kumina is also insufficient. Kumina is dynamic and with each generation contributes something novel to its
inherited past. My exploration of Kumina, then, is informed by its
expressions in contemporary Jamaica with relevant insights from
the existing literature on the subject. My research with Kumina
communities took place over six months (two visits in 1995 and
1996) in the parishes of St. Thomas and St. Catherine. During my

second research trip to Jamaica, in November 1996, I was fortunate enough to have an audience with Jamaica's former prime minister and leader of the opposition, Edward Seaga. Seaga, whose advanced training in sociology was truncated by his professional entry into politics, is nonetheless one of the most important researchers in the study of Revival Zion and Kumina. Seaga's contribution, however, has not been significantly felt, for most of his twenty-plus years of research materials may be found in Jamaican institutions waiting to be interrogated and analyzed by interested scholars.

During the course of the interview, Seaga expressed deep disappointment regarding the superficial studies of Jamaican religion that have informed the teaching and works of professional scholars and performance artists who replicate Kumina dances on stage. Since the 1960s Seaga had introduced a number of native Jamaican scholars to Revival Zion and Kumina practitioners with the hope that they would continue his legacy of research and, even more, publish substantially in the area. More than thirty-five years have passed since the publication of Seaga's noted article "Revival Cults in Jamaica," yet the scholarship on Jamaica's African-derived religions remains insufficient. When compared with the publications generated by a growing scholarly interest in the African-derived religions of Haiti, Cuba, and Brazil, we find the literature on African-derived Jamaican religions inadequate, as scholars base much of their interpretations upon unsubstantiated or inconclusive data.

One factor contributing to the emphasis on African-derived religions in Haiti, Cuba, and Brazil is the conspicuous and central appearance of African deities in those traditions. Esu or Ellegua; Ogou or Ogun; Sango; Yemoja, Yemanja, or Yemaya; Oya; and Obatala are only some examples of divinities which can be found in Yoruba and Vodun religious practices in West Africa as well as in Haiti, Cuba, and Brazil. Although Jamaican Kumina emphasizes continuity between the visible and invisible domains of the human and ancestral world, practitioners claim to worship one Deity, whom they call Zambi or King Zambi.[4]

Consequently, the African character of Jamaican religions is often depicted as less salient than that of Vodun in Haiti or of Yoruba derivatives in Cuba and Brazil. Perhaps the preoccupation with origins and nature in the study of African and African diasporic religions has encouraged the proliferation of scholarship on diasporic traditions that have identifiable parent cultures in Africa. While Haitian Vodun has been traced to its Dahomean, Yoruba, and Kongo sources; Cuban Yoruba and Santería to their continental Yoruba and Kongo sources; and Brazilian Candomblé and Umbanda to Yoruba and Congo sources; on the whole, African-derived Jamaican religious traditions offer less tangible evidence of direct continuity with parent cultures in Africa.

Furthermore, when we speak of African-derived religions in Jamaica, we are not referring to one or two widespread popular religions with markable beginnings and discernible trajectories of growth, transformation, or cross-fertilization. On the contrary, we are referring primarily to traditions with ambiguous origins, unpredictable evolutionary patterns, and, at times, regional significance. As discussed in previous chapters, Obeah, Myal, and the Native

Baptists emerged as islandwide traditions in Jamaica during the period of African enslavement; Kumina and Revival Zion traditions emerged, respectively, during the 1840s and 1860s.

Following the interpretation of Leonard Barrett, until recently, scholars held that Kumina was also a tradition practiced by enslaved Africans in Jamaica. However, Monica Schuler's research on African indentured labor in Jamaica between 1841 and 1865 and Bilby and Bunseki's field research on Kumina firmly establish it as a BaKongo-based religious practice that was introduced into eastern Jamaica by African indentured laborers just a few years after the abolition of slavery. Some studies have documented another tradition, Convince, which has been recorded as a spirit possession ritual practiced mostly by the Maroons and eastern Jamaicans.[5] More work is needed in this area, however, if we are to understand its history and evolution in Jamaica.

Some other African-derived religiocultural traditions are Jonkunnu or Burru, Gumbay, Ananse, Ettu, Tambu, Gerreh, Dinki Mini, Ni-Nite, Brukin' Party, and Zella.[6] Regional retentions have also been documented on the western end of the island in the Abeokuta village in the parish of Westmoreland, which derived its name from Abeokuta in Nigeria, as the community was able to retain fragments of Yoruba language and culture.[7]

In my view, one of the greatest challenges facing researchers is that of understanding and explaining how these diverse deposits of African religious cultures in Jamaica relate to Africa and to one another. With regard to Kumina, some would argue that it is not a religion but a dance or an ancestral "cult." I would argue, though, that Kumina is a religion inasmuch as it is a coherent system of belief, religious ritual, and spiritual practice structured upon the metaphysical principles and cultural norms of classical African societies. As Bilby and Bunseki write, "Kumina is indeed an African form of dance, but it is a great deal more than this. It is a religion, a worldview, and a living cultural preserve."[8]

Most of the research on Kumina is descriptive and derivative. Among scholars, there is a tendency to treat Kumina with some interpretive distance by focusing on its outward expressions of dance, song, drumming, and so on. For example, Rex Nettleford, founder and former director of Jamaica's National Dance Theater Company (NDTC), has emphasized the ritual dance component of Kumina both in his scholarship[9] and in the dance compositions performed by the NDTC. Joseph Moore has written about the songs and dances in Kumina ceremonies.[10] During the 1970s, Maureen Warner-Lewis undertook a deeper study of Kumina through the personality and religious lore of Imogene Kennedy, a Kumina queen from St. Catherine.[11] And in a more recent essay, "The Ancestral Factor in Jamaica's African Religions," Warner-Lewis makes a fitting attempt to identify African retentions in a wide array of Jamaican religiocultural traditions with specific African continental institutions. She also observes reciprocal patterns of influence in these traditions since the period of African enslavement. With regard to Kumina, Warner-Lewis discusses one of the interpretive tasks facing researchers if we are to deepen our understanding and appreciation of Kumina as an institution of knowledge, meaning, and contemporary relevance in Jamaican society. She maintains that we "need to ascertain what values [the Ancestors] hold for the present generations who invoke [them]."[12] Olive Lewin's treatment of Kumina is also a significant contribution of recent years.[13]

The truth is that most accounts of Kumina do not include enough detailed information about Kumina as an institution, including its theological and social significance to practitioners and to the larger Jamaican society. The earliest accounts of Kumina, by Zora Neale Hurston in the 1930s[14] and Madeline Kerr in the 1950s,[15] were informed by primary field research. Nevertheless, the experiences described in their works were based upon shallow appearances at a limited number of Kumina ceremonies. The most comprehensive study on Kumina as a structured religious institution was written by Kenneth Bilby in collaboration with Fu-Kiau Bunseki in 1978 as an unpublished master's thesis at the University of the West Indies (now published in *Les Cahiers du Cedaf*). The definitive import of their study is demonstrated by the unprecedented scope and depth of their research among a number of Kumina communities in Jamaica. Through attending ceremonies and intensive interviews, they collected a database of oral histories, folk stories, songs, and linguistic glosses. Thus, they offer a more developed portfolio of Kumina—one that contextualizes Kumina as a product of history, culture, and social transformation.[16]

As a system of ritual practice, Kumina is often described as an insular ancestral cult which places little, if any, significance upon analyzing and responding to social oppression. In one of her articles, Warner-Lewis compares Kumina with historic and contemporary Jamaican religious traditions, remarking:

> Myalism, the Native Baptist movement, Bedwardism, and Rastafari-anism all belong in one set of Afro-Jamaican religions which consciously aim to demolish the politico-economic evils of their age, whether slavery, colonialism, or neocolonialism. On the other hand, on the face of it, the ancestor cults adopt a neutral position vis-à-vis socio-economic conditions. With the exception of Convince, they appear to survive more out of a sense of clan identity and to foster feelings of spiritual fellowship within communities. Through them, communal history is relived in possessions, dreams, shared communions of food, and the immortalization of individuals and groups through song. But with time, the link between the living and ancestors at greater generational depth must become attenuated.[17]

Warner-Lewis suggests that the ancestral focus in Kumina is cultural and distinct from the kind of political consciousness fostered by other African-Jamaican religions such as Rastafari, Revival Zion, and Myal, which were explored in earlier chapters. My own research among Kumina practitioners is more consistent with Bilby and Bunseki's depiction of Kumina as a complex and cogently nuanced expression of religious ideas and ritual that govern the lives of adherents as they negotiate experiences that promote or compromise human potential for health (and general well-being) productivity, and fulfill-ment. For example, Bilby and Bunseki maintain:

> Kumina can neither be reduced to a quaint survival nor dismissed as a fantasy of Africa reenacted. It is a vibrant and fully living African-based religion. Those who belong to the "Bongo Nation" and prac-tice Kumina really *do* consider themselves Africans, regardless of what others might wish to believe about them. Their African identity and consciousness are not designed; they are rooted in the still-remembered historical experience of nineteenth-century African im-migrants who adapted their cultural pasts to the new surroundings in which they found themselves, and passed the product on to their children and their children's children. The end-result is that there exists today in eastern Jamaica, and particularly St. Thomas, a social and economic network of "Africans"—people who belong to a bona fide "subculture" based on an African-derived religion, ideology, and language.[18]

In identifying some of the limitations of former studies, I do not intend to trivialize the meaningful contributions that Warner-Lewis, Kerr, Hurston, Barrett, Moore, and others have made to the body of research on Kumina. Collectively, these scholars were the pioneers in documenting the ritual con-tent, language, and structure of Kumina as a religiocultural institution. The challenge before scholars today is to expand the understanding of the historical evolution and social significance of this 150-year-old cultural preserve in Ja-maica.

The only credible way of deepening our understanding of Kumina, as an oral-based transgenerational tradition, is through more intensive field research on practicing Kumina communities. My field research among Kumina com-munities in the parishes of St. Thomas and St. Catherine introduced me to a Jamaican worldview steeped in forms of African consciousness that I had only previously associated with Rastafari culture. I came to understand the saliency of Africa for Kumina communities during six months of attending Kumina ceremonies, interviewing practitioners, and collecting songs and lexicons.

It is important to acknowledge that the scope of my research involved a limited number of communities and, therefore, precludes any precise com-parative analysis, which will be required in the end for a definitive commentary on Kumina spirituality and cosmology. With this in mind, I attempt here to portray Kumina as I encountered it in the narratives, songs, rituals, and visible-invisible loci of the practicing communities. And I will do so sequentially, following the order in which I was permitted access to the essential compo-nents of Kumina identity. First, which people comprise the Kumina commu-nity? And what unifies them as a people with a shared past and a common destiny? Second, what is Kumina as religious practice? What is the purpose and significance of the various Kumina ceremonies to practitioners and non-practitioners?

The Kumina people are self-identified "Africans." They do not refer to themselves as Black, Jamaican, Afro-Jamaican, or even African Jamaican. They conceive of their African identity exponentially. They are simultaneously ethnic Africans[19] and Pan-Africans, thereby presenting themselves to be Africans ethnically, racially, culturally, and more specifically, spiritually. If we are to hear and understand what Kumina Africans intend by this assertion of identity, we must be willing to surrender, or at least suspend, postmodern critiques that render diasporic ethnocultural and racial identifications with Africa essentialist, romantic, and therefore inauthentic and contrived.

The African identity claims of people eight generations removed from ancestors who were born and buried on the continent of Africa disclose that Africanness has always signified something symbolic, intangible, and even inaccessible to many descendants of enslaved Africans in the Caribbean and the Americas. Yet it has also taken on a very specific meaning in the Caribbean and the Americas, one with which, at the end of the day, continental Africans must also identify—that is, Africanness, as an identity, is a consequence of the rise of the modern West. Europe's Africanization of distinct ethnic communities such as the Igbo, Yoruba, Fon, Mende, Asante, Hausa, and so on was essential to the proliferation of the racist ideological justifications for the transatlantic slave trade. Thus for many of the Igbo, Yoruba, Fon, Mende, Asante, Hausa, and so on, who became shipmates on slave vessels, African identity soon replaced or existed alongside ethnic identity in contexts of exile from family, clan, civilization, and ancestral homeland. For a significant number of diasporic Africans, "Africa" has been an all-encompassing symbol of the inaccessible ancestral homeland and the preservation or rearticulation of African continental institutions and worldviews in spite of slavery, Western cultural dominance, and their devastating impact on African diasporic cultures.[20]

For Kumina Africans, Africa (that intangible, inaccessible something) is also awesome and sacred, indeed something transcendent and deserving of reverence. And thus, in Kumina anthropology, we find clues for understanding why Kumina Africans do not experience the kind of ambivalence many diasporic Africans (especially those persuaded by postmodern critiques of essentialism) experience regarding their African heritage. Kumina devotees do not subscribe to a universal theological anthropology like that expressed by the Christian doctrines of Original Sin and universal redemption. They believe that each human being is essentially who she is due to the unique combination of her *kanuba* (spirit), *deebu* (blood), and *beezie* (flesh). The *kanuba* shapes the human personality and is patrilineally derived. The *beezie*, on the other hand, is matrilineally derived, and the *deebu* can be derived from either side. Some Kumina practitioners maintain strict taboos regarding these three components of their human makeup.

The *kanuba, deebu,* and *beezie* are the umbilical cord unifying the individual with his specific *nkuyu* (Ancestors) and unifying the larger community with the entire ancestral community.[21] The Ancestors are the departed who achieve spiritual status as members of the Divine Community and as Nzambi's messengers in the invisible world domain. They acquire power and use it to assist their living descendants in the visible world domain. Kumina devotees are in constant communication with Ancestors who validate and replenish their steadfast identification with Africa.

In Kumina anthropology, African identity is restored and epitomized in the transcendent yet accessible ancestral community. Through ritual possession and other acts of devotion, Kumina Africans constantly strengthen the metaphysical continuity between the living and the dead, the visible and the invisible, the Bongo[22] nation and the Bongo Ancestors. With the assistance of the Ancestors, Kumina devotees configure a space for accessing and applying African ideas and values to the concrete tasks and challenges they confront in the visible dimension of life. Pan-African theologian Josiah Young asserts that this process of reconciliation and empowerment has been an important aspect of African North American religiosity as well. In describing the underpinnings of his approach to theology, he writes:

> Those values that intrigue me most may be characterized as the communication between the living and the dead—a spirituality reappropriated in Pan-African theology today. I suspect that within certain cultures, namely those inherited by today's Gullahs, such communication was established through the liminality of ritual. Liminality has to do with the suspension of the prevailing sacred space, where a people discover, in the kinetic fervor of religious feeling, genuine liberation. Here social distinctions are eschewed in favor of a spiritual, transcendent state, in which devotees experience the intensification of community, and revel in their most heartfelt commitments.[23]

There is in Kumina a "heartfelt commitment" to African identity and its multivocal expressions in the oral cultural traditions, ceremonial possession rituals, and other acts of devotion. At the core of Kumina culture is a collective memory, grief, and indignation regarding African people's capture, exile, enslavement, and oppression by Whites or "the White supremacists," as one informant constantly remarked. All of the Kumina practitioners I interviewed identified their heritage in Jamaica with the period of African enslavement. Moreover, in each community, there were several elders and leaders who could give accounts of ancestral journeys from "Africa" to Jamaica, with specific details about the brutalities suffered on the slave ships and the hardships endured both during slavery and after Emancipation. One such narrative was recounted by Uncle P,[24] the sixty-seven-year-old grandson of a late Kumina queen in Port Morant, St. Thomas:

> Mi say, di White man, him wicked! Him tek fi wi ancestor-dem pon di ship an mek dem suffa. My grandmodda was rape[d] 'on di slave ship. Dem tek har, a fourteen-year-ole pickney, an rape har! . . . So di blood, it mix up because she get pregnant, and dem neva help har

wan bit (di White people I mean). . . . We no truss dem because dem wicked. But you cyaan blame di chile . . . a no har fault har fahdda White. We African a wan people.[25]

One's immediate reaction to Uncle P's story might be suspicion, for when we do the math, it could not possibly be the case that his grandmother was born before the abolition of slavery in the British Caribbean, let alone before the abolition of the slave trade in 1807. However, studies of the slave trade and the abolitionist movement in Britain show how and when the rape could have taken place. Monica Schuler's research on African emigration to Jamaica provides insight into this puzzling dimension of Kumina memory.

Schuler's study documents that 8,000 "recaptive [West and Central] Africans"[26] were sent to Jamaica from St. Helena and Sierra Leone between 1841 and 1865. Says Schuler, "Two categories of Africans arrived in Jamaica in numbers unanticipated by authorities—children orphaned by the slave trade, and Africans of all ages landed in Jamaica from Cuba-bound slave ships captured by the British navy in the Caribbean."[27]

The British navy rescued Africans from Portuguese-Brazilian and Spanish-Cuban slave ships throughout the 1860s. It is possible that Uncle P's grandmother was raped on a ship en route to Brazil or Cuba during the late 1860s before the British navy arrested its crew and rescued the Africans from their impending captivity as slaves. She could have survived to pass down her story to her children and grandchildren or to other members of her community, who helped to preserve the memory of her violation.

Ultimately, the rape narrative is the collective property of Kumina Africans, who are now bearers of their ancestral legacy in Jamaica. Uncle P's "grandmother" is the archetypal victim of sexual exploitation, a dehumanizing rite of passage experienced by African females throughout the Middle Passage and slavery. Members of the Kumina community, today apparently unaware of the unique sequence of events that led to their foreparents' arrival in Jamaica only *after* official emancipation, actually situate themselves within the broader collective history of African experience in pre-emancipation Jamaica and function then as retainers of national memory. For example, Edward Brathwaite cites an archetypal lynching story from a taped interview with one of the most celebrated and publicized Kumina queens, Imogene Kennedy. Kennedy described the lynching of African people on a cotton tree in Port Morant, St. Thomas:

> [I]s not dey-one came, is a whole heap-a-dem come 'ere in de slavery . . . because take for instant Morant Bay. . . . when dey came here . . . you 'ave a cotton tree out dere . . . what de buil' a gas station now . . . dat dey *use to heng people* . . . an' you husban' leave an come . . . after you . . . an' dey heng you; you husban' come to look fuh you . . . dey d'win de same . . . you children come out in de slavery time . . . but dose time it was still de African-dem . . . you understan' . . . ? Well dey hang dem out there, because at de las' time since I been here, an' when dey gwine to cut down dat cotton tree to buil' de gas station, it lick dung about four to five men . . . kill dem.[28]

In relating her version of countless African lynchings in Port Morant, Kennedy establishes that many Africans apart from her BaKongo Ancestors came to Jamaica as slaves. Thus, her report of these brutal executions concerns Africans both within and outside of her personal ancestral lineage, reflecting an inclusive and Pan-Africanist understanding of African community. Accordingly, we gain insight into the Pan-African motif as a probable recent development in contemporary Kumina culture for, as late as 1978, Bilby and Bunseki documented a strong consciousness and assertion of BaKongo ethnic identity among Kumina practitioners. "Like their ancestors," they write:

> many present-day "Africans" in eastern Jamaica maintain the concept of tribal affiliation, if not an actual genealogical map behind it. Individuals may assert, for example, that they are descended primarily from the Muyanji or Munchundi tribes. . . . Present-day descendants of the nineteenth-century Central African immigrants continue, in the tradition of their forebears, to set themselves apart—at least in theory—from the Afro-Jamaican majority surrounding them.[29]

At the time that I collected information from Kumina adherents in 1996, I observed a spirit of Pan-African unity in the attitudes of Kumina Africans toward nonpracticing Jamaican Blacks. They uniformly embraced nonpractitioners as kinfolk and held that any person of African descent from any cultural or geographic location has a right to claim allegiance to the Bongo Ancestors and a space in the Kumina-practicing Bongo nation. When I pressed informants to explain exactly what they mean by referring to themselves and the Ancestors as "Bongo," they often responded that Bongo is the African tribal or national place of origin. One informant, a Kumina queen well respected by fellow practitioners for her upkeep of the culture, also described the Ancestors as "Kongo" and explained that "Bongo" and "Kongo" are interchangeable names for the specific African lineage claimed by the Kumina community. The Kumina community's extension of membership in the Bongo nation to Blacks in the wider society synchronizes its particular sense of ethnic affiliation and its universal, Pan-African affinity with all Jamaican Blacks.

The depth of African identity consciousness in Kumina culture can also be assessed in the practitioners' perceptions of Whites. Kumina practitioners view Whites as culturally and spiritually Other. "White people can't hear the drum," said one Kumina queen when I asked if they are allowed to join Kumina bands. Another Kumina queen responded by asking of me, "How can White supremacists ask the Bongo Ancestors for help?"[30] Imogene Kennedy stressed the importance of speaking the "African language" in communicating with the Ancestors and responded, "Whites don't know the language or the rhythm of the dance. They can't talk to the Ancestors." Kumina practitioners are convinced that White supremacy is the dominant factor in African people's chronic suffering worldwide. They remain suspicious of Whites and blatantly critical of White religiocultural traditions. Even more telling of the anti-White ideological tendency in Kumina is the affirmative responses received when I asked those same informants if Indians and Chinese people are welcome to join Kumina bands (as Jamaica has a small Asian population). Kennedy responded that Asians could participate if they want because they are colored.[31]

The deep-seated African consciousness exhibited by Kumina devotees is generated as well by the community's resistance to and contempt for White supremacy and White oppressors. Their distrust of Whites is derived from the lessons taught by oral tradition. I take exception to Warner-Lewis's character-ization of Kumina as lacking in social consciousness when compared with Rastafari. I would argue that the memory of the violence and violation that their Ancestors endured during the late nineteenth century, when they were literally released from slave ships and accorded free status, has actually served to engender a type of pro-African consciousness among practitioners that Ras-tafari adherents would embrace. With each generation, recycled stories about their Ancestors' exploitation and confinement on the plantations, despicable wages, harassment, and intimidation had to have reinforced the Kumina com-munity's collective suspicion that the White person is an altogether different type of human being with a greater potential to harm Africans than to bring about any authentic liberation.

One informant (with the initials BH) attempted to recount the dreadful conditions under which Central Africans were brought to Jamaica. Her vague account was slightly incoherent, difficult to follow, and virtually indecipherable until I discovered documentation that corroborated the pieces of her memory that remained intact. A portion of our dialogue is translated below:

BH   They would tell them to join the line or they wouldn't get help. They really didn't have a choice.

DS   What line?

BH   They had to join the force and fight the war for the White man or stay slave.

DS   Where did this happen?

BH   Back in Africa.[32]

Our conversation took place within a larger discussion about the British navy rescuing Africans from slave ships, as I was attempting to discern if contemporary Kumina practitioners have retained any oral traditions about the specific details of their ancestors' extended Middle Passage from Sierra Leone and St. Helena to Jamaica under the indentured labor program. B.H. did not confirm or deny any of the information I shared with her about the conditions of her ancestors' passage to Jamaica during the postemancipation period. She immediately began talking about Africans having to "join the line." B.H.'s story always intrigued me but I did not know how to contextualize it. I initially assumed that when she discussed "the White man" she was possibly referring to colonial officers. I had also presumed that when she said the exchange occurred in Africa, she meant Central Africa. My conjecture was that she could have been describing Central African encounters with colonial officials or missionaries in the region. I was to discover some months later that B.H.'s story presented a fraction of the exchanges that took place between recaptured Africans and British government representatives ("the White man") in Africa, as she stated, but she meant Sierra Leone and not Central Africa. In her study of African immigration to Jamaica during the postemancipation period, Monica Schuler notes:

> By 1844 forced emigration of recently arrived recaptives from the Freetown Queen's Yard was an idea whose time had obviously come. In February the Colonial Secretary dispatched instructions to the Sierra Leone governor to offer recaptives the choice of immigrating to the West Indies or remaining in Sierra Leone without government assistance formerly offered. An older option, which had always existed for men—that of enlisting in the West India Regiments—remained. In reality the new dispensation read, "emigrate, enlist, or fend for yourself." The instructions made no exceptions for children.[33]

Schuler's research lends support to B.H.'s faded recollection and to the community's record of "the White man's" ill treatment of recaptive Africans. B.H.'s account suggests that the "older option" of military enlistment also noted by Schuler was not interpreted as a humane option by recaptive Africans. Schuler provides even further evidence for why this was so:

> Newly-liberated Africans had never before exhibited any interest in emigrating to the West Indies and were prone to take to the bush when emigration recruiters approached their villages. Recruiting in the Queen's Yard [Sierra Leone], therefore, was not simply a matter of inviting people to travel to the West Indies. . . . The standard practice was to isolate new arrivals from all except West India Regiment and plantation recruiters, and in some cases recaptives were detained in the Queen's Yard for one to three months awaiting the arrival of an emigrant ship.[34]

Faced with the options of "no help," "joining the line," or immigration to the Caribbean, recaptive Africans were forced to accept emigration. They never chose it. They had endured the hardships of torture and unsanitary conditions on slave ships and were rescued only to confront three basic options: abandonment in still a foreign country (Sierra Leone), the extended Middle Passage to the Caribbean as indentured laborers, or, for males, enlistment in the West India Regiments. It was unlikely that they would settle on boarding another ship under the direction of White men to labor in a country thousands of miles away. The oral traditions, songs, and rituals of the Kumina culture in Jamaica suggest that the only ships recaptured Africans desired to board were those that would take them back to their original birthplaces. Those ships never materialized and so they found ways to resurrect traditions from home in their new settlements in Jamaica.

Kumina narratives disclose a collection of experiences that have been extensively shaped by the sea. Their inclusive sense of shared peoplehood with all Jamaicans of African descent is salient in individual and communal identity formation. However, their sense of a shared situation of oppression with those in the Asian Jamaican minority who would participate in Kumina culture also points to an inclusive principle in the community's assessment of social oppression and to an acknowledgment of their extended Middle Passage as a context for identity formation and group solidarity. According to Schuler, the Central Africans who settled in St. Thomas displayed many levels of identification and group affiliations with all Africans, shipmates, all Central Africans in the parish of St. Thomas, Central African subethnic groups, and fellow villagers.[35] Ship records indicate that East Indians sailed to Jamaica as indentured laborers with Africans from depot stations in St. Helena.[36] The shared shipmate experience of transportation to Jamaica and subsequent experiences of working side-by-side on the plantation estates apparently shaped the Kumina community's perception of their Asian neighbors and their acceptance of those who have expressed interest in Kumina practices and ceremonies.

Through stories like Uncle P's, Kennedy's, and B.H.'s, Kumina Africans acknowledge the historical struggles of the Ancestors who withstood centuries of brutal violence in the African-Jamaican experience. They feel existentially connected to the ancestral narratives in that they too encounter violence, censorship, and religiocultural persecution in a Jamaican society that has absorbed the colonial Western Christian perception of African religions as pathological and uncivilized. Kumina practitioners are well aware of the battles they must fight on so many fronts if they are to protect themselves against cultural genocide.

More than anything else, Kumina ancestral narratives emphasize the indefinite quality of African suffering. For a community devoted to ancestral legacies, it is not surprising that the stories told reach back to the period of African enslavement, which is considered by many diasporic Africans to be the genesis of their collective oppression. The experiences of abuse, exploitation, social discrimination, and persecution recounted time and time again by narrators like Uncle P, Kennedy, and B.H. may well be orally recorded historical accounts of the conditions to which African indentured laborers (who were the actual carriers of Kumina culture to Jamaica) were subjected during their voyages from Africa to Jamaica and thereafter as exploited laborers in a post-emancipation plantation economy. Bilby and Bunseki's study contains testimonies in which Kumina informants actually do liken the experience of indentured labor to slave labor.[37]

Having said something about the heritage and identity of Kumina practitioners, I turn now to healing practices, the dimension of Kumina religiosity that appears to be most significant for practitioners and nonpractitioners alike. Healing and the sharing of healing remedies are constant activities in the daily journeys of Kumina practitioners. Although Kumina ceremonies, which are called by the same name (Kumina), are held to mark the significance of births and deaths, to express gratitude to the Ancestors, and to commemorate past struggles and achievements of the African Ancestors in Jamaican history, most of the Kumina ceremonies I attended were held for one or more sick persons. Kumina leaders, who are almost always female, are regularly sought out by the sick and troubled for their expert knowledge of therapeutic plants and access to ancestral power. When a person experiences grave misfortune, in terms of physical or psychological illness or any other personal problem, a Kumina queen may organize a ceremony at the request of the client or based upon her own assessment of the problem.

According to Kennedy:

> Wi do [Kumina] all di while in di smalla country [St. Thomas]. Wi jus tek di drum an wi gwan play. Who fi teach one annoda teach off di drum. An yuh have di ole people who will sid dung wid yuh an gwan home wid yuh. . . . But hear mi a tell yuh someting, mi no get no whole heap a teachment from nobody but di creator and my spirit dem who teach me.[38]

Kennedy also describes essential facets of Kumina religious practice that allow for healing, transformation, and equilibrium, through ritual sacrifice and food offerings, as well as possession trance and mediumship.

> In di African world when yuh gwine buil a sacrifice yuh use a ram goat, yuh use fowl, *malavu* which is rum . . . an when I making it now di yard full! People from all bout, people from foreign, people from all bout Jamaica, is here—cause mi mek it at watch night . . . when yuh gwine go buil a duty [ritual offering] now, yuh use bread, yuh use rice, rum, yuh get everyting dat yuh know dat yuh can travel unda; kyangle—peace an love; prosperity—blue an white. . . . Suppose yuh sick an yuh wan to buil someting as a tanksgiving or a uplifting or a deliverance yuh use blue an white, an yuh talk to yuh messenja . . . the Ancestors; dem tell yuh everyting.[39]

I had the opportunity to spend considerable time with one Kumina queen, with the initials HB, in Port Morant, St. Thomas, and observed her prepare for what she called a "double Kumina." "This is a serious work we have to do tomorrow night" were her words to the members of her bands, "and we have to start preparing from now."[40] HB delegated tasks to all in her group, and the community went to work. While I will not provide a detailed account of the rich experiences I had accompanying HB and her entourage into the mountains to gather the necessary plants and, later, attending the actual ceremony where an adult woman and a young man were treated for physical and psychological ailments, I will summarize my observations.

My most surprising discovery, which supports the claim that Kumina is actually a way of life steeped in religious traditions, was that collecting medicinal plants is a *religious* activity of supplication, libation, and absolute reverence for the natural elements in creation, the invisible forces that pervade the elements, and the person or persons seeking help. On the day before the Kumina,

I witnessed six members of the bands gather leaves from a wide assortment of plants, trees, and bushes. Some healing plants had to be extracted from the sands of shallow springs; others came from the huge limbs of pimento trees; and still others were gathered from the cracks of stony paths. The thread of consistency that for me characterized the exercise as religious ritual was the formulaic prayer and libation offered by every collector before picking each plant. For example, one prayer was recited as follows:

> Good morning, whosoever lives here, we come asking for health and protection. We come in peace; and we take life so as to give life to [the person for whom the medicinal plant is sought is named in full]. We seek not to destroy but to bless and uplift so that love and goodness will be spread throughout the nation. We ask for your help in this work. Let it be done.[41]

After the prayer, a libation of white rum is always poured onto the root of the plant or the stem of the leaf at the point of breakage. Kumina practitioners gave two reasons for doing this: the first was that rum has medicinal properties that, along with the prayer, help to wake up the sleeping plants; and second, rum is the sacrifice that must be offered to the Ancestors who might be buried directly below the trees and plants from which leaves are removed. This is done as a sign of respect for the sacred space occupied by the Ancestors. They also hold that leaves must be gathered with precision and care; they cannot be picked hastily, nor can they be carelessly discarded. Kumina practitioners retain oral traditions about the significance of the local geography to their oppressed Ancestors, to whom they refer as enslaved. They treat particular streams, rocks, bushes, and mountainous hiding spaces as shrines that provided safe haven for their African Ancestors when they were escaping from plantation slavery. They often recount stories of oppression and the emancipation provided by the natural surroundings as they travel along the same paths in search of therapeutic plants for their clients.

After about three hours of collecting plants, the party returned to the compound where HB used the leaves to prepare both liquid prescriptions and healing beds for her clients. On the following night, the Kumina began at 6:00 P.M. and was not officially completed until 6:00 A.M. the next morning. Through ritual acts of animal sacrifice, singing, drumming, and (Myal) spirit possession, the Kumina bands summoned the assistance of the Ancestors in restoring health and vitality to the sick clients. I had the opportunity to ask the clients how they felt after the Kumina. Both clients acknowledged that they were very satisfied with the results of the Kumina and confessed that they would not hesitate to seek out Kumina as a remedy for their troubles in the future.

The ongoing work of healing is one of Kumina's practical contributions to the larger society. Despite the popular culture's disdain toward Kumina practitioners, they are regularly consulted by nonpractitioners for solutions to their daily problems. In this regard, Kumina's contributions to Jamaican society, even today, appear to be indispensable.

Kumina was introduced to Jamaica only after Emancipation; yet, for years, scholars erroneously associated its Jamaican origins with the period of African enslavement.[42] Barrett identified Kumina with Akan culture, linguistically tracing the term to two Twi words: *akom* (the state of being possessed) and *ana* (relationship or ancestor).[43] Barrett opined that the Maroons, who were mostly of Asante heritage, introduced Kumina to the wider Jamaican society. In *Soul Force*, Barrett writes, "It is our intention here to show that myalism was the legitimate survival of the traditional religion of Africa and that myal and the Jamaican Cumina religion therefore are one and the same phenomenon."[44] Comparing Charles Leslie's eighteenth-century observation of PaPaw/Popo religious ideas with Melville Herskovits's research on Dahomean ancestral veneration, Orlando Patterson traces Kumina to a Dahomean origin.[45] Although his work precedes Schuler's research establishing Kumina's Kongo roots, Patterson's argument is unpersuasively (though understandably) supported by generic comparisons between Kumina and a Dahomean ceremony, comparisons which could probably be made between Kumina and any African religious tradition.

The chief issue giving rise to these and other misinterpretations of Kumina is the significance of Myal to Kumina adherents. Scholars have assumed that since Myal's eighteenth-century origins during the period of African enslavement are incontestable, then Kumina too was manifest during the same period. However, Kumina's regional appearance in eastern Jamaica, especially in the parish of St. Thomas, is consistent with the importation patterns pertaining to Central African indentured laborers in the same region. Second, Kumina oral tradition includes references to geographical locations and cultural traditions from the Central African region. Third, the most convincing evidence of Kumina's Kongo origin is linguistic. Kumina adherents have retained a significant vocabulary of Kikongo words. Bilby and Bunseki collected lexicons from a number of Kumina bands and found Kikongo cognates for nearly all of the words. Many of the Kumina songs are also unintelligible to native African Jamaicans because they are sung in a Kikongo-based language.[46] Today, Kumina practitioners call their ancestral language "African"; they also call the songs "African" or "country" songs—country being perhaps a reference to the African *country* of origin.

Another linguistic indication of Kumina's Kongolese African cultural location is the peculiar term *bands*, which serves to qualify a single Kumina or Revival band as well as multiple bands. *Bands* is used for both the singular and plural noun forms and so practitioners speak of a Kumina bands as well as Kumina bands. As a native Jamaican, I have always been perplexed by its appearance in the Kumina lexicon. In the past, I took it for granted that *bands* was an English term for it was commonly used to discuss groups of catechists, prayer circles, traveling singers, as well as rebels and criminals. I was never satisfied with this explanation, however, because syntactically the term is idiosyncratic in the grammar structures of the Jamaican Creole and English languages.

Specifically, in English, it is grammatically incorrect to use the term *bands* to describe a singular group, while in Jamaican Creole it is grammatically incorrect to use the term *bands* to describe either a single group or multiple groups. The plural form for nouns in Jamaican Creole is not realized by placing "s" at the end of a noun (as in English) but by placing the term *dem* after the noun. To illustrate the point most precisely, the plural form of the word band in Jamaican Creole would be *band-dem* or to take another example, the word *group* would become *group-dem* in the plural form.

Additionally, I noticed that Kumina practitioners would exaggerate the pronunciation of the vowels so that the vowel "a" sounded more like a long version of the term "ah" in English, while they de-emphasized the "d" at the end of the term. In other words, I heard the term *baahnz* rather than *bands*, which would have a slightly less stressed ah sound and a harder d sound (bahnd) in Jamaican Creole. So why all this fuss around bands, baahnz, and bahnd? I suspect that "bands" is actually a Central African cognate. When I was introduced to the Central African terms *mbanza* (house), and *inabanza* (possessor or head of the home), I heard the words spoken by a native Congolese.[47] I immediately recalled the Kumina term *baahnz*, for the pronunciation sounded exactly the same to me. As I inquired further about possible meanings for the term, I became convinced that "bands" (baahnz) is a bantu-derived term with parallel meanings in the Jamaican and Congo contexts. Most ethnic groups from Central Africa associate the term *mbanza* with primarily the household and town. There may be a difference in emphasis depending on the group. For example, with the creation of the Kongo kingdom, the term *mbanza* took on political significance as it became associated with the seat of power or the capital, and so one would hear *Mbanza Kongo*. In more remote areas of the kingdom and among neighboring cultural groups like the Luba in eastern and central Congo, *mbanza* is associated with the central position the wife has in the home. *Mbanza* was not necessarily associated with a centralized government but with the home. Even more intriguing to me is how the presence of and roles assigned to women in the home are what qualifies a home as *mbanza* and the female as the possessor (*ina*) of that home. In other words, a bachelor is not an *inabanza* for a bachelor's lifestyle may be random and inconsistent while a woman's presence and stature in the home give it stability, structure, and purpose.

The political and gender carryovers are obvious. Kumina female leaders hold the title of queen, connoting official governing power as in the Central African case of associating the term *mbanza* with the Kongo capital. *Modda* (mother) is also another title affectionately bestowed upon Kumina queens; however, I would argue that the mother/queen titles hold deeper meanings, connecting their status and role as ruler, head, decision maker, possessor with that of the *inabanza* in Central African households. And no doubt, the Kumina queen is central to the establishment, definition, and security of the *baahnz* in Jamaica. She is also a possessor of Myal secrets, leading many scholars to ponder the peculiar association between Myal and Kumina.

In Kumina rituals, the term *Myal* is used to describe the most powerful manifestations of ancestral possession. Myal is the highest state of mystical encounter between the Ancestors and humans, for when a medium "catches" Myal, the best opportunities for healing, fellowship, and reconciliation become available to the community. Thus the goal of any authentic[48] Kumina is to achieve Myal possession.

As noted by Kennedy: "Afta yuh in di trance dere and dem [the Ancestors] give yuh di prayers, yuh got di Myal, den now, yuh can know what yuh about. Because yuh suppose to get di African prayers, and den di bailo [Kumina songs and chants uttered in Jamaican creole] and den di country [African language/songs]."[49] Myal possession may manifest in any devotee and is not reserved for the Kumina queen; however, as is typical in religions where possession trance is salient, some devotees appear more susceptible to possession trance and mediumship than others.

> During an interview with Maureen Warner-Lewis (1970s) Kennedy described Myal as a somatic experience of aggressive intercourse with a possessing agent:

> > when de *myal* gwine *tek* you now
> > you' whole *body* be*comes*
> > like it *col'*
> > see?
> > and you *feel*
> > you' *feet* dem *draw*
> > an' you *neck* yah—
> > some*time* you' *neck*
> > fe away back yah *so*. . . .
> > *My*al is de *ting* dey call a *spirit*
> > where you' head *'pin* roun' an' you
> > *drop* an' you' *'kin* pupalick 'pon you *neck*
> > you see?
> > Dat a *myal spirit*
> > Dat a *bongo myal spirit*
> > which all de *hol' Af*rican dem—
> > de dead *Af*rican dem dem *come* roun'
> > an' dem *lick* you all a' you' *headside*
> > an' *ride* you 'pon you' *neck* an' you *drop*.
> > You see?
> > Dat dere mean to say *myal hol'* you *now*.[50]

Commenting on Myal as a mode of knowledge acquisition and fellowship, Kennedy asserted more recently:

> Myal is a spirit dat yuh get when yuh de pon di mada clay . . . bare-foot! Dat is a spirit dat yuh got. An dem give yuh dat. Dat a when di old time people dem dead, dem gwine pass it on to yuh . . . an when dem lick yuh wid dat, yuh gwine haf fi tell someting. Di first ting yuh know, yuh haf fi know how fi sing de African prayers. . . . When dem pass it on to yuh now, dem suppose to giv yuh someting dat when anybody aks yuh, yuh can tell dem something. . . . The first ting dat I get in mi African traveling is di prayers, di Our Father

prayers in di African language. Yuh get di prayers and yuh get di bailo [creole songs] to match it. Cause afta yuh say yuh prayers, yuh hafi sing, cause yuh kinda chant di messenja.[51]

The marriage between one of the oldest and one of the youngest African-derived religions in Jamaica might not be so perplexing if we situate this obscurity within our broader discussion of the Kongo antecedents of African-Jamaican religious cultures. In chapter 1, we considered the Kikongo term *mwela* (*miela*, plural), an apposite cognate for the term *myal*. We may do the same with regard to the term *kumina*, which Bunseki interprets as a derivative of the Kikongo noun *lusakumunu* (blessing) or its verb form *sakumuna* (to bless), which is only used in a spiritual context. There is also the term *sakumunwa* (to be blessed). Even more interesting is how Bunseki speaks of the link between *mwela/miela* and *lusakumunu*, for through *miela* (the energy of the elders and Ancestors primarily and of all entities in the cosmos) comes *lusakumunu*:

> A specific ritual will be done, and when the ritual is completed, you will be blessed. And this is a specific secret ritual, in the sense that specific words have to be used. There are songs involved and specific people who can speak during this ritual, specialists who are trained to do the ritual. Through sakumuna, the person receives the living energy of the ancestors. In the process, it is a ritual made between the living community, priest, person/s seeking to overcome a problem, and the ancestors and the cosmic world.[52]

Building upon Bunseki's remarks, I interpret Jamaican Myal and Kumina as symbiotic ritual processes that facilitate the distribution of cosmic energy for life-enhancing purposes. In the pre-emancipation period, African initiates eventually referred to this religious composite as Myal, while post-emancipation BaKongo laborers, who no doubt came into contact with Myalists during their settlement period (1840s–1860s), qualified their collection of rituals with the term Kumina. Bunseki's notation that religious specialists are empowered to sing and speak specific words during the ritual is no different from the eighteenth-, nineteenth- and early-twentieth-century testimonies about the secret practices and undecipherable songs and chants associated with Myal specialists and Bilby's late-twentieth-century discovery of "myal sing" in St. Elizabeth Gumbay Play rituals.[53] Kennedy also alludes to this esoteric ritual proficiency among Kumina queens when she describes the African prayers, the bailo (creole songs), as well as the country (African songs) that one must master in order to "chant di messenja." To be sure, many African religious cultures across ethnic societies would have fostered similar practices and rituals. My supposition though is that both Myal and Kumina, no matter which other religious cultures they have absorbed over time, are cognate religious institutions that bear the indelible signature of Kongo religious culture.

It would be misleading if I did not say for the record that my participant observation experiences tainted my interpretive location such that I could not resist inferring a link between eighteenth-century Myal and twentieth-century Kumina. I had read numerous descriptions of Myal before doing any fieldwork in Jamaica and, due to the racist tone of much of the descriptive literature, did not expect to find something "familiar" in the ceremonies I planned to attend. To my surprise, in the very first Kumina ceremony I attended, I felt transported back to the eighteenth century, almost as if the observers from that period were narrating the events unfolding before me. As I observed, I heard the missionaries and planters describing the Myal rituals of their time. Even those behaviors that were derisively and inaccurately portrayed as unbridled licentiousness or disingenuous performances were evident in the ceremonies I attended. Recalling this dimension of my research, the similarities were abundant then and continued to emerge as I read current ethnographic details from the research of scholars such as Kenneth Bilby and Maureen Warner-Lewis. For example, several Kumina devotees achieved Myal possession at the double Kumina healing ceremony discussed above. One young woman who went into Myal immediately reached for one of the sick clients for whom the Kumina was organized. Upon her touch, he fell unconscious to the ground and remained so for several hours while practitioners attended to his head and body. The client's healing included elaborate processions to ancestral burial grounds, while both the client and the healers were under the influence of the ancestral spirits; the client had to be carried in his unconscious state to each site. He did not regain consciousness until the climax of the ceremony had passed.[54] Such loss and revival of consciousness in the healing process was perhaps that component of Myal healing rituals during the period of enslavement which White observers often belittled as a feigned exhibition of death and resurrection. This was the ritual practice emphasized by William James Gardner when he wrote of Myal in 1842:

> Its first mode of development was as a branch of Obeah practice. The Obeah man introduced a dance called Myal dance, and formed a secret society, the members of which were to be made invulnerable, or if they died, life was to be restored. Belief in this miracle was secured by trick. A mixture was given in rum, of a character which presently induced sleep so profound, as by the uninitiated and alarmed, to be mistaken for death. After this had been administered to someone chosen for the purpose, the Myal dance began, and presently the victim staggered and fell, to all appearance dead. Mystic charms were then used; the body was rubbed with some infusion; and in process of time, the narcotic having lost its power, the subject of the experiment rose up as one restored to life.[55]

In the Kumina ceremony I attended, the sequence of events renders it highly unlikely that the young man was given any substance to induce his state of unconsciousness or restored consciousness. What appears more likely is that this Kongo-based healing procedure was only fortified in what became Kumina culture, as a result of the encounter between BaKong immigrants and African Jamaicans of Myal persuasion during the nineteenth-century.

The history of African-derived religions in Jamaica is, in the end, the reconstitution of Myal religiosity in Jamaica from slavery to the present. Myal has claimed a definitive place of authority in each of the African-Jamaican religious traditions, demonstrating its theological, spiritual, and political resilience. Within this spiritual orientation, I see indispensable resources for an African-centered, womanist theology of the cross which contests the traditional Euro-missionary theologies of the cross that were preached to Africans as the good news afforded them through their captivity.

African-Derived Religions in Jamaica: Toward an African-Centered, Womanist Theology of the Cross

In the first chapter I described six features of African-derived religions which signify reconstitutions of African religious traditions in the Caribbean and the Americas. These features deserve reiteration as the backdrop for my construction of an African-centered, womanist theology of the cross. I have discussed above how a Divine Community (communotheism), divination and herbalism, ancestral veneration, food offerings and animal sacrifice, possession trance, and neutral mystical power are universal orthodox components of African spirituality and ritual practice. And I have attempted to identify these features in the variegated expressions of African-derived religions in Jamaican history.

As a religious symbol, the cross is not the exclusive property of Christianity. It is one of the oldest religiocultural icons in Africa. The cross symbolizes the holistic spiritual and philosophical orientation regarding the visible-invisible sacred cosmos, which is normative for many classical African societies. It represents abounding theories of complementarity, opposition, and integration. The African (BaKongo) cross, with its surplus of meaning, also holds significance for practitioners of African-derived religious traditions in Jamaica. I suspect that by the time enslaved Africans began to hear the gospel preached as well as missionary reflections on the cross, the African cross was influential enough to subvert the perceived metasignificance of the Euro-missionary cross as they considered their situations as humans in bondage by capture or by birth. For example, Obeah oath rituals, which scholars maintain were enacted before every African rebellion, might very well have been influenced by classical Kongo cosmology, which uses the cross as its icon.

Moreover, in conversation with the womanist theological tradition, I see in Kumina and other African-derived religions important resources for constructing an African-centered theology of the cross that promotes the holistic liberation of Black women and Black communities. Taking seriously Delores Williams's argument that the Christian cross has been used to convince Black women that bearing crosses of constructed suffering and surrogacy is a Christian virtue,[56] I want to suggest some ways in which women's experiences in the Kumina religion point to another type of cross-bearing that might enhance African-Jamaican struggles to come to terms with the role of the Divine in human suffering.

Several African studies scholars have identified salient meanings in the Kongo Yowa cross that are pertinent to this discussion. For example, Wyatt MacGaffey's examination of the Kongo cross coheres with the theological meanings of both women's pragmatic focus upon problem solving in the Kumina religion and the pre-Emancipation African practice of taking Obeah oaths in preparation for revolts. According to MacGaffey:

> The simplest ritual space is a Greek cross [+] marked on the ground, as for oath-taking. One line represents the boundary; the other is ambivalently both the path leading across the boundary, as to the cemetery; *and* the vertical path of power linking "the above" with "the below." This relationship, in turn is polyvalent, since it refers to God and [humanity], God and the dead, and the living and the dead. The person taking the oath stands upon the cross, situating himself between life and death, and invokes the judgement of God and the dead upon himself.[57]

The cross is a fundamental symbol of religious life in classical Kongo civilization. Although we cannot be certain that this particular cosmological orientation informed the specific Obeah oaths that were taken during the period of Jamaican enslavement, MacGaffey's explication of the Kongo cross offers a view into the type of religious orientation that endowed ritual oath taking with sacrosanct meaning in the classical African societies from which enslaved Africans in Jamaica may have inherited such rituals. On the other hand, given that Kumina is a Kongo tradition, it could be argued that there is a specific connection between the Kongo religious orientation, symbolized by the cross as described by MacGaffey, and current Kumina rituals in Jamaica.[58] As such, Kongo cosmology is essential in determining the theological meaning of the African-derived religious practices of Kumina women.

The notion of incarnation, for example, may be applied to the shared religious orientation of BaKongo groups and their Kumina descendants. However, incarnation is not a christocentric doctrine in Kongo religious culture. Incarnation, in this context, points to the concrete embodiment of a Divinity or Ancestor for the benefit of the human community. This happens repeatedly in countless African religions and, as I have already discussed, in Jamaican Myal, Revival Zion, and Kumina. Robert Farris Thompson's reflections on Kongo theological anthropology of ancestorhood and reincarnation provide a backdrop for contextualizing what I call the Kongo "cross of incarnation," as evident in the Kongo spirituality of Jamaican Kumina devotees:

> This Kongo "sign of the cross" has nothing to do with the crucifixion of the Son of God, yet its meaning overlaps the Christian vision. Traditional Bakongo believed in a Supreme Deity, Nzambi Mpungu, and they had their own notions of the indestructibility of the soul: "Bakongo believe and hold it true that [a person's] life has no end, that it constitutes a cycle. The sun, in its rising and setting, is a sign of this cycle, and death is merely a transition in the process of

change." The Kongo *yowa* cross does not signify the crucifixion of Jesus for the salvation of [humanity,] it signifies the equally compelling vision of the circular motion of human souls about the circumference of its intersecting lines. The Kongo cross refers to the everlasting continuity of *all* righteous men and women.[59]

Here Thompson not only describes the place of the Ancestors and the human life cycle in Kongo cosmology, but he also correctly perceives that the Kongo sign of the cross does not signify the death of Jesus Christ. To be sure, the Yowa cross does not signify the death of any member of the Divine Community. With further analysis, it is evident that the Yowa cross counteracts death by mediating extended life, connection, and metaphysical continuity across the visible-invisible world domains. Thus the Yowa cross might be compared with what happens with the birth of Jesus Christ as embodied Deity rather than with the death of Christ.[60]

Yet, while the incarnation may be valid for Christians in terms of its christological focus, it is important to remember that, for BaKongo groups and other devotees of African-derived religions in Jamaica, the incarnation is the recurring event of embodied Deity/Ancestor made manifest in possession trance. From my study of Black religious formation, in several African diasporic contexts, I hold that the incarnational emphasis in African-derived religions provided a theological strainer, if you will, an aesthetic and discriminating theological device through which a majority of enslaved Africans filtered Christian symbols and religious ideas. Consequently, what emerged in both African-derived religions and the Black North American Christian traditions was an emphasis on the spirit (pneumatology).[61]

On Jamaican soil, the pneumatocentric dynamic is configured as spirit messengers within the Revival Zion tradition. In Kumina, Myal ancestral possession dramatizes the sign of the cross as the crossroads where the invisible meets the visible. This encoding of the cross through dance movements and ritual placement of objects at strategic points around a centerpole facilitates a process of collaboration among the inhabitants of the visible and invisible world domains. Both world domains then are represented in the image of the cross. The vertical pole, marking the invisible domain, is physically represented by the centerpole in Kumina ceremonies and signifies the sky and the locus of disembodied life.[62] The horizontal pole marks the visible domain, encapsulating the earth and embodied life. The point of penetration, the crossroads, symbolizes the event of incarnation.

Incarnations manifest as the disembodied living (Ancestors) unite with the embodied living (humans). Such an integrative and complementary show of divine power is the basis for a valuation of the body as an indispensable spiritual medium. This type of embodied spirituality can be observed in Black churches as spirit possession, despite the tendency in some churches to embrace popular dualistic Christian notions of the soul as good/sacred and the body as bad/profane.[63] Furthermore, this spirituality is the basis for a holistic anthropology which renders all people—females, males, elders, minors, the able, and the disabled—potential hosts of divine power, that is, participants in the event of incarnation. The African-derived religions of Jamaica testify through the body that health and well-being are restored when the embodied living and the disembodied living demonstrate their relational interaction, especially in its most concentrated expression, Myal. I suspect that this is the rationale for why Revival Zionists would testify to holding a Kumina when they are confronted with the gravest problems. They do not resort directly to Christ, for the power to restore temporal well-being is not derived from soteriological beliefs about Jesus' death but from African beliefs about recurring incarnation as the locus of life-sustaining power.

The exception, however, is the African-centered Rastafari tradition where incarnation is especially important because of its christological focus. As already discussed in chapter 3, Rastas view Haile Selassie as the incarnation of God—the Black messiah/Jesus Christ—and proclaim the divinity of all African people. In Rastafari theological anthropology, Black people are manifestations of the true God—the African God of Abraham, David, and Jesus. But Rastafari does not embrace Lutheran notions of cross-bearing. Indeed the Rastafari understanding of evil and *sufferation* as a concrete disruption of the temporal life to be enjoyed is much more consistent with Myal notions that evil offenses are acts against society and must be eradicated in this world.[64] Bob Marley's denouncement of the "preacher man's" theology illustrates how Rastafari Christology is most informed by Hebrew scriptural depictions of a political messiah who will not take up the cross per se but will lead the divine war against oppression and exile. Collectively, his songs dispute colonial missionary theology and profess the Rastafari belief in radical human agency and divine inspiration in the struggle for sociopolitical liberation.[65]

Rastas contend that divine incarnation in Africans inspires them toward sociopolitical resistance against oppression. Thus, the Rastafari notion of incarnation is congruent with that of the Kumina community in that it is explicitly related to practical, temporal experiences within the human community and eschews theologies of temporal suffering and subsequent eschatological reward.[66] Rastafari incarnational theology, however, reflects the intense Pan-Africanist political ideology that undergirds the religion's piety, doctrines, and praxes. Kumina's incarnational theology is subversive and therefore politically astute despite the tradition's nurturance of a subterranean Pan-Africanist ideology that is often overlooked or unrecognized by scholars because it is only subtly or conditionally expressed to outsiders.

Kumina's Kongo-based incarnational spirituality also underscores the point that, in spite of the resurrection, the cross becomes central in Christian theology because of the suffering and death of God. In Kumina and other African-derived religions, the cross is significant because it represents divine or ancestral incarnation for the concrete purpose of restoring health and wholeness within the community. This theology of the cross can never be related to the endurance of suffering as it is in Christian theology because it is based upon a religious view of life that is committed to the immediate alleviation of suffering.

By way of comparison, Kelly Brown Douglas speculatively suggests that enslaved Africans in North America made connections between what I call the classical African cross (of incarnation) and the Christian cross (of the crucified-and-resurrected Jesus). She posits this connection by alluding to the parallels between the stress on intimacy between the living and the dead in African religion and the intimacy between enslaved Africans and the crucified-and-resurrected Jesus in the context of exile from Africa and bondage in America.[67] I find this analysis intriguing and dialectically provocative as both a problematic and a resolve in the debate on Africanisms in Black religion (a problematic) and the lack of attention to Africanisms in Black theology (a resolve).[68] I differ with Douglas, however, in that I see no evidence that the crucified-and-resurrected Jesus (i.e., the Christian cross), interpreted through the matrix of the African cross (intimacy between the living and the dead), is most salient in forging the bond between enslaved Africans and Christ. The evidence suggests to me that the two crosses are actually oppositional if not antithetical while the African cross (of incarnation) and the Christian notion of incarnation are more compatible and infer reflection on pneumatology as a theological priority over reflection on Christology in African-derived religions that incorporate christianisms and in the sanctified Black churches that have linkages to the ringshout and hush harbor practices of enslaved Africans.[69] Delores Williams's discussion of the continuities between the Christian notion of incarnation and the African incarnational cross would seem to indicate the need for such a shift in black/womanist theological discourse: "The angel Gabriel tells [Mary], 'The Holy Spirit will come upon you, and the power of the Most High will overshadow you; therefore the child to be born will be called holy, the Son of God' (Luke 1:36). Translated in terms of African-American heritage from traditional African religions, one can say, 'The Spirit mounted Mary.' The word was first made flesh in Mary's body."[70]

In short, the resurrection of the deceased Jesus is less (if at all) compatible with the African cross than is the incarnation of God in Jesus via Mary's body.[71] The extant data on African American Christian formation support the position that some enslaved Africans forged intimate bonds with Jesus and Jesus' cross not because of their reverence for and intercourse with their Ancestors but because of the obvious parallels between their undeserved and unjust suffering and that of Jesus. The testimonies of enslaved converts to Christianity in Jamaica that were examined in chapter 3 are but a few examples.[72]

The suffering Christ in African American Christianity, prominent though it is, did not eclipse the African cross of divine incarnation. This normative feature of African religion survived in black North American Christianity as Black Christians found ways to reconcile it with the dominating Christian cross of divine death and resurrection. For example, in many traditional black churches a prevalent sermonic motif is the death and resurrection of Jesus the Christ (the Christian cross), yet another established religious practice in these same churches is spirit possession (the African cross of divine incarnation). The implications of the survival of the African cross within Black religious experience are not inconsequential for the sanctified and charismatic Black

Christian traditions of North America, and they deserve further attention in the works of Black and womanist theologians.

Comparative studies of incarnational spirituality in Black Christian and African-derived traditions might prove most useful in combating sexism, due to the prominence of women as mediums for Divine manifestations and as significant leaders in African-derived religions. Again Williams is instructive on this point as she challenges Black male theologians to incorporate more female-inclusive sources in their works. Williams specifically proposes that shifting from a christological-soteriological to an incarnational focus on the cross is more productive in addressing sexism within the Christian tradition:

> The critique of atonement views by womanist theology invites black
> [male] liberation theologians to begin serious conversations with
> black females about the black Christians' understanding of atone-
> ment in light of African-American women's experience of oppres-
> sion. Perhaps such a conversation can begin with the *incarnation*
> *and the cross.* By removing their sexist lens, black theologians can
> see that though incarnation is traditionally associated with the self-
> disclosure of God in Jesus Christ, incarnation also involves *God's self-*
> *disclosure in a woman*: Mary.[73]

Thus Williams suggests that if we are willing to view divine disclosure through Mary's body, we are compelled to raise questions about the essential meaning of the cross and resurrection to Christian faith and teaching. To begin with the incarnation in Mary's body indicates that the resurrection is no longer proof of divine disclosure and positions Mary, a woman, at the center of revelation. I would argue, though, that the Kumina approach to incarnation and the cross emphasizes the connection between women and divine revelation and offers even more promising antisexist symbols and concrete practices for a liberating and inclusive understanding of revelation, not only because women's bodies are hosts of the incarnation but also because any number of divine personalities manifested in human form are female. Furthermore, at the most elemental level, the incarnational focus in the Kumina tradition is a protest against any glorification of female suffering.

For example, because women are the keepers of the Kumina culture and of its esoteric meaning and religious rituals, Kumina queens are rendered unwavering respect within their communities for their multiple roles as psy-chologist, doctor, priest, and judge. Kumina queens take on tremendous re-sponsibility for managing and facilitating harmony and well-being in their communities as they serve people from diverse backgrounds and regions of the country. One must demonstrate a peculiar sensibility pertaining to both the visible and invisible world domains to ascend to the rank of Kumina queen.

The female leadership in Kumina is well established. Women are not sym-bolic figureheads; they are active participants along with other women and men in the worshiping community. Women are visible in Kumina because the com-munity's faith testimony is dramatized through their bodies. Theirs is a carnal rather than ideational testimony, which is experienced in the community's spiritual embrace of sensuality in prepossession dance, in the rhythms of drums, in the hyperbolized circular motion of bodies,[74] in the hands that sacrifice and anoint, and in the hands that rub medicines on the bodies of the sick and troubled. These are all aspects of embodied testimony from which one can derive important resources for womanist theological reflection. Indeed, Kumina's ritual focus on possession trance invites the womanist theologian to investigate the meaning of revelation, incarnation, and the cross in African-derived religions and underscores existing womanist/feminist critiques of those doctrines in the Western Christian tradition. Thus Kumina women's embodied spirituality emerges as a source for a theological interpretation of the cross as a fixation upon temporal well-being in Kumina and other African-derived religions.

In saying this, I actually see alternative approaches to human suffering, liberation, and revelation in the religious practices of Kumina tradition, which can address formidable concerns of both feminist and womanist theologies. Although Mary Daly writes from a White North American perspective, her scrutiny of traditional Christology is relevant to issues of oppression, survival, and liberation in womanist theology and corresponds with the religious practices of women in African-derived religions such as Kumina, Orisha/Yoruba, Vodun, and Candomblé. Daly contests the Christian teaching that the redemptive revelation of God occurred as a specific and unique, unrepeatable historical event. She contends that the idea that Jesus, a first-century Jewish man, was the Incarnation of God and therefore is the redemptive Christ, coupled with sexist Christological doctrines, is undeniably detrimental to women's liberation. Daly also opposes the tendency in Christian theology to hail Jesus, the sacrificial scapegoat, as a role model that women should emulate.[75]

Along similar lines, Delores Williams critiques traditional atonement theories as oppressive for Black women, who have been taught to ritually identify their surrogate experiences of sacrifice and suffering with Jesus' redemptive death on the cross. Although Williams turns away from the cross and toward Jesus' ministry for affirming examples of redemptive living, her critique of the cross and reconstruction of redemption does not address the problem of special revelation. Womanist theologians across the board have neglected to engage this doctrine, even when their evaluations of normative Christian traditions would logically necessitate a rejection of special revelation. For example, in one of her early essays on womanist Christology, Jacquelyn Grant is scathingly critical of the colonial missionary project. Nevertheless, she does not make the obvious link between the missionary enterprise and the doctrine of special revelation when she writes, "In the area of foreign missions . . . conversion to Christianity implicitly meant deculturalization and acceptance of the western value system on the part of Asians, Africans, and Latin Americans. Upon conversion, one had to withdraw from indigenous ways of imaging the divine reality."[76]

Through her prose and fiction, Alice Walker, who coined the term *womanist* in 1983, undoubtedly suggests that any thorough womanist treatment of Black female oppression must entail a critical assessment of Christianity as a tool of colonialism that has sponsored the centuries-long demonization of African and other non-Christian religious cultures. Walker, who is not a professional theologian, has been more forthright than any womanist theologian in addressing this theological problem on multiple levels in her works.[77] It may be that Christian systematic theological reflection is too much an exercise of apologetics to encourage this type of deconstruction. A comparative theological approach on the other hand would allow womanist theologians to examine non-Christian religious traditions as resources for theological reflection. For example, with regard to special revelation, Kumina women's spirituality of recurring incarnation offers a corrective to this theological conundrum as it implies an understanding of divine revelation that is expansive and inclusive. Devotees experience this in both tangible and symbolic ways.

In Kumina culture, God is African, the Ancestors are African, and they belong to the spirituality of Africa and the African diaspora. In the words of Imogene Kennedy: "Kumina, is just direc African kulcha, yuh know—di African kulcha. But yuh see, in dem tradition, dey say Kumina. Yuh understand? but di direc ting is African kulcha. Kumina now, dem jus put di Kumina but is African, is dy-rec African kulcha, cause wi a African children."[78]

Kumina devotees do not venerate the same deities and ancestors as those venerated in the White Christian tradition, and they do not have to engage in exercises of hermeneutical gymnastics to convince themselves that Christ is *really* Black and not White or that women can be hosts of divine power. In other words, Kumina provides an alternative approach to divine power for women like Celie in *The Color Purple*, who cannot reimagine God without whiteness or maleness because, as Celie says, "[H]e been there so long, he don't want to budge."[79]

The presence of African-derived religions in the Americas and the Caribbean demonstrates that some religious communities resisted Euro-Christian domination and the cooptation of their images of the Divine under the ubiquitous image of Jesus Christ as the only valid divine revelation. Kumina women's religious experience, then, contests Christian exclusivism, especially in terms of the doctrine of special revelation.[80] This is crucial for women of African descent because generations of European Christian authorities found justification in the doctrine of special revelation to support their exclusion of women from positions of leadership and authority in Christian churches and to anchor their condemnation of non-Christian religions, which do not recognize Jesus as the redemptive revelation of God.

The Christian perspective that the doctrine of special revelation necessitates the condemnation of African-derived religions and religious practices has also become normative for many African American and Caribbean Christians, who have uncritically accepted traditional European and Euro-American standards for evaluating Black religious experience. This condemnation intensifies the poverty and exploitation of female practitioners of African-derived religions because they are Black and female and because they partake in repressed religions that lack the cultural capital required for uncensored expression, progressive development, and public approval. This type of anti-Africanness or devaluation of African-derived religions is another facet of Black women's anthropological impoverishment.

Practitioners of African-derived religions, such as Kumina, Yoruba/Orisha, and Vodun, do not conceive of humans as being in need of any special redemption or salvation from some intrinsic depraved condition. They understand the human experience as susceptible to chaos, misfortune, disease, and ill will, and their religions are oriented toward identifying and overcoming the specific problems that compromise human fulfillment, well-being, and abundant life.

Cross-bearing is a Kumina ritual practice that validates women's bodies as capable of representing the Divine and exposes divine incarnation as a recurring event in human experience. And yet the "cross-bearing" women of the Kumina community serve as only one of many examples where women are reinforcing classical African ideas that affirm the value of meaningful life on earth. Taken as a whole, their spirituality directly challenges prevailing Christian beliefs that are oppressive to women of African descent while institutionalizing praxes of female empowerment and authority within the structures of African-derived religions.

In African-derived religions, the theology of the cross is a theology of the eternal manifestation of incarnation and can be understood as an emancipatory theology as it relates to the restoration of well-being (social, personal, spiritual, physical, material, political, and so on). This theology then invalidates the endurance of suffering as a spiritual quality favored by the Divine Community and stresses instead the Divine Community's role in addressing suffering. The political imperatives in Kumina and Revival Zion are not as explicitly stated as they are in Rastafari. However, it is instructive to recall the Myal/Native Baptist heritage of Revival Zion, which nurtured a political practice of militancy during the period of enslavement, contributing significantly to emancipation in the British West Indies.

In addition, the Paul Bogle Rebellion of 1865 is a pivotal event that may demonstrate, in the long run, a militant political strain in Kumina and Revival Zion. It might also prove to be a historical moment of intense collaboration among Native Baptists, Zionists, and Kumina communities. The socioeconomic context of the rebellion—increased labor exploitation in the face of growing economic decline—was mirrored in other parishes in the island. Yet the rebellion occurred after two decades of the recaptive/liberated African indentured-labor program in Jamaica. The year 1865 basically marked the final stage of more than twenty years of BaKongo (Central African) resettlement in Jamaica. The rebellion occurred four years after the end of the Great Revival, which gave birth to Revival Zion, a novel form of traditional African Myalism, and Native Baptist Christian Myalism. The rebellion also occurred in the parish of St. Thomas where most BaKongo (Kumina practitioners) worked as indentured laborers.[81] Monica Schuler maintains, "The voice of revival, because it partook of the Myal tradition, could also be revolutionary," as militant literature pertaining to the social oppression of the "Sons and Daughters of Africa" and their "day of deliverance" emerged from Revival circles in western Jamaica.[82]

Schuler concludes, however, that the Native Baptist and Revival Zion traditions provided religious inspiration for the Bogle rebellion without the involvement of BaKongo Kumina practitioners. Schuler describes the social context in St. Thomas as one where the Black creole population and BaKongo African indentured laborers had different responses to the changing economy. BaKongo indentured laborers, whose livelihoods depended upon maintaining positions on the estates where they worked, were less likely to take part in a revolt that would jeopardize job security. Although Schuler admits that at least one Ba-Kongo African was involved with the Bogle Rebellion, she notes that there are still a number of oral narratives that tell of African immigrants who, although they were not involved, were implicated as insurgents and brutally punished in the aftermath of the revolt.[83]

Today, Kumina practitioners have a strong attachment to the Bogle Rebellion and claim Paul Bogle as an Ancestor with whom they interact.[84] Kumina bands also commemorate the event with yearly celebrations in Morant Bay. It is possible that the Bogle Rebellion might have been (or might have provided) the context for a cross-fertilization and collaboration among Native Baptists, Revival Zionists, and Kumina practitioners. Is it plausible that Myal was introduced to Kumina during religious meetings that gave inspiration to the up-risers?

It will take more research before any conclusive statements can be made about the relationship between the Bogle Rebellion and the Revival Zion and Kumina religious traditions. What can be acknowledged now, however, is the pledge of solidarity that occurs among practitioners of the Revival Zion, Kumina, and Rasta religions. This was constantly affirmed during my field research in Jamaica. As one Zionist, Sister BT, said in response to my question about how she, as a Zionist, feels about Rastafari, "[D]en dem a no Zion too! Ahll a we a wan!"[85] Similarly, on another occasion, just before I was leaving the island to return to the United States, a Kumina informant told me about an important meeting that was to occur between some "Rasta bredren" and her Kumina bands. The meeting was called to discuss socioeconomic issues in the aftermath of the closing of one of Jamaica's national banks. Many Jamaicans, especially the poor, lost money in the process and had not been compensated. The agenda for the meeting was to organize protest groups and to plan strategies for collecting the money that was "robbed from the people." She went on to relate the plight of African Jamaicans to that of Africans on the continent and proclaimed that if Nelson Mandela called for an army of protesters for the struggle in South Africa, she could fill two airplanes with people ready to fight.[86]

The potential for sociopolitical praxis is so strong in the Kumina tradition because of its approach to human fulfillment and well-being and its explicit memory of African oppression in Jamaica. Since all of life is integrated and complementary, well-being is threatened if any aspect of life is jeopardized. In Kumina culture, there is no moral tension between the spiritual and the political. It might well be the case that some of the ripest ears for a Caribbean theology of liberation are to be found not only among the valiant male populations of Rastafari groups but also among female devotees across the Kumina communities.

The female voice is prevalent in Kumina leadership and appears to have been more prevalent in Zion traditions that met in balmyards as opposed to church structures.[87] For reasons not altogether known, women have by and large secured the posts of authority in Kumina. Unlike the Rastafari, who are suspicious of women's power, Kumina institutionalizes (1) the nurturing of Black female agency, (2) the empowerment of Black women as official leaders and teachers of their religious traditions, and (3) divine revelation via incarnation in female bodies as a recurring event. This is true in other African-derived religions of the Caribbean and the Americas as well.[88]

African religious practitioners in Jamaica's past and present appear to experience the incarnated Ancestors/spirit messengers/African political messiah (Haile Selassie) as a liminal gateway where humans meet divine emancipatory power. For Kumina devotees, the significance of the Ancestors is especially felt in the sign of the cross and is respected by their Revival Zion compatriots. Ancestral visitation through Myal possession forges a spiritual connection between present-day practitioners of Kumina and the enslaved Africans whose indigenous Pan-African religion was Myal. The diverse expressions of African-derived religions in Jamaica show that the Ancestors,[89] incarnation, and the cross of alleviated suffering are the center of African-Jamaican spirituality, *not* Jesus and Christology.

I think it is important at this juncture to emphasize that this spiritual orientation (the African sign of the cross) carries tremendous weight in shaping the cultural, psychological, and political dispositions of African religious practitioners across multiple traditions and social contexts. I imagine the cross-roads as an apposite theological concept, layered with meanings from which African and African-Caribbean/American scholars may extrapolate resources for constructive theologies of liberation. The Yoruba and Vodun traditions have a wealth of material on this subject, including textual, iconic, and performative resources. Both traditions honor Esu-Elegba (also known as Eshu, Elegba, Legba, or Ellegua), the manifestation of the Divine as the guardian of the cross-roads. Esu-Elegba is said to "open and close doors." He is the Deity who opens the doors of communication between humans and all other manifestations of divinity. Esu is the messenger of the deities. He is also the cunning trickster who, along with the Akan Ananse, became reconstituted in the personalities of Brer Rabbit[90] and Anancy the Spider.[91] This archetypal trickster Deity, the source of communication between the invisible and the visible, is the cross-bearer. Thus, when practitioners of Yoruba-based religions open ceremonies, they salute and pour libation first for Esu-Elegbara to petition for Orisha blessings in the form of divine possession—the crossroads (+).

Having examined the prominent sites and scenes of African people's religious journey in Jamaica, I pause at what I consider to be the crossroads between the social scientific documentation of African religious traditions in Jamaica and the history of theological commentary on African-Jamaican reli-

gious experience to interrogate the problems and concerns that will have impact upon my own theological prescriptions in the final chapter. One issue is
the persistence of anthropological poverty in the African-Jamaican experience
and its impact upon the multiple expressions of African-derived religions. Consequently, in the following sections, I aim to critically evaluate Jamaica's African religious inheritance with a focus upon external factors that have obscured
our present understanding of this inheritance, invalidated its life-giving focus,
discounted its integrity as a legitimate cultural contribution to Caribbean civilization, and exacerbated the multidimensional impoverishment of African
practitioners. It is my view that the Afrophobic and anti-African perspectives,
so deeply embedded within the Jamaican intellectual and popular imaginations, have cast a wide shadow over the range of conversations among theological scholars. Only by traversing this ideological crossroads can we attempt
to engage in theological discourse that is critical, constructive, and prophetic
in Jamaica and in the wider Caribbean.

African-Jamaican Religious Traditions: Ambiguous Sources, Sources of Ambiguity

African-Jamaican religions have managed to come through fires of persecution
and condemnation. They are survivors of colonial Christian anti-Africanness
and Afrophobia.[92] However, African-derived religions have been bruised and
burned by manifestations of anti-Africanness, first in European missionary
Christianity and later in the anti-Africanness of African-Jamaican Christianity.[93]

Within Jamaica, the context of enslavement and Christian evangelism
compelled African religions to operate underground, clandestinely beyond the
inspection of the White gaze. Yet with each opportunity for social toleration,
Myalists emerged with their agenda, appropriating and adapting Christian
sources to suit their moral imperatives and religious predilections. Myalists
were selective appropriators and independent interpreters of Christian sources.
For Native Baptists, John the Baptist was more appealing to the Myal personality than was Jesus. In John, Africans saw an archetypal forest or water priest,
empowered by the Creator Deity[94] to consecrate Jesus' mission. As Chevannes
notes:

> The Africans took rapidly and in large numbers to the new religion,
> but in doing so absorbed it into the Myal framework. African water
> rituals resurfaced in Christian baptism and missionaries had to
> wage theological battle to convince the people that John the Baptist
> was not greater than Jesus and should not be worshipped.[95]

William Wedenoja adds: "Myalist syncretisms, such as use of the Bible for
protection from spirits and a pantheon of Christian figures—John the Baptist,
the disciples, prophets, and angels—who replaced African gods in name but
not in form or function, were incorporated into Revival."[96]

For Myalists, the Christian Bible was a symbolic text with infinite hermeneutical potential. African-Jamaican appropriations of biblical symbols offer concrete examples to validate Paul Ricoeur's assertion that texts have a surplus of meaning.[97] In honoring John the Baptist as the (biblically legitimate) priest of the water deities, they were honoring and preserving classical African theological beliefs and practices. The Native Baptist (Myal) affinity for John the Baptist was probably inspired by the African idea that the natural elements (water, air, earth, fire) are invested with spiritual/mystical power.

The personality of John the Baptist has not lost significance for contemporary Revivalists and Kumina devotees. During my research among the two groups, several informants made reference to John the Baptist as an anointed prophet and spirit messenger. The centrality of John the Baptist in these traditions is evidence that the Native Baptist (Myal) religion is the progenitor of the Revival Zion religion.

Monica Schuler's persuasive analysis of the transformative moments in Myal evolution and the rich interaction between Myal traditions and Kumina is also pertinent. Her interpretation of African-Jamaican religious formation punctuates my view that the encounter between African-derived religions (Obeah and Myal) and Christianity was in large part an exercise in an African-oriented hermeneutics giving birth to more African-centered religions (Rasta and Revival Zion). Schuler writes:

> Myalists extracted and emphasized two central elements of the Baptist faith—the inspiration of the Holy Spirit, and baptism, in the manner of John the Baptist, by immersion—because they seemed to correspond with beliefs or symbols already familiar to them. Some members actually referred to their church as John the Baptist's Church. The leaders developed a technique for attaining possession by the Holy Spirit and "dreams" experienced in this state were crucial to a candidate's acceptance for baptism. Without them they could not be born again, "either by water or the Spirit." The Myalist emphasis on ritual immersion by water may be understood better by a comparison with beliefs of twentieth-century Kumina adherents (descendants of nineteenth-century Central African immigrants) concerning baptism. Kumina members profess a special attachment to Baptists and Revivalists who practice baptism by immersion in the river because the river is the house of African spirits who they believe protect Baptists and Revivalists as they do Kumina devotees. In addition, Kumina members deliberately seek Christian baptism for their children because the ritual is believed to provide the protection of a powerful spirit—the one the Christians call the Holy Spirit. The Afro-Jamaican religious tradition, then, has consistently reinterpreted Christianity in African, not European, cultural terms.[98]

The ambiguity surrounding the multiple expressions of African-derived religions in Jamaica is directly related to their subjugated and marginal status in Jamaican history. We know most about Rastafari because it has a received tradition of literature and songs (organic theology and hymns). In addition,

since the 1990s, Rastas have garnered wider sympathy and even social acceptance from a number of Christian compatriots.

Kumina and Revival Zion, however, are oral-based traditions. They are yet to
be accepted by the wider Christian community as legitimate sacred traditions.
Thus most Jamaicans have an investment in remaining culturally distant from
Kumina and Revival Zion traditions. Indeed too many are more culturally distant
from their native religions, Kumina and Revival Zion, than they are from the
imported religions and theologies of White North American Christian funda-
mentalists—Jimmy Swaggart, Oral Roberts, Jim Bakker, and the like.[99]

In the end, even with all of the unsolved puzzles pertaining to the intersecting roads among the African-derived religions in Jamaica, after worshiping
with and interviewing the Revival Zionists, Kumina practitioners, and Rastas,
I can assert without hesitation that these religious communities share a collective consciousness of the African-Jamaican struggle against anthropological
poverty (the censoring and vilification of things and peoples African) in the
forms of Afrophobia and anti-Africanness.[100] They also demonstrate religious
sympathy and solidarity for the spiritual values and cultural and political consciousness represented in varied configurations within each tradition. Their
ethical principle of religious solidarity is derived from shared theological assumptions about divine power, humanity, and human destiny. More than anything, the Rastas, Revival Zionists, and Kumina practitioners together recover
and re-member subjugated knowledges derived from the collective African-
Jamaican struggle to ensure freedom and well-being through religious autonomy and spiritual agency. Together these traditions present a strong case for
continued reflection upon the meaning of Africa in the African diaspora. Suppose, for instance, we said that in the past we had no convincing reason to
introduce the category "African religion" in the continental context, due to
religious distinctions that can clearly be drawn along ethnic, clan, or regional
lines. However, a study of African-Jamaican religions shows that, in the African
diaspora, Black religious formation within the acculturating rubric of Pan-
Africanization introduces a new logic for outlining composite features of what
we may call denominations of African religion or African-derived religion in
the Jamaican context. Over the centuries, the apparently slippery and elastic
margins of the various traditions, as they have encountered and traded resources within their informal institutional structures, have actually served to
protect them from the policing structures of the colonial state, proving the
resiliency of the Obeah-Myal religious framework as a tool of subversion even
into the twenty-first century.

Externally Imposed Anthropological Poverty:
The Stigmatization, Marginalization, and Exoticization of
Practitioners of African-Derived Religious Traditions

> The thing with any tradition is how it is used. If you use it for
> good you will get good; if you use it for evil you will get evil.[101]

> Before proceeding any further, I must give a description of the
> *obeahman*. He is the agent *incarnate* of Satan. The *Simon Magnus*
> of these good gospel days; the embodiment of all that is wicked,
> immoral and deceptious. You may easily at times distinguish him
> by his sinister look, and *slouching* gait. An obeahman seldom looks
> anyone in the face. Generally he is a dirty looking fellow with a
> sore foot. . . . The obeahman is to be feared in the system of
> poisoning which he carries on. He is well versed in all the
> vegetable poisons of the island.[102]

The Obeah practitioner, Revival Zionist, Kumina practitioner, and Rasta
remember, represent, and are often represented among anthropologically impoverished African Jamaicans who have been divested of land, heritage, language, religious/cultural significance, and the material profit of their labor.
Most Jamaicans are of African descent and poor (the legacy of African enslavement and colonialism). In the past, Third World theologians have identified
fundamental oppressions that compromise human beauty, dignity, and agency
as created by God. As a group, they have decried the manifestations of racism,
sexism, colonialism, and classism in the Christian church and in Christian
theology. They denounce these social sins as un-Christian abominations before
God.

In the Caribbean there is racism, sexism, heterosexism, neocolonialism,
classism, and anti-Africanness. Within the African diasporic context, anti-
Africanness is not reducible to racism but inclusive of it. Anti-Africanness and
Afrophobia concern not only the reality of discrimination against those who
have been racialized as Black but the hatred and negation of the origin and
heritage of the "Black race." Anti-Africanness is a moral problem for any theology of the African diaspora because it contributes to the multifaceted manifestations of poverty in African diasporic communities.

Historically, practitioners of African-derived religions have been doubly
jeopardized when it comes to economic impoverishment and social immobility.
It is not accidental that Haiti, the first Black republic in the Western Hemisphere (1801), is today the poorest, stricken with one affliction after another—
oppressive regimes, militarism, AIDS, imperialism, and so on. It must also be
remembered that Africans in Haiti wrested political control of the island from
the French under the leadership of Vodun priests and by the inspiration of
Vodun culture. As Western Europe evolved into a Christian civilization, Haiti,
by the time of the revolution, had become a Vodun civilization equipped to
manage the takeover of the island. In no other place has African religion
adopted the character and disposition of a people whose ancestral surname is
Exile. Haiti could achieve this as a result of its revolution. Not only was it a
successful revolution, it happened early in the exilic period when a critical mass
of Africans in the colony demonstrated a collective memory of their continental
heritages. And so African culture saturated the horizon of what Haitian culture
would become over two centuries and, within the boundaries of sovereignty
allotted for rebels, Vodun came to resemble its broken and raging populace,

its fierce and unrelenting exiles wrestling with modernity with little more than the tools of slaves.

Put another way, Haiti is poorest because its population is most conspicuously African not solely in terms of culture but also religion. The European and American powers punished Haiti for its show of African determinism. Haiti was immediately isolated from the global economy,[103] and its Vodun civilization has been targeted for derision and condemnation ever since.[104] The Haitian story is the quintessential story of anthropological poverty in the African diaspora. Mveng's notion of anthropological poverty, as depriving Africans of both what they possess and who they are, is well punctuated by Réné Depestre's reflections on the crisis in Caribbean identity. Depestre asks:

> In what way will [Black people] of the Caribbean come to terms with [themselves,] convert [themselves] to what [they are,] find [their] true [selves] in society and in history? . . . men and women have not yet been able to recover their social character[,] their profound personality, their humanity and beauty which colonization has alienated. Literature and the arts, just as science and education do not meet the immediate and future needs of our people. Our cultures continue to grow to the rhythm of western neocolonialism and lack the possibility of advancing in accordance with their own internal dynamism. With the sole exception of Cuba, the development of our nations is not conceived in terms of a decolonization of the alienating structures of the past. Our islands are victims of malnutrition, underemployment, illiteracy, intellectual underemployment and cultural hibernation.[105]

Most practitioners of African-oriented religions are poor. Their wealth is religiocultural, internally derived, and precapitalistic. Kumina and Revival Zion practitioners are especially impotent when it comes to navigating globalization and its market-driven culture that sustains socioeconomic stratification in Jamaican society. Within Rastafari, however, some individuals have been able to do just this through their involvement with the music industry. All the same, the two parishes most noted for their retention of African cultural traditions, St. Mary and St. Thomas, are also the poorest in the island.

The personal experience of interviewing Imogene Kennedy, for example, led me to raise ethical questions about the dispossessed woman in what might be called "performance" Kumina and the discrepancy between Kumina women's symbolic cultural wealth and their socioeconomic impoverishment within Jamaican society. In 1996, Kennedy was residing in the parish of St. Catherine in a small, squalid, dilapidated three-room shack. Kennedy was the subject of two significant articles on Jamaican Kumina, numerous taped interviews, and several video documentaries.[106] She was also responsible for introducing Edward Seaga, Jamaica's former prime minister, to the lore, music, and esoteric beliefs of Kumina culture.

During several conversations, Kennedy took pride in discussing her conversion from Revivalism to Kumina, which took place in the hollow base of a silk cotton tree when she was a young girl growing up in the parish of St. Thomas. There, for twenty-one days, the *Nkuyu* (Ancestors) taught her the "African" language and lore of Kumina. Kennedy reported that, during his tenure as Jamaica's first chief minister (1950s), Alexander Bustamante sponsored her relocation from Dalvey, St. Thomas to Kingston after her drums had been destroyed by local police during a Kumina ceremony.[107] "Jamaica treat African people-dem bad. . . . Dem treat we bad, man," Kennedy complained in a frail voice.[108] Confronted at once with the paradox of her prestige and deprivation, it was obvious that the decades of struggle against religious and cultural annihilation had taken their toll on her body and spirit. As she approached seventy, her pronounced impoverishment belied her public reputation as the famous "Miss Queenie," whom the Jamaican political leadership had displayed so proudly at government-sponsored Kumina competitions, presidential inaugurations, international "folk dance" competitions, National Heritage Weeks, and Devon House's[109] Friday night entertainment spots.[110]

Kennedy, with virtually no material possessions, had prize possessions—trophies, certificates, ribbons, and awards—to document her long journey as a Kumina exhibitionist. The quintessential symbol of the ironic joke Jamaica had played on her was her certificate of the Order of Distinction, which she received under Edward Seaga's administration on January 8, 1983. The Order of Distinction is one of the highest honors annually bestowed upon select Jamaican citizens for their distinguished service to the nation.[111] The point made is not one of discredit. One could argue that Kennedy deserved the honor after bringing visibility to a tradition that was subjugated and rendered invisible by the wider Jamaican society. For several centuries, the exotic mystique commonly associated with the tradition of exhibiting African peoples (especially women's bodies) and African religious cultures has no doubt facilitated the visibility of the marginalized and the colonized among large populations through museum displays, international world fairs, and the performing arts.[112] A womanist assessment of power, gender, and religion, however, contests the exhibition of African religious cultures through women's bodies.

Womanist theological method involves multidimensional analysis of oppression, religiocultural analysis, a sociopolitical analysis of wholeness, and bifocal analysis.[113] Each of these provides an important basis from which to critique performance Kumina as a colonial script that manufactures a reified notion of African religion in popular Jamaican thought. The collective work of womanist theologians suggests that womanist analysis of religion seeks to understand it as a product of culture. Thus, womanists insist that consistent critique of sociocultural traditions is a necessary task when attempting to analyze Black women's multidimensional oppression.

Because womanist theology is concerned about the liberation of Black communities, the principle of wholeness ensures that womanist sociopolitical analysis considers communal dynamics, but not at the expense of Black women's liberation. Wholeness compels womanist theologians to critically examine and respond to specific manifestations of oppression in a given Black community without prioritizing one manifestation over another. Furthermore, womanist theologians are bifocally critical of both external oppressive forces in the dominant society and internal oppression perpetuated within Black communities.

This womanist leaning toward intersectional analysis renders performance Kumina a complicated site of Caribbean cultural production that obscures Kumina's complex African religious foundations and women's mastery of its philosophical and theological system of thought. When *Kumina* and other African cultural practices are showcased in invented contexts of entertainment and cultural enrichment, their dignity and sanctity are compromised for an exotic visibility and cheap public recognition.[114] It is in this role, and this role only, that *Kumina* queens have found widespread yet compromised visibility in the larger society, which customarily seeks cultural and theological distance from much of what they represent. The festival venue in which Kumina is performed as a dance provides no opportunity for national reflection on Kumina's contribution to the making of African-Jamaican civilization.

Maureen Warner-Lewis, one of the first scholars to interview Kennedy, penned her thoughts about the underestimated resilience of the Kumina tradition, which has survived within a wider culture of hostility, and its import to reshaping the colonized consciousness of the Jamaican people. According to Warner-Lewis:

> [G]roups like Miss Queenie's kumina "bands" attempt to preserve a sense of historical continuity through spiritual and cultural means. At every kumina dance, each time an ancestral *nkuyu* possesses a devotee, this continuity is re-enacted. One wonders at the sense of purpose that could be unleashed in the West Indian people, if either through spiritual or secular means, or both, a sense of participation in a long historical process could be fostered. Despite its comparatively short existence in Jamaica, it is a miracle that kumina continues to flourish. It represents even more of a miracle of positive survival when one considers that this religion lives on, in the face of its non-visibility for so many in the total society, or indifference on the part of some, or scorn and disparagement from others. It is in fact a credit to the persistence of that traditional African awareness of the past as symbolized through the ancestors.[115]

The principal role of government organizations and initiatives in establishing performance Kumina as a permanent fixture of postindependence Jamaican nationhood cannot go unnoticed. No government official can take more credit for the evolution of a national agenda to recognize Jamaica's African cultural inheritance than former prime minister, Edward Seaga. Stemming in part from his ethnographic research on African-Jamaican religious cultures, Seaga's direct interest in exposing and celebrating Kumina and Revival Zion distinguishes him from other Jamaican heads of state.

Although Seaga is credited for bringing some legitimacy to Kumina and Revival Zion in the eyes of Jamaican Christians, his emphasis upon promoting

African religious traditions as staged public ceremonies has reinforced the trivialization of African-based religions as "folk culture." Thus, despite their periodic appearances before the Jamaican public, African-derived religions remain peripheral in the Jamaican collective consciousness where status is given to Christianity as a national religion and as the foundation of respectable culture. Seaga's contribution to African religious communities then is limited by the very contradictions in his approach to them. Entertaining performances of African religious practices in staged competitions, coupled with the distribution of champion ribbons and certificates, are, in the end, dramatic displays of Jamaican social stratification and colonialist consciousness. The negligible economic compensation offered to performers especially suggests that the Jamaican government's reductionist treatment of African-derived religion is no less than a recolonization of an imagined and symbolic "Africa," one that must be viewed as self-imposed if it is to be overcome in the future.

In his capacity as prime minister, Seaga missed a considerable opportunity to shape Jamaica's demonstration of national solidarity with practitioners of African-derived religions. A more productive initiative could entail the future investment of government funds and intellectual resources within African-based communities toward the development of local religious and cultural projects. This might prove to be much more valuable than performance-oriented initiatives of the past in promoting sustainable formalization and institutionalization of African-derived religious cultures in Jamaica.

Moreover, it could stimulate a respectful interest in and engagement with African-derived religious cultures like Kumina among the wider Jamaican citizenry. The Kumina queens I interviewed in 1996 lamented their plight as poor people with no resources to institutionalize and monitor the preservation of their culture. They have dreams of building Kumina schools where the "African" language can be taught systematically to each generation. They also expressed the desire to hold formal sessions on Kumina herbalism, spirituality, and theology.[116]

Government agencies such as the African Caribbean Institute of Jamaica and the Jamaica Cultural Development Commission have worked tirelessly to document and expose Kumina and other African-Jamaican cultural traditions, yet little has been done to support the formal institutionalization of African-derived religions in their local contexts. Only when this takes place can outsiders encounter Kumina and other religious traditions in their natural environment, where practitioners, especially women, maintain authority and credibility in transmitting knowledge about their traditions to the general public. Through deeper exchanges between Kumina practitioners and the outside world, we might discover that Kumina religious thought can, as Warner-Lewis suggests, "unleash" "a sense of purpose" and "foster" "a sense of participation in a long historical process" within the collective body of Jamaicans.

To the average Jamaican Christian, encountering Kumina culture outside of contrived settings would be a reach knowing that the repercussions for identifying with things and peoples African are still unbearable, even with 170 years of distance from enslavement. Thus, most Jamaicans would exempt themselves from Banbury's remark that "[s]uperstition, the belief in magic, witchcraft, the active intervention of ghostly or diabolic forces in the world of nature and the lives of men is surprisingly strong [in Jamaica]. It is of African origin but goes up the social scale much farther than one would expect."[117] African Jamaicans have learned the hard way that African religion and culture are incompatible with social status. Yet, while they publicly opt for the latter, the onset of crises or insurmountable tragedy sends many Jamaicans "down" the social scale to privately seek effective remedies from the former.

The African Religious Heritage: The Permanent Scapegoat for Evil and Pathology?

To many the word "religion" suggests, at first, something pertaining to the sacred, pious, or good life. Most would like to think that religion and evil are mutually exclusive, yet so much evil is committed by humans in the name of religion—all religions. Among the religions of the world, African religions and their diasporic derivatives have become the permanent scapegoat for evil and pathology. One would be hard-pressed to find sympathetic depictions of African-derived religions in Christian literature and lore or in popular Western culture from the period of African enslavement to the present day. Instead, one discovers the unmitigated vilification of Vodun, that is, "Voodoo," Yoruba, Kumina, and other African-derived religions in the Caribbean and the Americas. The stories about human sacrifice, cannibalism, zombification, sticking pins in dolls, and the like[118] have had definitive authority in rendering African-derived practitioners powerless to call the names of their deities; incapable of identifying the ideals, gifts, and life-sustaining potential within their traditions; and often defenseless against the condemnation of the worlds in which they find themselves.

Furthermore, the exoticization and mystification of the "evil" associated with African-derived religions induces Afrophobia, the most intense fear of and disdain for anything produced on the "dark" and "savage" continent. Indeed I have discussed in earlier chapters the African belief in mystical power, its omnipresence, and its moral and immoral appropriations by humans. Mystical power is *potentially* injurious. The enduring question is: why should *mystical* power be more feared and contested than *concrete* power? Aware of this mystical baggage of evil that attends the very word *Africa*, I have attempted to present African-derived religions from the starting point that they are life-giving traditions that nurture hospitable relations, life over disease and extinction, and the pursuit of freedom.

Perhaps I have betrayed the common expectation that the study of African-derived religions necessarily discloses something sinister and intolerable. The African-centered perspective finds nothing sinister or intolerable about Africans rebelling against those who kidnap, torture, and enslave them, nor does it see anything sinister about the movement of ancestral spirits and deities among African people in response to their petitions for help and protection.

Joseph Murphy also refuses to whet the general public's insatiable appetite for the antipathetic presentation of African religions. In his publication *Working the Spirit: Ceremonies of the African Diaspora*, Murphy prefaces his study with the following commentary:

> One of the highest hurdles to overcome in interpreting diasporan traditions to outsiders is the deep-seated popular image of them as "voodoo," malign "black magic." Hundreds of books and scores of films have portrayed the spirituality of millions of people of African descent as crazed, depraved, or demonic manipulations of gullible and irrational people. These images have their origin in the French colonial reaction to the revolt of Haitian slaves whose motive in liberating themselves from grinding and brutal enslavement was thought to rest in *vaudoux*. The success of the Haitian revolution sent shock waves through the white world that are still being felt today. I think that the relegation of "voodoo" to the horror genre reflects mass America's real horror of independent black power. If voodoo was powerful enough to free the slaves, might it not free their descendants?[119]

We should not think that Murphy is overstating the point. If Hesketh Bell's remarks about Haiti, almost a century after the Haitian Revolution, reflect the sentiments of his White contemporaries, we see how White people's commitment to anti-Africanness was harnessed into an ideology and, even worse, a presupposition. Bell writes:

> The [Haitian] monarchy did not last long, and was soon replaced by a republic; tumults and bloodshed were of constant recurrence. The negroes, jealous of the mulattoes, massacred or banished all the latter, and up to the present moment this beautiful island is constantly the scene of revolution and bloodshed, and the Haytians are frequently being called on to pay heavy indemnities to foreign traders and others for the damage done to their property in these constantly recurring riots. As may be expected civilization among the lower classes of Haytians is not very advanced, especially in the interior, where the authority of the Government is even less than nominal. Dreadful accounts reach us of thousands of negroes having gone back to a perfectly savage life in the woods, going about stark naked, and having replaced the Christian religion by Voodooism and fetish worship. Cases of cannibalism have even been reported, and nowhere in the West Indies has Obeah a more tenacious hold over high and low than in Hayti. Such a shocking state of affairs cannot be allowed to continue long, and covetous eyes are cast towards Hayti by more than one of the great powers.[120]

Bell's disdain for Haiti was indeed shared by Whites throughout the Americas, the Caribbean, and Europe. And Murphy is right: such disdain was and continues to be sparked by White people's "horror of independent black power." As demonstrated by Bell's comment, Whites have interpreted African religious and political power as a threat to international security. Thus Bell suggests Euro-imperialism (the forces of the "great powers") as the appropriate antidote for Haiti's "irreligion" and "barbarism." Against this established White portrait of Haiti and Vodun (or "Voodoo," which became the generic term for African-derived religions in the Caribbean and the Americas), we should not be shocked by Murphy's confession:

> Whenever I present this liberating view of diasporan traditions I will be reminded that there are genuine practices of malign sorcery within them. Yet I have grown tired of answering calls to present the less-salutary dimensions of diasporan spirituality in the interests of "balance." I take it for granted that peoples of African descent are as venal as anyone else, and charlatans and spiritual sadists might be readily located among them. I see my task in presenting the traditions to outsiders as practitioners might wish them to be presented, concentrating on the spiritual depth and beauty that practitioners find. As this spirituality is almost never reported by outsiders, this book may be a corrective toward a "balanced" view.[121]

The ultimate tragedy is that, as a general rule, African-Caribbean populations, having come under the influence of White Christian culture, perpetuate Afrophobic and anti-African ideas and attitudes regarding African-derived religious traditions. For example, in 1984 the African-Caribbean Institute of Jamaica sponsored a televised presentation of a Kumina ceremony in celebration of Jamaica's annual Heritage Week. During a taped interview (September 1996) the organizer of the program, Hazel Ramsay, recalled the general public's response to the presentation:

> We presented everything on the television. The drumming and the spirit possession and even the chicken sacrifice. I don't think I have recovered, after all these years, from the onslaught of negative responses we received after the program aired. People said we were an embarrassment—that we were promoting devil worship and heathenism. The Jamaican people were not ready to receive their own heritage—the very spirituality of people who live just beyond their own back yards. . . . It was devastating to experience.[122]

During formal interviews and informal conversations with Jamaican studies scholars, the theme of Black anti-Africanness constantly surfaces as an obstacle.[123] In fact, I believe that I was able to secure an audience with Edward Seaga due to familial connections. When sitting before him, he questioned me quite aggressively, attempting to understand my purpose in undertaking research on African-derived religions, especially as a theological student. He assumed that I approached the subject with a confessional Christian bias and that my aim was to discredit the traditions from that Afrophobic location. Even

White researchers have noted the pejorative views that Blacks hold about African religion and culture. For example, Laura Tanna conducted research on Jamaican folk songs and stories in eight parishes in the island. She recalled, "The Nago people, Yoruba descendants, lived in the village of Abeokuta in Westmoreland and were *one of the few* enclaves of immigrants who took pride in preserving their African culture."[124] Tanna, a White North American, also recounted an incident involving a man in Abeokuta, Jamaica, who was present when his compatriot agreed to sing folk songs and tell folk stories while being taped. "[J]ust as we were about to set up the tape recorder," Tanna writes, "the second farmer began to complain loudly about Whites exploiting the people and coming to make them look like monkeys."[125]

While Black anti-Africanness is alive and well in Jamaica, the truth is that it is Euro-derived. It did not emerge from practitioners of African religions but from the legacy of White Christian culture in Jamaica. The terminology used by contemporary Jamaicans to categorize Kumina practitioners, Revival Zionists, and Obeah practitioners is not African-derived. Rather, it was scripted into Jamaican cultural narratives by White traders, missionaries, and enslavers.

A critical evaluation of the extension of this Eurocentric, Afrophobic, and anti-African consciousness to diasporic Black thought and behavior in the Caribbean and the Americas invites one to consider which evil is worse: the nebulous mystical evil of the African antisocializer[126] or the concretized evil— enslavement, torture, murder, neocolonialism, and so on—historically perpetrated against Africans by Europeans. Somehow, the evil committed against African peoples by White missionaries, enslavers, and colonial authorities has been rationalized as a justified means to the righteous end of Christianizing African heathens and has managed to evade the notorious reputation automatically associated with Obeah and Kumina. White Christian evil appears less hazardous than African Obeah evil.

It is important to critique the intentional manipulation of human dependency upon religious ideas and beliefs as a dimension of human behavior in all religious systems. African religions, like all religions, offer their leaders opportunities to capitalize on the beliefs, fears, and anxieties of their adherents. However, African religions are often scapegoated as predisposed toward the abuse of power when compared with Christianity, where the evils committed by White Christians and their sustained impact on diasporic Africans are ignored,[127] justified, or excused as anomalous acts of morally corrupt individuals. For example, from the idea's inception, invested parties could not discuss the prospect of transporting indentured laborers to the British West Indies without somehow linking it to anti-African beliefs about African religion and culture. In deliberating on the pros and cons of endorsing the plan, Lord John Russell, the British secretary of state for the colonies, concluded:

> [T]he establishment of a regular intercourse between Africa and the West Indies, will tend greatly, not only to the prosperity of the British West Indian possessions, but likewise to the civilisation of Africa. A new epoch has arrived for the African race. We have in the

West Indies 800,000 Negroes, of whom perhaps three fourths are Christians in the enjoyment of practical freedom, of means of education and of physical comfort to a very high degree. There is no reason to suppose that their advances in wealth, knowledge and religious improvements may not be in proportion to the most hopeful anticipations. Nothing like this state of Society exists among the African race elsewhere. In Heyti there is a very low standard of government and Civilisation; in Cuba, in Brazil, and in the United States, slavery; in Africa, slavery, human sacrifices and the most degrading superstitions.[128]

African exposure to Euro-Christian culture emerges time and again in Jamaican history as the end that always justifies the means. In the case of indentured African laborers, the means were so treacherous and degrading it is no small wonder that Kumina culture is one of the most expressive memory sites of African enslavement in Jamaica.

The very fact that Myal is of marginal significance to the average Jamaican is evidence of the intentional demonization of African-derived religions in Jamaican culture. Why is it the case that, outside of the Revival Zion, Kumina, Gumbay, and Jonkunnu traditions, most Jamaicans are unfamiliar with the term *Myal*, let alone its roots and legacy in Jamaican culture? Yet every Jamaican knows very well the infamous name and legacy of Obeah. Where Myal was adopted, sheltered, and respected, it is known today by name and personality— in isolated regions across the island. However, Myal, the tradition historically noted (even by Whites) to counteract malicious uses of mystical power, has lost its name and positive influence in the broader contemporary Jamaican culture. Myal, the heartbeat and blood flow of Jamaica's African-derived religious traditions, is anonymous. This is why a scholar such as Edward Brathwaite, in seeking to nullify the Eurocentric conception of African-derived religions in Jamaican culture, focuses on a redefinition of Obeah. Obeah, with all of its negative associations, has come to signify any expression of African-derived religion in Jamaica, especially divination and herbalism. Although Jamaican Christians are repeatedly helped or healed by "Obeah" practitioners, they consult them in desperation, momentarily suspending their pejorative views about Obeah. At the end of the day, those same Jamaicans usually remain committed to anti-African ideas that stigmatize and denigrate the integrity of that which they call Obeah. Thus writes Brathwaite:

> According to [Matthew] Lewis [a nineteenth-century White Jamaican
> proprietor], however, it was difficult to know if the slaves had any
> real religious beliefs or practices, since the only external sign of a
> priest was the obeah man. Lewis was perhaps nearer than he knew
> to the truth about his slaves' religious beliefs and practices, but he
> did not understand the function of the obeah man, since he was as-
> sociated in the Jamaican/European mind with superstition, witch-
> craft and poison. But in African and Caribbean folk practice, where
> religion had not been externalized and institutionalized as in Eu-

rope, the obeah man was doctor [and] philosopher as well as priest.[129]

The Myal movement, which appeared in 1842, just a few years after Emancipation, has also been used to reinforce the antipathetic interpretation of Obeah. As discussed in chapter 1, I found no pre-emancipation descriptions of Myal independent of Obeah, and so firsthand accounts of Myalism as an independent tradition date back to this postslavery period. The 1842 outbreak was the most public expression of Myal, for before that time, Myalists and Obeah practitioners clandestinely combined their expertise to resist enslavement by any necessary means.

According to contemporary sources, some Myal groups of the 1840s had come under Christian influence (or at least publicly presented themselves in this manner), proclaiming that they were doing God's work and that they were clearing[130] the land for Jesus' return.[131] In many cases, Myal rituals interrupted plantation work, and aggravated proprietors had Myal organizers arrested. The missionaries also tried to suppress the movement but were met with vehement resistance. Hope Waddell, a Presbyterian missionary, confronted Myal resistance directly when he attempted to eradicate Myal activities on the Blue Hole estate. After he accused women in the movement of madness, enraged members retorted, "They are not mad. They have the spirit. You must be mad yourself, and had best go away. Let the women go on, we don't want you. Who brought you here? What do you want with us?"[132]

Monica Schuler duly notes that one of the strongest African tenets of this Myal movement was its insistence that evil made manifest necessitated a concrete human response. Myalists viewed evil as an "offense not against God but against society."[133] This African orientation toward evil[134] is significant, for it explains the "this-world" focus upon well-being and human fulfillment in each manifestation of African-derived Jamaican religions. Obeah, Myal, Native Baptist, Kumina, Revival Zion, and Rastafari all seek to combat disease, misfortune, dislocation, and *sufferation* by promoting well-being and reconciliation through practical, concrete means: divination, herbalism, armed resistance, animal sacrifice, ancestral possession, clearing rituals, and so on.

Because Africans generally believe that peculiar manifestations of misfortune can result from malicious assertions of mystical power, when economic decline and a large number of unexpected deaths struck the northern parishes of Trelawny and St. James, Myalists were summoned to cleanse the troubled estates of "Obeah." If it is true that the malicious assertion of mystical powers was the root cause of even some of the region's problems, according to my reinterpretation of Obeah outlined in chapter 1, the Myalists of this 1842 movement were actually combating the evil manipulation of Obeah, that is, *obeye* (neutral mystical power).[135] This interpretation contests the uniformly accepted notion that Myal and Obeah were contentious during slavery and especially during the 1842 Myal movement.[136] The equation of Obeah with immoral agency—including the 1842 context where Myalists proclaimed war against "Obeah"—is inconsistent with African people's beneficent use of Obeah/*obeye* to rebel against slavery, to procure remedies and antidotes for illnesses, and to secure protection against misfortune. By 1842, the automatic association of Obeah with immoral agency was deeply entrenched in White Jamaican popular culture. Apparently the ancient African association of moral agency with the human will as opposed to mystical power had lost saliency in the African-Jamaican community as Myalists declared open war against "Obeah." In ancient Akan societies, the struggle between good and evil was a struggle between good and ill human will, between persons who accessed *obeye* for beneficent ends (*obirifo/okomfo*) and those who accessed *obeye* for malevolent ends (*obay-ifo*).[137] Thornton identifies a similar ethical orientation among Central Africans, whose "theology did not usually envision evil as the provenance of specific supernatural beings, which were entirely evil, such as Christian theology of the Devil did. Rather, the African concept was more inclined to see the evil in the actions of people with wicked intentions enlisting some of the supernatural world in their projects."[138]

Remembering that, in the pre-emancipation period, any free African convicted of Obeah practice could be enslaved through judicial decree,[139] I am of the same mind as Brathwaite in his attempt to bring hermeneutical authenticity to a neutral interpretation of Obeah. Obeah, in its most comprehensive usage, represents African-derived religious traditions in Jamaica and as such needs to be redeemed from its criminal reputation. Obeah should be associated with the life-affirming spirituality, values, and goals of African-derived religions, as they have unfolded in Jamaica and must be reconceptualized to cohere with its legacy in ancient Akan, Kongo, and other African religious cultures because that legacy has also been established in diasporic manifestations of Obeah. Jamaican Obeah, like its Akan parent, *obeye*, is energy. In truth, Obeah is a scientific principle that is not foreign to any of us. We rely on this principle daily in our implementation of the various technologies that enhance our lives and facilitate our productivity. Yet, we also know that technology can be used to exploit and destroy life. A tangible comparison might be helpful at this juncture. We could conceive of a charged battery as one particular construal of the Obeah principle. As stored-up energy, a battery could be expended to supply electric current to a computer or a smoke detector. It may also be used to charge a stun gun, which could then be accessed as a weapon of self-defense (good intentions) or as a weapon of attack to disable a victim (negative intentions). When conceived in this sense, it is only in its application—the context in which, intentions with which, and means by which Obeah is deployed— that moral agency can be determined to be good or bad with reference to Obeah.

African studies research has probed the cultural determinants of power and agency within classical and contemporary African societies.[140] The diasporic presence of Obeah, Conjure, Hoodoo, and other African-derived traditions suggests that classical African conceptions of power and agency continue to permeate not only contemporary African communities but also African-American and Caribbean societies as well. As discussed above, power (as neutral) offered enslaved Africans avenues and vehicles for negotiating physical, emotional, psychological, and spatial confinement; static and monotonous work regimens; and sheer powerlessness over their bodies and social liberties. Enslaved Africans were inclined then to use mystical power to transform their lives in any number of concrete ways, including revolts and acts of sabotage against the slave regime. In comparing Western and African conceptions of power, Ivan Karp offers insight into why these systems of power and agency, with their transformative warrants, have been so resilient and salient in the lives of enslaved Africans in the Caribbean and the Americas. According to Karp:

> A different view of power is exhibited in African societies than in Western social science. The stress in Africa is not on the element of control but on the more dynamic aspect of energy and the capacity to use it. . . . African ideas of power . . . have to do with engaging power and creating or at least containing the world. They may allow for the possibility of transformations in a way that Western social science concepts of power do not.[141]

Obeah then is only one of the many approaches to transformative power in what might be called the African cosmos that captured the imagination and agency of countless enslaved Africans in the Caribbean and the Americas and continues to do so for many of their descendants today.

Anti-Africanness, Duplicity, and the Aesthetic Meaning of Masking

As a prolegomenon to my treatment of the theoretical and theological implications of African-based religions in Jamaica for Black religious studies, it seems appropriate to offer some closing thoughts about the transmission of anti-African values from Euro-Christianity to Afro-Christianity. Anti-Africanness, as I have defined it, is not the critique or modification of things African but the negation and denigration of things African, simply because they are African.

I am both intrigued and perplexed by the potent legacy of African religions in Jamaica and other Caribbean islands. I am intrigued because of the resilience of African people, who developed clever devices for disguising, protecting, and preserving their religions in response to the lethal measures taken by the planters and missionaries to exterminate their remnants in the Caribbean. I remain perplexed, however, by the cognitive dissonance in the attitudes of Caribbean peoples toward the African roots of their religious cultures. Very rarely does one find Caribbean people who feel comfortable accepting and appreciating their African heritage. As discussed above, Black anti-Africanness, or what I call a negative distance[142] from Africa, is a very real cultural attitude in the Caribbean, a consequence of the rise of the modern West. Black anti-Africanness has the effect of alienating and marginalizing the minority of Caribbean people who do not experience cognitive dissonance in relation to their actual daily religious habits, but who genuinely embrace and appreciate the traditions of their African ancestors. This is true not only in Jamaica but across the entire inhabited archipelago.

Stephen Glazier's 1984 publication on his study of the Spiritual Baptists in Trinidad offers broader insight into this negative distance between Caribbean peoples and their African heritage:

> Many Baptist leaders, in their quest for respectability, have tried to downplay African elements within the faith. Several Curepe informants, commenting on the published accounts of Herskovits and Simpson, complained that the accounts do not make their religion appear "as other faiths" (by which they meant London Baptists, Presbyterians, Anglicans, and so on). One leader who was extremely anxious that my book should "set things right," was very careful lest I visit churches with [Yoruba Orisha] Shango connections and get the "wrong impression." Ironically, his own church had Shango connections, and so he did not take me there.[143]

Glazier further observes, "[m]ost Shango leaders have Spiritual Baptist affiliations, while many Spiritual Baptists do not have Shango affiliations."[144] As in Jamaica, it is generally apparent in Trinidad that the most identifiably African religious practitioners are the least respected and accepted in "official" cultural scripts, both elitist and nonelitist. It is to the Shangoist's or Orisha[145] devotee's advantage to be open to alternative Christian traditions, for the Orisha devotee, or any representative of traditional African religion, must align herself with socially valued traditions if African traditions are to persist transgenerationally. I have noted above that African religions were traditionally dynamic and penetrable by cross-cultural encounters. However, the predicament of enslavement and the threats of African cultural extinction that pervaded the slave experience left Africans no choice but to open themselves even to undesired change and the opportunities for transgenerational survival that attended the most legitimate forms of Eurocentric religion and culture.

The representatives of African cultural traditions are not unaware of their pariah status in their wider cultures, and perhaps this is why defensive forms of Black nationalist consciousness continue to surface as nemeses of Afrophobic legacies in Black religion and culture. For example, Stephen Glazier's research indicates that, in some Shango services, African spirits are suspicious of attempts to mitigate or supplement African rituals with Christian ones:

> Sometimes Shango leaders conduct prayer meetings themselves. Most of the time, however, they ask the Baptist leader associated with that church to perform them. When a leader performs his own prayer meetings, he is in what one Baptist leader described as a "most discomfortable" position—he is a celebrant in two religious traditions at the same time. This is thought to be dangerous because at a later date the African powers might question his "sincerity."[146]

Some may understand these contradictions and cognitive dissonances as an indigenous and unavoidable dimension of African diasporic history and experience, which was poignantly articulated by W. E. B. Du Bois in his "double consciousness" or "twoness" theory.[147] I concur, but would argue that anti-Africanness is a persistent factor in our cultures of contradiction. And so, as long as African diasporic religiosity continues to compose variations on the dominant themes in continental religions, it might be helpful to understand the distinct diasporic flavor of African-Caribbean religious traditions like Obeah, Kumina, Orisha (Shango), and Vodun, not as truncated from their continental African roots but as illustrations of positive distance from Africa, marked by the consequences of exile, new types of cultural contacts, and the flow of innovations ignited by such encounters.

In view of the duplicity that deeply characterizes the consciousness of the Caribbean people, especially in the arena of negotiating Christianity and their African religious heritage, we might also examine this phenomenon from a slightly different and less tragic angle than that of double consciousness. I have already discussed how in contemporary Jamaica the official Christian populace scorns and fears Obeah and Kumina practitioners by day but respects and consults them by night. Ironically, such behavior, outlandish though it is, authenticates African religiosity as actual and necessary for the survival and well-being of Jamaican people. I would even dare to suggest that such inclinations are inspired by deeply embedded sensibilities for the beauty and the grotesque in things African. I am tempted to interpret these sensibilities as spiritual impulses. Camerounian philosopher and theologian Eboussi Boulaga identifies these types of human inclinations as "esthetic." His perspective is useful for understanding the penchant for things African that is consciously and unconsciously harbored within so many Black people throughout the diaspora. Boulaga maintains:

> One of the great events of our experience, and perhaps of our age is the advent of esthetic human beings. Their fashion of attaching to the past, to traditions, is neither dogmatic nor rationalistic. They have no intention of worshipping what their fathers venerated nor of burning it at the stake either. They are not concerned about choice between the thesis of the unsurpassable wisdom of the ancients and the Ancestor, and the antithesis of the antiquated imbecility of these same ancients or Ancestor. Their minds are elsewhere. For them, traditions are treasures of forms and models, and the most durable of them are styles that cannot be reproduced without fakery, but which ever inspire and enchant, which lend more zest to the present, our present, and more assurance to our own quest for the beauty that abides. For these styles procure for us the necessary space and distance to play our own game, ephemeral but unique. They refer us to the irreducibility of sensation, of the sense of situation. This sense is the presence of the human being to the simultaneous totality, momentary and epochal, of things and beings—a to-

tality that is the explosion of the origin, revealing human beings to themselves as a total part of the world.[148]

If Boulaga is correct, the African diasporic pursuit of things African may very well be an aesthetic quest to find freedom, meaning, security, and authenticity in an unfamiliar, yet familiar, past. And yet, given the devastating impact of slavery and Euro-Christianity upon African religions and cultures, such pursuit is akin to getting dressed in a completely dark room with the hope that, when exposed to the light, all of the clothing colors and styles will be well coordinated.

Two proverbs often uttered by Jamaicans bring home the initial point: "If yu wa-an good yu nuose ha fi run,"[149] and "Everything that glitters is not Gold." As African Jamaicans began to subscribe to the "glittering" official church doctrine and orthodox forms of Christian piety, they began to lose something as well. Lost was a connection to significant African-derived religions, the memory of the historical meanings and value of surviving African religious forms, the freedom and cultural legitimacy to affirm African religious traditions as worthy and beneficial for personal and communal health, and an awareness that some African values and practices continue to be expressed under the performance masks of Black Christian and quasi-Christian rituals. Boulaga's insights help us to see, however, that these performance masks are aesthetic conveyers of "epochal," "momentary," or even spontaneous experiences, which combat tragedy, exile, and dislocation in the African diasporic personality as they reconnect the performers with their African heritage time and time again.

5

Communion

Toward a Caribbean Theology of Collective Memory

Pluralism in the Caribbean means that its inhabitants, more that any-body else, can help Christians from around the world to appreciate that doing theology must take into consideration the presence of popular religions. In the Caribbean, one is dealing with expressions of religion which have often been written off as "demonic" because they do not come under the umbrella of Christianity. However these religions each have a contribution to make to the theological enterprise.[1]

I knew that before I could say anything theologically meaningful about the black situation of oppression, I had to discover a theological identity that was accountable to the history and culture of my people.[2]

The Moral Intent of Caribbean Theology

In the preceding chapters, I have attempted to examine the multiple expressions of African-derived religions in Jamaica in order to illustrate how it is that so many Jamaicans of African descent have come to accept Afrophobic and anti-African ideas about African-derived religions. As a critical aspect of my historical investigation of African-Jamaican religious experience, I have given special attention to Afrophobia and anti-Africanness as moral problems for consideration in any serious Caribbean theological project. If I have not fallen short of the task I set for myself in the introduction, it is appropriate to pause here to consider what I understand to be the moral intent of

Caribbean theology, especially with regard to the problem of anthropological poverty.

The association of poverty with things and peoples African is common-place in the narratives and symbols of the modern West: I would dare to submit that one of the effects of White supremacy has been acculturating people the world over to feel, at the very least, comfortable with African impoverishment. It might be said that Misery is Africa's middle name, and it takes intentional effort to divest the imagination of malnourished children, "warring tribes," HIV and Ebola viruses, "wild jungles," and corrupt dictators when the word "Africa" is invoked. The truth is that Africa *is* suffering from specific forms of impoverishment, apart from the manufactured stereotypes suggesting Africa's reducibility to poverty. As I see it, the moral imperatives of theology compel me to ask why Africa is so plagued with poverties and why so many people the world over accommodate Africa's struggle with impoverishment.

From the discussion above, we see that Africa's impoverishment is not only continental but diasporic as well. To begin with, the Caribbean plantation slave economy was bolstered by the material poverty of Africans. The mission-aries wrote disapprovingly about the wretched and squalid conditions in which Africans lived and suffered, and they complained that planters provided much better care for their animals than their (African) human property. Despite their observations and their knowledge that money was scarce among the enslaved populations, one visitor to Jamaica wrote that the missionaries were "cunning, intriguing, fanatical, hypocritical canting Knaves, cajoling the poor Negroes of all their little savings . . . under the pretense of saving them from the devil and everlasting damnation."[3]

To be sure, the missionaries, especially the Baptists, were willing to pur-chase land for the resettlement of emancipated African members of their con-gregations at reasonable rates, and as such they were instrumental in reestab-lishing some African communities. In postemancipation Jamaica, Africans stood on line to join the Christian religious organizations that could lend them financial and "legitimate" moral support. Officially, practitioners of African religion were excluded from the "blessings" bestowed upon the newly estab-lished African Christian communities. Emancipated Africans quickly discov-ered that African religion offered them no avenues out of poverty. As a result, most Africans concealed their allegiances to their ancestral heritage and opted for the benefits associated with the Christian religion.

It should not surprise us then that in Jamaica today the majority of Africans are members of the orthodox Christian churches, which, in most cases, were established under the authority of European missionaries. Obeah practitioners, Revival Zionists, Kumina devotees, and Rastas represent only a "remnant" among the "people of God." As echoed in the Hebrew Scriptures: "Yet, behold, therein shall be a remnant that shall be brought forth, *both* sons and daughters: behold, they shall come forth unto you, and ye shall see their way and their doings: and ye shall be comforted concerning the evil that I have brought upon Jerusalem."[4]

Although religious studies scholars tend to interpret the relationship between impoverishment and African-derived religions as the former causing the latter,[5] I maintain that it is the latter which gives rise to the former. It is here that I envision a new role for Caribbean theology if it is to be a morally accountable theology of liberation that speaks to and on behalf of the poorest and most oppressed of our region. It is fitting then to examine the theme of the African religious heritage in Caribbean theology in general and in related theologies of liberation.

The problem of the Eurocentric Christian bias as an obstacle to the formation of genuinely inclusive Caribbean theologies is so severe that the only way to address it is to expose it wherever it is found in liberation theological discourse. One example from Noel Erskine's early work on Jamaican theology might demonstrate the type of internal self-scrutiny required of Caribbean theologians if we are to surmount this oppressive Eurocentric bias, which shapes our individual and our collective consciousness in the African diaspora.

Noel Erskine was the first Caribbean theologian to articulate a developed theological perspective premised upon the African-Jamaican struggle for freedom. In his 1981 publication *Decolonizing Theology*, Erskine discusses the import of Revival Zion and Rastafari. With reference to Revival Zionists, he insists:

> To treat them as inconsequential is to fail these people theologically. The Revivalist cults must lead the Christian church, and any theology that would speak with cogency to the Caribbean, to use the symbols of black religious experience as expressive tools in structuring a religion that would have redemptive power for this community. Theology in the Caribbean must arise from the black religious experience if it seeks the redemption of these people.[6]

Erskine assigns an authoritative role to Revival Zion in shaping the voice of the Caribbean church and its theologians. However his assessment of African spirituality and its import for Caribbean theology is questionable when he writes:

> Revivalism in the Caribbean, apart from providing a context in which black people can identify themselves, also deals with their religious beliefs. This is an important function. These beliefs may seem strange because they are different and, admittedly, are the "cultural fragments" of primitive people, but they are a vital part of the world of the Caribbean.[7]

Unfortunately Erskine does not elaborate on what it is that he finds "strange" and "primitive" about Africans and their beliefs,[8] however his remarks invite the reader to suspect that his theological commitment to unorthodox and non-Christian expressions of the "black religious experience" is tenuous at best.

As I understand it, the moral intent of Caribbean theology compels those of us who would dare to speak about our people's walk with the Divine to take seriously the African-derived religions as sources for theological construction. I maintain that we cannot properly address the problem of Caribbean people's anthropological impoverishment without exposing and critiquing anti-African beliefs and attitudes in Black Christian culture, nor can Black Christians value that from which they are alienated.[9] But beyond this, if the task of African-Caribbean theology is to anchor our prophetic claims about God's preoccupation with the poor and oppressed in the religious history and legacy of our enslaved Ancestors, we have yet to complete this task.

Within the African-Jamaican experience, the connection between human freedom and the Divine Community was primarily expressed in Pan-African religious beliefs, rituals, and praxes. I have already discussed the hows and whens in the preceding chapters. The next step in Caribbean theology is to spend text time with the African-derived religions in their historical and contemporary expressions, which have inspired Africans to pursue freedom politically, spiritually, and culturally. The African pursuit of freedom in Jamaican history, whether overt or covert, is a testimony of faith (against the odds). If we seek to determine what it means to be faithful within the colonial context of bondage, it must be acknowledged that the faithful are those who remember not so much the specific content of "African culture," but the beauty in it, its value and beatitude, its potential to heal, fulfill, provide sanctuary, and produce miracles and miracle workers.

It is this faith testimony that I have tried to emphasize throughout this study—against the odds of audience expectations for something a little more Christian. A more holistic historical assessment of the African-Caribbean experience demands that the faith testimony of enslaved Africans and their descendants who have deliberately "kept up the culture"[10] should not be silenced by the metanarratives of the Christian faith. In the words of Korean feminist theologian Chung Hyun Kyung, "[T]he authentic memories of God's people were not completed two thousand years ago, and they cannot be imprisoned within the Christian canon. The text of God's revelation was, is, and will be written in our bodies and our peoples' everyday struggle for survival and liberation."[11]

To be sure, the pejorative Christian theological response to African-derived religions might be consistent with some aspects of Pauline teaching[12] but appear totally inconsistent with Jesus' teaching and practice. Jesus, it seems to me, was a "keeper of the culture." This is not to say that he endorsed everything his Hebrew Ancestors believed or practiced, for certainly part of his mission was to critique some oppressive dimensions of his inherited culture and religion. However, Jesus' commemoration of the sacred meaning of his culture on the night before his death is in my view the most poignant scriptural example of his respect for his heritage. According to scriptural testimony, Jesus, aware of his impending arrest and condemnation to death, sought closure and intimacy with his followers at a Passover meal. The Gospel of Luke says, "When the hour came, he took his place at the table, and the apostles with him. He said to them, 'I have eagerly desired to eat this Passover with you before I suffer.' "[13] In the Gospel of Matthew, Jesus instructs the disciples: "Go into the city to a certain man, and say to him, 'The Teacher says, My time is near; I will keep the Passover at your house with my disciples.' "[14] Jesus chose to celebrate the most sacred tradition in the history of his people, and he did so because that was where he could approach the God of his people—the God who inspired him on a prophetic mission among his people.

During the Passover meal, Jesus also identified his betrayer and exposed the evil in the community. As we have seen from the above discussion, it has been within the boundaries of African culture/religion that the Obeah practitioner, Myalist, Native Baptist, Revival Zionist, Kumina devotee, and Rasta have secured the courage and spiritual insight to expose and exorcise evil and affliction. I would suggest, then, that in the African-Jamaican context, the sacrament of Communion is authenticated when it orients us toward the life-affirming traditions of our Ancestors and situates us in community with the keepers of the culture. For example, the communal meal that is shared on the morning after a Kumina sacrifice is a sacramental celebration marking the holy and concentrated interaction between Ancestors and humans, and I would argue that the indigenous celebration of Kumina communion is actually more consistent with Jesus' "last supper" than the orthodox Christian celebration of the Eucharist in Jamaican churches today. Thus, while Caribbean theologians might neglect to see any connection between the Jesus of the Gospels and African-derived religions, a serious reexamination of Jesus and his Hebrew heritage might yield spiritual and ethical themes for a new theological project that considers the religious diversity across the various islands and the prominence of the African heritage in the region.

As I proceed to outline a Caribbean theology of collective memory for the Jamaican context, I pledge solidarity with the repressed Caribbean communities—those who remember the sanctity in African culture. As such, the nascent Caribbean theology I attempt here does not accommodate ideational, contemplative God-talk. It does, however, valorize the "subjugated knowledges"[15] of Africans who have died so slowly with culture in their veins and draws from them prophetic and critical theological statements. The precedence for this approach is best demonstrated within the liberation theological tradition. It is appropriate then to acknowledge the insights and limitations of liberation theology as it might critique and contribute to my articulation of a Caribbean theology of liberation.

The Rise of Liberation Theology and the Persistence of "Orthodoxy" in Liberation Theological Discourse

The theological camp known as contextual or liberation theology in the academy could rightly be identified with concurrent sociopolitical postcolonial struggles in the Third World and civil rights struggles in the United States. In order to fully appreciate the contributions that liberation theologians have made to the discipline of theology it is important to understand what they claimed to reject in the Western Eurocentric theological tradition. The theological reformation inaugurated by Third World theologians and oppressed groups in the United States rendered classical and modern approaches to the discipline inadequate. Since the Enlightenment, White male theologians had been preoccupied with the problem of belief in God versus doubt in God. How could one believe in a God who was no longer necessary to explain human experience and the natural world insofar as empirical science and philosophical reasoning provided the most adequate frameworks for understanding truth?[16] According to James Cone, theology in the modern West concerned itself with the problem of the unbeliever. The oppressed communities of the Third World and First World emerged with a novel theological agenda, that of relating God's revelation to the problem of nonpersonhood.[17]

There were two main points of contention between the European/Euro-American male theologians and the liberation theologians. First, White male theologians universalized their experience in claiming to write theology for all Christians. Second, White male theologians were not intentional about utilizing social context as an authoritative source for theological construction.[18] The liberation theological response was to resituate the moral purpose for theological reflection within concrete contexts of human suffering and social oppression.

Black theologians concentrated most on the problem of racism, while Latin American theologians concentrated on the problems of imperialism and classism. Thus Marxist theory has figured prominently in their analyses of the historical and sociopolitical context that informs their theological perspectives. Historically, African theologians north of the Zambezi River tended to emphasize cultural autonomy in Christian theology and piety. Their approach has also been termed inculturation, Africanization, or indigenization. African theologians south of the Zambezi River, namely those from South Africa, tended to emphasize political liberation and are often referred to as liberationists. And there are growing numbers of African theologians who emphasize both cultural and political liberation in their works.[19] As representatives of a minority religious group in Asia (roughly 3 percent), Asian theologians have focused on the problem of Christian identity and religious pluralism. They have also emphasized poverty, spirituality, and imperialism.

The earliest expressions of contextual theologies were penned by James Cone and Gustavo Gutiérrez. Cone published *Black Theology and Black Power* in 1969. In that preliminary text Cone sought to relate the imperatives of the Christian faith to the Black power struggle for racial justice and self-determination in the United States. One year later he published *A Black Theology of Liberation*. This was Cone's first systematic presentation of theology as a discourse and praxis grounded upon the historical and cultural sources of African-American Christian religious experience. The following year, in 1971, Peruvian Jesuit priest Gustavo Gutiérrez published his book *Teología de Liberación.*[20]

The most sustained dialogue among liberation theologies has emerged through the meetings and published literature of the Ecumenical Association of Third World Theologians (EATWOT). EATWOT was founded in 1976 in Dar es Salaam, Tanzania, when theologians from the Third World convened to discuss theological issues pertaining to the poor and oppressed in their respective countries. Since its founding, EATWOT has continued to hold general intercontinental assemblies and smaller intracontinental assemblies for the most part in Third World countries. Meetings have been held in Accra, Ghana (1979); Wennappuwa, Sri Lanka (1979); São Paulo, Brazil (1980); New Delhi, India (1981); Geneva, Switzerland (1983); Oaxtepec, Mexico (1986); Nairobi, Kenya (1992); and Manila, Philippines (1996) as well as in other countries. The proceedings from the EATWOT assemblies are documented in individual publications[21] and in EATWOT's journal, *Voices from the Third World*.

EATWOT theologians collaborate in order to respond to the specific economic and sociopolitical climate that consumes the resources of the Third World and denies a decent existence to most of the people in the Third World. Against the historicopolitical backdrop of slavery, imperialism, and neocolonialism, the liberation theologians have asserted that the epistemological orientation undergirding their theologies is radically different from that of the dominant theologies of Europe and Euro-America. They write in the interest of those who live and survive in "the underside of history,"[22] and they view the world from that perspective, giving priority in their theologies to the insights of the poor and oppressed, who know God as an ally in their struggles for liberation, responding to their concrete material and spiritual concerns in history.[23]

The emergence of Third World feminist and womanist theologies occurred within the context of liberation theological discourses and within their counterpart struggles in the social arena. It was also influenced by the twentieth-century women's movement in Europe and North America, which reached its zenith during the 1970s and 1980s, in terms of social activism and of academic feminist theorizing. The liberation movements and theological discourses of Third World and U.S. Black men and White feminists had something to contribute to the struggles of Third World and U.S. Black women. Yet they were both incapable of representing the multidimensional issues that characterized the life struggles of Third World and U.S. Black women. The male theologians from their respective communities addressed issues of poverty, imperialism, and racism without critiquing patriarchy and sexism, while the White feminists spoke to issues of sexism and patriarchy without critiquing racism and Western capitalist imperialism. Third World and U.S. Black female seminarians soon discovered that only they could bring adequate attention to their situations of oppression within the interlocking structures of classism imperialism, racism, and sexism.

Another significant factor in the development of feminist theologies across the continents has been the increased access that women have had to formal theological education especially after World War II. While there are still significant obstacles preventing some Third World women from entering the academy, others have been trained in institutions in their native countries as well as in Europe and North America.[24] In 1974 the World Council of Churches (WCC) sponsored two international conferences on women's issues. Four years later, the WCC began a three-year study (1978–1981) on gender issues and the church. Inspired by the United Nations' Decade for Women (1975–1985), the WCC also declared 1988–1998 as the Ecumenical Decade of the Churches in Solidarity with Women. Each of these activities contributed to the development of feminist consciousness and theologies in the Third World.[25]

Although some Third World women theologians, such as Marianne Katoppo and Mercy Oduyoye, had begun to articulate a feminist perspective from their respective Asian and African contexts, the first significant collection of Third World feminist theologies was the deliberate result of a collaborative endeavor at the EATWOT conference in Oaxtepec, Mexico, in 1986. By 1981, when EATWOT had met in New Delhi, India, the women participants discovered that the sexist traditions and patriarchal structures they opposed in the church and society were far from absent in the very organization that decried structural oppression and injustice in social and ecclesiastical institutions and relationships. The male theologians in EATWOT were sexist, and they belittled women's issues within the group. Virginia Fabella summarizes the experience:

> At the Delhi Conference in 1981 . . . it became clear to the women
> that for the majority of the EATWOT men, practice did not match
> the theory. As liberation theologians, they spoke against all forms of
> oppression and admitted their interrelatedness, but they remained
> basically sexist in their attitudes towards women's liberation and
> theological intervention.[26]

The women of EATWOT were determined to relate the imperatives of the Christian faith to the sexist oppression suffered by women in the Third World. Thus, they formed a Women's Commission of EATWOT at the 1983 Geneva Conference[27] and organized conferences in Latin America (Buenos Aires, Argentina, October 30–November 3, 1985), Asia (Manila, Philippines, November 21–30, 1985), and Africa (Port Harcourt, Nigeria, August 19–23, 1986, and Yaoundé, Cameroon, August 3–9, 1986). After Geneva, EATWOT women met to discuss their experiences and to frame a theological position on women's oppression in the Third World. As a result of that meeting, they produced *With Passion and Compassion: Third World Women Doing Theology*, a compilation of select papers from each of the smaller continental conferences. Several edited books containing some of the papers from the continental meetings were also published: Elsa Tamez's *Through Her Eyes: Women's Theology from Latin America* and Virginia Fabella and Sun Ai Lee Park's *We Dare to Dream: Doing Theology as Asian Women* were both released in 1989. In each regional conference and in the larger intercontinental meetings, the women gave deliberate attention to five aspects of theological construction: Christology, ecclesiology, spirituality, the Bible, and methodology.

On a wider scale, the EATWOT women have also identified focus issues for lasting theological attention. They encourage African, Asian, and Latin American women in theological studies to contribute to (1) analyses of the status and experiences of women in the Christian church and society; (2) comprehensive interdisciplinary analyses of their native countries, that is, the social, religiocultural, economic, and political circumstances that affect the quality of women's lives; and (3) theological reflection and biblical analysis using the tools of liberation theology and also indigenous religiocultural resources, such as folklore, myths, and other oral traditions.[28]

Although liberation theologians, male and female, made a radical hermeneutical departure from the Eurocentric theological tradition, they did not sever all methodological ties with their former teachers and academic interlocutors. For, even with the distinct focus on the experiences of the oppressed, liberation theologians derive their conceptual categories, that is, their structures for explaining the faith testimonies of the oppressed from Eurocentric theological discourse. Hence they provide us with repeated reflections upon Christology, ecclesiology, soteriology, revelation, eschatology, and so on. This is not altogether inappropriate, especially if they continue to do theological reflection that is exclusively based upon the orthodox Christian faith testimony of oppressed communities. This type of theological "orthodoxy," however, is inadequate for a Caribbean theology that is appropriately informed by African-derived religions.

My articulation of a Caribbean theology of liberation is African-centered and, therefore, methodologically unorthodox. Yet it stands hermeneutically in the same camp with the theologies of liberation referred to above. As such, its only starting point is African-Jamaican people's testimony, and their testimony of their liberative encounters with the Divine Community is the norm through which I understand the sources of their religious traditions. More than anything, I proceed to do critical theological reflection with the awareness that, as survivors of colonial Christian evangelism, practitioners of African-derived religions have scrutinized the sources of Christian faith and practice. As a result, their African-centered interpretations and, in some cases, appropriations of Christian sources undoubtedly challenge African-Jamaican identifications with orthodox Christian traditions.

Within the liberation theological discourse, then, the theology I attempt here claims space among the orthodox voices as a "subjugated" theology emerging from subjugated communities and buried knowledges that abound within them.[29] The Caribbean theology that I seek to construct is necessarily embodied and grounded in a somatic epistemology. It maintains critical distance from ideational theology as a Eurocentric articulation of faith testimony, which is false when applied to the African-Jamaican religious context. African-Jamaican faith testimony, for the most part, is not written in texts and therefore has not prompted a tradition of ideational theology. Rather it is embodied concretely in the lives of the testifying people. In this context, testimony is enacted, dramatized, and ritualized. Thus, an authentic African-Jamaican theology must begin with an assessment of embodied religious experiences in order to derive categories for proper systematic interpretations of their liberating content.

The point of departure between what is attempted in this Caribbean theology and what has come before in Eurocentric theologies is methodology. Christian theology, as conceptual theology, often characterizes Christian worship and practice. And in Eurocentric Christianity, theology has encouraged the belief that body and spirituality are contradistinct. Thus the polarization of religiosity as spiritual and sacred and sensuality as secular and profane encourages bodily denigration and alienation and consequently leads to stationary forms of worship. Within the context of African-derived religions, theological ideas emerge from concretized practice, ritual, and embodied spirituality. Because Africans understand the body to be a vehicle for spiritual expression, theological sources are composed in the "text" of corporeal mobility where a somatic memory of the community's heritage is recorded and recalled through ritual performance.

African-Derived Religions: The "Untouchables" in African Diasporic Theological Discourse

Silence is one of the most potent forms of protest or expressions of indifference. In any type of communication, what one does not say is as important as what one does say. Within the theologies emerging from regions populated by communities of African descent, conversations regarding the African religious heritage and its impact upon the African diaspora are less than satisfying. One reason for the lack of attention to the African heritage, especially as manifested in the African-derived religions, has to do with their status as subterranean traditions, which were forced into hiding and seclusion. Hence their invisibility, relative to the visibility of Christianity, contributes to their marginal treatment in African diasporic theological reflection.

In North America, the African character of Black people's religion was primarily debated outside the theological arena, within social science disciplines. Black theology concerned itself with Black *Christianity* and to some extent the Nation of Islam. Although Gayraud Wilmore has discussed the survival of specific African-derived religious trajectories in North America,[30] virtually no theologian associated with the Black liberationist discourse has attempted a comprehensive theological statement that is derived from the beliefs and practices of the African-based religions.

One notable exception is Josiah Young. Young defines his project, however, as a "Pan-African" theology. Where Black and womanist theologians have failed to draw theological insights directly from African-derived religions, Young specifically aims to interpret Black religion Afrocentrically, that is, in terms of its Africanness. Young acknowledges that Black religion is "related to Christianity" as is stressed in the theology of James Cone.[31] However Young's "perception is related to Pan-Africanization and to a theological perspective that does not attempt to Christianize religious dimensions that are independent of dogmatic categories."[32] With this statement, Young is not referring exclusively to African-derived religions but to "other forms of African-American 'orientation' " which, according to Charles Long, "have had great critical and creative power. They have often touched deeper religious issues than those of the church leaders of their time."[33] Thus, Young maintains, "Black religion, anchored in slave religion, signifies varieties of African-American expressions such as Vodun, San-tería, 'Hoodoo,' the Moorish Science Temple, the Black Jews, the Nation of Islam, the Shrine of the Black Madonna, Kwanzaa, as well as the black church."[34] Young also identifies African spiritual modalities in jazz music.

Young's approach to Pan-African theology is consonant with the theolog-ical approach I have attempted to develop in this work. Young addresses the issue of anti-Africanness in Black North American religion and in Pan-African theory and practice. His project denounces the scandal of anthropological pov-erty in Africa and African North America and suggests that a critical and pro-phetic Pan-African theology holds tremendous possibilities for liberating expressions of Afrocentric theology and praxis.

Young's Pan-African theology, however, will benefit from conversations with womanist and Caribbean theologians. Young makes tangential references to African-Caribbean religious experience but neglects to reflect specifically upon the Caribbean reality as a source for Pan-African theological construction. Acknowledging this limitation in his project, he writes:

> I focus on the transatlantic dimension of blacks of Africa and the United States. I am more familiar with the black experience of the United States and African history and culture than I am with the experiences of blacks of the Caribbean and South America. (I do, however, devote an entire chapter to a seminal progenitor of Pan-African tradition, Edward Blyden of St. Thomas, and know that much of Pan-African theory is owed to Jamaicans, i.e., Marcus Gar-vey and Harold Moody; and to Trinidadians, i.e., Sylvester Williams, C.L.R. James, and George Padmore.)[35]

Although womanist theology was well under way by the time Young pub-lished his work in 1992, he does not engage its exponents in his theological reflection. There are two issues to keep in mind with regard to women and the African diasporic religious experience. First, there is the task of identifying women as participants in the shaping of religious traditions and as agents of resistance to both external and internal oppression. Second is the issue of solidarity and vocational commitment to constructing liberating theologies that reflect the critical insights of womanist theologians. In his work, Young ac-knowledges, "I embark on no procrustean enterprise. I do not represent the totality of the Pan-African experience, which is a varied experience of oppressed women and men of diverse geopolitical contexts."[36]

To be sure, it requires a little more than patience to locate and retrieve a female legacy in the historical shaping of Pan-Africanist theory. However, the challenge before all African diasporic theologians, as posed by African-American womanist theologians, is to protest women's invisibility through careful works of recovery. Even in the absence of thick descriptions pertaining to women's specific experiences as religious subjects in history, it is incumbent upon us to interrogate the sources we do have and to subject them to the criteria of womanist theology. This might allow us the opportunity to make some con-nections between what we learn from history and what we know in the present moment about women's multidimensional experiences, religiosity, and agency in Black struggles for social change.

On this note I am challenged to demonstrate my commitment to womanist theological imperatives as they have been articulated thus far. Admittedly, this study is not a womanist project, per se. Additionally, in my focus upon the invisible constitutions of African religiosity in Jamaican culture, the invisibility of women and the subjugation of female agency abound in both primary and secondary sources. Even within the social science research, which features Jamaican women healers or practitioners of African-derived religions, emphasis is placed upon ritual processes and the cultural controversy regarding "African survivals," "creolization," or "syncretism." A serious focus upon the relationships among women's oppression, women's resistance to oppression, and African-derived religions is long overdue in the social science literature on African-derived religions of the Caribbean. I speculate that one reason for neglect in this area has to do with the defensive and apologetic nature of the discourse, which is often preoccupied with "proving" that Caribbean religiosity is deeply informed by "authentic" features or retentions from African religions. Although I presuppose the African sources of African-Jamaican religiosity, this work too is guided by an apologetic preoccupation with revaluing things and peoples African, especially African-derived religions. Within this framework, I discuss, although not exhaustively, some emancipatory and oppressive themes pertaining to women and to female imagery.

Like its native interlocutor, Black theology, womanist theology has not been shaped by the insights of African-derived religions. Womanist theologians have concerned themselves with the primary task of defining the relationship between the terms *womanist*, as derived from Alice Walker, and *theology*, as traditionally developed by Western Christian thinkers. In so doing, they have uniformly demonstrated their commitment to Black Christian women's experiences as their sources, norms, and categories suggest.[37]

It is fitting for our discussion to note that womanist theologians and ethicists such as Kelly Brown Douglas, Delores Williams, Cheryl Sanders, and others have launched scathing critiques against the androcentric focus in Afrocentric theory.[38] Womanist theologians, on the whole, appear reluctant to embrace the Afrocentric approach to scholarship not only because it is "thoroughly sexist"[39] but because it rejects Christianity as Eurocentric and incompatible with African religiosity.[40] Afrocentricity, however, is no more sexist than Black theology or Black Christianity, with both of which womanist theologians remain affiliated.

For the most part, womanist theologians have been wedded to the church and Christian theology through their faith and vocational commitments, representing a prophetic tradition that constructively critiques sexist traditions in Black theology and the Black church. I admire the tenacity of womanist theology in testing and questioning the validity of Afrocentric theory for Black women. I also suspect that men will never lead the way in articulating a liberating social theory or Black theology that satisfies the concerns of womanist theorists and theologians.

This notwithstanding, as womanist theologians wrestle with sexism and patriarchy in Black theology and the Black church, a next and important step in womanist theology might be the exploration of African-derived religions, where feminine images of the Divine appear more promising than the Christian male Trinity (even with Grant's Black female Christ).[41] The practice of Yoruba, Vodun, Akan, and other African-derived religions is not the exclusive property of African or even Caribbean immigrants. African-American women and men have sojourned, in many cases, from Christian backgrounds into these traditions to meet manifestations of the Divine that heal, fulfill, liberate, and empower.

In addition, the moral problem of anti-Africanness afflicts many of them as they navigate the embattling terrain of Christian Afrophobia. I have heard testimony after testimony from African-American women who are tired of hiding their religious identity as Yoruba practitioners from their families for fear of rejection. African-American women who choose such paths have testimonies to share with Christian women, and womanist theologians can participate in facilitating that sharing by diversifying their theological categories and reflecting on Black women's African-derived religiosity and spirituality in ways that are liberating for Christian-identified and non-Christian women. In fact, an inclusive approach is more consistent with Alice Walker's articulation of womanism.[42] My African-centered womanist theology of the cross, inspired by Kumina women's spirituality, is an attempt to do just this.

In the last decade novel voices in Black theology have also emerged with questions that are relevant to the study undertaken here. Anthony Pinn, for example, has made one of the most recent controversial contributions to Black theological discourse in North America. Pinn revisits the issue of theodicy, initially debated by first-generation Black theologians in response to William Jones's scrutinizing text, *Is God a White Racist?*[43] Pinn expands upon Jones's critique of Black theology, arguing against its professed liberationist norm and purpose, given its inability to critically address the theodical contradictions in the Black Christian religious experience. Pinn argues that Black humanistic responses to Black suffering have been marginalized within Black culture, especially due to the dominant influence of Black Christian traditions—the Black church, spirituals, popular notions of redemptive suffering, and so on. As a corrective, Pinn contends that Black humanism provides more realistic and ethical foundations for a liberation praxis that will enable African Americans to make comprehensive critiques of their collective suffering and respond with effective strategies that sincerely enhance Black people's quality of life and well-being.

While I concur with Pinn in his critique of Black Christian traditions that promote unethical and problematic views on Black suffering and the theodical contradictions in Black Christian religious experience, Pinn constructs his argument too narrowly around a dichotomy between Black Christianity and Black humanism. It is here, I would argue, that both Black Christian theologians and Pinn, as a Black humanist, exclude African-derived religions from the conversation about theodicy and the Black religious experience. For example,

Pinn appropriately critiques Dwight Hopkins for interpreting primary historical sources pertaining to the Black slave experience through a Christian theological lens, without convincing justification. "All too often," says Pinn:

> non-Christian resources are forced into the parameters of theistic expression. And so, even non-Christian expression must point to the workings of God. Dwight Hopkins demonstrates this tendency when discussing trickster figures . . . in Black literature. Hopkins does not entertain the possibility that these figures represent human efforts at liberation owing to the nonexistence of God. Rather, he asserts that "savior intermediaries" point to God working with humans and nature, and thereby confirm the strict theistic nature of Black religion.[44]

Despite this poignant insight, there is a lingering hermeneutical problem if we neglect to explore how African-derived religions provide resources for what Pinn interprets in the trickster, Brer Rabbit stories as Black humanism. In fact, Brer Rabbit stories point to the very understudied phenomenon that I have been outlining here in the Jamaican religious context. Brer Rabbit, like Anancy the Spider in the Caribbean, is a signifier for African theistic power and points to the Divine or invisible personalities in classical African religions, which were attacked for obliteration by Euro-Christian missionaries and Eurocentric Black converts. The secularization of African religious resources developed as one of the most effective strategies for protecting and sustaining the value and viability of African theism and religiosity in Christian contexts that fostered anti-Africanness, Afrophobia, and hostility toward African religious cultures. Because White and Eurocentric Black Christian evangelists understood African communotheism and religious practices as antithetical to Christian trinitarianism and religious practices, they were officially forbidden. The consequences have been that classical African religious resources have both subtly informed the Black Christian tradition and explicitly influenced the evolution of what we might term Black secular culture.

Pinn acknowledges that Hopkins and other Black theologians admit that the Black religious experience "can be Christian and non-Christian; but it must be theistic."[45] Following the insights of Charles Long, who argued that sacred and secular experiences together comprise Black religiosity, Pinn maintains that "such thinking is myopic and . . . leaves a wealth of Black expression untapped as religious insight. Hence in considering what Black theology says about Black suffering, it is irresponsible to limit the investigation to theistic responses—irrespective of the relative volume and majority status of theistic responses." Although Pinn follows this comment with the assertion that "this epistemologically based expansion must . . . eventually include a conversation with other nonmajority Black religious traditions (such as the Nation of Islam, Spiritual churches, and Voodoo),"[46] by neglecting to explore the invisibility and aggressive repression of African-derived religions in the history of the Christianization of African Americans and African Caribbeans, Pinn only delays the conversation that would compel Black theologians, Pinn included, to begin to consider African communotheistic responses to suffering and evil.

In the end, while I find Pinn's denunciation of Black Christian theistic responses to Black suffering convincing, without a proper analysis of African-derived religions, he is unjustified in making conclusive statements about the hazardous impact of Black theistic religious experience upon Black people's interpretations of Black suffering. I think Pinn is misguided when he uses evidence from a Brer Rabbit narrative to argue in favor of "strong humanism,"[47] which according to Pinn, "considers theistic answers to existential questions simplistic and geared toward psychological comfort without respect for the complex nature of the human condition."[48] In the narrative, Brer Rabbit petitions God for a long tail, and after some exchange, God reluctantly promises to furnish it if Brer Rabbit can accomplish three difficult tasks. When Brer Rabbit shows competence in completing each task, God becomes annoyed, slams the door to the "Big House," and scares Brer Rabbit into hiding under a tree. In response, God strikes the tree with lightning and tells Brer Rabbit to get his own long tail if he is so smart.[49]

The exchange between Brer Rabbit (the secularized African trickster deity) and God (the African Supreme Deity) does not represent the struggle between humanism and theism because both characters in the narrative are members of the Divine Community. Pinn appropriately sees ultimate value in the narrative's humanistic motif because humanism is essential in African religiosity and ethics. Pinn is apparently unaware, though, that humanism also coheres well with theism in African and African-derived religions. In fact human agency, that is, effort, work, sacrifices, and transformation, is necessary for all religious solutions to human suffering. Furthermore, divine involvement is categorically coupled with human effort or manifested through human mediums, who act as divine agents in helping to alleviate human suffering and in solving human problems.

Dominique Zahan's research on African religions, which is based upon multiple continental studies, lends support to this claim. He concludes, "African religion is a kind of humanism, one which, moving away from [the human being] only to return to [the human being], seizes in the course of its voyage all that is not of [humanity itself] and which surpasses [the human being]. This humanism is the basis for an individual and social ethic."[50] Zahan goes on to say:

> [Humanity] was not made for God or for the universe; [humanity] exists for [itself] and carries within [itself] the justification of [its] existence and of [its] religious and moral perfection. It is not to "please" God or out of love for God that [the African person] "prays," implores, or makes sacrifices, but rather to become [oneself] and to realize the order in which [one] finds [oneself] implicated . . . when [a person] venerates the divinity, it is not for the glory of God but for [one's] own personal development.[51]

If the Brer Rabbit narrative must be interpreted polemically, the struggle, I would argue, is not between humanism and theism but between African-derived religious values (which affirm humanism and theism as compatible) and Christian hostility toward African culture, as implied by "God's"[52] attitude toward Brer Rabbit. Furthermore, in petitioning God for a long tail, Brer Rabbit appears to operate with the type of African humanistic consciousness of "personal development" or self-improvement described above by Zahan and portrayed by the activities and attitudes of the Divine Community in many African myths. The claim that the Brer Rabbit narrative points to tensions between African religiosity and Eurocentric Christianity might appear to be mere conjecture. However, in the broader context of African-American culture it is more than plausible. Again, Pinn furnishes evidence from the blues tradition that supports this position. For example, he examines the following lines, noting that the "blues promotes a raw religiosity which includes African practices in various forms—hoodoo, voodoo and conjure":

> Yes I went out on the mountain, looked over in Jerusalem, (2×)
> Well, I see them hoodoo women, ooh Lord, makin' up in their
>   low-down tents.
>
> Well I'm going to Newport to see Aunt Caroline Dye, (2×)
> She's a fortune-teller, oh Lord, she sure don't tell no lie.[53]

Confronted with the historical evidence of African religiosity in African-American culture, in this case the blues, Pinn recognizes its value and significance when he writes (in response to Muddy Waters's references to his "mojo"), "[T]he merit of hoodoo as a system responsive to existential need is highlighted. And in this way, an alternative to mainstream Black Christianity is offered."[54] Yet Pinn's discussion is weakened by his truncated analysis of African-derived religions, which were not being offered as "an alternative to mainstream Black Christianity" at all. African-derived religions were the primal religions of enslaved Africans in North America (not an alternative), which White and later Eurocentric Black Christian evangelists endeavored to extinguish. With reference to Black religious experience, the tension in the blues and other historical Black cultural productions is not humanism versus theism or the secular versus the sacred but non-Christian, African-derived religious traditions versus Christianity. It is true, though, that where the Black church was constructed as sacred, African-derived religious traditions were constructed as secular. In the social commentary of the blues, we hear the Christian condemnation of secularism, sex, and African-derived religious traditions as belonging to the devil's domain. Hence, people who sing and dance the blues are lewd and promiscuous, inclined toward Hoodoo/Voodoo, and thus are not saved but sinners.

The complex nature of Black cultural evolution in North America is one that requires extensive research on African-derived religious traditions in their variegated forms of Conjure, Hoodoo, Vodun, and so on. Without a proper investigation into the legacy of African religious resources in North America and their impact upon Black religious experience, Pinn's Black humanism only promotes the muteness and erasure of African-derived religions in the Black religious experience. Whereas traditional Black and Caribbean Christian theologians have used Christian theological categories to interpret Black religious experience from slavery to the present day, Pinn uses Black humanism to categorically interpret voices of protest against Christian traditions, especially Christian theism, without fairly considering the significance of the explicit and subtle presence of African religious (including theistic) traditions among those protest voices. Pinn's narrow and dualistic structuring of the debate as humanism versus theism does not permit him to consider the possibility that African Americans, represented by such protest material, may have rejected Christianity not because they were atheists or strong humanists but because of its Afrophobic and anti-African theology, piety, and ecclesiology. Thus, in response to Pinn, who "offer[s] Black humanism as an important aspect of Black religious reflection which resolves the problem of evil (i.e., Black suffering) without collapsing into redemptive suffering argumentation,"[55] I argue that African-derived religions offer life-affirming *theistic* resources that function in consort with *human* efforts in addressing multiple forms of suffering, evil, and oppression, as reflected in my extrapolation of an African-centered womanist theology of the cross.

Before concluding with theoretical and theological reflections on African-derived religions in Jamaica, it is important to raise questions about Latin American liberation theological responses to anti-Africanness in the Latin American context. While Latin American theologians make passing references to "racism," "Blacks," or "African culture" in their works, on the whole, they have resigned the race problem to African North Americans.[56] If there is any place that Africanness is unquestionably subjugated and rendered invisible or trivial in the African diaspora, it is Latin America. As Lloyd Stennette, a Costa Rican Episcopal priest, writes:

> The problem of blacks in Latin America is practically the same [as that of the indigenous people]. Often people simply try to evade the issue. It seems as if we, as members of the black race, don't even exist on the continent. But there are millions of blacks in Latin America, in Brazil especially but also in the Caribbean, the countries of Central America, Venezuela, and Colombia.[57]

Latin American theology has yet to acknowledge the insidiousness of racism and anti-Africanness in Latin American sociocultural beliefs and attitudes. What is more, Latin American theologians have neglected to make the connection between anti-Africanness and poverty in their countries. Africans comprise some of the poorest communities in Latin America while Whites comprise some of the wealthiest. This is a social problem for which Latin American theology should show concern as it decries socially constructed oppressions, especially economic injustice.

To be sure, some of the Latin American theologians have introduced critical questions about racism and African Latin Americans. Writing about challenges confronting the Latin American church, Leonardo Boff declared in 1984:

> The church in Latin America, and especially that in Brazil, faces a theological challenge of unprecedented historical magnitude. Our continent's races bear witness to great cultures such as those of the Incas, the Mayas, the Aymaras, etc. It is also populated by European immigrants, primitive indigenous peoples, and millions of blacks and mulattos. Brazil, with almost forty million blacks is, after Nigeria, the largest black nation in the world. Very few elements from Afro-Brazilian or Amerindian cultures have been incorporated into Christianity. Blacks are in the process of developing an immensely rich cultural and religious vitality. They want to be Christians within their own cultural milieu, one that will allow their own experiences [to be] incarnated in a way that will permit a new model of Latin-Afro-Indigenous Catholicism to be born.[58]

Others have also called attention to the general posture of indifference toward addressing racism and the African experience among Latin American theologians. In the fifteenth-anniversary edition of the English translation of Gustavo Gutiérrez's *A Theology of Liberation*, Gutiérrez acknowledges in the new introduction:

> One of our social lies has been the claim that there is no racism in Latin America. There may indeed be no racist laws as in some other countries, but there are rigid racial customs that are no less serious for being hidden. The marginalization of Amerindian and black populations, and the contempt in which they are held, are situations we cannot accept as human beings, much less as Christians. These populations themselves are becoming increasingly aware of their situations and are beginning to claim their most basic rights. . . . The racial question represents a major challenge to the Christian community, one to which we are only now beginning to respond. The approaching five hundredth anniversary of the evangelization of America should be the occasion for an examination of conscience regarding the immense human cost historically connected with that evangelization—I mean the destruction of individuals and of cultures. Such an examination will help us define a commitment of the church to races that have for centuries been neglected and mistreated.[59]

It is a sobering probability that the Latin American people will have to rely on the concerted effort of African–Latin American theologians to produce extensive treatments of racism, the African–Latin American experience, and African-derived religions in Latin America. Unfortunately, they are not yet represented among the cadre of theologians who have been definitive in the shaping of liberation and feminist theology in Latin America.

One of the most forceful articulations of the estrangement between Latin American liberation theology and the African experience in Latin America was penned by a regional Latin American section of the Association of Third World Theologians (la Asociación de Teólogos del Tercer Mundo, ASETT). Their publication of *Cultura Negra y Teologia (Black Culture and Theology)* in 1986 brought visibility to racism and anti-Africanness in the sociocultural institutions and economic structures in Latin American countries. In several essays, contributors discuss syncretism and the African character of some Latin American expressions of Christianity. The significance of this collaborative work is that it applies the imperatives of Latin American theology to the situation of Black people's anthropological impoverishment in their respective countries. The summary on the back cover conveys it best:

> Liberation theology cannot be reduced to a generic theology as, for example, theologies of peace, politics, hope, etc., but points to a real and concrete compromise in doing theology. From the theological point of view, the Black issue demands an empowerment of theology that will address the concrete situations of oppression, discrimination and racism in which the Black community lives. Liberation theology has to address the relative themes of this issue. It will have to divorce itself from the White oppressive perspective and will have a new cosmology from the Black perspective. The issue of Black identity and theology also states more radical demands. It demands the empowerment of theology, so that it takes on a deep sensibility for sharing the problems of the Black community. Only the one who is Black knows what it means to be Black in Afro-America.[60]

The essays comprising this volume have yet to be taken seriously by some of the most prominent liberation theologians. Most important, they explicate the problems of racism and the negation of Black culture as they relate to women and the poor and their sociopolitical struggles for liberation. This is a welcome and, I would argue, genuine perspective as we await theological reflections that emphasize the relationship between cultural oppression and material poverty. *Cultura Negra y Teologia* indicates to me that the classic divide between inculturationists and liberationists is a false one.[61]

Although the face of Latin American feminist theology is by and large "mestizo," Ana María Tepedino's remarks at the 1992 EATWOT General Assembly on spirituality are encouraging. She maintains:

> I have some friends who tell me about their experience: they are Black and have been raised in the Catholic faith, and they believe in God, in Jesus and the Holy Spirit. These last few years, with the appearance of Black movements, their consciences have been aroused about their roots, and they begin to have a double way of relationship to God, but little by little they are integrating the two ways in a new way of living spirituality. The Black spirituality is matriarchal, and the priesthood of women is another way of working religiously;

they create community and they influence the spirituality of a part of society.[62]

Tepedino's comments lend some support to my perspective regarding the emancipatory womanist resources in African-derived religions. Here it appears that she speaks with reference to unorthodox Christianities and not directly to African-derived religions that are not deeply penetrated with Christian symbols and rituals. Even as we see growing theological support for "unorthodox" expressions of Christianity in the African–Latin American experience, the expanse of the discourse has not generated enough specific discussion on the African-derived religions that bear the names of Vodun (Dominican Republic), Yoruba/Santería (Cuba, Puerto Rico, Venezuela), Candomblé (Brazil), and so on.

Theologians from the African diaspora, especially the Americas (North, Central, South) and the Caribbean, appear convinced by the public face of Christian piety that African religious traditions are dying if not dead. The mask of Christian piety in African diasporic religiosity might well be the African survivalist response to what the Catholic Brazilian priest Mauro Batista calls "the ideology that seeks to make Black people white, the ideology of *branqueamento*." Batista goes on to say that this ideology

is present and powerfully operative in our multiracial society. How might we describe this ideology? Basically it is profoundly dualistic and Manichean [sic] in its view of reality. It says that white is good, black is bad. Being black means embodying everything that is worthy of discredit and hate and that should be discarded rather than given recognition. The human ideal is being white, or being human and being white are completely equated. This ideology is not just to be found in the white population. It has penetrated every level of society and struck deep roots in blacks as well. As a result, blacks reject their own blackness, their selfhood, and their real identity as black human beings.[63]

Theologians of the African diaspora might want to consider, then, that some manifestations of African-derived religious traditions have not yet come out of hiding. This is true especially in places like the United States, where Black theologians ought not presume that virtually all African Americans are Christian devotees with sprinkles of Black Muslims across Black communities.[64]

Perhaps the exaggerated perception of the Christianness of African-American religiosity could be rectified if theologians develop the necessary interest and patience to explore and acknowledge the symbolic, presuppositional, and ideological foundations of African-American and African-Caribbean religious behavior. In other words, we should not be convinced of African-American and African-Caribbean religiocultural distance from ancient African traditions because, on the surface and in plain view, we may not find the parental sources for sundry religiocultural traditions across the African diaspora. This approach is a search for tangible evidence that proves, beyond a shadow of a doubt, the African authenticity of African-Caribbean and African-American identities. Yet, even where particular religiocultural practices may be seen both in Africa and in the Caribbean/America, is it not incumbent that we ask other questions about the contexts in which practices were preserved and about how those varied contexts have been influencing and modifying the value and expressions of such practices?

The truth is that our awareness of specific conspicuous African retentions, which are traceable to their continental sources, is only an elementary step in our endeavors to decipher and understand the legacy of Africa in the African diaspora. What is further required is a sensibility for detecting and apprehending that which is intangible within African diasporic culture and religion. The intangibles and invisibles of human experience—one's intuitive inclinations, one's presuppositions and ideas, one's judgments and (emotional) sentiments, one's perception and "sense of situation,"[65] one's gestures, modes of expression, movements, sense of time, rhythm, silence, beauty, and tragedy—in total, one's approach and attitude toward world experiences must be probed before we can do justice to African retentions and Africanness as controlling factors in the shaping of African-Caribbean and African-American identities. By "controlling factors" I do not mean they are unamalgamated or unfused with European, Amerindian, or Asian traditions. Considering the experiences of cultural interactions and interpenetration among these traditions, the Africanness of Black religiocultural experience is like a thread stitching all of the African, European, Amerindian, and Asian cultural elements together into one garment, which is still recognizable if one examines the garment carefully, especially its underside. Jamaican sociologist Barry Chevannes's approach to the study of African retentions is insightful here. He argues:

> The question is not whether Revivalism can be found in Africa or not, or even the matter of spirit possession, the drumming and the dancing. It's not whether Voodoo is traceable to Dahomey, as it is, or Santería to the Yoruba and Kumina to the Congo. That's not the point. The point is to understand the outlook of the people on the world and how that outlook has shaped their institutions.[66]

In another article, Chevannes forwards a sound analysis of the conspicuously institutionalized and inconspicuously disseminated African-derived traditions that characterize Jamaican religion and culture. He maintains that "the small and numerically insignificant sects, which can still be found in the little nooks and crannies of a country like Jamaica, and which seem to be so remote from the mainstream of religious activity in the country, are indeed the organized expression of a much deeper consciousness."[67] Chevannes became convinced of the relationship between the "deeper consciousness" and the "small and numerically insignificant sects" as he began to look critically at contemporary events[68] which "reveal how deep-seated are the beliefs which we normally trace to our African past, despite the years, decades and even centuries of Christian, European indoctrination, and despite repression of beliefs and practices which have been condemned as contrary to Christianity." And he correctly points out that "many of these beliefs and practices do not appear in the normal day-to-day life of Church members but, under emotional stress brought on by crisis, they sometimes assume ascendancy over Christian orthodox beliefs."[69]

Chevannes's conclusions complement the findings of my research and the claim that constructing theology in the Caribbean context is a new kind of prophetic task which presupposes the integral role of spirituality and religious experience. But, when I say "religious experience," I am now referring to the invisible and intangible experiences which retain the quality of invisibility as a result of Eurocentric Christian anti-Africanness and its credence among Caribbean populations. The prophetic task calls for a specific type of insight, which might be called a gift of discernment or perception. This gift can be harnessed as theologians search for the "evidence of things unseen."[70] I would submit, though, that the insight into "things unseen" is already harnessed among the African diaspora's anthropologically poor—in their spiritual struggles to defy Otherness[71] and in their religious respect for invisible power (their Ancestors, spirits, and deities). As such their religious institutions are extensions of the type of "faith" described in the Christian Scriptures' Epistle to the Hebrews:

> the assurance of things hoped for,
> the conviction of things not seen.
> Indeed, by faith our ancestors received approval.[72]

From Selective Memory to Collective Memory in Caribbean Theological Construction

In the preceding chapters, I have stated the problem of anthropological poverty and defined it more precisely as anti-Africanness and Afrophobia in the history of African-Jamaican religious experience. Before arriving at this point, I explored significant motifs of African-derived religiosity as they pertain to problem solving. In many African religious traditions, when a person experiences misfortune he asks for a consultation with a diviner. During divination the problem and the method for rectifying it are stated as was proposed in the introduction to this project. Rectification rituals almost always include libation (invocation), incantation (prayers), offering (sacrificial food, beverages, implements, and so on), visitation (ancestral or divine incarnations or manifestations), and communion (partaking of the offering). And so, with the problem stated, I proceeded through each chapter and through each motif with the aim of trying to explore more deeply the problem of anti-Africanness and Afrophobia in the Jamaican religious experience toward the end of gathering possible solutions.

As I turn now to suggest directions for a Caribbean theology of collective memory, I return to the issues raised in the introduction regarding the compatibility or incompatibility between African-derived religions and the discipline of theology. And I do so in conversation with Caribbean theologians, especially with the two most prominent Jamaican liberation theologians, Noel Erskine and Lewin Williams.

Toward a Theoretical Analysis of African-Jamaican Religions

Noel Erskine's contribution to Jamaican theology and to Caribbean theology in general should not be understated. Before Erskine's concentrated study on the African-Jamaican religious experience (1981), English-speaking Caribbean theologians attempted to frame and respond to the problem of identity in the church and society. Their discourses were published under the auspices of the Caribbean Conference of Churches in 1973. *Troubling the Waters* exposed the detrimental effects of Eurocentric Christianity on the shaping of African-Caribbean Christian identity. As stated by Ashley Smith, "[T]he intensity of black self-hatred, body-shame and fatalism is due mainly to the use of religion as an instrument for the inculcation of the 'white bias' in non-European peoples of the region."[73] Reflections on liturgy, doctrine, colonial theology, the church, and family explore specific manifestations of the identity crisis and the church's identification with the oppressed as essential to healthy assertions of identity in the Caribbean. However, as Erskine duly notes, *Troubling the Waters* "does not deal in any significant way with the history and theology of Caribbean spirituality."[74] Erskine introduces his work, then, as "a response to *Troubling the Waters* as the study of oppressed people and their search for freedom in history seeks to provide a window through which many Caribbean peoples will be able to see themselves and hence better understand their quest to be more fully human."[75] In this regard, Erskine's *Decolonizing Theology* is an indispensable contribution to the search for identity and freedom in Jamaica and in the larger Caribbean.

With particular reference to the problem of anti-Africanness, Erskine's historical inquiry leads him to the African roots of "Black religion." However, his text traces mainly the Christian expressions of the African religious heritage in Jamaica. Although I locate Revival Zion and Rastafari within the framework of African-derived and African-centered religions, respectively, Erskine emphasizes the unorthodox "Christian" content of both traditions. The main difference between our interpretive approaches is that, based upon my field research and contemporary scholarship, I understand the African appropriation of symbols from Christian sources, or the African appropriation of Christian sources in themselves (for example, the Bible or biblical concepts and icons), to be the persistence of African-derived religion through oppressive time/history. Erskine, however, values this hermeneutical strategy in that it yields Black cultic[76] expressions of Christianity, that is, "Black religion." Perhaps Erskine neglects to draw any theological insights from the Kumina tradition because it is so conspicuously African-identified and exists alongside Christianity. In other words, Kumina does not wear a Christian performance mask as does Revival Zion and, therefore, cannot be interpreted as an (unorthodox) expression of Christianity.

Theophus Smith's theoretical analysis of African North American religious experience as *conjured* lends significant support to my critique of Erskine's concept of Black religion with reference to African-Jamaican religious experience. According to Smith:

> [C]onjuring culture by means of biblical figures operates covertly in black America because conjure, in its traditional form as folk magic, has been censured and marginalized since the earliest days of missionary supervision of black Christianity. In reaction to such censure, the use of biblical figures to conjure culture involved a collective strategy to cloak, mask, or disguise conjurational operations by employing approved religious content—namely biblical and Christian content. In this connection the historian Albert Raboteau has reprised the much debated thesis of the anthropologist Melville Herskovits that "some elements of African religion survived in the United States not as separate enclaves free of white influence but as aspects hidden under or blended with similar European forms." Such legitimation strategies are rarely explicit and conscious, of course, and may even be forgotten or repressed if ever rendered transparent.[77]

Smith's remarks are especially important for my interpretation of the Native Baptist and Revival Zion religions as African-derived religions that have, under the pressure of censorship, covertly and perhaps unconsciously used "approved religious content—namely biblical and Christian content" to "cloak, mask, or disguise" African religious traditions. In connection with this, we may recall that I use the term *Christian* Myalist to refer to the Native Baptist and Revival Zion religions in order to acknowledge the differences between eighteenth-century expressions of Myalism, which were derived from classical African sources, and many nineteenth-century expressions of Myalism, which were Christian-influenced. More important, however, is that I still interpret the nineteenth-century Christian-influenced Myal traditions as African-derived because of the presence of the six African features that transgress orthodox Christian traditions but correspond harmoniously with orthodox features of classical African religions.

Also helpful is Smith's exploration of iconics, as a conjurational strategy for producing recognizable expressions of African spirituality in North America. This leads him to consider its application for Rastafari. According to Smith, "[I]conographic modes [of conjuring religion] allow for increased openness and transparency."[78] Not only is Smith on target here, his notion of iconics can be directly applied to my interpretation of Rastafari's (iconic) appropriation of the biblical Zion concept and especially its aim to make transparent and explicit the values and aspirations invoked by the image of Zion in emphasizing what its Revival Zionist progenitors had not, that is, the relevance of Africa as a tangible political rather than mystical symbol most pronounced in its glorification of a specific African geographic place and political region—Ethiopia.

Is it fair to say that my "African-derived" and "African-centered" religions and Erskine's "Black religion" amount to the same thing with reference to

Revival Zion and Rastafari? I think not. The point of contention is a herme-neutical one. For me, "Black religion" becomes a nebulous category when discussing traditions that access both African and Christian sources for mean-ing in their struggle against anti-Africanness. I am not exactly sure what to make of his use of the term *Black*. Does it mean not quite African, not quite White, not quite Christian, or not quite all of them? *Religion*, on the other hand, seems to suggest something broader than Christianity. If "Black religion" is employed to refer to traditions that access both African and Christian sources for meaning, then we are still left with the task of explicating how those sources are appropriated, prioritized, aesthetically expressed, and hermeneutically con-veyed. Erskine's rendering of Revival's African character as " 'cultural frag-ments' of primitive people" obscures, all the more, his elaboration of Black religions as systems of belief, reflection, and coherency. In my view, Erskine's lack of attention to these religious "identity" issues is a limitation in his treat-ment of Black religion, which I have attempted to address in this work.

To be sure, my interpretation of African-derived religions in Jamaica and in the diaspora at large protests the prevailing assumption that African tradi-tional religions are static and resistant to dynamism. Black cultures of the Caribbean and the Americas make the case for an understanding of African-ness as the extension of continental modes, mannerisms, styles, orientations, and meanings into new environments and repressive contexts (of exile, slavery, and attending oppressions) that modify and reconfigure various expressions of African religion among diasporic populations. Thus the reality of exile and distance from Africa is marked by extension not severance and is punctuated with creativity, innovation, and memory rather than rupture, fragmentation, damage, and deterioration.

Again, the interpretive insight of African philosopher Eboussi Boulaga is critical to conversations about identity and Africanness in the Caribbean. With reference to contemporary analyses of African religion, Boulaga asserts, "[W]e are not piecing together a fossil, we are dealing with something living, some-thing that reacts, mobilizes and creates antibodies to resist aggression from without."[79] If we take for granted that African-derived religion is not a trans-planted fossil from ancient Africa nor a relic of the slave period but a living organism with its innate dynamism, energy, and "antibodies," we might be able to see traditions such as Native Baptist and Revival Zion as types of African-derived religious expression imbued with codes and symbols, or chris-tianisms. These christianisms are innoculants insofar as they function collec-tively as a vaccine, stimulating the production of antibodies that allow practitioners "to resist aggression from without."

Another significant Jamaican theologian, Lewin Williams, has contributed not just to the construction of Jamaican theology but his *Caribbean Theology* is a comprehensive rendering of theology within the Caribbean context. The strength of Williams's theology is indeed its relevance to the entire Caribbean region as opposed to a few countries. According to Williams, "[I]t is the hope of this investigative effort that indigenous theology will speak for the corporate self-awareness which will foster unity of purpose if not uniformity."[80] Williams's work complements Erskine's as he situates the identity question within the context of theological discourse in the Caribbean. To what should Caribbean theology respond in the geopolitical world order? and in the history of Christianity in the region? Moreover, how does one determine the sources and methods for indigenous articulations of Caribbean theology? These are the chief questions guiding the discussion in Williams's *Caribbean Theology*.

Given his focus, Williams does not elaborate a theology that is rooted in what he would call its "pre-Caribbean"[81] African heritage. Williams's anthropological and cultural starting point is that since virtually all of the indigenous populations were exterminated during the colonial period, what we have now in terms of culture and religion is uniquely composed of imported "pre-Caribbean" traditions (African, European, Asian). While I find merit in this perspective, I suspect that it does not lead to a critical assessment of White supremacy, which is vital in a region that suffers from deep denial about the institutionalization of racism and anti-Africanness in its social structures, cultural milieux, and popular attitudes. I agree with Williams that we must generate theologies that reflect the comprehensive and common experiences of the Caribbean as a region. In so doing we are compelled to consider macro-level geopolitical and socioeconomic issues affecting the region and their implications for the people of the Caribbean. Yet we belie the imperatives of an indigenous theology if we fail to acknowledge that racism, anti-Africanness, and Afrophobia are comprehensive, commonplace, and *indigenous* in every Caribbean country in the region. Williams's perspective on culture neutralizes what should be an uncompromising antiracist/pro-African agenda in whatever goals we state for our indigenous Caribbean theology.

Consequently, I find Williams's reflection upon "folk religion" to be an overly simplified portrayal of the complex issues regarding the historical encounter between Christianites and African-derived religions in the Caribbean. Williams duly acknowledges, "The problem between the missionary church and folk religion is that the church has taken no opportunity to understand it and has therefore treated it as heathenism."[82] However, in categorizing that which the missionary church "treated as heathenism" as "the non-European pre-Caribbean 'leftovers,' " Williams (even more than Erskine) generalizes in such a way that he obscures the fact that the protracted, pernicious censoring and vilification of African culture and religion across the Caribbean is the heart of the matter. To launch a generic critique against missionary opposition to "folk religion" is like decrying the Nazi regime and concentration camps without mentioning the specific extermination of six million Jews.

In the end, Williams does make specific references to Jamaican Kumina and Trinidadian Shango (Orisha). And he is on point in declaring, "The question is whether there are tenets in these or any other parts of folk religion capable of enhancing Caribbean liberation praxis." Indeed, the answer is yes, if we are persuaded by my exploration of African-derived religions (Williams's "folk religions"/"leftovers") in the preceding chapters. To his credit, Williams appears hopeful when he describes the "tremendous reciprocity between the Shango religion and Black militancy which had its upsurge [in Trinidad] about the same time [mid-1970s]."[83] Williams actually confesses "quite freely the difficulty in unlearning even the learned prejudices against one's cultural experiences." This follows an anecdotal account of a yearly ritual enacted by his grandmother, which Williams includes as an example of her "African leftovers."[84] Williams's task in *Caribbean Theology* is broad, methodological, and hermeneutical. He asserts nonetheless that "Caribbean theology cannot continue to ignore its folk experience as the missionary church did. It must explore and utilize it to the enhancement of the liberation struggle."[85]

With reference to my introductory remarks about theology and African-derived religions, I understand Williams's final analysis of the relationship between Caribbean theology and folk religion (African-derived religions) as an invitation to demonstrate their compatibility.[86] In order to do so, I submit that Barry Chevannes's understanding of anthropology and culture with regard to the Caribbean region provides a better and more accurate starting point for an indigenous theology of liberation in the Jamaican context and perhaps in the wider British and French Caribbean context. Chevannes is a contributing author to the collection of essays *Caribbean Theology: Preparing for the Challenges Ahead.* In "Our Caribbean Reality," he writes:

> In this paper I focus on those Caribbean cultures shaped predominantly by the Africans. The justification for this approach is that in terms of mass movements they were the first, and now constitute the majority. In one aspect, namely population, Trinidad and Tobago and Guyana are currently the exceptions, boasting East Indian majorities. But even here, the folk languages spoken by all the people is that formed by the Africans. It is important to recognize this, because of the popular theory that the Caribbean is a melting pot: a little bit of Arawak, a little bit of Chinese, Lebanese and Portuguese, a large amount of India and the most of Europe and Africa. This is a misunderstanding. Caribbean reality is shaped by Africa.[87]

The weaknesses in the theologies of Erskine and Williams point to both the Christian biases in their works and a false anthropological and cultural starting point (in the case of Williams). However, they also stem from the lack of a proper theoretical framework for interpreting the African religious phenomenon in Jamaica and the broader Caribbean. While theorizing about the nature and characteristics of African-derived religious traditions is customarily undertaken by scholars in the social sciences, it is indispensable for Caribbean theologians who want to premise their reflections upon emancipatory religious traditions, given their orientation toward Africa. In the case of Jamaica, my research compels me to challenge established theories and historical assumptions concerning the manifestations of African-derived religions there and perhaps elsewhere in the Caribbean and the Americas.

With regard to African-derived religions as a general category, a majority of scholars are comfortable using theories of syncretism to interpret their historical, contemporary, and future significance in the Caribbean and the Americas. For example, the African-derived religions of Haiti (Vodun), Brazil (Candomblé), Trinidiad (Orisha, Spiritual Baptist), and Cuba (Lucumi, Santería) are understood as New World religions that were spawned by an amalgamation of Old World African traditional religions and Christianity, especially Catholicism. While a number of established scholars are committed to the view that African-derived religions are syncretistic traditions, emerging from correlations of traditional African religious and Euro-Christian sources, I maintain that the Euro-Christian features in these traditions have minimal influence upon the significance of ritual life and religious meaning. As my review of the history of the encounter between Africans and European missionaries in Jamaica makes clear, there is overwhelming evidence demonstrating that practitioners of African-derived religions have incorporated Euro-Christian traditions into their belief systems and ritual behavior to either complement African spirituality or to disguise and conceal African religious practices. This is true for other parts of the African diaspora as well. For example, Theophus Smith bases his entire theoretical interpretation of African North American religion and culture upon the premise that conjuring (not syncretizing African and European traditions) accounts for both tangible and intangible expressions of African spirituality in systematic and unsystematic configurations in Black North American cultural productions. Thus, it comes as no surprise that Smith eschews the simplistic and myopic category of syncretism and instead opts for multidimensional categories that warrant a hermeneutics of complexification[88] to decipher and interpret the covert and transparent strategies that have been at work in Black religiocultural production in the United States.

On the other hand, diverging from the most developed insight of Melville Herskovits, who introduced syncretism as a category for Black religious studies, a number of scholars have promoted or reinforced the current commonly held view that syncretism emerged as the natural outcome of interreligious encounters while noting a tangential relationship between syncretism and religious persecution in the African diaspora. This perspective has encouraged truncated analyses and interpretations of African-derived religions. For example, James Houk has completed one of the most recent studies on the Yoruba-based Orisha religion in Trinidad. In his book *Spirits, Blood, and Drums*, Houk maintains that syncretism must be understood as a process of both camouflage and voluntary incorporation. The camouflage theory of syncretism takes the social factor of religious persecution into account, and the voluntary incorporation theory is based upon parallelisms between Yoruba religion and Catholicism. In the former, Houk argues that Africans in Trinidad have concealed their devotion to the Orisha (the community of divinities) by feigning their devotion to the Catholic saints during times of persecution. In the latter, Houk argues that Africans have recognized similar patterns of belief and practice in the Yoruba and Catholic religions and have voluntarily included Catholic traditions in their practice of Yoruba religion.

The camouflage theory of syncretism corresponds with my thesis that syncretism signifies conflict and oppression in the encounter between African-derived religions and Christianities. And the voluntary theory of syncretism accounts for African absorption of Euro-Christian themes and practices to accentuate their indigenous traditions. I disagree, however, with Houk's working definition of *syncretism* as "the integrating or blending of selected meanings (ideology) and/or forms (material culture) from diverse sociocultural traditions, resulting in the creation of entirely new meanings (ideology) and/or forms (material culture)."[89] In my view, Houk does not support his definition with convincing evidence, yet he concludes that "syncretism and spirit possession are perhaps the two most important and salient characteristics of Afro-American religions. Syncretism, in fact, perhaps more than any other cultural process, has been the mechanism behind the development of such a diverse and broad group of religions."[90]

Houk's notion that syncretism is a "characteristic" of African-derived religions, and a "most important and salient" one at that, is highly controversial and represents the type of simplistic analysis of African-derived religions and assumptions about their structures and belief systems that I find suspect. I have already noted six features that I maintain are salient in both classical African and African-derived religions. My list is not exhaustive but serves as an entry point into analyzing the religious systems of Africans in the diaspora from slavery to the present day. More than anything, my study of African-derived religions in Jamaica challenges Houk's thesis that syncretism gives rise to African-derived religions or that syncretism is their main characteristic, for, in so doing, African-derived religions tend to be interpreted as fragmented traditions displayed as dance, art, musical instruments, psychological responses to crises, and so on. As Mervyn Alleyne maintains, "[R]ather than treat Jamaican religion as a pathological reaction to extreme social-psychological deprivation, as many other studies do, [I] begin by looking at African religious belief and practice and [go] on to examine how it was transformed on Jamaican soil."[91]

I argue that syncretism (if used at all) should be viewed first as a process that has taken place among various African religious cultures as they encountered each other in exile during the period of African enslavement in the Caribbean and the Americas. It should also be understood as a process that has modified African-derived religious expressions over time as they have encountered Christianity and other religious systems of belief and practice. However, my research on African-derived Jamaican religions yields no evidence that the process of syncretism necessarily changes the substance of African religious identity and theological meaning for practitioners of African-derived religions. Houk's application of Herskovits's categories of syncretism and reinterpretation is modified in that he views the Orisha (Yoruba-based) religion in Trinidad as a new religious product of two major spiritual heritages, the African and the Euro-Christian. Herskovits, on the other hand, argues for retentions and Africanisms that implied continuity between African religions and African diasporic religions, if not in comprehensive systematic configurations then in terms of specific patterns, structures, styles, and institutions.

Alfred Métraux provides a convincing example from his study of Haitian

Vodun, which points to the inadequacy of syncretism theories concerning African-derived religions. Responding to a Catholic priest's claim that Vodun practitioners "worship the pictures of the saints," Métraux writes:

> Although we cannot really talk of a true assimilation of *loa* [divinities] to Catholic saints it remains none the less true that Voodooists have not failed to notice analogies between their respective functions. . . . All the same, even if the two groups do resemble each other in exercising similar powers, they still stand apart and belong to two entirely different religious systems. Whereas the *loa* reveal themselves in possession, no one to my knowledge was ever possessed by a saint. In the same way *loa* do not borrow the attributes and characters of the saints to whom they are supposed to correspond. It is, as we have seen the other way about: The saint, stripped of his own personality, takes on that of the *loa*.[92]

Métraux's observation is of critical significance given that the classic syncretism example most noted by scholars is that of associating African divinities with Catholic saints in ritual life. The aesthetic and theological import of ritual life and its protocols to devotees of African-derived traditions is not diffused even among groups (such as Revival Zionist or Trinidadian Spiritual and Shouter Baptist) that explicitly incorporate Christian elements into their religious practices. As I reflect upon my fieldwork among these Christian-influenced, African-derived religions in Jamaica and Trinidad, it is becoming increasingly apparent to me that Jesus Christ is not profoundly central in ritual processes and ritual enactments. Jesus Christ and other christianisms are significant symbols or signifiers that function as codes for multiple dimensions of African spirituality and that intensify African aesthetic rituals. For example, the vigorous ringing of a bell, especially in the Spiritual and Shouter Baptist religions in Trinidad, is often done in patterns of threes by devotees as they approach the space of concentrated sacred power around the center pole. Although devotees explain this act through Christian Trinitarian reasoning, namely, that it represents communion with the Father, Son, and Holy Spirit, the act itself is aesthetically pronounced and ritually efficacious in the experience of hearing, seeing, and feeling the penetrating sound, motion, and rhythm of the bell when devotees attempt to connect with the Divine Community by invoking the gods spirits.[93]

My nascent analysis of this type of symbolization is that it allows for an aesthetically intense and endless encoding process where christianisms do not introduce new meanings but actually hyperbolize African spirituality. Aesthetic encoding through the ritual resources of African religious cultures makes the Spiritual/Shouter Baptist or Revival Zion religions distinctively what they are and utterly meaningful to devotees. The remarks of Funso Aiyejina and Rawle Gibbons are theoretically instructive on this point and for the larger debate on syncretisms in African-derived religions. In analyzing the Christian elements within the Trinidadian Orisha religion, they conclude:

On the strength of the details about the Orisa which have survived in Trinidad, we would like to suggest that syncretism, if defined as a method of conflating two religions into one, is an inadequate term. What the African did was to use the dominant and socially accepted form of theology to preserve his systematically despised world view and its theology. The saints and the prayers, therefore, became mere "alphabets" with which the African recorded the stories of his Orisa for posterity.[94]

Even more troubling is that syncretism arguments tend to be biased toward Eurocentric notions of civilization and progress. The European elements of African-derived religions and other cultural productions are interpreted as providing structure, organization, and new meanings to dismembered, inferior African traditions, which would be as good as dead without input from unimpaired, superior Western cultures.

Against this backdrop, my treatment of Jamaica's African-derived and African-centered religions attempts to refocus the theoretical discussion to include contextual evidence of sociohistorical and cultural factors that account for the pattern of what scholars have been calling syncretism in African-derived religions and their assumptions about the process of syncretism. In so doing, I have given particular attention to the African cultural background of African Jamaicans and to issues of religious censorship and religious legitimacy in Jamaica where practitioners of African-derived religions have struggled to maintain their cultural and spiritual integrity, indeed their humanity, in a society dominated by Christian anti-Africanness. Mervyn Alleyne also seeks to debunk theories that "inferiorize" African culture when compared with Western culture in Caribbean and American situations of encounter. In the preface to his book *Roots of Jamaican Culture*, Alleyne writes:

My own belief, argued, in this book, is that not just "pitch, intonation and timbre" but entire functioning languages were carried to Jamaica and can still be found there even now. Not just "general cultural orientations" or "religious beliefs" but entire religions were carried to Jamaica and struggled to maintain themselves in hostile conditions; not just "artistic or aesthetic orientations and preferences" but African musical instruments and a repertoire of songs and performances for religious and secular occasions.[95]

Preferring to start from the same premise as Alleyne and Theophus Smith, I endorse the view that African-Jamaican religiosity has unfolded from African religious systems into Obeah, Myal, Native Baptist, Revival Zion, Kumina, and Rastafari religious traditions via conjuration or, more appropriately, *Obeahic* strategies of cultural production. I want to argue, though, for a theoretical category that is particularly helpful in understanding the contested terrain of covert Black religious culture in the specific context of Jamaica. This is precisely because covert trajectories of African religious culture are coded and thus naturally lend themselves to misinterpretation in popular culture and scholarly research. I hold that the complex web of controversy surrounding and often concealing the identity and significance of African religious experience to African-derived practitioners in Jamaica is best interpreted by a theory of masquerading.[96] A theory of masquerading allows, then, for a decoding of covert trajectories of African religious culture, while explaining its innovative and constructive character.

Covert Jamaican Religions: Masquerading as Modus Operandi

Broadly speaking, a *masquerade* is "a festive gathering of people wearing masks and costumes." The term is also used to refer directly to the actual costume that is worn at such gatherings. Other definitions include "false outward show; pretense . . . to represent oneself falsely . . . to disguise oneself."[97] Masquerading traditions can be traced to many regions across the globe. On the continent of Africa, masquerading is commonplace within countless societies and has religious significance in traditional contexts. Anthropological research has shown that, in Africa, masquerades are especially important for initiation rites and social governance.[98] In many cases masquerades represent the appearance of the Ancestors. The masquerader who dances fully concealed by the masquerade (costume) loses his[99] identity and becomes an incarnated Ancestor. The facial construction (mask) of the masquerade is most potent in some societies for interaction with the Ancestors. For example, art and archaeology professor Frank Willett has observed that, for the Dan of the Upper Cavally River in the Ivory Coast, the mask is a

> channel of communication with the [supreme] god Zlan, but the
> real intermediaries are the spirits of the ancestors who are invoked
> through the masks. The power of the mask to influence the ances-
> tors depends on the social prestige of the owner, since a man can
> only reach prominence with their help, and his very success shows
> that the ancestors favor him.[100]

Benjamin Ray also notes the relationship between masks/masquerades and the Ancestors among the Dogon of Mali and the Yoruba of Nigeria. The Dogon, as do many other African societies, enact elaborate burial and ancestorhood rituals. The *Dama* rite, which concludes a "long period of mourning and spiritual transition . . . begins with a sacrifice to the Great Mask" after which a "group of masked dancers climbs up to the flat roofs of the homes of the deceased and dances vigorously to . . . compel the dead to join the assembly of the ancestors in the afterworld."[101] The Yoruba represent the deceased male family head "by a masked *egungun*[102] dancer who will appear to the assembled members of the family and tell them what has happened in the household since his death." Special masks are made and named for deceased persons of public prominence in civic society or in the *egungun* society: "Under this guise he will appear at yearly festivals together with other ancestors."[103]

In traditional African settings, the Ancestors return to render blessings and celebrate the accomplishments of the community. They also come to warn, scold, admonish, and pass commentary on social and political matters that pertain to the governance of civil society.[104] This necessarily places the human mediums who become possessed by ancestral personalities in vulnerable positions. Thus the appearance of the Ancestors as masquerades (concealed anonymous dancers) preserves their sacrosanct status and protects the human medium from social castigation.

The ritualization of masking as a concealing device that protects the integrity and authority of the Ancestors and ancestral traditions makes masquerading more than a traditional institution in Africa. The institution of masquerading provided enslaved Africans in Jamaica with an aesthetic mode of concealment and protection that allowed them to preserve Obeah, Myal, and other African-derived religious traditions in variegated forms masked as Christian traditions. By the same token, Myal was also preserved literally within the Jonkunnu masking tradition. African religious practitioners who instituted the Native Baptist and Revival Zion traditions made a Jonkunnu out of Christianity—a performance mask that they could wear and control in their efforts to safeguard African religious culture. Masquerading, it seems to me, is an appropriate theoretical category for interrogating Black religious formation in this instance because Obeah, Myal, and other African-derived religious traditions are ancestral traditions wielding hermeneutical authority in the process of African-Jamaican religiocultural production. For example, masquerading, as a modus operandi, is shown in contemporary Revival Zionist appropriations of (1) the Psalms as avenues to neutral mystical power; (2) Trinitarian theism to justify (conceal) the communotheism implicit in their devotion to spirit messengers; and (3) Old Testament Hebrew practices of animal sacrifice to justify their African ritual practice of animal sacrifice, which is required for food offerings to the Divine Community. These are all aspects of Revival Zion religiosity that are essential to working with the invisible powers toward concrete ends. The correlation of what the dominant censoring culture had come to view as illegitimate African ideas and practices with legitimate Christian or biblical ideas and practices facilitates the essential spiritual work that practitioners conduct on a daily basis. One Revivalist stated it this way: "If wi did fi really go like certain rituals, people would a seh 'den a wha Kin'a church dis.' "[105]

Like their Revival Zion descendants, in the nineteenth century, the Native Baptists also masqueraded as Christians and thus were able to win support for their resistance movement from enslaved Africans who were members of Euro-missionary Christian churches. Concealed within the Native Baptist and Revival Zion traditions (which self-consciously identify as Christian) Obeah and Myal traditions are given immunity from external attack and censorship and are preserved for their sustaining impact upon the health and well-being of African Jamaicans.[106]

Rather than viewing them as syncretisms, I prefer to name the innovations or christianisms responsible for transforming African traditional Myalism into Native Baptist and Revival Zion traditions "antibodies," as suggested by Boulaga[107] in his analysis of continental African independent churches. The term *syncretism* only accounts for what happens when two or more cultures interact, and one can erroneously infer, from scholarly employment of the term in African diasporic studies, that the dominant European culture provides coherency for the subdued and disintegrated African culture(s) or even equally contributes to the formation of a new culture. On the other hand, the term *antibodies* accounts for not only what happens in terms of cultural borrowing but for the processes by which such cultural borrowing occurs, under which types of sociopolitical and historical contexts and toward which ends. It also acknowledges the subversive agency of enslaved and colonized Africans to simultaneously modify yet preserve themselves and their African heritages under conditions conducive for religiocultural and human extinction.

Masquerading, then, as I understand it, is more than just a New World strategy as some have argued syncretism is. Masquerading is an aesthetic cultural mode or disposition of religious significance that ensures the protection and preservation of African people's most treasured, authoritative ancestral institutions both on the continent of Africa and in the African diaspora of Jamaica. Again, Funso Aiyejina and Rawle Gibbons caution against any reductionist reading of African diasporic openness to cultural innovation as syncretism. From their studies of the Orisha religion in Trinidad, they note an ironic compatibility between the secrecy coerced by censorship and the secrecy governing classical African approaches to esoteric ritual knowledge:

> Against the background of the authoritarian control imposed on the New World . . . [t]he African took his religion underground. This would have been very easy to accomplish since significant aspects of religious rituals of Africa are generally opened only to the initiated. So, while affirming the general truth to the effect that when a people are denied the opportunity to express themselves openly, they are forced to go underground, they were also affirming a practice that is an integral aspect of African religious tradition.[108]

I specifically interpret masquerading as one "integral aspect of African religious tradition" that suited the needs of enslaved and colonized Africans in Jamaica as they too negotiated the secrecy and invisibility demanded by the Eurocentric Christian-based culture of domination. In the area of religion then, masquerading can be conceived as a subversive mannerism of African-Jamaican religiosity and perhaps as a mannerism of the broader African-Caribbean religious complex, which is simultaneously aesthetic and political in expressing an Africanist conscious, subconscious, or even unconscious disposition that ancestral traditions are worthy of repetition. Thus, as Dominique Zahan explains:

> For Africans, tradition is above all the collective experience of the community. It constitutes the totality of all that successive generations have accumulated since the dawn of time, both in spiritual and practical life. It is the sum total of the wisdom held by a society at a

given moment of its existence. If we admit that the ancestors do not constitute a closed community, but that they are seen as an assembly which is perpetually increasing and incessantly evolving, then we must recognize that tradition too is not at all static. . . . Tradition for Africans is, then, a means of communication between the dead and the living, as it represents the "word" of the ancestors.[109]

As a component of African tradition, African religions render the "Word"[110] of the Ancestors transparent for human application to daily life experience. And Africans in diasporic contexts of enslavement and colonial conquest have struggled to find innovative ways of transmitting the Word from one generation to the next for empowerment and victory over corporeal, cultural, and spiritual death. In Jamaica we see that, from Obeah to traditional African Myal, to Native Baptist and Revival Zion Christian Myal, to Kumina, to Rastafari, the transmission of the Word of the Ancestors, which is life-affirming rather than death-dealing,[111] promotes social liberation over captivity and health over disease, and it recycles African culture for the personal development of the individual and positive enhancement of the community. In Jamaica, masquerading, as a modus operandi, has functioned covertly in the history of encounters between African practitioners and European colonial and ecclesiastical authorities to ensure the space and opportunity for the aesthetic repetition and unfolding of African-derived religious traditions, re-expressing the epochal Word of the Ancestors and the "momentary"[112] or spontaneous experiences of the present generation. It should come as no surprise then that masquerading was most pronounced within the nineteenth-century Native Baptist and Revival Zion religions, when missionary activity was at its peak and African religious traditions were most vulnerable to ruin.

Even the manner in which Revival Zionists unmask in private spaces, among fellow adherents and clients who consult them clandestinely, speaks to masquerading as a subconscious or perhaps unconscious religious modus operandi. By "unmask," I mean the explicit or, as Theophus Smith would say, transparent expression of African spiritual and religious traditions. Practices like feeding the Ancestors at clearings in the privacy of a client's home or using African divination techniques in sessions with clients held privately in a reading room reserved solely for such purposes tend to be suppressed during public Sunday morning church worship services. For at Sunday church services, the Christian masquerade of evangelical testimonials, sermonizing, christological faith confessions, and scriptural authority is most publicly dramatized.[113] Moreover, given the antibiotic utility of these and other christianisms in Revival Zion religion, devotees masquerade through these types of public services unmolested by existential questions about cultural integrity and spiritual authenticity.

During the pre-Emancipation period, the practice of Obeah oath taking among Native Baptists, who masqueraded as Christians in public, constituted too an unmasking in private and secluded contexts where antislavery conspirators plotted their rebellious labor strike under the direction of Samuel Sharpe.

The chief difference between contemporary Revival Zionist unmaskings and nineteenth-century Native Baptist unmaskings is that while the former points to masquerading as an unconscious modus operandi, the latter points to it as a conscious, perhaps even superconscious, modus operandi necessitated by the oppressive fact of slavery and the purpose of political and social transformation toward which Obeah and Myal activities were specifically oriented. In other words, within the context of slavery, Native Baptist insurrectionists were conscious of their need to mask their spiritual and political pro-African liberation praxes to ensure success and the perpetuation of the ancestral Word.

In traditional African settings, members of masquerading societies also unmask themselves in private venues among fellow initiates before and following public displays of the masquerades for their communities. The efficacy of their performances as ancestral mediums is dependent upon prior and posterior ritual acts that take place among initiates in classified meetings off-limits to the wider public. Similarly, the efficacy of African-Jamaican people's efforts (both conscious and unconscious) to secure emancipation and well-being has been contingent upon the unpublicized practice of ancestral rituals such as Obeah oath taking, Kumina healing ceremonies, and Revival Zion readings and clearings. In continental Africa and the African diaspora of Jamaica, privacy and seclusion allow for and even require transparent manifestations of ancestral practices, while masquerading is required in order to protect and preserve those same ancestral traditions within public social contexts, especially ceremonial settings.

Dominique Zahan provides further insight into why protecting and preserving ancestral traditions remain significant to people of African descent. According to Zahan:

> For the African, time is inconceivable without generations as its framework. The succession of human beings issuing one from another offers to African thought the ideal basis for establishing the three fundamental correlative stages of duration: past, present, and future. However, contrary to what we might expect, a succession of individuals linked by ties of birth appears on the ideal axis of time facing not the future but the past. The human being goes backward in time: [the human being] is oriented toward the world of the ancestors, toward those who no longer belong to the world of the living.[114]

The historical expressions of African-derived religions in Jamaica, I maintain, disclose an ancestral orientation in the traditions examined in this text. And masquerading as modus operandi especially punctuates the ancestral orientation when one considers the covert Native Baptist and Revival Zion African religious trajectories.

As a transparent African-centered religion, Rastafari transgresses masquerading as a modus operandi, as does Kumina, a transparent African-derived religion, perhaps due to its postemancipation origin in Jamaica. It is important to establish, however, that Kumina devotees participate in the masquerading operations of Revival Zionism when performed as a Christian tradition for the general public. What Kumina adherents do not do (if it is an authentic Kumina) is combine masquerading traditions with Kumina traditions. Kumina adherents, then, are dually aligned,[115] practicing two distinct traditions alongside one another. Kumina practitioners, however, are most transparent in their transmission of the Word of the Ancestors. They are, as Zahan writes, undeniably "oriented toward the world of the ancestors, toward those who no longer belong to the world of the living."[116]

The Prophetic Word of African-Jamaican Religious Traditions

How might a Caribbean theology of indigenization be informed by the cosmologies, anthropology, spirituality, and religiosity of the African-derived religions (the Word of the Ancestors) in the context of postcolonial Jamaica? In his reflections on enculturation and acculturation in the Caribbean, Lewin Williams considers the significance of the encounter between African-derived religions and missionary Christianity, discussing the devaluation of African-derived religions as an outgrowth of missionary "misevangelization":[117]

> [W]hile drastic changes have taken place in the areas of liturgy and mission strategy in the so-called "mother" churches in Europe and North America, the missionary churches in the Caribbean have remained almost as colonial as the day they were started. It is not unusual for denominations to be "enlightened" to hold "missionary services" during which one can hear vivid renditions of songs, written a century and more ago to encourage those who would bring the light of the gospel to their ancestors, which are replete with the missionary presumption of godlessness and ignorance. Even today people seem to derive spiritual blessing from lyrics such as these: *"In heathen lands afar / Thick darkness broodeth yet; / Arise, O Morning Star, / Arise and never set."*

Williams identifies misevangelization as a contemporary issue as he goes on to say:

> The problem of misevangelization should not be considered as something that took place in the past and therefore is now among the innocuous relics of ancient history. The problem is as alive today as when the conquistadors arrived with the Bible in one hand and the sword in the other to conduct a "violent evangelism."[118]

Williams's analysis of the encounter between Africans and European missionaries in colonial Jamaica and its impact upon the Jamaican Christian community today is consistent with my own conclusions about Africans who came to accept Euro-missionary Christianity. With this acknowledged, however, Jamaican and other Caribbean theologians have neglected to explore the critical commentary evident in the various expressions of African-oriented religions which have existed alongside the expansion of Eurocentric orthodox Christianity among Black populations. Although Caribbean theologians have begun to identify the destructive legacy of colonial Christianity in degrading the cultures and non-Christian practices of their various populations, their evangelical perspectives are still saturated with the theology and missiology of Europe. As Carlos Cardoza maintains, "They are good traditional evangelical theologians for sure. Yes, they understand the cultural context of the Caribbean and assert its value for the indigenous populations but then they want to sing 'Rock of Ages.' To be sure, they will welcome *Rock of Ages* sung to Caribbean rhythms in a Caribbean style, but it must be *Rock of Ages*."[119]

Because theology in Europe, the Americas, and the Caribbean is decisively Christian, there is no precedence in the West for the type of African-centered liberation theological reflection demanded by the record of Black struggles for authentic emancipation in the Caribbean. In other words, if any religious tradition has been a viable force in African liberation struggles in the Caribbean, it is African-derived religion and not Christianity. Indeed in those cases where we observe a cohabitation of Christianity with African religion in a single tradition, the evidence demonstrates the primacy of African-derived spirituality and religiosity in shaping the identity of the practitioners, even if the practitioners claim to be Christian. Ultimately, the case of Jamaica requires a paradigmatic shift in the discipline of theology, one that expands the categories for theological thinking beyond Christian doctrines and the centrality of Jesus Christ.

Given the history of missions in the Caribbean, I would argue that to do Caribbean theological reflection that is liberation focused with the Christian God and Christ[120] mind is oxymoronic; but this is exactly what has been done thus far in Caribbean theologies. My assessment that the sources and methods of theological reflection in the Jamaican context, for example, must include historical analysis (method) and African-derived religious traditions (sources) insists that theology must not be held captive to Christianity. I concur with Juan Luis Segundo then when he makes the case for the liberation of theology from his Latin American perspective. The Caribbean too needs the liberation of theology generated by an even more specific local awareness[121] of the permanence of African religiosity in the struggles for freedom among its African populations. Thus, as a resolve to the posed introductory problematic of theology's compatibility with African religiosity, theology *has* to be understood in broader terms than Christian theology.

Since Eurocentric concepts, images of, and symbols for God and God's self-disclosure in Jesus litter the theologian's conceptual landscape with obstacles that prevent a new approach to theology, it is essential to modify the iconic and conceptual pretext[122] with which theologians approach the context of Caribbean experience in their work. Shifting the theistic symbol from the Christian God and Christ to the classical African Divine Community is one important move in emancipating Caribbean theologians from subconscious anti-African proclivities in their approaches to the theological task. In the Caribbean context, the Divinity of the Crossroads, Esu-Elegba (Legba) is a figurative metonym for a hermeneutic that epitomizes the Word of the African Ancestors. This is especially appropriate because Esu-Elegba is the divinity who communicates thoughts, intentions, ethics, judgments, and wisdom—that is, the Word—which prescribe appropriate options and limitations for human behavior. Like the Greek messenger and trickster divinity, Hermes, from which the term *hermeneutics* is derived, Esu, as a metaphoric lens for elucidating an African, ancestrally oriented hermeneutics, brings into focus a critical interpretation of messages from the Divine Community.

The message that Jamaican theologians must hear condemns Eurocentric Christianity as an impediment to African liberation and exposes colonial-based Christianity as hostile to and therefore incompatible with African-derived religions. Christianities in Jamaica are the products of Eurocentric missionary activity, and as Laurenti Magesa duly notes, "looking upon Africa, [Christian missionaries] compared the continent's practices (its real culture) with the ideals of Europe (its ideal culture). The conclusion was, of course, that African culture was inferior."[123] Black Christians across the African diaspora, as a whole, have never adequately addressed how the problem of anti-Africanness, most conspicuously expressed in the Christian condemnation of African practices, continues to promote the fallacious notion that European ideal culture is Europe's real culture, which Blacks should endeavor to approximate. Yet the Native Baptist, Revival Zion, and Rastafari religions have attempted to address this very problem in signifying Christianity[124] as Other and situating it outside of the Word of the Ancestors. In each of the three cases, Africans utilize sources from the Christian tradition (christianisms) especially the Bible, for their iconic value. Yet their appropriations are not accommodative in the direction of orthodox Eurocentric Christianity but transformative toward altogether different African-based and African-centered religions, Rastafari being the most explicit example.

To maintain that Native Baptists and Revival Zionists are Christian because the Bible is an important source for their religiosity is as outrageous as believing that Christians, Jews, and Muslims practice the same religion because they use overlapping sacred texts as religious sources. In the case of the latter, they are all Abrahamic religions, but they are different Abrahamic religions that utilize and interpret scriptural sources according to the norms and principles of their specific traditions. The Native Baptists and Revival Zionists have Myal (not Christianity) as their common base while they masquerade as Christians to protect and sustain that common base. The Bible is also a significant source for Rastafari doctrine and religiosity perhaps even more so than it is for Revival Zion. Yet Rastafari, as a transparent African-centered religion, explicitly condemns Christianity as oppressive and enslaving.

The theological implications of the contemporary conversation among Revival Zion, a masquerading, covert, African-derived religion; Rastafari, a transparent, Jamaican-derived, African-centered religion; and Kumina, a transparent, African-derived religion, are crucial for any Jamaican theology of liberation. Each tradition has fashioned a distinct response to Christian anti-Africanness and Afrophobia that stands in critical opposition to their compatriots who, in large part, have embraced orthodox Christianity as established by the European missionaries in the island.

Revival Zion

Revival Zionists responded by masquerading as Christian to protect the Obeah- and Myal-based traditions they inherited from the Native Baptists and traditional African Myalists. Thus, along with their Native Baptist progenitors, Revival Zionists raise questions about *Christian* identity. Although Noel Erskine speaks for most who would interpret Revival Zion as an Afro-Christian tradition, I reject this interpretation in that it suppresses the fact that Revival Zionism was born from the struggle between defensive African-derived religions and offensive Christianities. Thus, when interpreting them as Afro-Christian traditions, theologians are not apt to reflect upon the ethical problems of anti-Africanness and Afrophobia and how they elicit masquerading as an embodied aesthetic mode encoding cultural and spiritual memory, which protects and preserves Myalism. To be sure, my use of the category *Christian Myalist* to describe Revival Zionists mirrors the use of the term *Judeo-Christian* to describe Christians. In Revival Zion religion, christianisms influence the tradition as a vaccine that protects its Myal foundation and characterizes the Revival Zion tradition as, nonetheless, an altogether different religion than the Christian religion. In the same vein, Christianity is a distinguishable religion from Judaism, despite the latter's influence upon the former.

Rastafari

Rastafari responded by destroying the masquerade and eliminating explicit African-derived religious practices. As suggested earlier, the Rastafari response unfolded as a critique of both Christianity and covert African-derived religion as masqueraded by Revival Zion. I have already explored the destructive impact of missionary Christianity on the Jamaican soul, body, spirit, and psyche. It appears that, when masqueraded as Christianity by Revival Zionists, African-derived religion was limited by its covert operations in ways that quelled its potential as an explicitly militant religiopolitical movement.

From my hermeneutical perspective, I do not agree with the Rastafari tradition which holds that Christianity in any form must be oppressive (Babylon) and anti-African. However, the Rasta repudiation of Christianity cannot be dismissed as erroneous. Their prophetic Word of condemnation exposes the anti-Africanness and Afrophobia that characterize Christianity in its various manifestations. For even Black expressions of Christianity in Jamaica have spoken the language and have nurtured the consciousness and theological values of the missionaries as they pertain to the condemnation of African religions. As such, they are Babylon and can never liberate African Jamaicans from anthropological poverty.

Through their Africanist appropriations of Christian sources, Rastafari and

Revival Zionism (and Native Baptist religion before them) suggest that Christianity can be reconceived and expressed in multiple cultural contexts, including those of Africa and the African diaspora.[125] Christianity has not always been known through the symbols and cultural fabric of Western Europe. Yet, Western European expressions of Christianity are dominant across the globe in African, Asian, Caribbean, and Amerindian cultures. Africans the world over can take hermeneutical authority away from Euro-missionary-based Christianities and nurture Christian identities that in no way promote anti-Africanness and Afrophobia. However, there is little encouragement for this type of reformation from Western ecclesiastical authorities. And although continental and diasporic theologians of African descent have categorically rejected Eurocentric Christianity in their theologies of liberation, inculturation, contextualization, and decolonization, as a whole, they have maintained a critical distance from controversial doctrinal issues that make anti-Africanness and Afrophobia appear inherent in Christianity. Lewin Williams's analysis of the colonial missionary church is a case in point. He understands the colonial missionary church as one that engaged in misevangelization and declares that it is "as alive today as when the conquistadors arrived with the Bible in one hand and the sword in the other."[126] While I agree with the tenor of Williams's critique, I would push it a bit further and claim that evangelism as a Christian obligation has always involved personal faith convictions about Jesus Christ's relevance for all people, which includes, in the worst cases, hegemonic and, in the best cases, covert strategies for winning converts.

The centuries-long encounter between African-derived religions and Euro-missionary Christianity in the Caribbean requires any Afrocentric or African-oriented Christianity to reject outright evangelization and another central tenet of orthodox Christianity, the doctrine of special revelation. The doctrine of special revelation—that Divine incarnation in Jesus was a unique historic event that alone offers forgiveness of sin, salvation, and eternal life to all human beings—has, along with the missionary example of Paul in the New Testament, inspired the belief that evangelism is a Christian responsibility. By *evangelism*, I mean the attempt to convince others that Jesus is the unique divine incarnation who saves the world from sin and promises eternal life to those who confess faith in him. I am aware that evangelism might involve many other humanitarian activities. However, evangelism, as I have defined it here, is alive and rampant in the world today and has functioned in consort with colonialism, imperialism, and neocolonialism in Africa, the African diaspora, and other parts of the Third World, crippling human achievement at personal, communal, and national levels and violating the sanctity of human life and other forms of creation.

Although there are other traditions and tenets that people of African descent must reject if their Christianities are to cohere with the emancipatory Word of the Ancestors, I would argue that the doctrine of special revelation and the practice of evangelism are most problematic. This type of revolutionary turn has not come to fruition in Christian doctrinal analysis, which is of paramount significance when considering the various expressions of imaginative and constructive genius in the African-oriented religious traditions. More specifically, Revival Zion and Rastafari demonstrate that Africans can appropriate Christian-derived sources (the Bible/biblical content, Christology, and so on) and use them to fashion non-Christian religions. Together, Revival Zion and Rastafari recognize the significance of the liberationist Christian sources that Black, womanist, Pan-African, Caribbean, and Latin American liberation theologians have used to structure their prophetic theological statements. However, Revival Zion and Rastafari make it clear that authentic liberation requires extricating those sources from a corrosive (Eurocentric) Christian religion and resituating them in non-Christian, African-derived, or African-centered religions. Thus, for the Revival Zionist and Rasta, the Bible and other select Christian traditions are religious resources for the symbolic exaggeration of African-centered, cross-bearing theological ideas (+).

In other words, Black people's rejection of Christianity does not necessarily indicate that they reject the Christian-derived traditions or sources of Christian belief that have been significant in their Ancestors' liberation struggles across the African diaspora. For example, in Revival Zion, God, Jesus, and the Holy Spirit are members of the Divine Community, but the spirit messengers are also present and oftentimes more significant than the Christian Trinity. In Rastafari, Divine incarnation in Jesus Christ is an indispensable doctrine. However, Jesus' declared African identity, his reincarnation in Haile Selassie, and the proclaimed divine nature of all Africans is equally indispensable for a proper interpretation of the doctrine. In the end, the possibilities for rethinking what Christianity will mean to Black people in the twenty-first century are numerous. In Jamaica, that rethinking should be done with an eye toward an African-centered womanist theology of the cross and articulations of the Word of the Ancestors in the Revival Zion and Rastafari traditions. Nathaniel Murrell and Burchell Taylor reinforce this point in their analysis of the Rastafari tradition:

> Whether one accepts any or none of the specific conclusions that the Rastafarians have arrived at in their exegetical work, one must yet admit that, in an uncanny way, they have paved the way for the kind of liberating exegesis sought and undertaken in contexts where the theology of liberation is being done. No theological project that is relevant to the Caribbean reality can truly ignore this Rastafarian exegesis as a source and paradigm for theological engagement in the region.[127]

Rastafari then and, for that matter, Revival Zion are "antibiotic" African-centered and African-derived traditions. As noted earlier in the discussion of Revival Zion, the christianisms within the tradition are best understood as a preventative vaccination that provides concrete immunization—antibiotics—to counteract the Eurocentric Christianization of Black people. These christianisms are material gathered from the Eurocentric Christian tradition and injected into Revival Zion religiosity to counteract the epidemic expansion of

Euro-missionary Christianity and the extinction of African-derived religious traditions in Jamaica.

Kumina

Kumina responded to Christian anti-Africanness and Afrophobia through what Barry Chevannes calls "dual membership."[128] Kumina practitioners often maintain official or informal affiliations with Revival Zion or sanctified Baptist churches where spiritualities of the crossroads (possession trance) are nurtured. This method of participating in two distinct religious traditions allows practitioners of African-derived religions to transmit the Word of the Ancestors as transparently as possible, that is, without masquerading in one setting. It also allows them to present themselves publicly as members of legitimate or more tolerated (in the case of Revival Zion) churches. Dual membership or dual allegiance is also very popular in other parts of the diaspora, and African practitioners of Christian heritage in the United States often remain dually aligned with a Christian denomination in order to conceal their involvement with African-based religions from Afrophobic and anti-African Christian relatives and friends. I have an African-American friend who puts it this way: "Christianity is the religion I pose in; Yoruba is the religion I practice."[129]

Dual allegiance usually has two consequences for African practitioners. In some cases, practitioners emphasize common aspects between Christianity and African-derived religions (especially spirit possession) and focus on those as a way of avoiding contradictions that promote Afrophobia and anti-Africanness. In other cases, practitioners feel inauthentic when they "pose" as Christians and cannot reconcile the doctrine of Christian exclusivism with African inclusivism. In other words, Christianity emphasizes Jesus' redemptive power as unique and superior to any other powers[130] from all other religions. African practitioners view power exponentially, believing that spiritual power multiplied by spiritual power equals *more* intense spiritual power. Thus Africanists are more likely to combine powers from whichever traditions are available to achieve their goals. Again, the focus on combining African and Christian mystical power for personal and communal enhancement is one of the reasons African practitioners are apt to be dually aligned without feeling disingenuous.

Many Christian-identified Blacks also unknowingly practice a type of dual allegiance; they officially identify as Christian, but during times of crisis show ultimate faith in African-derived religions for resolving their problems. The irony is that dually aligned Christians appear to be grossly offended by African-derived religions and often express Afrophobia and anti-Africanness in their language of condemnation with reference to African-derived religions. The Kumina practice of dual allegiance (in which adherents engage with general respect for the ideals of Christianity and without denouncing Christianity as evil or pathological) points to the hypocritical attitudes of some Christians, who are conveniently dually aligned with an African-based religion yet Afrophobic in their characterization of African-based religions.

The only ethical response to this type of hypocrisy is for Christian theologians to expose this manner of dual allegiance as lukewarm and deceitful. Jamaican and other Caribbean theologians might begin by raising questions about why many Black Christians need African-derived religions for crisis resolution. The "apostasy" of the ancient Hebrews who constantly violated the commandment to exclusively worship Yahweh by worshiping Baal and participating in Canaanite religious traditions offers an interesting biblical parallel. Theologians might have to explore whether the problem is apostasy or a coercive monotheism that excludes and condemns the Other and that which does not comply with monotheism. The best place to start, it seems to me, is within discussion groups and workshops in local church communities. First, theologians must ask themselves: Have I ever accessed African-derived religions for personal benefit? And second, has any other person ever utilized African-derived religions for my benefit? Then theologians must encourage their Black Christian communities to answer the same questions. These questions represent a courageous beginning that can potentially yield new popular theologies and practices of inclusion among the church communities across the Caribbean (and the Americas as well) and that can stimulate novel academic theological reflection among Caribbean and American theologians.

Ultimately, the Black Christian community, which suffers from Eurocentric theologies (for example, Manichaean anthropologies and docetic soteriologies) that impede liberation struggles, will have to come to terms with its ambivalent and duplicitous relationship with African-derived religions. In so doing, Black Christians will inevitably begin to address the problems of double consciousness and divided selfhood that, in the end, keep the collective community anthropologically impoverished because they jeopardize Black authenticity and self-integrity especially with regard to the question of Africanness and African heritage.

But there is another dimension to this practice of dual allegiance among Kumina and other devotees of African-derived religions that is instructive and corrective for the future of comparative theology and global interreligious dialogue. In the introduction, I noted the conspicuous absence of commentary on African religions as a dialogue partner in comparative theological scholarship. Although there is also a notable absence of scholars of African descent in this religious studies discourse, this does not excuse the appalling record of religious exclusion in comparative theological conversations. Indeed, it reveals all the more how deeply the primitive-civilized dichotomy has influenced the Western Christian mind[131] and specifically the Western Christian comparative theologians' particular selection of dialogue partners among the global religions acknowledged by the guild as "world religions." Even a cursory study of African and African-derived religions should speak to the interests of the comparative theologian in that African and African-derived religions have no normative traditions of religious condemnation, persecution, or devaluation of non-African religions.

There is overwhelming evidence throughout the centuries that African religiosity is hospitable to other spiritualities and religious traditions. This can be observed across the continent of Africa and in the African diaspora, where practitioners approach other religious traditions with openness and a willingness to appreciate their value to humanity and creation. This is true even when the bearers of foreign religions such as Islam and Christianity have engaged African peoples with no respect for their classical religions and with the intention of converting them from what they deem to be heathenism to monotheism. As examined here in the Jamaican context, African-derived practitioners often accommodate and incorporate resources from non-African religions in order to exaggerate or reinforce their most entrenched values and institutions bequeathed to them via classical African religions. This points to their ability to recognize common ground and perhaps a common humanity even with their oppressors, who lacked the profundity to see something similar when they encountered African traditions and African peoples.

The study of African ethics and philosophy in the light of the question of interreligious dialogue and global peace would make for a profound restructuring of the categories and parameters of comparative theological discourse in the twenty-first century. For example, in his 1994 article, "Being a Transformationist in a Pluralistic World," John Cobb offers a scholarly Christian response to the limitations in exclusivist, inclusivist, and pluralist comparative theological approaches to global religious diversity. Noting that "[b]oth inclusivism and pluralism fail to do justice to the depth of diversity among the traditions," he advocates that Christians must instead opt for "transformationism." More specifically, he writes:

> [Christian] [t]ransformationists have faith that most of the strong commitments to diverse positions have Christian grounds, and that there are elements of wisdom and value in all the major positions represented. . . . For transformationists, the fact that the diversity is to be treated as an opportunity does not mean that the denomination should simply rest in diversity. On the contrary, the opportunity should be seized. Representatives of the several theologies need to dialogue openly with one another, not with the goal of finding something in common, or of defeating each other in debate, but with the goal that each be challenged by the insights of the other so that a new consensus can emerge that does justice to the basic commitments of all.[132]

While Cobb posits his category of transformationism from a prophetic Christian standpoint, it is possible to read his commentary with African and African-derived religions fully in mind and not from a prophetic theological point of view but from an African theological point of view that seeks to formally articulate that which is normative and consistent in African-based religiosity. Cobb attempts to persuade Christians to adopt transformationism, an ethical approach to religious diversity that is already omnipresent in African and African-derived religions. Devotees of African-derived religions, within various contexts that range from religious repression to quasi religious freedom, have demonstrated the normativity of transformationism in their traditions as they repeatedly affirm that "diversity is to be treated as an opportunity [which] does not mean that the denomination[/tradition] should simply rest in diversity. On the contrary, the opportunity should be seized." Although it is tempting to probe African-derived religions for valuable contributions to comparative theology in terms of their pharmacological foci,[133] the transformationist disposition of devotees to African-derived and African religions is no less compelling if scholars are willing to engage them as complex religions with philosophical, theological, and ethical imperatives of worth to comparative theological discourse.

Kumina: The Integrative Power of a Tradition for Jamaican Collective Memory

During the nineteenth century, liberated and recaptive African indentured laborers, who established Kumina culture in Jamaica, were either promised outright or given the impression that they would be transported back to Africa upon completion of their terms of service. In actuality only a handful of liberated Africans from Sierra Leone were able to obtain passage home. There are Kumina stories about indentured African Ancestors who overcame their exile by simply flying back to Africa. They acquired the power to do this after abstaining from salt intake. Today, Kumina devotees, as do other African religious practitioners in the Caribbean, prepare ancestral food offerings without adding salt.[134] Rastafari groups also maintain fairly rigid food taboos, including restrictions against salt intake and the use of salt in the preparation of *ital* (natural) food.[135]

Although flying narratives abound in Kumina lore, amnesia concerning the religiocultural experiences of African Jamaicans during slavery persists, especially with regard to African-based practices and customs. It might be the case that the Kumina community offers tremendous resources for confronting the problem of historical erasure with regard to the African experience in Jamaica. Kumina is a site of African historical consciousness where the experience of slavery and African oppression are tangibly remembered through cultural institutions and the natural terrain—the mountains where the Maroons and Bongo nation lived and took asylum, in the sanctuary of forests where healing power is stored in every plant, in the shallow streams that Africans crossed in flight from captivity, and at the grave sites and extant "slave shacks" of the African Ancestors.[136] Kumina practitioners retain local knowledge of both significant events and conventional traditions that characterize much of eastern Jamaica's history. Their narratives carry multivalent meanings for local residents and for the African-Jamaican citizenry.

Kumina challenges the contrived selected memories Jamaicans have been conditioned to retain regarding the nation's sociopolitical and religious history, memories that would credit certain forms of Christianity rather than African-derived religions as the religious source of progress and emancipatory praxis among Blacks in their history on the island. Kumina culture belongs to the spirituality of Africa and the African diaspora, to those who can "hear the drum." I believe that a thorough engagement with Kumina culture within Kumina territory has the potential to make Jamaican Blacks uncomfortable about their Afrophobia and anti-Africanness, which is an important first step in overcoming our alienation from Africa, from our history, and from our very selves.

Kumina presents a religious tradition that is the property of Jamaican Blacks. The Kumina tradition persists today in spite of its marginalized and illegitimate status in Jamaican society. It remains an unfinished document about African people's struggle to surmount the horrors of slavery and its aftermath in Jamaica. Studies of this resilient tradition render the subtle connections among African heritage, the slave trade, abolitionism, and dislocation transparent.

First, with regard to the African heritage, Kumina, a post-Emancipation tradition, has reinforced and helped to preserve some of the oldest African-derived Myal practices in the island. This phenomenon in Jamaican religious history illuminates our understanding of religious repression and religious formation among African Jamaicans from slavery to the present. Second, when evaluated alongside historical documents, Kumina lore brings credibility to the subjugated narratives of indentured African laborers, to their individual and collective memories of captivity and compromised liberation. Finally, Kumina traditions offer insight into an indispensable dimension of post-Emancipation identity formation among Africans in Jamaica. Hence, Rastafari is not the only or the original site for the cultivation of self-conscious Pan-African ideals and convictions in Jamaica. My impression is that the Kumina tradition, which predates Rastafari by almost a century, has indeed contributed to Rastafari political consciousness and wields historical influence over more areas of the *livity* (Rastafari way of life) than those already noted by scholars, namely, music[137] and dietary taboos. Kumina demonstrates that contemporary expressions of African-derived religions can also nurture Pan-Africanist values within their adherents while striving to preserve the specific continental African ethnic foundations of their traditions. Through their identity consciousness then we see that Monica Schuler's identification of a Pan-African macrocosm encompassing an ethnic-based microcosm within Jamaican and other African diasporic slave societies is also a current phenomenon in the Jamaican experience. In these pre-emancipation and post-Emancipation contexts, organic constructions of identity that neutralize the politics intrinsic to either/or positions could engender a rethinking of the relationship between African heritage and Jamaican identity in the twenty-first century.

A Final Word on Theological Construction

Caribbean theologians, particularly those from the English-speaking islands, have fashioned a critical discourse primarily upon the problem of methodology. Within the Jamaican context, I am persuaded by the decolonization of theology

(Erskine) and the indigenization of theology (Williams). However, I have yet to be convinced that we can construct decolonized and indigenized theologies without sincerely addressing the history of antagonism between African-derived religions and Christianities in our island.

For this reason Caribbean theology must begin with sociohistorical analysis. The extensive treatment of historical context in this work is not intended to avoid the prophetic responsibility of theology. On the contrary, our communities' historical marriage to oppression and disaster compels Caribbean theologians to revisit our people's journey in the diaspora for a careful assessment of how we have come to believe that which we believe about the African and Christian identities and religions of our Ancestors and of the Caribbean and Caribbean-American populations today, and the implications of both.

It is a disappointing reality that prophetic (liberation, decolonization, and indigenization) theologies both in the United States and in the Caribbean, which call Black people to identify with and practice the "best of" the African diasporic Christian tradition (that which insists that challenging and resisting oppression authenticates Christian faith), have not had a significant impact upon the identities, liturgies, and praxes of most Black North American and Caribbean churches. It will be all the more disappointing if we discover that remembering and revaluing our African-derived religions in specific detail, with the twofold intention of understanding and critiquing those traditions based upon the norms and values of the African diasporic liberation theological tradition and recovering meaningful life-enhancing strategies and institutions—that is, signs of the cross that will alleviate African diasporic anthropological poverty in all of its dreadful manifestations—proves a vain task in the end. Yet we should not abandon the project of revaluing African-derived religions for fear of failure[138]—lest we are overcome by Afrophobia.

My study of Jamaican Christianities and African-oriented religions illustrates a point that should not be overstated but should also not be taken for granted. No religion is innately liberationist in doctrine, ritual, text (oral or written), religious symbolization, or piety. Furthermore, what might serve to liberate in one context may not have the same function in another. It follows then that oppressive theological or religious interpretation has existed and will continue to exist alongside and within the reflections of liberation theologians. A Caribbean theology of collective memory, then, must be self-critical in every generation. As Cuban theologian Aldolpho Ham maintains:

> The individual and collective consciousness of the people is expressed through culture, therefore the struggle for liberation has to be expressed also in the cultural realm. Theology has to discern those elements in culture that can better contribute to liberation, self-determination and authenticity. It has to be conscious also of those elements in which we share and communicate elements of the culture of domination and hinder or conceal elements of popular culture. We have to help the people to re-discover their collective memory as an account of these struggles.[139]

A promising start toward a collective remembering of African/indigenous Caribbean religions and cultures took place during a ground-breaking ecumenical conference on popular religion at the close of the last century (1995). Perhaps it was Esu-Elegba who inspired the title of the resultant publication, *At the Crossroads: African Caribbean Religion and Christianity*,[140] for indeed the Caribbean churches, theologians, and communities of faith are at a crossroads. The cross-bearing children of the Divine Community (Esu/the Ancestors/the spirit messengers) know exactly where the roads meet and why. Their testimonies of faith just might inspire the churches and theologians on a new cross-bearing mission in years to come.

Conclusion

What can be experienced as the good—the redemption and salvation—that Western Christianity extends to people of African heritage? Where do we find St. Augustine's *beatitudo* and Terrell's sacramental value of the sacrifice,[141] required of Africans in both their resistance and acquiescence to Western Christianity? The most appropriate response is not to locate and celebrate "pure" ideals as the redeemable essence of Christianity nor to discover an equally commanding pre-Western, ancient meaning of Christianity in East Africa, although there are compelling reasons for pursuing both of these projects. It is to uncover the dynamics of the encounter and to make central the practices and beliefs of the people as they have withstood Western Christianity and its Eurocentric ideological trappings. This path of resistance, which Josiah Young calls "re-Africanization,"[142] cannot be assumed but is discerned in our evaluation of the history of African exiles in Jamaica and other regions of the African diaspora. This is why any liberation theology that emerges from the African diasporic context must be, if nothing else, historical theology. It must seek to examine the path of resistance charted by the oppressed people who suffer and struggle for abundant life. In this, liberation theologians must be willing to hear and accept the judgment that colonial Christianity (slaveholding, plantation, and missionary) is evil and Afrophobic.

The trivialization or marginalization of African-derived religions in Caribbean theology exposes the theological incompetence and scholarly deficit characterizing our intellectual argumentation on the legacies of oppression and liberation in the Black experience. The focus on Jamaica in this work makes clear that we cannot reduce Obeah and Myal to magic and Revival Zion and Kumina to thaumaturgical cults while classifying the reigning expressions of orthodox missionary Christianity as "legitimate" religion. This approach to Jamaican religious history is theologically oxymoronic. A focus upon liberation in theological construction punctuates all the more the inherent problem in this approach to African-derived and missionary Christian religious traditions; the records indicate that in Jamaica, as well as in Haiti, Cuba, and other countries in the Caribbean, African practitioners who rejected missionary Christianity were the first, the leaders, the organizers, the carriers of African values and Black consciousness to the center of social transformation and political liberation praxis. The discrepancy between history and theology in this region leads us to conclude that Caribbean theology today requires a new pretext for investigation.

The Black religious experience in Jamaica has much to offer the Caribbean and the larger African diasporic theological community as scholars continue to ponder the meaning of Black religion and liberation in the twenty-first century. In Jamaica we encounter African people's resistance to dehumanization. The documentation of Black Jamaicans' struggle with death is nowhere more detailed than in the religious traditions both preserved and spawned within the context of exile and bondage. If we are to embrace the dynamism of Africa and reject static representations of African religion, as called for by Jacob Olupona,[143] we can identify in the religious history of Jamaican Blacks the transportation of African religions to a hostile and foreign geographic place and their translation into African diasporic languages under repressive and alien sociopolitical conditions.

Obeah, Myal, Native Baptist, Revival Zion, Kumina, and Rastafari are not just religions of people of African heritage, they are African religions in an oppressive New World. They are not Asante, Fante, Popo/Papaw, and Kongo religions but as African-derived or African-oriented religions, they instate the meaning of African religion and religiosity in diasporic terms. To be African in the diaspora is not a nebulous or contrived state of existence. It is, for Black people of African heritage in the Caribbean and Americas, to be a synthesis of many encounters among the various ethnicities and cultures comprising the African continent, in spite of the mystery surrounding the ethnocultural heritage of any particular person, community, or tradition. And it is not just any religious expression of Black people that qualifies as such. The Blackization of the missionary church in Jamaica does not qualify it as African. The missionary church in Jamaica, which is overwhelmingly Black in population, has a European heritage and established its foundation in Jamaica as the salvific and ethical alternative to what it interpreted as the barbaric heathenism promoted by African-derived religions. The missionary church competed with African religion in Jamaica and succeeded in forcing African practitioners underground and in stigmatizing African religiosity in the consciousness of its Christian converts. This church is essentially Euro-derived and Euro-oriented in theology, liturgy, piety, and consciousness. Caribbean theological scholars, as a collective, have acknowledged this time and time again as they endeavor to find a corrective to this unresolved "gospel and culture" problem in the region.

Theology in the Caribbean and in all regions of the African diaspora lacks creative genius and second sight, the third eye, the piercing perception needed to detect the stifled powers of subversive epistemologies from the underground experiences of African-oriented religious practitioners. This deficiency, this inability to recognize the ancestral Word as a source for theology, is crippling the prophetic voice in our discourses. The ancestral Word has materialized in African-derived traditions such as Obeah, Myal, Native Baptist, Revival Zion,

Kumina, and Rastafari. Comprehensively they have rejected the Euro-Christian Word of God. In spite of Eurocentric Christianity's dominance, these traditions together have expressed and restated transgenerationally the following imperatives:

- Afrophobia and anti-Africanness constitute a toxic cultural ethos characterizing the modern encounter between Africans and Europeans via racial slavery, colonialism, and their aftermath; such toxicity must be resisted.
- Freedom and liberation are legitimately defined and affirmed in terms of our African heritage.
- Indigenous knowledge, especially somatic epistemologies (body memory), are essential to our comprehensive wellness—the ultimate aim of abundant living.
- Life spent on earth is intended for human enjoyment; misery and disease are the enemies of life.
- The afterlife is a hostel for relational existence and reconnection and also offers elite knowledge and power to the disembodied living; it does not offer compensation for unmerited earthly suffering.
- Creation is sacred and demands respectful attention and care.
- Religion and spirituality are lived rather than confessed, thus religious and spiritual responsibilities are honored through actions not through proclamations.
- Humans are empowered to exercise their agency in concrete ways for social and personal transformation.
- The Divine Community assists the human community in its efforts to preserve wellness, transmit humanity pursue liberationist transformative action, and establish countercultural codes of civilization in anti-African and Afrophobic environments.
- African ancestral traditions are worth preserving transgenerationally even within severely repressive social contexts that censor such traditions.
- Religious pluralism and interreligious encounters should enhance human potential for hospitable communion with all creation. Thus religious diversity is a welcome remedy to division, stratification, and xenophobia in the human family.

These imperatives (in no specific order of importance) emerge from the struggles of anthropologically impoverished Jamaican Blacks. Through their struggles, they have managed to encode their indigenous wisdom and cultural knowledge within various Black religious configurations from slavery to the present day. This text represents one attempt to decode aspects of that wisdom and knowledge by dismantling some of the most troublesome theological blindspots that obscure a clarity of vision and by encouraging the piercing perception of Caribbean theological scholars who attempt to present the prophetic and liberationist trajectories in Caribbean religious experience.

When Caribbean theological scholars are able to take hold of such ancestral wisdom traditions and cultural knowledges, when we embrace the vulnerability of the Africans who love their Africanness regardless of the deep waters of separation and trauma, we are able to define resistance from the standpoint of the oppressed. The implications for academic theological reflection are momentous. Thus we should expect theologies that will shed the skins of inherited doctrinal reflection when they belie the major questions and paths of inquiry guiding our comprehensive research on African-Caribbean religiosity. This does not mean that we should not use classical doctrinal categories at all nor does it mean that we should not engage the Christian tradition of doctrinal analysis. However, Caribbean and other Black theologians will need to scrutinize our deeply ingrained disciplinary training, which functions like a blindfold preventing us from apprehending the intellectual resources present in African-derived religions and other non-Christian Black religious traditions. The reflections of the postcolonialist Nigerian scholar Chinweizu are helpful to consider on this point. In *The West and the Rest of Us*, he assesses the implications of his colonial academic training:

> It was a miseducation which, under the mystique of "modernizing" me into some "civilized" condition had worked to infect me with an intellectual meningitis that would twist my cultural spine, and rivet my admiring gaze upon Europe and the West. . . . It was a miseducation which, by encouraging me to glorify all things European, and by teaching me a low esteem for and negative attitudes towards things African, sought to cultivate in me that kind of inferiority complex which drives a perfectly fine right foot to strive to mutilate itself into a left foot.[144]

As new scholars with diverse interests in Black diasporic religious studies emerge, it will become increasingly apparent to theologically trained scholars that we must arrest the impulse to mutilate the right foot of Black (African diasporic) religions into a Christian left foot. Indeed, we have to be willing to allow the bearers of second sight, the coconut readers, and four-eyed women and men to speak to our rational minds in such a way that we give ourselves permission to relinquish Christian doctrinal categories as the pretext of our research.

This shift in sources and methodology does not displace the need for constructive Christian theology. However, it demands that space be made in theology for neglected knowledges or "resource zones" with regard to diasporic struggles against Afrophobia and anti-Africanness, a certain form of anthropological poverty that has been virtually ignored in the liberation theologies of the Americas and the Caribbean. Indeed Christian theology will have to be different if Christian theologians begin to regard the African heritage as a worthy subject of scholarly merit. African-derived and African-centered religious communities such as Revival Zion, Kumina, and Rastafari might be interrogated as resource zones even for Caribbean theologians of orthodox Christian persuasion who aim to do constructive liberation theology for the twenty-first century. Vernon Robbins has coined the term *resource zone* to signify the processes that produce sacred texts within and across interactive communities such as Judaism, Christianity, and Islam.[145] These processes indicate selective borrowings, shapings, and literal recordings of shared narratives within the scared texts of the three traditions and could be compared with the processes of religious formation among African Jamaicans, where Obeah, Myal, Native Baptist, Revival Zion, Rastafari, and Kumina communities, as they have interacted with Euro-missionary Christianity and with each other, emerge as resource zones with equally compelling, authoritative, overlapping and independent textual[146] materials for theological consideration.

The suggested methodological shift also imagines a variety of theological projects that will redefine how theology is done when it is focused upon non-Christian traditions such as Rastafari, Black Islamic and Judaic religions, as well as African-derived religions like Kumina, Vodun, and Orisha. The next phase of the theological enterprise in the African diaspora will be saturated with conversations about Black religious pluralism, an especial outcome of our focus on liberationist hermeneutics. As we exit this current phase of liberation theological discourse, the energy generated by its pathfinders is already producing voices of reflection on singular traditions that are not Christian.

Most promising is the pregnant state of our queries and debates, which will inevitably yield theological discourses on the problematic of Christian dominance and arrogance in comparative, collaborative, or integrative theologies that consider the interaction and interfacing of multiple heritages, collective memories, and religious traditions among African diasporic peoples and other peoples of Africa, Asia, and the Americas. This pluralistic historical composition is, in the end, our inheritance and our debt. Furthermore, liberationist approaches to the sources of Black people's religious histories expose the assumptions of previous generations—that Christianity is our inheritance (wealth) and African religion our debt (impoverishment)—to be perilously deceptive and indeed a heresy of our double consciousness that no longer holds merit. Through the sight of the third eye, we see ourselves more clearly and are free to embrace what we do not yet see.

Notes

PREFACE

1. See Patricia Hill Collins's feminist analysis of migration and boundary crossing in the Black North American experience, *Fighting Words: Black Women and the Search for Justice* (Minneapolis: University of Minnesota Press, 1998), 3–5, 231–234. Also see Gloria Anzaldúa's theory of boundary crossing in Anzaldúa, *Borderlands/La Frontera* (San Francisco: Spinsters/Aunt Lute, 1987).

2. Daniel Payne, *History of the African Methodist Episcopal Church* (New York: Arno, 1969).

3. Alexander Crummell and Wilson J. Moses, eds., *Destiny and Race: Selected Writings, 1840–1898* (Amherst: University of Massachusetts Press, 1992).

4. Martin Delany, "Report of the Niger Valley Exploring Party," in *Search for a Place: Black Separatism and Africa, 1860*, ed. Howard Bell (Ann Arbor: University of Michigan Press, 1969), 133–134.

5. Kelly Brown Douglas, *The Black Christ* (Maryknoll, NY: Orbis, 1994), 105–106.

6. George Brandon, *Santería from Africa to the New World: The Dead Sell Memories* (Bloomington: Indiana University Press, 1993); Michel Laguerre, *Voodoo and Politics in Haiti* (New York: St. Martin's, 1989); Monica Schuler, *"Alas, Alas, Kongo": A Social History of Indentured African Immigration into Jamaica, 1841–1865* (Baltimore, MD: Johns Hopkins University Press, 1980); Leonard Barrett, *Soul Force: African Heritage in Afro-American Religion* (London: Heinemann, 1976).

7. See E. Franklin Frazier, *The Negro Church in America* (New York: Schocken, 1964); and Melville Herskovits, *The Myth of the Negro Past* (Boston: Beacon, 1990).

8. Liberation theologians commonly use this term, which carries the same meaning as the term *liberationist*.

9. Islam as carried from Africa to the Caribbean and the Americas by

enslaved Africans is a minor trajectory that deserves more attention in studies of slave religion, especially given the formation of the Nation of Islam in North America and the phenomenon of conversion among African North Americans to other Islamic traditions in the twentieth century.

10. *Transmitting humanity* refers to something very specific and significant in African diasporic contexts like Jamaica. When a group faces dehumanization in literal, symbolic, physical, psychological, and cultural terms, the transmission of humanity as defined by their being-in-the-world—however that is—is of ultimate significance to the group. Religion serves this purpose in the Jamaican context and in other African diasporic contexts as well. F. Eboussi Boulaga's discussion of the nature of being human in African religiosity stimulated this discovery (in my research) of the transmission of humanity in African diasporic religions. See his *Christianity without Fetishes: An African Critique and Recapture of Christianity* (Maryknoll, NY: Orbis, 1984), esp. 79–83.

INTRODUCTION

1. I use the term *African(s)* to represent the autochthonous peoples and cultures of the land mass which came to be known as "Africa" in the modern period. Included in this representation are peoples of the African diaspora, especially those who self-consciously identified and continue to self-consciously identify as such. I also use the terms African Caribbean, African American, and Black to refer to the descendants of enslaved Africans in the Caribbean and the Americas.

2. This aphorism was popularized by Jomo Kenyatta during the time of the Mau Mau revolution in Kenya. I expand it here to demonstrate how widespread the trajectory of dominance via Christian imperialism is in European history. See David Lamb, *The Africans* (New York: Vintage, 1987), 59.

3. This was certainly the assertion of one of the most influential theologians of the twentieth century, Karl Barth. In this regard, Barth stood on the shoulders of numerous forerunners for whom this line of thought was a presupposition and requisite of the faith. See Barth's "The Revelation of God as the Abolition of Religion," in *Church Dogmatics*, vol. 1, pt. 2, ed. G. W. Bromiley and T. F. Torrance (Edinburgh: Clark, 1936–1940), 280–361.

4. Englebert Mveng, "Third World Theology—What Theology? What Third World? Evaluation by an African Delegate," in *Irruption of the Third World: Challenge to Theology*, ed. Virginia Fabella and Sergio Torres (Maryknoll, NY: Orbis, 1983), 220.

5. Liberation theologians have collectively embraced this hermeneutical approach, which must be attributed to Paul Ricoeur. Ricoeur examines "interpretation as an exercise of suspicion" in his *Freud and Philosophy: An Essay on Interpretation* (New Haven, CT: Yale University Press, 1970), 32–36.

6. Mercy Oduyoye, "Reflections from a Third World Woman's Perspective: Women's Experience and Liberation Theologies," in *Irruption of the Third World*, ed. Fabella and Torres, 246–255.

7. Josiah Young, who defines his project as "Pan-African" theology, is the only exception. More will be said about Young's approach and the shared and divergent aims of our projects in chapter 5. See Josiah Young, *A Pan-African Theology: Providence and the Legacies of the Ancestors* (Trenton, NJ: Africa World, 1992), and Young, "God's Path in Pan-Africa," in *Black Theology: A Documentary History*, Vol. 2, ed. Gayraud Wilmore and James Cone (Maryknoll, NY: Orbis, 1993), 18–25.

8. See especially Gayraud Wilmore, *Black Religion and Black Radicalism: An In-*

terpretation of the Religious History of Afro-American People (Maryknoll, NY: Orbis, 1990); Cone, *Martin and Malcolm and America: A Dream or a Nightmare* (Maryknoll, NY: Orbis, 1991); Cone, "An Interpretation of the Debate among Black Theologians," in *Black Theology: A Documentary History, 1966–1979,* ed. Gayraud Wilmore and James Cone (Maryknoll, NY: Orbis, 1979), 609–623.

9. The motif of African heritage in African diasporic religious experience is short-lived in the works of most theologians. Commentary on the legacies of African religious and cultural expressions in the diaspora are usually limited to the introduction or initial chapters of most Black and Caribbean theologies.

10. By *classical,* I am referring to the ancient African cultures that have emerged over centuries in ethnic societies across the continent. I use *classical* with specific reference to indigenous African religions, which are customarily termed "African traditional religions" by most scholars.

11. Mercea Eliade, *The Quest: History and Meaning in Religion* (Chicago, IL: University of Chicago Press, 1969), 2.

12. Eric Sharpe, *Comparative Religion: A History* (La Salle, IL: Open Court, 1990), 280.

13. See Hans Küng, "No World Peace without Religious Peace," in *Christianity and the World Religions: Paths of Dialogue with Islam, Hinduism, and Buddhism,* ed. Hans Küng et al. (New York: Collins and Doubleday, 1986), 440–443; Wilfred Cantwell Smith, *Towards a World Theology: Faith and the Comparative History of Religion* (Maryknoll, NY: Orbis, 1981); Paul Knitter, *No Other Name? A Critical Survey of Christian Attitudes toward the World Religions* (Maryknoll, NY: Orbis, 1990), 1–54.

14. Smith, *Towards a World Theology,* 128.

15. Küng, "No World Peace without Religious Peace," xv.

16. Smith, *Towards a World Theology,* 6.

17. In the case of Wilfred Cantwell Smith, he undoubtedly supported the view that the classical African religions as "primitive religions" do not contain "religion's highest and truest development." See his essay "Comparative Religion: Whither—and Why?" in *The History of Religions: Essays in Methodology,* ed. Mircea Eliade and Joseph Kitagawa (Chicago, IL: University of Chicago Press, 1959), 37–38. Also see Jacob Olupona's discussion of Smith's perception of African religions. According to Olupona, after receiving criticism from other scholars, Smith recanted. Jacob Olupona, "Major Issues in the Study of African Traditional Religion," in *African Traditional Religions in Contemporary Society,* ed. Jacob Olupona (St. Paul, MN: Paragon House, 1991), 25–26.

18. Gordon Colin, ed., *Power/Knowledge: Selected Interviews and Other Writings, 1972–1977, by Michel Foucault* (New York: Pantheon, 1980), 82–83.

19. Borrowing from Michel Foucault's concept of "local knowledge," the term *local awareness* is intended to be inclusive of persons, both internal and external to a context of *constructed* suffering, who acknowledge the concrete sociopolitical factors that qualify the suffering as constructed. See Colin, ed., *Power/Knowledge,* 78–92.

20. "Final Statement of the Fifth EATWOT Conference, New Delhi, August 17–29, 1981," in *Irruption of the Third World,* ed. Fabella and Torres, 202–203.

21. Colin, ed., *Power/Knowledge,* 82–83.

22. Kongo/Kongolese refers to BaKongo ethnic subgroups occupying regions within the Democratic Republic of Congo (DRC/former Zaire), the Republic of Congo, and Angola. Congo/Congolese can refer to any ethnic group or culture found in the DRC and in the neighboring Republic of Congo. In referring to BaKongo culture, linguists sometimes use the spelling Koongo, stressing the long "o" in pronunciation.

CHAPTER ONE

1. Testimony given by an enslaved African, Mrs. Brooks, to the wife of a missionary, Mrs. Coultart. Cited in Religious Tract Society, *Missionary Records: West Indies* (London: Religious Tract Society, 1834–1838), 109.

2. Jamaica was called *Xaymaca* by the indigenous people of the region.

3. Colón is believed to be the first European to visit Jamaica and establish a European presence in the island. Colón landed in Jamaica on May 5, 1494, during his second voyage to the Caribbean region. During Colón's first voyage, he and his ninety-person entourage initially disembarked at today's Watling Island (Bahamas) on October 12, 1492.

4. Eric Williams, *Capitalism and Slavery* (Chapel Hill: University of North Carolina Press, 1944), 3.

5. The only notable exception is the Kongo kingdom, which was influenced by the Portuguese culture and Christian religion as early as the last decade of the fifteenth century. See Chinweizu, *The West and the Rest of Us: White Predators, Black Slavers and the African Elite* (New York: Random House, 1975), 27–30.

6. It is important to acknowledge that Europeans held a variety of opinions about the evangelization of Africans. While there were many who supported it for any number of reasons, Whites who were (personally) economically invested in the plantation system—as distinct, say, from Whites invested in the trade of buying and selling Africans as slaves, that is, the planters, overseers, attorneys, and so on—tended to oppose evangelization. K. S. Malden addresses some of the reasons for White opposition to missionary work among enslaved Africans in his book *Broken Bonds: The S.P.G. and the West Indian Slaves* (Aberdeen, Scotland: Aberdeen University Press, 1933), 18–34. This issue will be discussed later in the chapter.

7. Spanish governorship was established in 1509, only five years after a dejected and destitute Colón left the Caribbean with about 100 survivors and headed for Spain. He never returned to the region again. See J. H. Parry and P. M. Sherlock, *A Short History of the West Indies* (London: Macmillan, 1956), 1–11.

8. This was the same year that Bartolomé de Las Casas suggested to King Charles V that Africans should be imported to replace the slave labor of a dying population of native Indians in the Spanish territories. The first shipment of Africans to the Caribbean took place in 1502 in Hispañola. See Michael L. Conniff and Thomas J. Davis, *Africans in the Americas: A History of the Black Diaspora* (New York: St. Martin's, 1994). Malcolm Cowley cites 1518 as the date when "the slave trade proper began with the landing in the West Indies of the first black cargo directed from Africa." See Daniel Mannix and Malcolm Cowley, *Black Cargoes: A History of the Atlantic Slave Trade, 1518–1865* (New York: Viking, 1965), vii.

9. For a concise treatment of the Spanish regime in Jamaica, see Patrick Bryan, "Spanish Jamaica," *Caribbean Quarterly* 38 (1992): 21–31.

10. The Spanish, French, Dutch, Italians, Portuguese, and English were rivals over Jamaica and other Caribbean territories during this period. For a thorough historical account of the European competition for sovereignty in the Caribbean, see Parry and Sherlock, *Short History of the West Indies*, esp. 1–94.

11. Mannix and Cowley, *Black Cargoes*, xii.

12. By 1768, Jamaica sustained 648 sugar estates. For a comprehensive sociohistorical overview of Jamaican plantation systems, see Orlando Patterson's chapter. "The Slave Plantation: Its Socio-Economic Structure," in Patterson, *The Sociology of Slavery:*

An Analysis of the Origins, Development and Structure of Negro Slave Society in Jamaica (Teaneck, NJ: Fairleigh Dickinson University Press, 1975), 52–69.

13. Williams, *Capitalism and Slavery*, 54–55.

14. Parry and Sherlock, *Short History of the West Indies*, 69. This pattern can be traced into the nineteenth century as well. For example, in 1820, there were 839,000 persons of African descent and 57,000 Whites in the entire British Caribbean.

15. Philip D. Curtin, *The Atlantic Slave Trade: A Census* (Madison: University of Wisconsin Press, 1969), 53. Compare with Horace Campbell, *Rasta and Resistance: From Marcus Garvey to Walter Rodney* (Trenton, NJ: Africa World, 1987), 15. Campbell maintains, "Over a million slaves were brought to Jamaica during the period of slavery, of which 200,000 were re-exported." J. E. Inkori also quotes higher numbers than does Curtin in his edited work, *Forced Migration: The Impact of the Export Slave Trade on African Societies* (London: Hutchinson, 1982).

16. The British landed in Jamaica in 1655. In 1660, Spanish forces left for Cuba, and by 1670 the British had complete sovereignty over the island.

17. Parry and Sherlock, *Short History of the West Indies*, 1–94.

18. Penalties for rebellion were devastating. Both during and after the 1831 rebellion in Jamaica, at least 707 Africans were killed as compared with 14 whites. See Patterson, *Sociology of Slavery*, 273. The same pattern can be observed in other Caribbean islands. For example in Barbados, "during a dreadful insurrection in 1816 . . . about 1,000 negroes were massacred, either as actual insurgents, or on unfounded suspicion." See Religious Tract Society, *Missionary Records: West Indies*, 145.

19. Parry and Sherlock, *Short History of the West Indies*, 151.

20. Richard Hart's book, *Slaves Who Abolished Slavery* (Kingston, Jamaica: Institute of Social and Economic Research, UWI, 1985), is an extensive treatment of African rebellions against the Jamaican slave regime.

21. As early as 1684, only fourteen years after the British acquired official sovereignty over the island, the Jamaican Assembly passed an "Act for the better ordering of slaves," which said, "[I]t is further enacted by the authority aforesaid, that every master or mistress or overseer of a family in the island shall cause all slaves houses to be diligently and effectively searched once every fourteen days, for clubs, wooden swords, and mischievous weapons, and finding any, shall take them away and cause them to be burnt." We might infer then that organized revolts were incessant enough to invite this legislative response. See Joseph Williams, *Voodoos and Obeahs: Phases of West India Witchcraft* (New York: Dial, 1932), 160.

22. Patterson, *Sociology of Slavery*, 260.

23. Ibid., 274. Patterson evaluates this information comparatively, noting, "The most serious revolt in [the United States]—that of Nat Turner—involved only seventy slaves." Compare with Horace Campbell, "Jamaica acquired special significance during the period of slavery, not only because it was the most prosperous of the British colonies, but also because it was the area of the most slave revolts in the New World. There were more than 400 revolts with major confrontations in 1729–39, 1760, and 1831–32, each involving over a thousand slaves." See Campbell, *Rasta and Resistance*, 26.

24. During the seventeenth and eighteenth centuries, enslaved Africans outnumbered Europeans in Jamaica ten to one, and during the nineteenth century, thirteen to one. The ratio of enslaved Africans to Europeans in Barbados was approximately four to one. The ratio never exceeded eight to one in the Leeward Islands, save for Antigua, even after African importation increased in the early eighteenth century. Patterson, *Sociology of Slavery*, 274.

25. Ibid., 275–276.

26. For example, Drax Hall was founded in 1669 on Jamaica's north coast (just east of St. Ann's Bay). By 1691, the estate comprised more than 3,000 acres. Between 1760 and 1821, the ownership changed and the plantation's operations were carried out without direct supervision from the owners, William Beckford and William Beckford, Jr., who resided in England. John Pink purchased Drax Hall from the Beckfords in 1821 and resided there throughout the remainder of the slave period. As an eighteenth-century sugar-producing estate, Drax Hall was sustained by the labor of 320 enslaved Africans on average. For a more descriptive historical account of the sugar plantation, see Douglas V. Armstrong, "Afro-Jamaican Plantation Life: An Archaeological Study of Drax Hall," *Jamaica Journal* 24 (June 1991): 3–8. Also see Patterson, *Sociology of Slavery*, 34–45, 50–51.

27. Ibid., 276–279.

28. Barrett, *Soul Force*, 1–2.

29. See ibid.; Vincent Harding, *There Is a River: The Black Struggle for Freedom in America* (New York: Vintage, 1983); Albert Raboteau, *Slave Religion: The "Invisible Institution" in the Antebellum South* (Oxford: Oxford University Press, 1978); Wilmore, *Black Religion and Black Radicalism*; George Simpson, *Black Religions in the New World* (New York: Columbia University Press, 1978); Young, *A Pan-African Theology*; Barry Chevannes, *Rastafari: Roots and Ideology* (Syracuse, NY: Syracuse University Press, 1994). Other sources include Lawrence Levine, *Black Culture, Black Consciousness: Afro-American Folk Thought from Slavery to Freedom* (Oxford: Oxford University Press, 1977); Sterling Stuckey, *Slave Culture: Nationalist Theory and the Foundations of Black America* (New York: Oxford University Press, 1987); Schuler, *"Alas, Alas, Kongo"*; Laguerre, *Voodoo and Politics in Haiti*.

30. A Jamaican legislative act passed in 1696 includes in clause 32: "And Whereas divers slaves have of late attempted to destroy several people, as well white as black, by poison; the consequences of which secret way of murdering may prove fatal, if not timely prevented: Be it enacted by the authority aforesaid, That if any Negro, or any slave or slaves, before the making of this Act, have maliciously given or attempted to give, or shall hereafter maliciously give, attempt or cause to be given to any person whatsoever, free or slave any manner of poison, although the same was never taken, or if taken, death did not or shall not ensue upon the taking thereof; the said slave or slaves, together with their accessories, as well before as after the fact, being slaves, and convicted thereof . . . shall be adjudged guilty of murder . . . and shall be condemned to suffer death, by hanging, burning, or such other way or means as to the said Justices and freeholders shall seem most convenient." See Williams, *Voodoos and Obeahs*, 160–161, and see 198–199 for several examples of Africans who were caught or criminally tried for poisoning/attempted poisoning of White overseers and slave masters.

31. It is rare to find references to African "religion(s)" in the Eurocentric literature associated with the slave period. Europeans had a tendency to view Africans as irreligious or prereligious and therefore often used labels such as "superstitious," "fetishistic," "sorcery," "witchcraft," "black magic," and the like to signify African religiosity.

32. Walter Rodney framed the question as follows: "One of the uncertainties concerns the basic question of how many Africans were imported. This has long been an object of speculation, with estimates ranging from a few millions to over one hundred million." *How Europe Underdeveloped Africa* (Washington, DC: Howard University Press, 1982), 96.

33. Although Curtin is a credible authority, his demographic and import-export estimates pertaining to the slave trade appear conservative when compared with the findings of more recent research. For a deeper discussion of the discrepancies among scholars, see Inkori, *Forced Migration*, 19–38.

34. In the 1990s, the Du Bois Institute at Harvard University sponsored the production of a comprehensive CD-ROM on the demographics of the slave trade. This collaborative scholarly effort appears to be the most meticulous and comprehensive to date and will surely advance African diasporic studies across disciplines. See David Eltis and G. Ugo Nwokeji, *The Trans-Atlantic Slave Trade: A Database on CD-ROM* (Cambridge, UK: Cambridge University Press, 1999).

35. Mervyn Alleyne, *Roots of Jamaican Culture* (London: Pluto, 1988), 37; Parry and Sherlock, *A Short History of the West Indies*, 95–111.

36. One example of this unintentional yet erroneous collapse of ethnic identities into regional identity is seen in Patterson's discussion of the Ananse folk tradition in Jamaica. In his chapter "Social Institutions of the Slaves," Patterson notes that "much has been made of this etymology by writers who wished to substantiate the untenable argument that *the Coromanti Negros culturally dominated the rest of the slave population*" (italics mine). See *Sociology of Slavery*, 250.

37. See map on xxvii for a comprehensive list of European holding forts and posts along the "Gold Coast" and "Slave Coast."

38. Patterson's study is well researched and particular to Jamaica, thus I find it very persuasive. See *Sociology of Slavery*, 113–144.

39. Mannix and Cowley, *Black Cargoes*, 100.

40. Eric Williams, "Caribbean Slavery and the Capitalist World Economy," in *Caribbean Slave Society and Economy: A Student Reader*, ed. Hilary Beckles and Verene Shepherd (Kingston, Jamaica: Randle, 1991), 120–129.

41. Alleyne, *Roots of Jamaican Culture*, 39.

42. Ibid., 41.

43. Ibid. See map on xxvii for information on these and other slave forts.

44. The Company of Royal Adventurers, trading to Africa, was incorporated in 1663. The company was reformed and its name was changed to the Royal African Company in 1672. See Williams, *Capitalism and Slavery*, 30–31.

45. Ibid., 30–32.

46. Alleyne, *Roots of Jamaican Culture*, 42.

47. Ibid., 28. Africans were transported from the British settlements of Sierra Leone and St. Helena and from intercepted slave ships en route to Brazil and Cuba.

48. Monica Schuler, "The Experience of African Immigrants in 19th Century Jamaica" (unpublished manuscript, 1972), 7. Cited by Alleyne in *Roots of Jamaican Culture*, 43.

49. Alleyne, *Roots of Jamaican Culture*, 44. Compare with Patterson's chapter entitled "The Tribal Origins of the Jamaican Slaves," in *Sociology of Slavery*, 113–144.

50. See John Mbiti, *Introduction to African Religion* (London: Heinemann, 1975), and *African Religions and Philosophy* (London: Heinemann, 1969); Bolaji Idowu, *African Traditional Religion: A Definition* (London: SCM, 1973); Dominique Zahan, *The Religion, Spirituality, and Thought of Traditional Africa* (Chicago: University of Chicago Press, 1979); Robin Horton, *Patterns of Thought in Africa and the West* (Cambridge: Cambridge University Press, 1993); Simon Ottenberg, ed., *African Religious Groups and Beliefs: Papers in Honor of William R. Bascom* (Meerut, India: Archana, 1982).

51. My intention is not to skirt the obvious polemic concerning the *African authenticity* of African diasporic religions and cultures as such. Debates about the Afri-

canness of Blacks in the Americas and the Caribbean are significant in my estimation insofar as they expose an often unverbalized sentiment—that there is no true benefit in identifying with Africa. In this study, I de-emphasize the set of questions and issues that attends the problematic of African identity for dispersed peoples whose ancestors were undeniably "African" at some recent point in the history of humanity. See Herskovits, *Myth of the Negro Past*; Simpson, *Black Religions in the New World*; Robert Farris Thompson, *Flash of the Spirit: African and Afro-American Art and Philosophy* (New York: Random House, 1983); Leonard Barrett, *Soul Force* and *The Sun and the Drum: African Roots in Jamaican Folk Tradition* (London: Heinemann, 1976); Roger Bastide, *The African Religions of Brazil: Toward a Sociology of the Interpenetration of Civilizations* (Baltimore, MD: Johns Hopkins University Press, 1983); Sidney Mintz and Richard Price, *The Birth of African-American Culture: An Anthropological Perspective* (Boston: Beacon, 1976); John Mason, *Black Gods: Orisa Studies in the New World* (Brooklyn, NY: Yoruba Theological Archministry, 1985); Stuckey, *Slave Culture*.

52. The view that Africans are communotheistic, have a relational view of deities, and understand them as operating within a community has been forwarded by A. Okechukwu Ogbonnaya in his book *On Communitarian Divinity* (New York: Paragon House, 1994). This notion is significant because it accents a central aspect of African theism that is undermined when emphasis is placed upon a hierarchic ordering of deities in African religions. I maintain that the hierarchic ordering of deities, often conceived ontologically, has been exaggerated in the discourse on African religions. For example, see E. Bolaji Idowu, *Olodumare, God in Yoruba Belief* (London: Longmans, Green, 1962); R. S. Rattray, *Religion and Art in Ashanti* (Oxford: Clarendon, 1927); Emefie Ikenga Metuh, *God and Man in African Religion: A Case of the Igbo of Nigeria* (London: Chapman, 1981).

53. Young, *A Pan-African Theology*, 103.

54. Jonathan Z. Smith, *Imagining Religion: From Babylon to Jonestown* (Chicago: The University of Chicago Press, 1982), 18.

55. Ibid., 8.

56. Charles Leslie, *A New History of Jamaica: From the Earliest Accounts to the Taking of Porto Bello by Vice-Admiral Vernon* (London: Printed for J. Hodges, 1740), 306–307. Later in the chapter (p. 311), Leslie provides more specific details of the African origin of the enslaved population: "They [slave traders] trade from *Sierra Leona* to *Cape Negro*, [original emphasis] a vast Territory on the Coasts near 1500 Miles in Length, in which are a great Multitude of petty Kingdoms."

57. See David Hall, *Worlds of Wonder, Days of Judgment: Popular Religious Belief in Early New England* (Cambridge: Harvard University Press, 1990); also see David Hall, ed., *Lived Religion in America: Toward a History of Practice* (Princeton, NJ: Princeton University Press, 1997). See the following works by Robert Orsi, *The Madonna of 115th Street: Faith and Community in Italian Harlem, 1880–1950* (New Haven: Yale University Press, 1985); *Thank You St. Jude: Women's Devotion to the Patron Saint of Hopeless Causes* (New Haven: Yale University Press, 1996); *Gods of the City: Religion and the American Urban Landscape* (Bloomington: Indiana University Press, 1999). See also Charles Long, *Significations: Signs, Symbols, and Images in the Interpretation of Religion* (Philadelphia: Fortress Press, 1986).

58. See, for example, Richard Madden's comparison between African (Obeah) rituals performed in Jamaica and European pagan rituals, especially those of "Scotch witches." Also see his discussion of mob violence and corporal punishment of "witches" in England and Scotland on pp. 72–73. Madden was a stipendiary magistrate who served in Jamaica in 1833 and wrote two volumes about his experience. See

his *A Twelvemonth's Residence in the West Indies*, vol. 2 (Philadelphia: Carey, Lea and Blanchard, 1835), reprinted (Westport, CT: Negro University Press, 1970), 69–70.

59. Ibid., p. 70. Madden describes a ritual for detection of theft involving a Bible and a key and concludes: "This is a singular instance of an African superstition ingrafted on Christianity."

60. I will take up this issue more extensively in chapter 3 when I discuss Revival Zion.

61. Examples are Haitian Vodun, Brazilian Candomblé, Cuban Santería, and Surinamese Winti.

62. This last rationale, blessing, was relayed to me by Stanley Stewart, a native Jamaican of fifty-four years, during a formal interview, Kingston, Jamaica, October 4, 1996.

63. Patterson's findings support my own. In his discussion of African religion in pre-Emancipation Jamaica, he maintains, "This aspect of the slaves' lives may be considered under two heads. First, the survivals of African supernatural behavior as they were reshaped during slavery; and secondly, the impact of Christianity on the slaves. The latter was of no real significance until the last three or four decades of slavery." See *Sociology of Slavery*, 182.

64. Barrett, *Soul Force*, 79–80.

65. Malden, *Broken Bonds*, 17–18.

66. Alfred Caldecott, *The Church in the West Indies* (London: Cass, 1898), 70, 72.

67. Ibid., 70–76.

68. Walter Hark, *The Breaking of the Dawn; or, Moravian Work in Jamaica* (London: Strain, 1904), 1–26. Evidence of planter and overseer opposition to the work of the missionaries among enslaved Africans is overwhelming throughout the entire document; see esp. 29, 32–33, 38. For other examples of planter and overseer opposition to Presbyterian, Baptist, and Wesleyan missionaries, see George Blyth, *Reminiscences of Missionary Life, with Suggestions to Churches and Missionaries* (Edinburgh: Oliphant, 1851), 44–50; Mary Turner, *Slaves and Missionaries: The Disintegration of Jamaican Slave Society, 1787–1834* (Urbana: University of Illinois Press, 1982), 1–37. Religious Tract Society, *Missionary Records: West Indies*, contains reports about planter and overseer opposition to missionary work throughout the British and, in some cases, French Caribbean. See esp. 83–84, 86–94, 128–139, 187–188, 279–296, 299–304; also see 172–184 for an apparently rare example of planter support for missionaries, which occurred in the island of St. Christopher (St. Kitts) during the late eighteenth century.

69. Hark, *Breaking of the Dawn*, 13.

70. Ibid., 17.

71. Caldecott, *The Church in the West Indies*, 84. Compare with Malden, *Broken Bonds*, 31: "[I]n 1696 'an Act of Jamaica' laid down that 'masters were to instruct their slaves and have them baptized when fit for it,' and this was repeated in an act of 1788, but as there was no pretence of punishment, or remedy for neglect of this injunction, it remained a dead letter."

72. G. H. Rose, *A Letter on the Means and Importance of Converting the Slaves in the West Indies to Christianity* (London: Murray, 1823), 4–5. Also Malden, *Broken Bonds*, 32, who provides important data on the dearth of Christian teaching throughout the British Caribbean: "At the beginning of the nineteenth century the whole of the Bahamas were under the charge of one priest living at New Providence. In 1784 Grenada and Carriacou, with a slave population of 24,000, had only five clergymen. Demerara and Essequibo had, in addition to their free population 77,376 slaves, one

church and one clergyman. Berbice, with a population of 25,959, had no English church or priest, and only one Dutch minister for the entire colony. As late as 1818 there was no church or church establishment in the whole of the island of Trinidad. On the fortunate islands which boasted of churches, many of the vicars were plural-ists, and had two or three parishes to look after; and what churches there were, were intended for the white population, not the black."

73. Hark, *Breaking of the Dawn*, 20.

74. Thomas Coke, *A History of the West Indies, Containing the Natural, Civil and Ecclesiastical History of Each Island*, vol. 2 (Liverpool, England: Nuttall, Fisher and Dixon, 1808–1811), 89–104.

75. For example, two of the most prolific chroniclers of African religious prac-tices during slavery, Edward Long and Bryan Edwards, expressed unmitigated racist sentiments about Africans and African culture. Their racist discourse will be dis-cussed in chapter 2.

76. Religious Tract Society, *Missionary Records: West Indies*, xii.

77. Ibid., 94–95.

78. Charles Leslie, *A New History of Jamaica*, 307–310.

79. Ibid.

80. Hans Sloane, *A Voyage to the Islands Madera, Barbados, Nieves, St. Christo-phers and Jamaica*, vol. 1 (London: Printed by B. M. for the author, 1707–1725), Special Collections and Archives, Robert W. Woodruff Library, Emory University, xvi.

81. Patterson, *Sociology of Slavery*, 196.

82. Religious Tract Society, *Missionary Records: West Indies*, xiii. Portions of this quote are apparently derived from James Phillippo's text *Jamaica: Its Past and Present State* (Westport, CT: Negro University Press, 1970, originally published in 1843), 269. Note the reference to enslaved Africans of different religious orientations, including Islam and Coptic/Ethiopian Christianity. This, along with other testimonies, should peak the interest of any Caribbean religious historian and invite novel evaluations of the pluralistic religious heritages of the Africans who came to the Caribbean as slaves.

83. Most scholars cite what appears to be a 1740 edition of Leslie's text. I also have a copy of a 1740 edition and have not been able to acquire an earlier edition. Frederic Cassidy's and R. B. Le Page's bibliography in the *Dictionary of Jamaican En-glish* (Cambridge: Cambridge University Press, 1967) notes that the 1740 text is a sec-ond edition but does not provide the date or publication information of the first edi-tion. In *The Sociology of Slavery*, p. 199, Orlando Patterson states that Leslie published his *New History of Jamaica* in 1730. However, his first citation of Leslie's text on page 31 provides a publication date of 1740 with no other publication information. Patter-son does not include a bibliography and all other references appear to be to the 1740 edition. I believe this incongruence is an oversight because after further investigation I discovered that two editions of Leslie's *New History of Jamaica* were released in the same year and so it is unlikely that Leslie published a 1730 copy of the text.

84. Thus far I have read all of the seventeenth-century publications that I could acquire, none of which comments upon the religious lives of enslaved populations in Jamaica. Texts examined include: Edward Ward, *A Trip to Jamaica: With a True Char-acter of the People of the Island* (London: J. How, 1700, first printed in 1698); Richard Blome, *A Description of the Island of Jamaica* (London: Milbourn, 1672, reprinted by J. B. for Newman, 1678); *The Laws of Jamaica, Passed by the Assembly* (London: Hills for Harper, 1683); Fr. Clark for Malthus, *The Present State of Jamaica* (London: 1683). In the cases of Ward and Blome, I read both editions of their texts.

85. Charles Leslie, *A New History of Jamaica*, 307. Orlando Patterson's line of

reasoning in connecting these terms to Dahomean ancestor rituals, if correct, would prove Leslie incorrect here in identifying these names with deities. I discuss Patterson's interpretation on p. 57. Although very compelling, Patterson's interpretation is not conclusive and so I do include Leslie's description of Naskew and Timnew as African deities in Table 1.4 of this chapter, which catalogues general African-derived beliefs and practices. Also see Charles Leslie, *A New and Exact Account of Jamaica* (Edinburgh: Fleming, 1739).

86. Edward Long, *The History of Jamaica or, General Survey of the Antient and Modern State of that Island with Reflections on its Situation, Settlements, Inhabitants, Climate, Products, Commerce, Laws and Government* (London: Frank Cass and Company, 1970, First edition, 1774), 416.

87. The only pre-emancipation literature I know of that mentions Myal without introducing the topic of Obeah is a four-line diary entry that offers no descriptive detail about Myal and so I did not deem it necessary to create a chart for the following: "Wednesday, 22nd March 1769: Egypt Lucy acquainted Phibbah privately, that the Myal dance has been held twice in Phibbah's Coobah's house, at Paradise Estate, as also Egypt Dago, and Job, who are both Myal-men attend these dancings." See Douglas Hall, *In Miserable Slavery: Thomas Thistlewood in Jamaica, 1750–86* (Barbados: The University of the West Indies Press, 1999), 217. For the last nineteen years of his life, Thistlewood held 30 slaves on his 160-acre property in the parish of Westmoreland.

After reading a wide array of documents from the slave period in Jamaica and the wider British Caribbean, I have noticed that a number of writers quote or paraphrase earlier writers without citing them. In such instances, I have tried to avoid duplication by not citing those passages or by omitting the source altogether. The descriptions in Tables 1.2, 1.3, and 1.4 are paraphrases and direct quotes of the noted sources, which contain varying spellings for the same term. I deliberately retain multiple spellings for the same word (e.g., Obia, Obeiah, Obeah) because I thought it important to present the actual words from each writer so that readers could have access to the exact language used, which may be particularly helpful to linguistic scholars. I also hope that scholars from Africa will do more work on African diasporic religions by examining historical records from the slave period in connection with other methodological strategies. And so I believe it is important that, as scholars access archival materials on slavery, they make efforts to expose the actual descriptions and observations of African religious and cultural practices for wider scholarly and popular audiences. In each table, the letter "P" placed after a date designates the publication date of the cited source in contrast with the date of observation. I was not able to determine the actual date of observation for every text.

Relevant sources for Tables 1.2, 1.3, and 1.4 are Edward Long, *The History of Jamaica*, vol. 2, 416–425; 489; Richard Madden, *A Twelvemonth's Residence in the West Indies*, 65–77; Bryan Edwards, *The History, Civil and Commercial, of the British Colonies in the West Indies*, vol. 2 (New York: AMS Press, 1966, first published in 1793), 85–86; 108; 111–112; 114–117; Frederic G. Cassidy and R. B. Le Page eds., *Dictionary of Jamaican English*, 326–327; Peter Marsden, *An Account of the Island of Jamaica* (Newcastle: Hodgson, 1788), 40; Author Unknown, *The Koromantyn Slaves or West Indian Sketches*, (London: J. Hatchard and Son, Piccadilly, 1823), 177–178; Richard Hart, *Slaves Who Abolished Slavery* (Kingston, Jamaica: Institute of Social and Economic Research UWI, 1985), 234–236; H. T. De la Beche, *Notes on the Present Condition of the Negroes in Jamaica* (London: Cadell, 1825), 30–31; Alexander Barclay, *A Practical View of the Present State of Slavery in the West Indies* (London: Smith, Elder, 1826); Matthew Lewis, *Journal of a West-India Proprietor* (London: Murray, 1834), 294–295; 354–355;

James Phillippo, *Jamaica, It's Past and Present State*, 243–249; Charles Leslie, *A New History of Jamaica*, 306–308.

88. In his reflections on his residency in Jamaica, Peter Marsden recounts how the explanation "negroes" offered for the failing health of a "poor black wench, called Juno" was that " 'somebody had given her *obea*.' " See Marsden, *An Account of the Island of Jamaica*, 40.

89. Some important texts that offer insights into neutral mystical power in African religious cultures are Sophie B. Oluwole, *Witchcraft Reincarnation and the God-Head: Issues in African Philosophy* (Lagos: Excel Publishers, 1992); M. J. Field, *Religion and Medicine of the Ga People* (London: Oxford University Press, 1937); Wande Abimbola, *Ifa Will Mend Our Broken World: Thoughts on Yoruba Religion and Culture in the Diaspora* (Roxbury, MA: Aim Books, 1997); John Anenechukwu Umeh, *After God is Dibia: Igbo Cosmology, Divination & Sacred Science in Nigeria* (London: Karnak House, 1997); T. Uzodinma Nwala, *Igbo Philosophy*, vol. 1 (Lagos: Literamed Publications, 1985); Maya Deren, *Divine Horsemen: The Living Gods of Haiti* (Kingston, NY: McPherson & Company, 1953); Simon Bockie, *Death and the Invisible Powers: The World of Kongo Belief* (Bloomington: Indiana University Press, 1993); and Kola Abimbola, "Yoruba Diaspora," in Melvin Ember, Carol R. Ember, and Ian Skoggard, eds., *Encyclopedia of Diasporas: Immigrant and Refugee Cultures Around the World* (New York: Kluwer Academic/Plenum, forthcoming 2005).

90. Ivan Karp, "African Systems of Thought," in P. O'Meara and P. Martin, eds., *Africa* (Bloomington: Indiana University Press, 1986).

91. Monica Schuler, "Afro-American Slave Culture," in Michael Craton, ed., *Roots and Branches: Current Directions in Slave Studies* (Toronto: Pergamon Press, 1979), 128–129, also see 122–123.

92. Mary Turner, *Slaves and Missionaries*, 56.

93. Obeah is still employed for these and for other purposes today in Jamaican society: Jamaicans resort to Obeah for personal success in court cases, health maintenance, business ventures, resolving problems in intimate relationships, and the like. They also use Obeah to take revenge on enemies and to protect themselves from external harm or danger, including danger from another's Obeah work.

94. Instances can be cited from the entire Caribbean region. For example, Obeahmen led one revolutionary plot in Trinidad in 1808. Their intent was to kill all of the Whites on the entire island. See Lionel M. Fraser, *History of Trinidad, from 1781 to 1813* (Port of Spain: Government Printing Office, 1891–1896).

95. Hart, *Slaves Who Abolished Slavery*, 236.

96. Gordon Lewis, *Main Currents in Caribbean Thought: The Historical Evolution of Caribbean Society in Its Ideological Aspects, 1492–1900* (Baltimore, MD: Johns Hopkins University Press, 1983), 224.

97. Ibid., 234–235.

98. Some of the most famous surviving accounts about the Windward Maroon leader Nanny, even in contemporary Jamaica, pertain to her achievements as an effective Obeah practitioner. Hart reflects upon Nanny's legacy within Maroon society: "In Maroon oral tradition Nanny has a reputation of being not only a great military tactician but also personally invulnerable. She is alleged to have turned her back to the fire of her adversaries and, bending over, to have attracted the bullets to a portion of her anatomy where they were caught and rendered harmless. Explaining to the Catholic priest J. J. Williams how Nanny did this, Colonel Rowe showed a touch of delicacy: 'Nanny takes her back to catch the balls.' He added that she 'had a lot of science about her.' " "Science" is employed here as a euphemism for Obeah, perhaps because

it does not call to mind the historical baggage of immorality which cannot be avoided with the term "Obeah." See Hart, *Slaves Who Abolished Slavery*, 80.

99. I became acquainted with the term "Afrophobia" through a conversation with Dr. Elias Farajaje-Jones in May 1997. Since then, I have heard it used in informal conversation among activists in New York City. While my definition of it here might correspond with other understandings of Afrophobia, it is not derived per se from Farajaje-Jones who, at the time, had not yet defined it in published literature, nor is my definition derived from any other source.

100. Today Obeah is almost always viewed as evil and menacing, even by persons who have been helped by Obeah practitioners. To "work Obeah" on somebody is to deliberately injure another. Thus, to avoid social castigation, many practitioners of Obeah (African religion) will not claim the label.

101. Influenced by African conceptions of the soul complex, the "shadow" is viewed as one aspect of the soul complex in Jamaican religious cultures, and Obeah practitioners were often accused of literally "stealing" and/or "catching" (restoring) a victim's shadow, leading to slow death in the former case or rejuvenation in the latter case. I use the term here as an apposite metaphor for the cultural genocide Africans confronted in colonial Jamaica. Maureen Warner-Lewis argues that there is evidence that enslaved Africans viewed their enslavers as "thieves" and practitioners of the "witchcraft" of enslavement. In *Central Africa in the Caribbean: Transcending Time, Transforming Culture* (Barbados: The University of the West Indies Press, 2003), 196, she writes: "There is oral evidence that the enslaved perceived the captors and owners as thieves, a perception that recurs at the folkloric and popular level but is absent or muted in the scribal medium which hardly reflects the views of the subaltern." See also p. 195.

102. In contemporary Jamaican culture, the term "spirit thieving" is more common than "shadow thieving." As a dimension of the soul complex, it follows that over time spirit might have replaced shadow in the popular culture. I find the term "shadow" an apposite metaphor in this context because it was widely used in the pre-Emancipation period and it keeps before us the opacity of slave religion in Jamaica and the Afrophobic context in which derivations of clandestine African religions unfolded in Jamaica. George Blyth, a postemancipation missionary writer, interprets the term "shadow" to mean spirit. See note 109 and corresponding page in this chapter for printed citation.

103. "Alternate states of being" is a deliberate choice of language. I do not find alternate states of "consciousness" helpful in this context, for it introduces a host of assumptions about the mind/body split and it implies that emic interpretations of divine manifestation or spirit travel are not the most reliable interpretations of ecstatic trance experiences.

104. Cassidy and Le Page, *Dictionary of Jamaican English*, 314.

105. Edward Long, *The History of Jamaica*, 416–417.

106. Bryan Edwards, The *History, Civil and Commercial, of the British Colonies in the West Indies*, vol. 2, 107–108, reprint from 1819 edition. Edwards originally published his first two volumes in 1793.

107. Matthew Lewis, *Journal of a West Indian Proprietor*, 294–295.

108. In attempting to assess the contents and roles of Obeah and Myal during the slave period, I have deliberately refrained from using postslavery commentary with this exception. This is because, as I will argue below, the dualistic and antagonistic portrayal of Obeah and Myal is definitively reported in the postslavery literature. Every scholarly interpretation that I have read attempts to explain the functions of

and relationship between Obeah and Myal by using the postslavery descriptions as a standard for evaluating the workings of Obeah and Myal during slavery. This approach might yield some credible insights. However, I will argue that scholars neglect to account for glaring inconsistencies between the presumption that Obeah and Myal were antagonistic traditions during the slave period, and the actual data that pertain to the period.

109. Blyth, *Reminiscences of Missionary Life with Suggestions to Churches and Missionaries* (Edinburgh: Oliphant, 1851), 172–175.

110. Although I think Orlando Patterson assents to the scholarly tendency of establishing a strict demarcation between Obeah and Myal, Patterson lends support to my interpretation when he writes of Myal: "The most important difference from obeah, however, was the fact that it was not an individual practice between practitioner and client, but was organized more as a kind of cult with a unique dance ritual." I still interpret Obeah as more dynamic and broad, which includes space for solo-practitioner work as well as communal ritual practice. See *Sociology of Slavery*, 188.

111. Cassidy and Le Page, *Dictionary of Jamaican English*, 313.

112. See F. Cassidy, *Jamaica Talk* (London: Macmillan, 1960), 241; Cassidy and Le Page, *Dictionary of Jamaican English*, 326; Joseph Williams, *Voodoos and Obeahs*, 120–121; Leonard Barrett, *Soul Force*, 64. For a synopsis of the different interpretive approaches here referenced, see Patterson, *Sociology of Slavery*, 185–195.

113. Barrett, *Soul Force*, 68.

114. Monica Schuler, "Myalism and the African Religious Tradition in Jamaica," in Hilary Beckles and Verene Shepherd, eds., *Caribbean Slave Society and Economy: A Student Reader* (Kingston/London: Ian Randle and James Currey, 1991), 295–296, also see note 85 on 301; compare with Alleyne, *Roots of Jamaican Culture*, 85.

115. See Dianne Stewart, "African-Derived Religions in Jamaica," in Stephen Glazier ed., *Encyclopedia of African and African-American Religions* (New York: Routledge, 2001), 165–169; Dianne Stewart, "Womanist Theology in the Caribbean Context: Critiquing Culture, Rethinking Doctrine and Expanding Boundaries," *Journal of Feminist Studies in Religion* 20, no. 1 (Spring 2004): 61–82.

116. See especially Linda Heywood, *Central Africans and Cultural Transformations in the American Diaspora* (Cambridge: Cambridge University Press, 2002); Warner-Lewis, *Central Africa in the Caribbean*.

117. Maureen Warner-Lewis, *Central Africa in the Caribbean*, 190–198; Kenneth Bilby and Fu-Kiau Bunseki, *Kumina: A Kongo-Based Tradition in the New World*, Cahiers du CEDAF 1983/8 (Brussels: Centre d'etude et de documentation africaines, 1983).

118. Fu Kiau Bunseki, interview with author, Atlanta, GA, April 23, 2004.

119. Ibid.

120. Trees have spiritual significance in many global religious cultures, for example, ancient European and Amerindian cultures; see M. J. Field, *Religion and Medicine of the Ga People* and Patrice Malidoma Somé, *Of Water and the Spirit: Ritual, Magic, and Initiation in the Life of an African Shaman* (New York: Jeremy P. Tarcher/Putnam, 1994) and Somé, *The Healing Wisdom of Africa: Finding Life Purpose Through Nature, Ritual and Community* (New York: Jeremy P. Tarcher/Putnam, 1998). Note especially pp. 43–57 and pp. 259–260. Also see chapter 6, "Tree Worship" in James George Frazer, *The Illustrated Golden Bough*, abridged by Robert K. G. Temple (New York: Simon & Schuster, 1996), 89–103.

121. Maureen Warner-Lewis, *Central Africa in the Caribbean*, 190.

122. Kenneth Bilby, "Gumbay, Myal, and the Great House: New Evidence of the Religious Background of Jonkonnu in Jamaica," *ACIJ Research Review: 25th Anniversary Edition* (1999/4): 64.

123. Martha Beckwith, *Christmas Mummings in Jamaica* (New York: American Folk-Lore Society, 1923), 11.

124. Kenneth Bilby, "Gumbay, Myal and the Great House," 53–54.

125. Ibid., 56.

126. Ibid., 57.

127. Ibid., 55.

128. See, for example, Maureen Warner-Lewis's discussion of possible linkages between Jonkunnu and Kongo culture, where she builds upon the research of Beckwith and Bilby in *Central Africa in the Caribbean*, 223–224.

129. Williams, *Voodoos and Obeahs*, 159.

130. The most extensive volume I know of on the subject includes contributions from English- and French-speaking authors. See Colloque international sur la notion de personne en Afrique noire, *La notion de personne en Afrique noire, Paris 11–17 octobre 1971* (Paris: Éditions du Centre national de la recherche scientifique, 1973). Also see Mary Cuthrell-Curry, "African-derived Religion in the African-American Community in the United States," in Jacob Olupona, ed., *African Spirituality: Forms, Meanings and Expressions* (New York: Crossroad, 2000), 450–466; Kwame Gyekye, *An Essay on African Philosophical Thought: The Akan Conceptual Scheme* (Philadelphia: Temple University Press, 1995); Wande Abimbola, *Ifa Will Mend Our Broken World*; Maya Deren, *Divine Horsemen*; Joseph van Wing, *Études Bakongo: Sociologie, Religion et Magie* (Bruges: Desclée, De Brouwer, 1959).

131. Charles Leslie, *A New History of Jamaica*, 306–307; Edward Long, *The History of Jamaica*, vol. 2, 404–434.

132. Melville Herskovits, *Dahomey: An Ancient West African Kingdom*, vol. 1 (New York: J. J. Augustin, 1938), 211. Cited in Patterson, *Sociology of Slavery*, 200.

133. Melville Herskovits, *Dahomey*, vol. 1, 209–238. Charles Leslie's and Orlando Patterson's distinct interpretations should be noted. Coming from a Western Christian bias that God is the primary mover and shaper of world events and the force behind the laws of nature may have influenced Leslie's belief that these ancestral labels were theistic titles of African deities. It is also possible that Patterson's thesis may not be incorrect, although I am convinced of its veracity.

134. Edward Long, *The History of Jamaica*, vol. 2, 420.

135. In the United States, there is a significant corpus of testimonies from formerly enslaved Africans, which were collected by interviewers working for two distinct agencies at different time periods. Interviewers employed by the American Freedmen's Inquiry Commission collected testimonies during and immediately following the Civil War, and interviewers employed by the Works Progress Administration conducted 2,194 interviews between 1936 and 1938. For a critical discussion of these collections, see the introduction to *Slave Testimony: Two Centuries of Letters, Speeches, Interviews, and Autobiographies*, ed. John Blassingame (Baton Rouge: Louisiana State University Press, 1977), xiii–xv. Blassingame's entire book serves as one of the most comprehensive examples of "slave testimony" in North America. Also see B. A. Botkin, *Lay My Burden Down: A Folk History of Slavery* (Chicago: University of Chicago Press, 1968).

136. Williams, *Voodoos and Obeahs*, 145.

137. Charles Long, *Significations*, 153.

138. "They would sometimes make a sudden halt, put their ears in a listening

attitude against the coffin, pretending that the corpse was endued [sic] with the gift of speech, and was determined not to proceed to burial until some debts due to him were paid, some slanderous imputation on his character removed, some theft confessed . . . they would leave the corpse at the door, or even in the house of a neighbour, from which they would not remove it until the demands were satisfied." See citation on p. 31 of this chapter.

139. The comparison might be made to the Korean ritual of *Han-pu-ri* as explored by Hyun Kyung Chung in her book *Struggle to Be the Sun Again: Toward an Asian Feminist Theology* (Maryknoll, NY: Orbis, 1992). Chung argues that the Korean shamanistic tradition of *Han-pu-ri* should be a source for feminist theology and praxis, which remembers and honors the Ancestors by demanding justice on their behalf and on behalf of the living community. For Jamaicans who surrender religious authenticity and authority to Euro-Christian orthodoxy, it especially serves as a fitting cross-cultural example of how some Korean Christians continue to make use of their indigenous religious heritage. See especially 42–44 in *Struggle to Be the Sun Again*.

140. In his diary entry of May 20, 1838, the Scottish Presbyterian minister Hope Waddell describes the "Myal system" as one "wholly opposed" to "Obea." This detail suggests that Myalists were distinguishing themselves from practitioners of Obeah even before the 1840s, when the anti-Obeah Myal campaign gained widespread attention in the island. I will examine the implications of this development in the Myal institutional framework in greater detail in chapter 4. See Hope Waddell, *Twenty-Nine Years in the West Indies and Central Africa, 1829–1858* (London: Frank Cass, 1970), 137. First edition, 1863.

141. See Williams, *Voodoos and Obeahs*, 145–175, for a full discussion of this campaign.

142. Mbiti, *African Religions and Philosophy*, 213.

143. Monica Schuler, "Afro-American Slave Culture," 132–133.

144. Mbiti, *African Religions and Philosophy*, 197–198, 202–203. Chukwunyere Kamalu compares this philosophical orientation with that of the modern West. Kamalu writes, "In African belief, which many authors have referred to as 'animistic,' the *Life-force* or *Vital-force* is the essential force which moves everything. This force exists in everything and, disguised as everchanging matter, it is the dynamic manifestation of an All-Pervading Energy or Spirit. One can, if one wishes view it as a form of pantheism. It can alternatively be viewed, if one is a puritanical materialist, as a form of atheism depending on whether one prefers to be more scientific and substitute the term 'energy' for 'spirit.' . . . There is, however, an important and fundamental aspect in which African beliefs differ from modern Western science which relates to the living nature of all matter. In the African universe nothing is dead, not even a stone, which is in stark contrast to the Western idea of matter. What will be known here as the 'Dead Matter Thesis' in Western thought probably began with Isaac Newton and may well have evolved more as a result of political and theological necessity than intellectual necessity, in order to avoid being persecuted for heresy like his forerunner, Galileo, by a church whose theological doctrine pronounced God as creator external to His creation. Such a doctrine was plainly contradicted by any idea of animate matter and Newton, who had much respect for Egyptian knowledge, was bound to base his science on the notion of passivity or lifelessness of matter." *Foundations of African Thought: A Worldview Grounded in the African Heritage of Religion, Philosophy, Science and Art* (London: Karnak, 1990), 86.

145. Mbiti, *African Religions and Philosophy*, 204–215.

146. Patterson, *Sociology of Slavery*, 183. In Yoruba religion the term for morally neutral mystical power is *àshe*. See Thompson, *Flash of the Spirit*, 5–9.

147. Melville Herskovits, *Dahomey: An Ancient West African Kingdom*, vol. 2 (Evanston, IL: Northwestern University Press, 1967), 282.

148. Simon Bockie cites Buakasa's definition of *kindoki* as "power or force. . . . It is susceptible to being exercised in any sense, in a good sense as well as evil. It is a question of an ambivalent, ambiguous power." *Death and the Invisible Powers*, 43.

149. Wyatt MacGaffey, *Art and Healing of the BaKongo Commented by Themselves: Minkisi from the Laman Collection* (Stockholm: Folkens Museum-Etnografiska and Bloomington: Indiana University Press, 1991).

150. See Riggins Earl, *Dark Symbols, Obscure Signs: God, Self, and Community in the Slave Mind* (Maryknoll, NY: Orbis, 1993); Robert Hood, *Begrimed and Black: Christian Traditions on Blacks and Blackness* (Minneapolis, MN: Fortress, 1994).

151. The Nation of Islam reverses the categories and assigns innate goodness to Black people and innate evil to Whites. By critiquing this anthropology, I do not reduce it to a mere reversal of White *racist* anthropology, for the former is a defensive essentialism, inspired by overwhelming experiential and historical evidence from African encounters with Europeans, while the latter is aggressive and unsubstantiated.

152. Joseph Williams is the only author who actually proposes that Obeah practitioners and Myalists cooperated in opposition to slavery with some explanation. Although he does support the view that Obeah and Myal were antagonistic traditions, he writes, "In early legislation we find accentuated the danger from fanaticism aroused by religious assemblies and nothing more. Then appears due provision against the menace of poisonings and finally formal condemnation of Obeah. But through it all the secret phase of Myalism and its confederation with its archenemy Obeah against the oppressor of both, never seems to have been suspected." See *Voodoos and Obeahs*, 160. Monica Schuler assumes Obeah and Myal collaboration in slave revolts but provides no evidence or explanation to support her claim. The description of an Obeah practitioner believed to be Nanny, the legendary military commander of the Windward Maroons, might suggest connections between Obeah and Myal. According to Hart: "The obeah woman referred to may or may not have been the famous Nanny. Thicknesse described Quao's obeah woman as an 'old Hagg' wearing 'a girdle round her waste with (I speak within compass) nine or ten different knives hanging in sheaths to it' " *in Slaves Who Abolished Slavery*. Myal practitioners, both during and after slavery, were portrayed as wearing waist belts from which instruments, including shears, were hung. Madeline Kerr, *Personality and Conflict in Jamaica* (Liverpool, England: University Press, 1952), 114–136.

153. For example, K. S. Malden disparages midwifery among enslaved Africans in this remark: "Expectant mothers . . . were usually only attended by some old black mammy who was completely ignorant of all the laws of hygiene and pinned her hopes on charms and lucky omens." Nonetheless, he offers evidence that, within the enslaved African populations of the British Caribbean, the medical practice of delivering babies and nursing expectant and lactating mothers involved religious rituals and observances, underscoring the connections among medicine, divination, and religion. See Malden, *Broken Bonds*, 55. See also Patrice Malidoma Somé, *Of Water and the Spirit*, for a narrative portrayal of the exchanges among religion, medicine, and divination from the perspective of an African healer. Also see Mbiti, *African Religions and Philosophy*, especially 166–212; and Zahan, *The Religion, Spirituality, and Thought of Traditional Africa*.

154. I concur with Mervyn Alleyne's analysis of the relationship between religion and resistance in Jamaica. Alleyne argues that the "resistance" thesis "focusses on slavery and the environment, and the culture generated thereby. It neglects the time dimension, and considers neither the culture of Africans before enslavement, nor the different stages within the period of slavery, nor the aftermath of slavery. It refuses to consider the possibility that pre-slavery cultures may have largely determined the response and adjustment of slaves to slavery. . . . Slave religion . . . was—certainly in the case of Jamaica—first and foremost the continuity of an ancestral religion. True, there was an important link between religion and resistance; but religion was taken to Jamaica from Africa and was an important basis for resistance; it was not created during the course of that resistance." Alleyne, *Roots of Jamaican Culture*, 21–22.

155. Hesketh Bell, *Obeah: Witchcraft in the West Indies* (London: Low, Marston, Searle & Rivington, 1889), 31. A similar account about her experiences in Cuba is given by the Swedish author Fredrika Bremer in an 1853 publication: "Formerly, it is said, might be heard every evening and night, both afar and near, the joyous sound of the African drum, as it was beaten at the Negro dances. When, however, it was discovered that these dancing assemblies had been made use of for the organisation of the disturbances which afterward took place, their liberty became very much circumscribed." *The Homes of the New World: Impressions of America*, vol. 2 (New York: Harper, 1853), 346.

156. Alfred Métraux, *Voodoo in Haiti* (New York: Shocken, 1972), 42.

157. See C. L. R. James, *The Black Jacobins* (New York: Vintage, 1963), 87. According to James, "The symbol of the god of the whites was the cross which, as Catholics, they wore round their necks." The cross will be discussed further in chapter 4.

158. Laguerre, *Voodoo and Politics in Haiti*, 62.

159. Ibid., 69.

160. Ibid., 63.

161. The exchanges and interaction among African-Caribbean religious cultures during the period of enslavement are defensible due to the patterns of cross-importation and deportation within the islands. Jamaica was especially active in this regard. Of the 745,500–1,000,000 Africans imported into Jamaica, 200,000 were reexported to other islands in the Caribbean and to the Americas. See Patterson, *Sociology of Slavery*, 289–292; Campbell, *Rasta and Resistance*, 15.

162. I use the term *praxis* here in the sense that it is used by liberation theologians to signify the application of one's religious faith in struggles against oppressive regimes or systems of injustice, or acting out one's religious convictions in opposition to social oppression or injustice.

163. Anna Pescatello, *Old Roots in New Lands: Historical and Anthropological Perspectives on Black Experiences in the Americas* (Westport, CT: Greenwood, 1977), 27–28. Pescatello summarizes the significance of African-derived religions in the Caribbean as loci for social cohesion, collective empowerment, and resistance to the varied manifestations of Eurocentric domination: "Religious ceremonies, beliefs, and other elements associated with Afro-Caribbean life have been the most residual African elements in the Caribbean. It was in the religious sphere that a leader could emerge who could transcend ethnic boundaries and garner support from the diverse groups. In that role, religious leaders provided an alternative to the white ruling class representatives and a channel for preserving African values. The European efforts to eradicate Africanisms were strongest in the area of religion, for it made good political sense to undercut the base of support for the growth of African leaders in their servile environment. Not until after abolition did many Africans move to the established Eu-

ropean churches, since the need for ethnic leadership had, presumably, been removed."

164. Mbiti, *African Religions and Philosophy*, 210. We must read Mbiti with caution here. I cite Mbiti because African religious cultures tend not to adhere to rigid and exacting concepts of judgment in the afterlife, as we may find in a number of Christian religious cultures. This is not to suggest that African religious cultures have no concept of judgment in the afterlife, for more than just a few African religious cultures have definite ideas about judgment as an evaluation period in the afterlife, not so much for individual actions committed as for the life led on earth. Some of these ideas are connected to elaborate views about reincarnation, ancestorhood, and the possibility of extinguishment of the soul complex, for example, the Yoruba and Kongo cultures would apply here.

CHAPTER TWO

1. Johann Gottfried von Herder, *Ideas on the Philosophy of the History of Mankind*, trans. T. Churchill (New York: Bergman, 1800). Cited by Emmanuel Chukwudi Eze, ed. *Race and the Enlightenment: A Reader* (Cambridge, MA: Blackwell, 1997), 74.

2. Alvin Thompson, "Race and Colour Prejudices and the Origin of the Transatlantic Slave Trade," *Caribbean Studies* 16, nos. 3–4 (1976–1977): 59. Also see Cornell West, *Prophesy Deliverance! An Afro-American Revolutionary Christianity* (Philadelphia: Westminster, 1982), 47–65.

3. Winthrop Jordan addresses this issue in his acclaimed study *White over Black: American Attitudes toward the Negro, 1550–1812* (Baltimore, MD: Penguin, 1969).

4. Thompson, "Race and Colour Prejudices and the Origin of the Transatlantic Slave Trade," 33. The original commentary is published in *Diodorus of Sicily*, bk. 3, vol. 2, trans. C. H. Oldfather (London: Heinemann, 1953), 103–105.

5. Ibid., 34. Pliny (23–79 C.E.) who, according to Thompson, produced "the most detailed extant work by a classical writer on the 'monstrosities' found in black Africa," published his views in *Natural History* (77 C.E.), trans. H. Rackham (London: Heinemann, 1947). See esp. bk. 6, vol. 2, 477–487.

6. Ibid., 34–35.

7. Ibid., 36. Ptolemy was a second-century scientist and philosopher who lived in Alexandria.

8. Jordan, *White over Black*, 18, 36.

9. Origen, *The Song of Songs: Commentary and Homilies*, trans. R. P. Lawson (London: Longman, 1958), 103. Robert Hood's interpretation of Origen's commentary leads him to conclude that Origen generally held positive ideas about Black people. Yet Hood clearly notes, "Origen was ambivalent about the moral significance of blackness. Blackness means sin and privation." I do not agree with Hood's view that Origen "transform[ed] blackness from a negative affirmation of evil to a positive witness to the divine good by linking blackness to Jesus Christ." Even within the passages Hood cites to support this claim, Blackness is othered and negated except by association with the Gentile church. I remain unpersuaded because in the commentaries of Origen and other Christian writers, antiblackness, i.e., negative significations of the color black, becomes an ontological problem when such significations are applied to people—their complexions, cultures, ethnicities, and moral dispositions. See Robert Hood, *Begrimed and Black: Christian Traditions on Blacks and Blackness* (Minneapolis, MN: Fortress, 1994), 80–82.

10. Origen, *Song of Songs: Commentary and Homilies*, 278.

11. Hood, *Begrimed and Black*, 82–83.

12. Cited by C. H. Haskins, *The Renaissance of the 12th Century* (Cleveland, OH: World, 1970), 303–306.

13. Thompson, "Race and Colour Prejudices and the Origin of the Transatlantic Slave Trade," 40–41.

14. Ibid., 42.

15. Quoted in James Walvin, *The Black Presence in England: A Documentary History of the Negro in England, 1555–1860* (London: Orbach and Chambers, 1971), 36–37. Cited by Thompson in "Race and Colour Prejudices and the Origin of the Transatlantic Slave Trade," 30–31.

16. Thompson, "Race and Colour Prejudices and the Origin of the Transatlantic Slave Trade," 43–44.

17. Ibid., 46.

18. Ibid., 45.

19. Jean Bodin, *Method for Easy Comprehension of History*, trans. Beatrice Reynolds (New York: Columbia University Press, 1945), 105.

20. Thompson, "Race and Colour Prejudices and the Origin of the Transatlantic Slave Trade," 48–49.

21. James Muldoon, *The Expansion of Europe* (Philadelphia: University of Pennsylvania Press, 1977), 4.

22. From an anonymous author, published c. 1788–1789, cited by Malden, *Broken Bonds*, 52–53.

23. Cited by Eric Williams, *British Historians and the West Indies* (New York: Africana, 1972), 25.

24. Ibid., 26.

25. The recent case of Jeffrey Dahmer, a White North American who savagely killed, dismembered, fetishized, preserved by freezer, and ate the corpses of African-American men, when contextualized within the history of Europe's racist preoccupation with African bodies, appears to be a twentieth-century manifestation of what has come before. Dahmer and the remains of his victims were discovered and made known to the public in July 1991. Dahmer was later prosecuted and sentenced to life imprisonment. One year into his sentence, Dahmer was killed by an African-American inmate.

26. De Gobineau's French text was published in Paris by Firmin-Didot. No date is given, however, many scholars date the first printed French edition as 1854. See English, translation, Arthur de Gobineau, *The Inequality of Races* (New York: Putnam, 1915), 51–52. Also see Eze, ed., *Race and the Enlightenment: A Reader*, for evidence of anti-African ideas in the writings of Enlightenment thinkers.

27. Thompson, "Race and Colour Prejudices and the Origin of the Transatlantic Slave Trade," 32.

28. Williams, *Voodoos and Obeahs*, 113–114.

29. Consequently, some of the French slaveholders escaped and resettled in Jamaica with enslaved Africans. See Turner, *Slaves and Missionaries*, 13.

30. Williams, *Voodoos and Obeahs*, 159–161.

31. Ibid., 164.

32. Ibid., 165–166.

33. See chapter 1. It bears repeating here that Gordon Lewis notes that "a sense of social cohesion . . . was reinforced by the imposition of the collective [Obeah] oath, again African in origin, holding the conspirators to secrecy and loyalty: a practice mentioned by all the extant accounts of uprisings." See *Main Currents in Caribbean*

Thought, 224. Lewis's claim that "all" extant accounts "mention" collective oaths in enslaved African rebellions may or may not be an overstatement for he does not claim to have read "all" extant accounts of uprisings. All of the accounts I have read support Lewis's assertion.

34. Williams, *Voodoos and Obeahs*, 177.

35. Quoted in ibid., 176.

36. Ibid., 180. Richard Dunn also documents the poor health condition of enslaved Africans, which was exacerbated by insufficient and unprofessional medical care. See chapter 9 of his book *Sugar and Slaves: The Rise of the Planter Class in the English West Indies, 1624–1713*. Chapel Hill: University of North Carolina Press, 1972. See esp. 308–309, where Dunn notes, "Though the English were contemptuous of the medical practices brought from Africa by their slaves, there seems to have been little essential difference between the two methods of doctoring. [One doctor] saw the slaves administer herbal potions, draw blood, cup and scarify—all standard techniques in his own practice."

37. See Orlando Patterson's chapter "The Treatment of Slaves in Law and Custom," in *Sociology of Slavery*, 70–93, for specific citations of laws enacted between 1662 and 1834.

38. In 1744, the power of White enslavers was extended over even the *thoughts* of Africans. After a "frustrated rebellion wherein 'a general massacre of the white people was intended,' " an act was passed rendering as criminal and punishable by death "compassing and *imagining* the death of any white person by any slave or slaves" (italics mine). Williams, *Voodoos and Obeahs*, 162.

39. Patterson, *Sociology of Slavery*, 92.

40. Ibid., 52–69.

41. See Turner, *Slaves and Missionaries*, 43–47, for more information on the provision grounds of enslaved Africans. Also see Robert McLarty, "Jamaica Prepares for Invasion, 1779," *Caribbean Quarterly* 4 (January 1955): 62–67, for an important assessment of the impact of the American Revolutionary War on food shortages in Jamaica. McLarty notes that provision grounds for enslaved Africans were particularly encouraged because of the food shortages during which many Africans died of starvation and from diseases related to malnutrition. Ivy Baxter's study on the vast assortment of African-derived festival and cultural traditions in Jamaican society is perhaps the most comprehensive discussion of this subject. See *The Arts of an Island: The Development of Culture and of the Folk and Creative Arts in Jamaica 1494–1962* (Metuchen, NJ: Scarecrow, 1970).

42. Cited by C. Jesse, "The Papal Bull of 1493 Appointing the First Vicar Apostolic in the New World," *Caribbean Quarterly* 11 (September–December 1965): 62.

43. Ibid., 63.

44. Ibid., 63–64, 66. Also see Muldoon, *The Expansion of Europe*, 3–15. On 4–5, Muldoon confirms, "From Urban II [who proclaimed the first Crusade in 1095] to Columbus, those who planted European flags outside of Europe claimed religious reasons."

45. Jesse, "The Papal Bull of 1493," 70–71.

46. November 28, 1816, entry. Cited by Hark, *Breaking of the Dawn*, 23.

47. Blyth, *Reminiscences of Missionary Life*, 175–176.

48. See Lewis, *Main Currents in Caribbean Thought*, 203. In his chapter on the ideology of the evangelical missionaries, he asserts that "even the most cautious of them saw the intrinsic evil of the system; it is impossible to read the accounts of the typical plantation workday by Buchner and Ramsay and feel otherwise. All of them— Smith, Phillips, Knibb, Ramsay, Cernick, Lang, Dober and many others—as they

fought for amelioration, education, and, at times, abolition, became, in Ramsay's phrase, rebel convicts against the interest and majesty of plantership."

49. My use of the term *religious* to describe African practices should not be confused with the missionary interpretation of African practices. Europeans categorized African religion with what they conventionally called "superstition" in their culture. "Religion" was synonymous only with Christianity and perhaps Islam; everything else was superstition or paganism. Note, for example, Alfred Caldecott's reference to "European irreligion and Negro heathenism" when describing the moral condition of the West Indies at the beginning of the nineteenth century. See *The Church in the West Indies,* 77.

50. Francis Cox, *History of the Baptist Missionary Society from 1792–1842,* vol. 2 (London: Ward, 1842), 11.

51. Ibid., 183–184.

52. Ibid., 74. See a Baptist missionary's description of the most essential doctrinal ideas that enslaved Africans had to understand and accept before they could be received for baptism and membership in the church: "The nature of our examination is to ascertain what led the candidate first to think of serious concerns—his views of sin—of himself as a sinner—his danger as a sinner, with respect to futurity—his deserts as a sinner—his views of God—the holiness of God—the justice of God in his hatred and punishment of sin—the love of God in the gift of his Son—his views of his own unworthiness—his inability to effect his own salvation—the way of salvation—the person of Christ—the atonement—the love of Christ—the evidence he has that he loves Christ, that he is a new creature—his views of religion, its duties, its holiness, &c.—the effect it has had upon himself—baptism and the Lord's supper, &c." Also see chapter 3 of Turner, *Slaves and Missionaries,* 71, for an extended discussion on the efforts of Christian missionaries to convince Africans to abandon their religious practices in favor of Christian salvation. Turner examines primary sources and concludes that conversion was a difficult process as it was hard for the missionaries to induce uncompromised allegiance from the enslaved Africans who frequented their services. Turner notes, for example, that the missionaries "were trying to implant entirely new ideas about the nature of the spirit world and the nature of God. Nothing in the slaves' theology prepared them for the idea of God the law giver. The slaves also proved resistant to the basic Christian concept of sin; it tended, when first confronted, to intensify their feelings of inferiority induced by the slave system. Though the 'wages of sin' was the text of innumerable sermons to newly founded groups, the missionaries found it was generally 'a long time before a Negro would admit himself to be a sinful creature,' and welcomed storms and earth tremors as means of rousing from 'the sleep of sin those who would not be wakened by gentler methods.' " Albert Raboteau supports Turner's claim that "sin" was a foreign concept to enslaved Africans. See his *Slave Religion,* 27.

53. Cox, *History of the Baptist Missionary Society from 1792–1842,* 83.

54. Ibid., 185–186. Also see Cox's reference to the execution of the leader of the rebellion, Samuel Sharpe, who "attest[ed] with his last breath, the innocence of the missionaries [in the rebellion]; and declare[d], that if he had listened to their instructions, he never should have come to that awful end" (182). Missionary Christianity also functioned as a mode of social control even when unsuspectingly operating as a central institution sympathetic to the plight of the enslaved. Cox, writing about the role of the church on the day of full Emancipation in Jamaica, says: "The christian church hailed with inexpressible delight this great sabbath of the slave; and met in every place, to mark it with *appropriate* celebrations. There was joy *without riot;* tri-

umph *without reproach*; multitude *without confusion*; while religion assumed the undisputed presidency over the soul-exhilarating scene" (italics mine; 246).

55. Lewis, *Main Currents in Caribbean Thought*, 201. See Shirley Gordon, *God Almighty Make Me Free: Christianity in PreEmancipation Jamaica* (Bloomington: Indiana University Press, 1996), 88, where he writes: "[s]ome of the older missionaries went so far as to beg their societies in Britain to conduct their anti-slavery activities less prominently lest the plantocracy in Jamaica retaliate by driving out their missionaries." Also see Cox's reference to Mr. William Thompson, a "person of colour" who was questioned in court about "whether he had not heard his ministers say and preach to the negroes, that the king had given them their freedom, and they were to set fire to the estates, and fight for it. He answered, 'he had heard the ministers preach contrary to that; namely, that they must be obedient to their earthly master, whom they saw, otherwise they could not be obedient to their heavenly Master, whom they could not see.' " Cox, *History of the Baptist Missionary Society from 1792–1842*, 153. The Shipman catechism, devised by a Wesleyan missionary, also demonstrates how "obedience to divine law" was propagated. The following excerpt from the catechism is cited by Mary Turner. "Is it right for servants to steal from their masters? No, because God has commanded us 'Thou shalt not steal.' Even if they are not observed? But God sees and will punish them. How are thieves punished in this world? By being whipped, confined, banished and sometimes hanged. But, is this all the punishment they are subject to? No, if they repent not God will punish them in hellfire forever." Turner, *Slaves and Missionaries*, 76–77.

56. Blythe, *Reminiscences of Missionary Life*, 57–58.

57. Religious Tract Society, *Missionary Records: West Indies*, 77–78.

58. Ibid., 78.

59. Turner, *Slaves and Missionaries*, 76.

60. John Boles, *The Great Revival: The Origins of the Southern Evangelical Mind, 1787–1805* (Lexington: University Press of Kentucky, 1972). See esp. chap. 2.

61. Ibid., 24.

62. Scholars of the slave period in the Caribbean note that enslaved Africans were continuously imported to replace the steadily dying population. The habit of working enslaved Africans literally to death and importing new Africans to replenish the labor pool as opposed to working enslaved Africans into old age was most profitable in the Caribbean. See Patterson, *Sociology of Slavery*, 97–104; Dunn, *Sugar and Slaves*, chap. 9.

63. Turner, *Slaves and Missionaries*, 71.

64. Ibid., 75.

65. Religious Tract Society, *Missionary Records: West Indies*, xiii.

66. Ibid., 123.

67. Ibid., 114–115.

68. Although his is a treatment of the propagation of the "curse of Ham" myth in antebellum North America, Thomas Virgil Peterson's book *Ham and Japheth: The Mythic World of Whites in the Antebellum South* (Metuchen, NJ: Scarecrow, 1978) is a thorough study on the emergence and proliferation of this anthropology in modern White racist culture. Also see David Goldenberg, *The Curse of Ham: Race and Slavery in Early Judaism, Christianity, and Islam* (Princeton, NJ: Princeton University Press, 2003).

69. Coultart comments upon the physical suffering endured by another African woman on her deathbed, saying, "Religion, had it done no more than this, has procured one happy exit from death to life, one glorious triumph for a daughter of Ham,

on whom the curse of slavery rested heavily for many years." Religious Tract Society, *Missionary Records: West Indies*, 116.

70. Ibid., 52.

71. Ibid., 171.

72. Ibid., 191–192.

73. Ibid., 93. *Missionary Records* does not provide the missionary's name.

74. Williams, *Capitalism and Slavery*, 47–48.

75. See Hark, *Breaking of the Dawn*, 16–17: "In order to provide the necessaries of life, [the Moravian missionaries] had to grow ground provisions and to keep a cattle-pen at Old Carmel. This again was impossible without slave labour. Consequently, the missionaries became slave-holders! Free servants could not be procured. And the wrong of slavery itself had not yet been fully realized by the Christian conscience— not even by the missionaries' conscience! Old Carmel estate was worked by thirty to forty slaves. . . . Though it is evident, from all the diaries still preserved, that the Old Carmel slaves were treated with the utmost kindness: such kindness was often abused, and then, 'slaves that feigned sickness had to be punished'; others 'ran away, and must wear an iron chain around their necks.' . . . 'They are a spoiled race—this is not to be wondered at, for nobody ever yet was able to bring good out of evil, to gather grapes off thorns, or figs off thistles—to make the bitter sweet.' "

76. Charles Long's collection of essays *Significations: Signs, Symbols, and Images in the Interpretation of Religion* is an insightful study on cultural contact between Europeans and Africans. He discusses Blackness as Other and argues that it is the experience of Otherness that will enable Black people to rearticulate the meaning of "human being."

77. Quoted in Turner, *Slaves and Missionaries*, 75. Also see Cox, *History of the Baptist Missionary Society from 1792–1842*, 122, 127, and 143, for court testimonies of enslaved Africans. Many identify themselves as regular attendants at the missionary services but clearly state that they were not official members. In chapter 1, I provided data attesting to the low numbers of African converts to Christianity throughout the period of enslavement.

78. Williams, *Voodoos and Obeahs*, 142–208.

79. Turner, *Slaves and Missionaries*, 158–159.

80. Mason, *Black Gods*, 1–7; Sidney Mintz and Richard Price, *An Anthropological Approach to the Afro-American Past: A Caribbean Perspective* (Philadelphia: Institute for the Study of Human Issues, 1976), 23.

CHAPTER THREE

1. The epigraph is from a song which was sung during a Rastafari *groundation* (meeting) held by Prince Emmanuel in Kingston in March 1958.

2. Cited in Religious Tract Society, *Missionary Records: West Indies*, 114.

3. The *abeng* is a hornlike instrument, African in origin. It was used by enslaved Africans in ceremonies to send messages back and forth from distant locations. Its use was repeatedly outlawed in Jamaican legislative history, for insurgents used it to send coded signals to one another. The Maroons still blow the *abeng* today. The *goombah* or goombay drum was made from a hollow wood barrel and covered with sheepskin. It was played by enslaved Africans in Jamaica and is associated with African religious customs. See Patterson, *Sociology of Slavery*, 234.

4. Religious Tract Society, *Missionary Records: West Indies*, 109–110.

5. Jeremiah 13:23.

6. Cox, *History of the Baptist Missionary Society from 1792–1842*, 225, 229, 231–233; Turner, *Slaves and Missionaries*, 84.

7. Religious Tract Society, *Missionary Records: West Indies*, xvi, 75–76. With regard to the establishment of missionary schools for recently emancipated Africans, Caldecott describes the punctured hopes of Africans who believed that literacy would allow them access to a better life. He writes: "But deeper down than this lay the disappointment of some foolish but very natural expectation on the part of the simple Negroes. They had been inclined to suppose that ability to read and write would lead to immunity form agricultural labour." See *The Church in the West Indies*, 114.

8. Religious Tract Society, *Missionary Records: West Indies*, 234–235.

9. The status of enslaved Africans changed in 1834 from chattel to apprenticed labor, which, from the testimonies of the ex-enslaved, was only a four-year continuation of a stratified social relationship with White planters. The year 1838 is cited by most Caribbean studies scholars to mark legal emancipation in the British West Indies.

10. Cox, *History of the Baptist Missionary Society from 1792–1842*, 245–247. It is worth noting the governor's exhortation that, on the eve of full emancipation, Africans should "[r]ecollect what is expected of you by the people of England, who have paid such a large price for your liberty." Although the planters and missionaries had ample evidence of how widespread the impulse to strike for freedom was among enslaved Africans, here and elsewhere, Cox's report shows that both planters and missionaries wanted desperately to believe that the instinct for freedom was beyond the natural inclinations of enslaved Africans, and as such, the "idea of freedom" had to originate from Europeans. In the case of the planters, they resolved that the missionaries were culpable and in defense of themselves the missionaries returned the accusation, claiming that it was the planters' stubborn and tenacious grip on slavery, unwilling to concede to any ameliorative recommendations, that incited rebellion among the slaves. See Cox (142, 188–190) for specific examples. This tendency toward myth making and constructing reverse truths is prevalent in White racist culture. West African philosopher Anthony Appiah identifies this pattern as the consequence of what he calls the "cognitive incapacity" of Whites to understand and thoroughly critique their racism (public lecture, Colgate University, February 17, 1989). Also see his collection of essays *In My Father's House: Africa in the Philosophy of Culture* (Oxford: Oxford University Press, 1992) for a more developed critique of White racist ideology.

11. Sloane, *Voyage to the Islands*, vol. 1, 57. The amputation of body parts was a common penalty inflicted upon the enslaved, including penile castration. See Dunn, *Sugar and Slaves*, chaps. 7–9; Patterson, *Sociology of Slavery*, 70–93, for specific examples.

12. Boles, *The Great Revival*, 113.

13. Cox, *History of the Baptist Missionary Society from 1792–1842*, 39–40.

14. I have not found any scholars who understand the communion between African deities and human persons as "incarnation." Most scholars use the term *spirit possession* to refer to any possession of a human being by a deity, Ancestor, or any spirit. I find it useful and appropriate to talk about divine possession of human subjects in African religion as "incarnation." My study of, and experience with, this phenomenon in continental and diasporic forms of African religion have encouraged me to use the term *incarnation in* African religious contexts. Sheila Walker's study *Ceremonial Spirit Possession in Africa and Afro-America: Forms, Meanings, and Functional Significance for Individuals and Social Groups* (Leiden: Brill, 1972) is helpful in exploring the role and function of this phenomenon in African-derived religions.

15. I have experienced the incarnated deities performing these roles in numerous

Santería, Yoruba, and Vodun services in the United States, Nigeria, Cuba, the Dominican Republic, and Trinidad. I have also witnessed the Ancestors, spirit messengers, and Holy Spirit functioning this way (expressing prophecy and healing) in Kumina, Revival Zion, and other Black worship services in the United States, Jamaica, and Trinidad.

16. It seems to me that the ritual of conversion also put to rest a plethora of anxieties and internal conflicts in some Africans. See Cox, *History of the Baptist Missionary Society from 1792–1842*, 42. Mintz and Price's analysis is helpful here: "[T]he [slave] system itself, since it was rooted in inherited inequality, produced conflict as an integral feature of continuing control, whatever the nature of adjustment or accommodation between slaves and masters." See *An Anthropological Approach to the Afro-American Past*, 14. Such conflict was the order of the day; it pervaded all aspects of the slave experience—both embodied and extrabodied experience. Hence it was physical, psychological, emotional, social, political, and economic. Religion and particularly Christian religion as the legitimate moral system assuaged some of the effects of such conflict, namely, anxiety, nervousness, paralysis, depression, self-negation, and addictive self-destructive habits like the ones identified in the quoted testimony.

17. Cox, *History of the Baptist Missionary Society from 1792–1842*, 59–60.

18. Boles discusses how evangelical Christianity was, in the eyes of many itinerant preachers and missionaries, an "answer to the problem of coldness in religion." See *The Great Revival, 1787–1805*, 25. Also see his chapters 2 and 3 for a more developed discussion of the evangelical response to the decline of religion in the American South.

19. Cox, *History of the Baptist Missionary Society from 1792–1842*, 37.

20. Ibid., 40.

21. Kelly Brown Douglas, *The Black Christ* (Maryknoll, NY: Orbis, 1994), argues that, historically, White theology has been a "confessional theology" which allowed slave masters to own Africans, confess Christ, and thus secure eternal salvation. On the contrary, Black theology, emerging out of the slave experience, has been praxis-oriented. Douglas asserts that enslaved Africans judged a person's Christian integrity by how she conducted herself. See chapters 1 and 2 for a developed treatment of her thesis. I believe Douglas's thesis has merit especially within the context of slavery. My experiences with classical African religions have taught me that African religiosity demands constant acts of devotion and has very little use for confessional expressions of faith. Wande Abimbola, a renowned scholar and practitioner of Yoruba religion, once told me that sacrifice is central to African religion because the deities and the Ancestors expect devotion or repentance to be acted out through concrete rituals and not through verbal confessions of "belief." See his book *Ifa Will Mend Our Broken World* (Roxbury, MA: Aim, 1997).

22. Mary Turner provides insightful commentary upon this aspect of missionary theology in chapter 3 of *Slaves and Missionaries*; see esp. 84–85.

23. Cox, *History of the Baptist Missionary Society from 1792–1842*, 199. For other examples, see 41, 46–47.

24. Ibid., 199.

25. Ibid., 220.

26. In some cases, it was apparently worth a lot. The following accounts illustrate why the missionaries and the new Christian life may have been so appealing to some Africans. Writing about the consequences of the 1831–1832 revolt, Blyth remarks, "Many of the incendiaries were executed, and others who had committed no crime, terrified by the threats which they heard, or examples of vengeance which they

witnessed, escaped to the mountains. I warned several of my members against pursuing such a course, but one of them ran off without informing me of his intention,
and remained in the high mountains for three months, shunning every human being
and habitation, lest he should be betrayed and executed, and seeking a precarious
subsistence among the provision grounds which had been deserted. At last, feeling
solitude intolerable, and suffering from want of salt—which he described as his
greatest affliction—he resolved to deliver himself up in any way his minister might
advise. Accordingly one Sabbath evening he presented himself before me, half-dead
with terror and want, and asked if there was any hope of his life being spared? . . . On
my interceding in his behalf . . . the authorities . . . sentenced him to three months'
labour in the penitentiary, after which he returned to his family without any molestation from his master." See Blyth, *Reminiscences of Missionary Life*, 63–65. Another example of missionary influence upon slave masters was recounted by Cox: "After
having revolved the matter in his mind, and praying earnestly for divine direction,
Mr. Knibb mentioned to his church his conviction of the sinfulness of holding apprentices, who were really slaves, and desired them to think upon the subject. All,
excepting three, promised at once to free them; which involved a pecuniary sacrifice
on the part of those who were already poor. They assured their pastor that they had
long thought of it, but as it was their *all*, they were fearful of not being able to procure food for their children. A firm conviction, however, of the sin, determined them
in the self-denying resolution, and their noble example was very extensively imitated."
See *History of the Baptist Missionary Society from 1792–1842*, 239. With the power to
influence White Christian planters to free African captives, it is no small wonder that
some African Christians expressed such gratitude and devotion to the missionaries
and to the Christian God who sent them their way. By contrast it is important to acknowledge that there is substantial evidence that Catholic missionaries in the islands
and the Americas, especially in the seventeenth and eighteenth centuries, were often
as brutal as the conquistadors and the slaveholders. For example, Gordon Lewis
maintains, "The Catholic religious saw [proselytization] as a war against paganism
and superstition, summed up in Pére Labat's astonishing story of how he was driven
to fury by discovering an obeahman secretly practising his rites and he himself merci-
lessly beat the offender." See *Main Currents in Caribbean Thought*, 195.

27. See chaps. 4–6 in Turner, *Slaves and Missionaries*. Missionary documents
also offer pertinent information which shows that the enslaved did respond with both
hope and despair to their Christian faith, depending on the successes or failures of
their attempts to resist slavery. For example, immediately after the rebellion, when Africans realized that the English government would not mandate their legal emancipation, one person had this to say: "It is no use minister; what can church and prayers
do for we again?" See Hope Waddell, *Twenty-nine Years in the West Indies and Central
Africa 1829–1858*, 70–71. The prayers cited later in this section occur, however, immediately after the 1838 Emancipation legislation. Any number of social, economic, and
political factors were constantly recontextualizing the Sitz im Leben of Africans
within the confines of a slave society.

28. Cox, *History of the Baptist Missionary Society from 1792–1842*, 213.

29. Ibid., 214.

30. The sincerity of some enslaved Africans' commitment to missionary Christianity is shown in their willingness to risk flogging and punishment to attend meetings. Missionary documents commonly discuss how some Africans were severely
punished by their owners for attending meetings. See Religious Tract Society, *Missionary Records: West Indies*, 17–18, 50–51, for some examples.

31. Ibid., 198.

32. Ibid., 84–85.

33. Caldecott notes: "Another immigrant was Moses Baker, who was careless about religion when he arrived, but was drawn to the Baptist congregation, and became a pastor. He was less judicious in the difficult circumstances than Liele, and made some mistakes; but he acquired a great influence over the smaller congregations. These men and some others who became pastors were left to work without any support or guidance from either America or England up to some years after 1800." See *The Church in the West Indies*, 75.

34. Adam Clark coined the term "primordial Blackness" during a discussion at Union Theological Seminary, November 8, 1994.

35. See especially Bob Marley's "Time Will Tell," *Bob Marley, Songs of Freedom* (Island Records, 1992. Originally released on *Kaya*, 1978).

36. Turner, *Slaves and Missionaries*, 93. Also see Cox's citation of a Baptist missionary, Mr. Candler, who noted, "The denomination called native Baptists, are under the teaching of black and coloured men, who were once leaders in other congregations, but have broken off and set up ministers for themselves." *History of the Baptist Missionary Society from 1792–1842*, 16–17. Also see James Washington, *Frustrated Fellowship: The Black Baptist Quest for Social Power* (Macon, GA: Mercer University Press, 1986), 10.

37. Hark, *Breaking of the Dawn*, 26–27.

38. Ibid., 27.

39. William Gardner, *A History of Jamaica from Its Discovery by Christopher Columbus to the Year 1872* (London: F. Cass, 1971 [1873]), 357.

40. Phillippo, *Jamaica: Its Past and Present State*, 273.

41. Ibid., 270.

42. Cox, *History of the Baptist Missionary Society from 1792–1842*, 182.

43. Italics mine; ibid., 187.

44. African blood oaths were enacted not only in Obeah rituals in Jamaica but also within Vodun ceremonies prior to the Haitian Revolution and during the Mau Mau ceremonies in preparation for guerrilla resistance against colonialism in Kenya. See Robert Edgerton, *Mau Mau: An African Crucible* (New York: Ballantine, 1989), 54–56, 61–63, 217–218. Sacred oaths continue to be important to many African societies. For more information, see Mbiti, *African Religions and Philosophy*, 171, 212, 214. See especially Rattray's chapter "Oaths" in *Religion and Art in Ashanti*, 205–215.

45. Gordon Lewis's analysis of the "Afro-Baptist" religious values that sparked the rebellion supports my own. See his discussion of Sam Sharpe as a practitioner of "Afro-Baptist" faith in *Main Currents in Caribbean Thought*, 225–228.

46. Cox, *History of the Baptist Missionary Society from 1792–1842*, 186.

47. Turner, *Slaves and Missionaries*, 154–155. Sharpe was also, and I think strategically, a member of Thomas Burchell's mission chapel in Montego Bay. See Shirley Gordon, *God Almighty Make Me Free: Christianity in PreEmancipation Jamaica* (Bloomington: Indiana University Press, 1996), 41–55 for a concise synopsis of Native Baptist formation in Jamaica.

48. Ibid., Turner discusses the evolution of the rebellion and the expectations of enslaved Africans in detail in chap. 6 of her book.

49. The Divine Community included the Christian God, the Myal spirits, and the Ancestors.

50. Gordon, *God Almighty Make Me Free*, 13–14.

51. Ibid., 41–55.

52. Gardner, *History of Jamaica from Its Discovery by Christopher Columbus to the Year 1872*, 358.

53. In the past, scholars identified two traditions emerging from the Great Revival: Zion and Pocomania, or Pukkumina. As Obeah is used to refer to explicit forms of African-derived religions, Jamaicans tend to use Pocomania or "Poco" to refer to any Revival group. However, scholars have documented significant differences between Zion and Poco. Interestingly, Poco is most associated with African traditions and consequently has a notorious reputation even among some Revivalists, who distinguish their practice from Poco. According to Barry Chevannes, since the late twentieth century, Poco practitioners have been merging with Zion practitioners, giving rise to dynamic expressions within the various Zion churches. I was reluctant to endorse the use of the terms Pocomania, Pukkumina, or Poco because in my research I found no Revivalists who would claim ownership of these labels. I came to the conclusion that these terms were always externally derived and derisively employed to humiliate and belittle Revivalists when Edward Seaga admitted in an interview that, during his research in the 1950s and 1960s, he too never found anyone who claimed the labels. Ironically, it is Seaga's publication on Revival traditions that identifies definitive characteristics and traditions belonging to Zionists and Pukkuminists. I have since revised my view after conducting further research. I now believe that the term *poco* may be a Revival Zion term that was corrupted by antipathetic Whites, who attached "mania" to it to classify Revival Zion religiosity as Pocomania.

At times, I use the terms *Zion* or *Zionist* especially to refer to contemporary practitioners because that is how they consistently identified themselves to me during my field research in 1996. Several of my informants did make the distinction between "Revival 60" practitioners and "Revival 61" practitioners, claiming that the latter are more steeped in the African traditions. It has been suggested that the origin of those identifiers are chronologically determined by the year that each trajectory emerged during the Great Revival of 1860 and 1861. In his edited text, *Rastafari and Other African-Caribbean Worldviews* (New Brunswick, NJ: Rutgers University Press, 1994), Barry Chevannes notes a new trend in Revival Zion interaction with North American Christian groups. He explains that "the religion has entered into a new, modernizing phase. The main feature of this development, which is yet to be fully documented and analysed, is the affiliation by the small groups and bands with overseas churches, almost entirely North American, and most of them Pentecostal, Church of God or AME Zion" (9).

54. Grace Hamilton, "The History of Jamaican Revival Religion," unpublished paper (Kingston: African-Caribbean Institute of Jamaica, 1959).

55. Italics mine. Gardner, *History of Jamaica*, 331.

56. John Thornton, "Religious and Ceremonial Life in the Kongo and Mbundu Areas, 1500–1700," in *Central Africans and Cultural Transformations in the American Diaspora*, ed. Linda Heywood (Cambridge: Cambridge University Press, 2002), 84.

57. Barrett, *Soul Force*, 115–116. We should not think, however, that the 1860 revival did not win some African converts to Euro-Christianity. Barrett himself offers evidence of this when writing about a famous Revivalist healer: "The mother of Mammie Forbes was an African slave who is said to have been an expert in bush remedies, but seems to have given up her practice when she was converted to Christianity in the 1860 Revival." See Leonard Barrett, "The Portrait of a Jamaican Healer: African Medical Lore in the Caribbean," *Caribbean Quarterly* 19 (September 1973): 9.

58. Barrett, *The Sun and the Drum*, 58.

59. In my six months of field research in Jamaica, I never encountered a Revival Zion pastor or priest who was not a "reader" (diviner) or who did not have an impressive knowledge of Jamaican plants and their healing properties. During a taped interview on November 3, 1996, Edward Seaga, who has conducted the most comprehensive studies of Revival Zion, acknowledged that his informants also demonstrated the same gifts and expertise. Funso Aiyejina and Rawle Gibbons see a connection between the ritual phenomenon of herbal bathing in the African-Trinidadian Orisha religion and propitiatory sacrifice in classical Yoruba religion. Propitiatory rituals are also found in a number of other classical African religions and may have influenced the religiocultural tradition of bush bathing in Jamaica and across the wider Caribbean. See Funso Aiyejina and Rawle Gibbons, "Orisa (Orisha) Tradition in Trinidad," *Caribbean Quarterly* 45 (December 1999): 48.

60. Chevannes, *Rastafari: Roots and Ideology*, 18–19.

61. William Wedenoja, "The Origins of Revival, a Creole Religion in Jamaica," in *Culture and Christianity: The Dialectics of Transformation*, ed. George Saunders (Westport, CT: Greenwood, 1988), 107.

62. I will submit interpretive comments about Revival Zion later with regard to Rastafari and Kumina, based upon data derived from my research in Jamaica between June and November 1996.

63. I have not yet found enough evidence to substantiate the connection between the "Dove" in Revival Zion and the Dove who was one of Sam Sharpe's chief aides. Dove, along with two others, Johnson and Gardner, took the military title of "colonel" in preparation for armed resistance to enslavement. If the association proves true, this would be a significant example of the relationship between the Native Baptist religion and Revival Zion. It would also be a specific example of ancestral veneration in the contemporary Zion religion.

64. Emanuela Guano, "Revival Zion: An Afro-Christian Religion in Jamaica," *Anthropos* 89 (1994): 521.

65. Mbiti, *Introduction to African Religion*, 11–86; 131–143.

66. Revival Zion worship is not static in terms of locus. Worship takes place inside the church structure but also on the grounds surrounding the church—at the sacred pools, center poles, and other constructions. Center poles are also standard in Haitian Vodun. See Maya Deren, *Divine Horsemen*, esp. 34–36, 238.

67. Guano, "Revival Zion: An Afro-Christian Religion in Jamaica," 523. Here Guano makes important comparisons among the Yoruba, Vodun, and Candomblé riverine deities—Osun, Yemoja/Yemaya, Erzulie, and so on—who are also venerated in similar ways by their adherents.

68. George Simpson, "Culture Change and Reintegration Found in the Cults of West Kingston, Jamaica," *Proceedings of the American Philosophical Society* 99, no. 2 (April 15, 1955), 90.

69. It appears that Zionists do not usually talk about the Ancestors in relation to worship. However, I participated in a number of extrachurch services that were performed to address problems at the request of clients. In such cases I found that they made constant references to the Ancestors. Ancestral veneration may not be explicitly and uniformly embraced by all Zionists in the twenty-first century. More research is needed before drawing any conclusions.

70. Edward Seaga, "Revival Cults in Jamaica," *Jamaica Journal* 3 (1969): 8–9. This entire description of Revival Zion is also informed by my fieldwork among Zionists in Kingston and St. Thomas.

71. Ibid., 8.

72. Ibid., 11.

73. Guano, "Revival Zion: An Afro-Christian Religion in Jamaica," 522.

74. Barrett, *Soul Force*, 123.

75. Ibid., 95–127.

76. Chevannes, *Rastafari and Other African-Caribbean Worldviews*, 9.

77. Joseph Murphy, *Working the Spirit: Ceremonies of the African Diaspora* (Boston: Beacon, 1994), 114.

78. Catherine Duncan, personal communication, October 6, 1996. Kumina will be treated within its historical and cultural context in chapter 4. For now it is important to know that scholars interpret Kumina as the "most African" and the "least Christian" of all of the Black religious traditions in Jamaica. Kumina practitioners are generally belittled and despised by orthodox Christians, especially in public discourse.

79. Mrs. Lileth Grant, interview with author, Holy Mount Zion Baptist Church of Holiness, Yallahs, St. Thomas, October 17, 1996.

80. Chevannes, *Rastafari and Other African-Caribbean Worldviews*, 2–3.

81. This would account for the exaggerated emphasis upon Christian piety in Joseph Murphy's treatment of Revival Zion. Murphy's discussion of Revival Zion spirituality does not appear to be informed by any weeknight healing services or extra-church "work" with clients. See *Working the Spirit: Ceremonies of the African Diaspora*.

82. I witnessed and participated in several of these rituals.

83. Donald Matthews has argued this point well in his critical review of scholarly treatments of slave religion in the United States. See his *Honoring the Ancestors: An African Cultural Interpretation of Black Religion and Literature* (New York: Oxford University Press, 1998).

84. Fu Kiau Bunseki, interview with author, Atlanta, GA, April 23, 2004.

85. Bockie, *Death and the Invisible Powers*, 36–82.

86. Thomas Banbury, *Jamaica Superstitions, or the Obeah Book* (Kingston: de Souza, 1895), 21–22.

87. Beckwith, *Christmas Mummings in Jamaica*, 32.

88. Martha Beckwith, *Black Roadways* (Chapel Hill: University of North Carolina Press, 1929), 144.

89. Warner-Lewis, *Central Africa in the Caribbean*, 190–198.

90. Fu Kiau Bunseki, interview with author, Atlanta, GA, April 23, 2004.

91. Campbell, *Rasta and Resistance*, 70.

92. Quoted in Chevannes, *Rastafari and Other African-Caribbean Worldviews*, 10.

93. See Robert Hill, "Leonard P. Howell and Millenarian Visions in Early Rastafari," *Jamaica Journal* 16, no. 1 (1983): 24–39. Also see Wilson J. Moses, *The Golden Age of Black Nationalism, 1850–1925* (New York: Oxford University Press, 1978).

94. The *livity* is the Rasta term for the Rastafari understanding of the world and its attending lifestyle and culture. This discussion of the three phases of Rastafari is informed by Barry Chevannes's research. See *Rastafari and Other African-Caribbean Worldviews*, 9–16.

95. Haile Selassie (1916–1974) ruled Ethiopia from 1930 to 1974. *Daily Gleaner*, December 16, 1933. Cited by Campbell, *Rasta and Resistance*, 71.

96. *Daily Gleaner*, March 14, 1934.

97. Leonard Howell and Claudius Henry are two examples. See Chevannes, *Rastafari and Other African-Caribbean Worldviews*, 11–14; Barry Chevannes, "The Repairer of the Breach: Reverend Claudius Henry and Jamaican Society," in *Ethnicity in the Americas*, ed. Frances Henry (The Hague: Mouton, 1976), 263–269.

98. Rasta term for suffering.

99. I had firsthand experience with members from the Bull Bay Bobo community in March 1996.

100. This information was collected while I was doing research in Jamaica, September 1996.

101. Emmanuel Edwards, "The Black Christ Salvation: With Joy and Peace Internationally," in his *Black Supremacy in Righteousness of Salvation Jesus Negus Christ Emmanuel "I" Selassie "I" Jah Rastafari in Royal Majestiy Selassie "I" Jahovah Jah Rastafari "I"* (Bull Bay, Jamaica: Ethiopia Africa Black International Congress, n.d.), 26–27.

102. Chevannes, *Rastafari and Other African-Caribbean Worldviews*, 14.

103. *Ganja* is the local term for marijuana.

104. Ibid., 18.

105. Dr. Leahcim Semaj, interview with author, Kingston, Jamaica, September 27, 1996.

106. See Sheila Kitzinger, "Protest and Mysticism: The Ras Tafari Cult of Jamaica," *Journal for the Scientific Study of Religion* 8 (Fall 1969): 252–255.

107. Judy Mowatt, "Only a Woman," *Only a Woman* (Shanachie Records, 1988). The words of Mowatt's song are slightly altered to reflect her change of consciousness about gender bias as it relates to the status of women in Jamaican and other global societies. In a letter to the author granting permission to use her lyrics, Mowatt wrote the following: ". . . on our journey in life there are places where we have found ourselves and may have rest[ed] there for awhile because of our circumstances and relationships, but knowledge and truth are two progressive elements that would not allow us to tabernacle there. What I [am] trying to say, is the title *'Only a Woman'*, is something that I would not want to associate with anymore. God made woman, not 'only' a woman. I would much prefer if where *'Only a Woman'* appears in the song, you would eliminate the word 'only' and please write, *'Just because we are woman'*."

108. Maureen Rowe, "The Woman in Rastafari," in *Caribbean Quarterly Monograph: Rastafari*, ed. Rex Nettleford (Kingston, Jamaica: Caribbean Quarterly, University of the West Indies, 1985), 19.

109. Chevannes, *Rastafari: Roots and Ideology*, 255–262.

110. "Daughter Loi," *Rasta Voice* 94 (Ras Historian, September 1985). Cited by Chevannes in *Rastafari: Roots and Ideology*, 257.

111. For important insights into the negative impact of White supremacy on Black popular culture and the Black personality in Jamaica, see Clinton Hutton and Nathaniel Samuel Murrell, "Rastas' Psychology of Blackness, Resistance, and Somebodiness," in *Chanting Down Babylon: The Rastafari Reader*, ed. Nathaniel Samuel Murrell, William David Spencer, and Anthony Adrian McFarlane (Philadelphia: Temple University Press, 1998), 36–54, esp. 47–50.

112. Goldenberg in biblio. For a thorough study of the myth of Ham, especially as it evolved in the United States, see Goldenberg, *The Curse of Ham*. Also see Peterson, *Ham and Japheth*.

113. Western Christian anthropology was established by Augustine of Hippo (354–430) who concluded that the human being is a rational substance composed of a body and a soul and created in God's image. While Augustine's doctrine of humanity was not dualistic per se, it was hierarchical and has been reduced to support dualistic thinking with regard to the doctrine of humanity in the history of Christian thought. Augustine believed that the body and soul, as created by God, are both good. However, he maintained that the soul is a *greater* good and the body a *lesser* good. He also concluded that the soul's higher powers were of ultimate importance and allowed for wisdom (*sapentia*) or knowledge of God and contemplation as its outcome, while the

soul's lower perceptive powers led to a useful but inferior cognitive knowledge (*scientia*), action being its outcome.

114. See page 95 for the full citation of the testimony of an enslaved African who converted to Christianity.

115. This remark, of course, pertains to the modern period, when Africans in the Americas and the Caribbean were introduced to Western European Christianity. In the ancient world, East Africans and North Africans comprised some Christian communities and were participants in shaping orthodox Christian doctrine and traditions.

116. Lucius Outlaw, "Language and Consciousness: Toward a Hermeneutic of Black Culture," *Cultural Hermeneutics* 1 (1974): 403–404.

117. Gordon, *God Almighty Make Me Free*, 41–55.

118. This practice was denounced as fetish worship by White missionaries. See page 102 for testimony that the Native Baptist George Lewis discouraged the practice among African converts.

119. Schuler, "Myalism and the African Religious Tradition in Jamaica," 297. Also see entire article for a full discussion.

120. I stand by this interpretation also because there is some evidence, although anecdotal until confirmed by further research, that Revival Zionists were making distinctions between themselves as spiritualists and other Christian churches during the first half of the twentieth century. I have been told this by several informants who are descendants of Revival Zionists but are not themselves adherents.

121. See the previous section on Revival Zion, which explores these features as present in contemporary Jamaican expressions of the tradition.

122. Zora Neale Hurston, *The Sanctified Church*, 103.

123. Rupert Lewis, "Marcus Garvey and the Early Rastafarians: Continuity and Discontinuity," in Murrell, Spencer, and McFarlane, eds., *Chanting Down Babylon* (Philadelphia: Temple University Press, 1998), 145–149.

124. Chevannes, *Rastafari: Roots and Ideology*, 127.

125. Ibid., 22.

126. Lewis, "Marcus Garvey and the Early Rastafarians," 154.

127. Chevannes, *Rastafari: Roots and Ideology*, 21.

128. Rowe, "The Woman in Rastafari," 78.

129. Chevannes, *Rastafari: Roots and Ideology*, 130.

130. Kelly Brown Douglas submits that womanist theology is "bifocal" in its "religio-cultural analysis." See her article "Womanist Theology: What Is Its Relationship to Black Theology?" in *Black Theology: A Documentary History, vol. 2: 1980–1992*, ed. Gayraud S. Wilmore and James H. Cone (Maryknoll, NY: Orbis, 1993), 290–299.

131. See Theophus Smith, *Conjuring Culture: Biblical Formations of Black America* (New York: Oxford University Press, 1994), 126–139. On 134, Smith notes, "[W]e may describe the iconic dimension of African American spirituality as a tradition of enactive interpretations or performances; the tradition features, preeminently, interpretive appropriations of *religious* figures and biblical narratives."

132. George Eaton Simpson, "Personal Reflections on Rastafari in West Kingston in the Early 1950s," in Murrell, Spencer, and McFarlane, eds., *Chanting Down Babylon*, 219.

133. See Long, *Significations*, 176–179.

134. Abyssinia is the ancient name for the kingdom that became known as Ethiopia in the modern period.

135. Psalms 68:31. From *The New Revised Standard Version of the Holy Bible* (New York: Oxford University Press, 1989).

136. See chap. 1.

137. See chap. 1.

138. My use of *Zionism* here refers to the Jamaican Revival Zion spirituality and iconography. It in no way refers to twentieth-century Jewish Zionism.

139. King Alpha is a Rastafari title for Ras Tafari Makonnen/Haile Selassie I, emperor of Ethiopia.

CHAPTER FOUR

1. Barrett, *Soul Force*, 87.

2. Some Kumina songs have been recorded by researchers over the years.

3. On my first Kumina site visit, I stopped at a home where a neighborly looking woman was sitting on the front porch. I asked her for directions to the home of my intended informant. The woman responded by waving her hand at me and saying that she wanted nothing to do with those "devil people" who lived up the road. She pointed to the left with a suspicious look on her face. Later, some time after I had developed a relationship with my informant, I told her about the incident. She smiled and responded that the woman's husband is a Jehovah's Witness minister who condemns Kumina culture any time he has a public platform to do so. Ironically, one day he became very ill and sent his son to my informant to snoop around and see if anyone would prescribe some natural medicine for his malady (as Western medicine had proved to be ineffective). My informant wasted no time; she cured the man that very day, yet he continues to condemn Kumina and Kumina practitioners. These types of incidents—of stigmatization and condemnation from Christians—were repeatedly confirmed by Kumina and Revival Zion practitioners.

4. This deity is Nzambi in Central African Kongo culture. See Simon Bockie, *Death and the Invisible Powers*, 108.

5. Donald Hogg, "The Convince Cult in Jamaica," *Papers in Caribbean Anthropology* 58 (New Haven, CT: Yale University Publications in Anthropology, 1960); Chevannes, *Rastafari and Other African-Caribbean Worldviews*, 19. Chevannes specifically associates the practice of Convince with the parish of St. Mary in Jamaica. The year 1867 is sometimes mentioned as the official termination date for the indentured labor program.

6. For a developed discussion of these traditions, see Ivy Baxter, *The Arts of an Island*; also see Patterson, *Sociology of Slavery*, 231–259.

7. See Laura Tanna, *Jamaican Folk Tales and Oral Histories* (Kingston: Institute of Jamaica Publications, 1984), for insight into the music, song, and folklore of these traditions and cultures.

8. Kenneth Bilby and Fu-Kiau Bunseki, "Kumina: A Kongo-based Tradition in the New World" (Brussels: Les Cahiers du Cedaf, 8 (1983): 1.

9. Rex Nettleford, *Inward Stretch, Outward Reach: A Voice from the Caribbean* (London: Macmillan, 1993). See chapter entitled "Cultural Resistance in Caribbean Society: Dance and Survival," 91–115.

10. Joseph Moore, "Religion of Jamaican Negroes: A Study of Afro-American Acculturation" (Ann Arbor: University Microfilm Publication 7053, Doctoral Dissertation Series, 1953).

11. Female Kumina leaders are often given the titles queen and/or mother. Maureen Warner-Lewis, "The Nkuyu: Spirit Messengers of the Kumina" (Kingston, Jamaica: Savacou, 1977).

12. Maureen Warner-Lewis, "The Ancestral Factor in Jamaica's African Relig-

ions," in *African Creative Expressions of the Divine*, ed. Kortright Davis and Elias Fara-jaje Jones (Washington, DC: Howard University School of Divinity, 1991), 74.

13. Olive Lewin, *Rock It Come Over: The Folk Music of Jamaica* (Barbados: University of the West Indies Press, 2000), 215–303.

14. Zora Neale Hurston, *Voodoo Gods: An Inquiry into Native Myths and Magic in Jamaica and Haiti* (London: Dent, 1939), and *Tell My Horse* (Berkeley, CA: Turtle Island for the Netzahualcoyotl Historical Society, 1983).

15. Kerr, *Personality and Conflict in Jamaica*.

16. Bilby and Bunseki, "Kumina: A Kongo-based Tradition in the New World," 2.

17. Warner-Lewis, "The Ancestral Factor in Jamaica's African Religions," 74.

18. Bilby and Bunseki, "Kumina: A Kongo-based Tradition in the New World," 3.

19. In 1978, Bilby and Bunseki discovered a pervasive awareness of cultural continuity with BaKongo culture among Kumina practitioners. See Bilby and Bunseki, "Kumina: A Kongo-based Tradition in the New World," esp. 11–13.

20. See Appiah, *In My Father's House*, for a discussion of Europe's construction of Africa. While I agree with Appiah's critical assessment of the European construction of "Africa," he misperceives the problem of exile from Africa and African diasporic responses to that problem. Appiah does not give enough credit to the reasons that many people in today's African diaspora hold tenaciously to less than "factual" ideas about Africa, nor does he give proper consideration to the religious meaning of the symbol "Africa" for Africans in the diaspora. Compare with V. Mudimbe, *The Idea of Africa* (Bloomington: Indiana University Press, 1994).

21. Moore, "Religion of Jamaican Negroes: A Study of Afro-Jamaican Acculturation," 115–117.

22. Bongo, I was told by several informants, is the actual name of the African ancestral homeland and the ethnic identity of the Kumina Ancestors.

23. Josiah Young, "God's Path and Pan-Africa," in *Black Theology: A Documentary History*, vol. 2: 1980–1992, ed. Wilmore and Cone (Maryknoll, NY: Orbis, 1993), 22.

24. Some informants chose to be represented by pseudonyms or initials to protect their identities.

25. Uncle P, interview with author, Port Morant, St. Thomas, Jamaica, September 19, 1996.

26. Schuler employs the term *recaptives* "to describe recent African arrivals in St. Helena or Sierra Leone who still resided in reception depots." Some of the recent arrivals came from intercepted slave ships en route from Africa to Cuba. See "*Alas, Alas, Kongo*," 5.

27. Monica Schuler, " 'Yerri, Yerri, Koongo': A Social History of Liberated African Immigration into Jamaica, 1841–1867" (Ph.D. diss., University of Wisconsin, Madison, 1977), 138.

28. Edward Brathwaite, "Kumina: The Spirit of African Survival in Jamaica," *Jamaica Journal* 42 (1978): 47.

29. Bilby and Bunseki, "Kumina: A Kongo-based Tradition in the New World," 11.

30. Maureen Smith and Hortense Bailey, personal communication, Port Morant, St. Thomas, Jamaica, November 9, 1996. A Kumina group is referred to as a "bands." In 1969, Seaga noted that Revival groups also used the term self-referentially. See "Revival Cults in Jamaica," 6.

31. Imogene Kennedy, interview with author, St. Catherine, Jamaica, October 7, 1996.

32. Translated from audio-recorded material, Port Morant, St. Thomas, Jamaica, October 23, 1996.

33. Schuler, " 'Yerri, Yerri, Koongo,' " 74.

34. Ibid., 75.

35. Ibid., 175.

36. Ibid., 78, 183.

37. Bilby and Bunseki, "Kumina: A Kongo-based Tradition in the New World," 17–21.

38. Imogene Kennedy, interview with author, St. Catherine, Jamaica, October 17, 1996.

39. Ibid.

40. Cited from field notes, Port Morant, St. Thomas, Jamaica, October 10, 1996.

41. Cited from audio-recorded material, Port Morant, St. Thomas, Jamaica, October 10, 1996.

42. Monica Schuler could not be more correct in her contention that "[m]ost social studies of English- and French-speaking Caribbean societies, preoccupied with the persistence of certain African cultures, have tended to assume, until recently, that they must be retentions from the slave period. Sufficient evidence exists to show that this is an incomplete explanation, however. Besides Jamaica, other territories that received African indentured laborers in the nineteenth century, such as Trinidad, Grenada, and Martinique have recognizable Yoruba or Central African cultures. The same late arrival, large numbers, and group cohesiveness that conditioned their survival in Jamaica account for the preservation of these cultures elsewhere." Schuler also identifies some scholars who have miscontextualized Kumina within the period of enslavement. See "Alas, Alas, Kongo," 9.

43. Barrett, Soul Force, 69.

44. Ibid., 68.

45. Patterson, Sociology of Slavery, 201. See the broader context of Patterson's interpretation of Leslie and Herskovits in chapter 1.

46. I also collected lexicons and songs similar to the ones included in Bilby and Bunseki's article "Kumina: A Kongo-based Tradition in the New World."

47. I am thankful to Dr. Kalala Ngalamulume for taking the time to discuss these terms with me.

48. I use this qualifier to distinguish between Kuminas that are exhibited on stage at national celebrations, competitions, and other public appearances as demonstrations of Jamaica's "African heritage" and those organized within the legitimate boundaries and authority of Kumina communities. I understand the former to be inauthentic and by and large exploitative.

49. Imogene Kennedy, interview with author, St. Catherine, Jamaica, October 17, 1996.

50. Original emphases. Warner-Lewis, "The Nkuyu: Spirit Messengers of the Kumina," 59–60.

51. Imogene Kennedy, interview with author, St. Catherine, Jamaica, October 17, 1996.

52. Fu Kiau Bunseki, interview with author, Atlanta, GA, April 23, 2004.

53. Two important details from an early twentieth-century description are germane to this discussion. Martha Beckwith describes the Pukkumerian tradition as a derivation of Revival Zion and Obeah, noting that they "hold their meetings near a graveyard, and it is to the ghosts of their own membership that they appeal when spirits are summoned to a meeting 'They jump and dance and sing and talk in a secret language because the spirits do not talk our language.' " See Martha Beckwith, Black Roadways, 176–177. In chapter 1 of this text, I include Bilby's discussion of the

importance of the graveyard in Gumbay Play/Myal rituals. Carrying sick victims to ancestral burying grounds and communing with their spirits at the burial sites were also essential in the Kumina ceremonies I attended.

54. I was convinced of the authenticity of events as they unfolded, in part because the young man's mother had requested the Kumina to correct what appeared to be a psychological affliction of her son. The young man cooperated but seemed unprepared for what was to happen. When one of the young women caught Myal, the young man began to laugh hysterically. Within seconds he had collapsed on the ground in an unconscious state. At first, I thought he was dead, but later learned that his collapse into unconsciousness was the work of the Ancestors which was necessary for the healing process.

55. Gardner, *History of Jamaica*, 192.

56. Delores Williams, *Sisters in the Wilderness* (Maryknoll, NY: Orbis, 1993).

57. From unpublished work cited by Thompson, *Flash of the Spirit*, 108.

58. The contemporary Kumina community maintains a memory of oath-taking rituals which is tangential to this discussion. According to Kumina oral tradition, the oaths were followed even after Emancipation. Several practitioners gave accounts of the "sacred oath" that was sealed before the Paul Bogle Rebellion of 1865, which occurred in the parish of St. Thomas, the home of (Kongo-based) Kumina. It is not clear whether the oath was taken based upon the authority of the Bible, or whether Obeah rituals were involved, or both.

59. Thompson, *Flash of the Spirit*, 108. Thompson cites from John Janzen and Wyatt MacGaffey, *An Anthology of Kongo Religion: Primary Texts from Lower Zaire* (Lawrence: University of Kansas Press, 1974), 34.

60. Although it might be tempting to interpret the resurrection of Jesus Christ as coherent with the cross of recurring incarnation in Kongo traditions, the enfleshing of the Divine within the human corpus is absent in the resurrection, and thus I make a clear distinction between the two.

61. Zora Neale Hurston's research on the sanctified (Pentecostal) church in the early twentieth century documents that the sign of the cross as incarnated spirit/Divinity has also dominated the religiosity of Blacks who accepted Christianity in the United States. Hurston argues that there is a definite connection between the phenomenon of spirit possession in the sanctified church and in African-derived religions like Vodun. See her *The Sanctified Church*, 79–107. Also see Herskovits, *Myth of the Negro Past*.

62. I use the term *disembodied life/living* to refer to the "living dead" or the Ancestors. This domain of the Ancestors, which is under the earth, is known as *Kalunga* in Kongo cosmology. Through its icon, the cross, the Kongo Cosomogram shows the Kalunga where the "invisible" vertical pole sinks beneath the "visible" horizontal pole. *Kalunga* is reconceived among BaKongo Kumina descendants in Jamaica as the Atlantic Ocean. See Thompson, *Flash of the Spirit*, 109; Schuler, "*Alas, Alas, Kongo*," 95.

63. I submit that this was not the intention of St. Augustine, who conceptualized the soul and body as hierarchically created by an ultimate good God. In Augustine's anthropology nothing about human nature is actually bad or evil because everything has its source in God's goodness. Augustine appraised the soul as good and the body not as bad, but as a lesser good when compared to the soul.

64. See Schuler, 182–183 for a fuller discussion of her argument.

65. See especially Robert Marley, "Get Up, Stand Up" (Burnin' Island Records, 1973).

66. This has been a defining characteristic of Rastology since the beginning of the movement and continues to distinguish the Rastafari ethos from local Jamaican expressions of Christianity.

67. Douglas, *The Black Christ*, 22–29.

68. In other words, although I do not support her conclusions on this matter, the connections that Douglas makes between classical African spirituality and Black North American Christianity is an important move in Black and womanist theological discourse. In this way she takes steps toward addressing the apparent lack of interest among far too many Black and womanist theologians in the African religious heritage and its significance to Black religious formation in North America.

69. The ringshout and other hush harbor practices were aspects of slave religion whereby possession trance and other forms of ecstatic religious expression, consistent with features of African religion, were nurtured and expressed within concealed spaces away from and outside the purview of White authority. See Raboteau, *Slave Religion*.

70. Williams, *Sisters in the Wilderness*, 168.

71. See note 60 above.

72. See also Raboteau, *Slave Religion*, and Clifton H. Johnson, ed., *God Struck Me Dead: Voices of Ex-Slaves* (Cleveland: Pilgrim, 1993) for similar testimonies among North American African captives. Although several contemporary constructive African Christologies have imaged Jesus as ancestor par excellence, I am not persuaded that, in the context of slavery, Africans, who were introduced to Jesus Christ as God, would have reinterpreted this perhaps intriguing and inviting yet exotic White Christian deity as an ancestor. Ancestorhood in classical African religions concerns the family unit—its ethical codes, taboos, and protocol, generativity in the family lineage, and the continuity of life, along with the acquisition and assertion of knowledge (wisdom), ontological status, and power. An analysis of the complex theology of ancestorhood falls most appropriately within the rubric of theological anthropology, for ancestors are departed family members whose names are remembered, and invisible presences felt through ritual acts of veneration and through the sacramental experiences of mundane living: eating, harvesting crops, giving birth, fishing, hunting, fighting wars, curing diseases, and so on.

73. Emphases added. Williams, *Sisters in the Wilderness*, 168.

74. Consistent with BaKongo cosmology, in Kumina ceremonies, circular motion represents the continuity of life. This motion is hyperbolized as devotees make simultaneous circular motions with multiple parts of their bodies. This is done as they move around the center pole and drummers move in the same direction and configuration of the sun (a counterclockwise circle) and as they spin around on their feet intermittently within that circle.

75. See Mary Daly, *Beyond God the Father* (Boston: Beacon Press, 1970), 75–81.

76. Jacquelyn Grant, "Womanist Theology: Black Women's Experiences as a Source for Doing Theology, with Special Reference to Christology," in *Black Theology, A Documentary History*, Vol. 2: 1980–1992, ed. Wilmore and Cone, 273.

77. Besides *In Search of Our Mothers' Gardens*, see, for example, Walker's *The Color Purple* (New York: Pocket, 1982); and Walker, *Anything We Love Can Be Saved: A Writer's Activism* (New York: Random House, 1997).

78. Imogene Kennedy, interview with author, St. Catherine, Jamaica, October 17, 1996.

79. Walker, *The Color Purple*, 204.

80. JoAnne Terrell examines the theme of Christian exclusivism more closely

than many other womanist theologians in her text *Power in the Blood? The Cross in the African American Experience* (Maryknoll, NY: Orbis, 1998).

81. This is not to say that there were no other expressions of protest against the rising socioeconomic problems. For example, there were strikes on several other sugar estates in 1863 and 1864. See Campbell, *Rasta and Resistance*, 34.

82. Schuler, " 'Yerri, Yerri, Koongo': A Social History of Liberated African Immigration into Jamaica, 1841–1867," 105.

83. Ibid., 105–110.

84. I have slides of a "duty" (shrine) of four colossal statues of Marcus Garvey, Paul Bogle, Nanny, and Cudjoe, which are on Imogene Kennedy's front lawn. Kennedy built the duty in the early 1990s at the instruction of the Ancestors. "They must be remembered" is what she reported to me during a personal interview, St. Catherine, Jamaica, October 25, 1996.

85. Interview with author, Yallahs, St. Thomas, October 20, 1996. Translation: Rastafari and Zion affirm the same values and principles. We are all one.

86. Paraphrased from research journal, November 4, 1996.

87. See Barrett, *The Sun and the Drum*; Kerr, *Personality and Conflict in Jamaica*, 114–136.

88. See Karen Brown, *Mama Lola: A Vodou Priestess in Brooklyn* (Berkeley: University of California Press, 1991), 156–157, 189–190, 220–221.

89. Josiah Young makes this argument for the African North American context in his assertion that the Ancestors were the norm of enslaved Africans' religion. Young refutes James Cone's claim that Jesus was the norm of enslaved Africans' religion. See Young, *A Pan-African Theology*, 106–116.

90. See Linda Gloss and Clay Gloss, eds., *Jump Up and Say! A Collection of Black Storytelling* (New York: Simon and Schuster, 1995).

91. See Daryl Dance, *Folklore from Contemporary Jamaicans* (Knoxville: University of Tennessee Press, 1985).

92. See Robert Marley, "Survival," *Songs of Freedom* (Island Records, 1979).

93. Contemporary manifestations of anti-Africanness are discussed and responded to in a publication of the Caribbean Conference of Churches: Burton Sankeralli, ed., *At the Crossroads: African Caribbean Religion and Christianity* (Trinidad and Tobago: Caribbean Conference of Churches, 1995).

94. The Creator Deity is known as Onyame or Nyankpong among the Akan, Olodumare in Yoruba culture, Chukwu in Igbo culture—to name a few.

95. Chevannes, *Rastafari and Other African-Caribbean Worldviews*, 8–9. Also see Waddell, a contemporary of the movement, in *Twenty-nine Years in the West Indies and Central Africa*, 190ff.

96. Wedenoja, "The Origins of Revival, a Creole Religion in Jamaica," 106.

97. Paul Ricoeur, *Interpretation Theory: Discourse and the Surplus of Meaning* (Fort Worth: Texas Christian University Press, 1976).

98. Schuler, "*Alas, Alas, Kongo*," 36.

99. North American fundamentalist religion has won mass numbers of converts among the Jamaican people. Jamaicans have access to their televised sermons through both local and cable network television. Lewin Williams raises this issue as a moral problem to be addressed by Caribbean theology. See *Caribbean Theology* (New York: Lang, 1994), 14–18, 24–27.

100. I saw countless examples of fellowship, affirmation, and support among the three groups. In addition, the three communities share the same beliefs about a variety of religious practices. The Zionists and Kumina devotees use the coconut,

fresh water, and rum for the same purposes in their religious rituals. Rastas, Revivalists, and Kumina practitioners shun the use of salt in food prepared for ritual and in some cases even in nonritual dietary consumption. Monica Schuler persuasively identifies the taboo against salt with the nineteenth-century BaKongo immigrant belief that salt intake would prevent them from flying back to Africa. See *"Alas, Alas, Kongo,"* 93–96. Compare with Chevannes, *Rastafari: Roots and Ideology,* 34–35. Chevannes convincingly argues that the persistence of the taboo against salt in the Kumina, Revival, and Rastafari religions is a symbol of African resistance to European culture.

101. Homer Lobban, pastor of Mount Zion Baptist Church of Holiness, interview with author, Yallahs, St. Thomas, Jamaica, October 19, 1996.

102. Banbury, *Jamaica Superstitions, or, The Obeah Book: A Complete Treatise of the Absurdities Believed in by the People of the Island,* 7.

103. For an extensive treatment of this issue, see Paul Farmer, *The Uses of Haiti* (Monroe, ME: Common Courage, 1994).

104. For a thorough treatment of this subject, see Laguerre, *Voodoo and Politics in Haiti.* Also see Sidney Mintz's introduction to Métraux, *Voodoo in Haiti,* 1–14. Eric Williams cites the derisive commentaries forwarded by Thomas Carlyle in 1849 and by J. A. Froude in 1887 with regard to Haiti's sovereignty as a Black nation in *British Historians and the West Indies,* 82, 182–183.

105. Réné Depestre, "Problems of Identity for the Black Man in Caribbean Literatures," *Caribbean Quarterly* 19, no. 3 (September 1973): 51.

106. The African Caribbean Institute of Jamaica (ACIJ) has sponsored and supported numerous research projects on Kennedy. Over the years, the ACIJ has acquired a significant collection of materials on Kennedy and the Kumina tradition. Also see Maureen Warner-Lewis, "The Nkuyu: Spirit Messengers of the Kumina," Savacou Publications Pamphlet No. 3, 1977; and Edward Brathwaite, "The Spirit of African Survival in Jamaica," *Jamaica Journal* 42 (1978), 44–63.

107. See Edward Seaga, "Revival Cults in Jamaica," *Jamaica Journal,* 3/2 (1969), 5. "Revivalist groups are not forbidden by any Statutory Law but Cultists sometimes infringe the Night Noises Prevention Law of 1911 and the so called Obeah Law of 1898,—the latter defines the consultation with practitioners of Obeah and the publication and distribution of any material 'calculated to promote the superstition of Obeah.' " According to my informants in both the *Kumina* and Revival Zion traditions, these laws were brutally enforced until Edward Seaga "cut the ribbon" and "gave the license" for them to practice their religions without molestation from the Jamaican police.

108. Imogene Kennedy, interview with author, St. Catherine, Jamaica, October 17, 1996.

109. Devon House is a historic colonial local attraction, located in the heart of Kingston, which sponsors a number of social and cultural activities.

110. Edward Seaga described the Friday night Kumina and Revival Zion performances to me as venues for "cultural expression." Edward Seaga, interview with author, Kingston, Jamaica, November 3, 1996.

111. By way of comparison, the Jamaica Order of Distinction catalogue lists as corecipients for the Order of Distinction: Charles Hyatt, actor, broadcaster, and producer (August 6, 1980); Lt. Col. Ian Jameson, commanding officer, Third Battalion, Jamaica Regiment (August 5, 1974); Dr. Horace Keane, dental surgeon and past president, Jamaica Dental Association (August 1, 1978); Arthur Jones, marine pilot, superintendent of pilotage, Port Authority, Kingston (August 6, 1980). Imogene Kennedy is listed as a "folklorist" and is honored "for services in the development of African heri-

tage." See Chancery of the Order of Distinction, *The Order of Distinction* (Kingston, Jamaica: Chancery of the O.D., 1988), 35–36, 87, 123.

112. For a thorough treatment of the ethics, politics, and controversy surrounding the exhibition of cultures in a global context see Ivan Karp and Stephen D. Lavine, eds., *Exhibiting Cultures: The Poetics and Politics of Museum Display* (Washington, DC: Smithsonian Institute Press, 1991). Also see Rachel Adams, *Sideshow U.S.A: Freaks and the American Cultural Imagination* (Chicago: University of Chicago Press, 2001).

113. See Kelly Brown Douglas, "Womanist Theology: What Is Its Relationship to Black Theology?", in *Black Theology: A Documentary History*, Vol. 2: *1980–1992*, ed. Wilmore and Cone, 290–299.

114. This is exactly what happened at Jamaica's October 1996 Caribbean Heritagefest, where a number of African religiocultural dances were performed. The organizers introduced each tradition with sketchy references to their historical background. To say the least, the dances were misunderstood by a crowd that was alienated by time and memory from their significance as religious worship. I witnessed several people gawking and laughing at the presenters. This subject is thoroughly treated from a global perspective in Karp and Lavine, eds., *Exhibiting Cultures*. Also see Edward Brathwaite's critique of the performance of Jamaican culture in Brathwaite, "Kumina: The Spirit of African Survival in Jamaica."

115. Warner-Lewis, "The Nkuyu: Spirit Messengers of the Kumina," 77.

116. Fieldnotes, Port Morant, St. Thomas, Jamaica, September 23, 1996 and October 5, 1996, Yallahs, St. Thomas, Jamaica, October 17, 1996 and November 3, 1996.

117. Cited by Cassidy, *Jamaica Talk*, 240–241. Leonard Barrett offers insight into this issue in the following passage: "There are few Jamaican elites now alive who can truthfully say that their lives have never been affected in some way by [folk healers]. A particular individual might not have had personal contact with them, but if pressed hard enough he generally admits that either his parents or some of his relatives have been cured or helped in some way by an African practitioner. The writer recalls quite vividly a medical doctor and graduate of a prestigious British university, who, on learning of the author's plan to study the healer, Mother Rita, declared with all sincerity 'the woman saved my life!' He then proceeded to tell the story. As a small boy his older sister (age five) died of vomiting sickness and following her death, he too came down with the illness. The family became greatly alarmed because all the professional treatment that was available had not saved his sister's life. His father, a school teacher and a catechist in the mission church, could not openly associate himself with the folk specialists in the community, but his maternal uncle was a believer in the folk tradition and his mother was also very sympathetic to them. This uncle prevailed upon the father to consult Mother Rita. He finally decided, and under much secrecy he went for consultation. One bottle of medicine was all that was necessary. The doctor in question is convinced that it was through the work of this folk healer that his life was saved. Numerous stories of this type could be told among Jamaican elites but few are as honest as the doctor in acknowledging these experiences." See Barrett, "The Portrait of a Jamaican Healer: African Medical Lore in the Caribbean," 7.

118. For thorough documentation of these ideas, see Métraux, *Voodoo in Haiti*; Williams, *Voodoos and Obeahs*.

119. Murphy, *Working the Spirit*, x.

120. Bell, *Obeah: Witchcraft in the West Indies*, 58.

121. Murphy, *Working the Spirit*, x.

122. Hazel Ramsay, interview with author, Kingston, Jamaica, September 29, 1996.

123. The problem was raised during conversations with Rex Nettleford, Olive Lewin, Barry Chevannes, and Edward Seaga.

124. Italics mine. Tanna, *Jamaican Folk Tales and Oral Histories,* 6.

125. Ibid., 12.

126. I elect to construct a distinct term to signify a person who uses mystical power for antisocial purposes. I prefer *antisocializer* because I find terms such as "witch," "sorcerer," "magician," and related compounds or derivations inadequate to describe the person who manipulates mystical power for antisocial purposes. Although the latter terms are widely used across religious studies to describe this phenomenon in a variety of settings, they have been overused to describe African religion and religious practices. Indeed they have also been erroneously maligned within Western Christian discourse with reference to pre-Christian European traditions.

127. This is especially true in White academic theology—a moral and prophetic vocation which calls on the theologian to expose and denounce evil. For centuries White theologians in Europe and America wrote about God, Christ, human destiny, salvation, sin, evil, and justice in most cases without even mentioning the slave trade and African enslavement.

128. Cited by Schuler, *"Alas, Alas, Kongo,"* 4.

129. Edward Brathwaite, *Folk Culture of the Slaves in Jamaica* (London: New Beacon, 1981), 9–10.

130. "Cutting and clearing destruction," that is, discovering and eradicating evil, is one of the chief foci of contemporary Revival Zion religiosity.

131. Waddell, *Twenty-nine Years,* 188.

132. Ibid., 190–192.

133. Schuler, *"Alas, Alas, Kongo,"* 36.

134. See J. Omosade Awolalu, "Sin and Its Removal in African Traditional Religion," *Journal of the American Academy of Religion* 44, no. 2 (1976): 275–287. Awolalu argues that the African response to evil is immediate and concrete. When confronted with evil, Africans exorcise it through concrete ritual acts and attempt to restore harmony and well-being.

135. See chapter 1 for a full discussion.

136. This is the interpretation endorsed by every scholarly study of Obeah and Myal that I have read. Schuler, Chevannes, Barrett, Patterson, and others opt for this interpretation even after acknowledging the significance of Obeah in the African pursuit of liberation from slavery, as well as the role of the Obeah practitioner in exorcising evil and restoring health.

137. See chapter 1 for a full discussion of Obeah. Another puzzling dimension of this scapegoating of African traditions as innately evil or negative is the use of the term *Nkuyu* by Kumina devotees themselves to refer to the Ancestors. Given traditional KiKongo terms for the living dead, the legitimate term for Ancestors (residents of Mpemba or the Community of the Dead) is *Bakuyu*, while *Nkuyu* specifically refers to a living dead who has been exiled from Mpemba. The *Bankuyu* (plural form of *Nkuyu*) "are evil dead who in their lifetime in this world were engaged in negative acts . . . adultery, murder, theft, and all other major crimes." This development among BaKongo descendants is worth more study. Perhaps semantic nuances in terminology by region might account for the variation. However the survival of the negative term for the living dead (*Nkuyu*) and the apparent absence of the term for revered Ancestors (*Bakuyu*) among Kumina devotees in Jamaica is intriguing. See Bockie, *Death and the Invisible Powers: The World of Kongo Belief,* 131.

138. John Thornton, "Religious and Ceremonial Life in the Kongo and Mbundu

Areas, 1500–1700," 81. Thornton's comparison of European and African conceptions of "witchcraft" demonstrates the contrasting views even more poignantly on 81–82.

139. Bryan Edwards, *The History of the British West Indies*, vol. 2, 122.

140. See, for example, W. Arens and Ivan Karp, *Creativity of Power: Cosmology and Action in African Societies* (Washington, DC: Smithsonian Institution Press, 1989).

141. Ivan Karp, "African Systems of Thought," in *Africa*, ed. P. O'Meara and P. Martin (Bloomington: Indiana University Press, 1986), 199–212.

142. I use the terms *negative distance* and *positive distance* to capture the different attitudes or responses of diasporic Africans to continental Africa. The neutral factor in the diasporic African experience is "distance" (from continental Africa). What is interesting and important to note are the positive and negative ways in which Blacks in the Caribbean and the Americas understand and interpret their "distance" from continental Africa. See 186 where I conclude that African-Caribbean religious traditions are examples of positive distance from continental Africa.

143. Stephen Glazier, *Marchin' the Pilgrims Home: Leadership and Decision-Making in an Afro-Caribbean Faith* (Westport, CT: Greenwood, 1984), 122.

144. Ibid.

145. Since the late 1980s, the tradition formerly known as Shango in Trinidad has been renamed "Orisha" by devotees, taking the name that signifies the collective Yoruba divinities. Like Glazier, after five years of research in the island (1998–2003), I have encountered deeply entrenched anti-African and Afrophobic attitudes among the wider Christian Trinidadian population with regard to the Orisha tradition.

146. Glazier, *Marchin' the Pilgrims Home*, 133.

147. W. E. B. Du Bois, *Souls of Black Folk* (New York: Bantam, 1989), 3.

148. Eboussi Boulaga, *Christianity without Fetishes*, 205. Cited by Josiah Young, *A Pan-African Theology*, 117.

149. This particular aphorism is indigenous to black Jamaicans and in English translates as "If you want something good your nose has to run." In pursuing any desired end, one must sacrifice something to achieve that end. In the case of Jamaican farmers expecting a good harvest, they have to work not only in the sun but also in the rain, which often brings on the discomforts of the common cold.

CHAPTER FIVE

1. George Mulrain, introduction to Sankeralli, ed., *At the Crossroads*, 2.

2. James Cone, "The Vocation of a Theologian," *Union News* (Winter 1991): 3.

3. Cynric Williams, *Tour through the Island of Jamaica* (London: Printed for Hunt and Clarke by C. H. Reynell, 1826), 37. Cited by Patterson, *Sociology of Slavery*, 210.

4. Ezekiel 14:22. From *The New Revised Standard Version of the Holy Bible*.

5. See Simpson, *Black Religions in the New World*, 16–17; Barrett, *Soul Force*, 95–98; Kerr, *Personality and Conflict in Jamaica*, 118–136, esp. 135–136. See also Chevannes' discussion of the interpretive approaches used by prominent scholars to explain the presence of African-derived religions in the Caribbean and the Americas, "Some Notes on African Religious Survivals in the Caribbean," *Caribbean Journal of Religious Studies* 5, no. 2 (September 1993): 20. The standard argument is that African Jamaicans form or join these institutions because of their low economic and marginal social status in the society. This interpretation, however, is unsatisfying and not altogether true. As I have shown above, Africans in Jamaica have always practiced African religions in some form. African-derived religions did not emerge on the scene be-

cause Africans were poor and enslaved; they emerged because Africans continued to be religious according to the cultural norms and spiritual values of religious traditions they inherited from Africa. Both during and after slavery, practitioners of African religion were denied access to opportunities for economic and social advancement.

6. Noel Erskine, *Decolonizing Theology* (Maryknoll, NY: Orbis, 1981), 106.

7. Ibid.

8. I am not convinced that there is anything more "strange" and "primitive" about the Revival Zion belief that God's help, protection, and love are experienced through spirit possession than the Christian belief that Jesus' death on the cross was an act of love redeeming those who confess him as Savior.

9 Christians cannot claim to *love* their neighbors if they do not know anything *true* about them.

10. Kumina devotees show a lot of respect to those in the community who "kept and keep up the culture."

11. Chung, *Struggle to Be the Sun Again*, 111.

12. The Ghanaian biblical scholar Kwesi Dickson has examined the issue of Christian exclusivism and the biblical controversies giving rise to both judgmental and tolerant trajectories in the Christian church's behavior toward non-Christians. See *Uncompleted Mission: Christianity and Exclusivism* (Maryknoll, NY: Orbis, 1991), esp. 46–48, 50–53, 56, 68, 71, for his discussion of these motifs in Pauline theology.

13. Luke 22: 14–15.

14. Matthew 26:18.

15. Michel Foucault's term. See Michael Foucault, *Power/Knowlege*, edited by Colin Gordon (New York: Pantheon, 1980), 78–92.

16. Jeffery Hopper, *Understanding Modern Theology I: Cultural Revolutions and New Worlds* (Philadelphia: Fortress, 1987), 5–30.

17. Cone, *A Black Theology of Liberation*, xiii–xxii.

18. Theo Witvliet, *A Place in the Sun: An Introduction to Liberation Theology in the Third World* (Maryknoll, NY: Orbis, 1985), 24–42.

19. See the works of Jean Marc Ela, Englebert Mveng, and Eboussi Boulaga.

20. It was translated into English in 1973. Although Cone and Gutiérrez pioneered the revolutionary turn toward sociohistorical context as a significant source for theological constructions, other significant contributors to the development of Black theology include J. Deotis Roberts, Gayraud Wilmore, Cecil Cone, and the late Major Jones. Other major contributors to the development of Latin American liberation theology include Jon Sobrino, Pablo Richard, Juan Luis Segundo, Leonardo Boff, and José Míguez Bonino. There are four important texts which document the historical development of Black and Latin American liberation theologies: Gayraud Wilmore and James Cone, eds., *Black Theology: A Documentary History: 1966–1979* (Maryknoll, NY: Orbis, 1979); Alfred T. Hennelly, ed., *Liberation Theology: A Documentary History* (Maryknoll, NY: Orbis, 1995), a compilation of major writings in the history of Latin American liberation theology (1970–1988); and Gayraud Wilmore and James Cone, eds., *Black Theology: A Documentary History* (Maryknoll, NY: Orbis, 1993). Both volumes of this corpus offer a thorough presentation of the evolution of Black theology from the mid-1960s to the rise of womanist theology in the late 1980s. Volume 1 is an abridged edition of the 1979 edition, which eliminates some important articles from the 1979 edition.

21. These are in sequence: Virginia Fabella and Sergio Torres, eds., *The Emergent Gospel: Theology from the Underside of History* (Maryknoll, NY: Orbis 1978); Kofi Appiah-Kubi and Sergio Torres; eds., *African Theology en Route* (Maryknoll, NY: Orbis, 1979);

Virginia Fabella, ed., *Asia's Struggle for Full Humanity* (Maryknoll, NY: Orbis, 1980); John Eagleson and Sergio Torres, eds., *The Challenge of Basic Christian Communities* (Maryknoll, NY: Orbis, 1981); Virginia Fabella and Sergio Torres, eds., *Irruption of the Third World: Challenge to Theology* (Maryknoll, NY: Orbis, 1983); Virginia Fabella and Mercy Oduyoye, eds., *With Passion and Compassion: Third World Women Doing Theology* (Maryknoll, NY: Orbis, 1986); and K. C. Abraham and Bernadette Mbuy-Beya, eds., *Spirituality of the Third World* (Maryknoll, NY: Orbis, 1994).

22. Virginia Fabella and Sergio Torres, eds., *The Emergent Gospel.*

23. Virginia Fabella and Sergio Torres, eds., *Doing Theology in a Divided World* (Maryknoll, NY: Orbis, 1985), and *Irruption of the Third World.*

24. On the issue of theological education for women, see Mercy Oduyoye and Roina Fa'atauva'a', "The Struggle about Women's Theological Education," in *Feminist Theology from the Third World: A Reader*, ed. Ursula King (Maryknoll, NY: Orbis, 1994), 170–175.

25. See Mercy Oduyoye, *Who Will Roll the Stone Away? The Ecumenical Decade of the Churches in Solidarity with Women* (Geneva: WCC Publications, 1990).

26. Virginia Fabella, "Third World Women Doing Theology: An Introduction to the Women's Document," *Voices from the Third World* 11, no. 1 (June 1988): 172–174.

27. See Fabella and Oduyoye, eds., *With Passion and Compassion*, x.

28. "Final Document: Intercontinental Women's Conference," in Fabella and Oduyoye, eds., *With Passion and Compassion*, 184–190.

29. See the introduction of this volume, where I employ these terms derived from Michel Foucault's theoretical works.

30. See Wilmore, *Black Religion and Black Radicalism*, 220–241.

31. Young, *A Pan-African Theology*, 107.

32. Ibid., 116.

33. Ibid., 107. See also Long, *Significations*, 7.

34. Ibid., 106.

35. Ibid., 11.

36. Ibid.

37. See, for example, the section on womanist theology in Wilmore and Cone, eds., *Black Theology: A Documentary History, Volume 2: 1980–1992*, 257–351, featuring articles about sources and categories by Jacquelyn Grant, Delores Williams, Kelly Brown Douglas, Katie Cannon, Toinette Eugene, Cheryl Townsend Gilkes, Diana Hayes, Cheryl Sanders, and Renee Hill.

38. Cheryl Sanders, ed., *Living the Intersection: Womanism and Afrocentrism in Theology* (Minneapolis, MN: Fortress 1995).

39. Delores Williams, "Afrocentrism and Male-Female Relations in Church and Society," in Sanders, ed., *Living the Intersection*, 50.

40. Cheryl Sanders, "Afrocentric and Womanist Approaches to Theological Education," in Sanders, ed., *Living the Intersection*, 166–175.

41. See Jacquelyn Grant, "Womanist Theology: Black Women's Experience as a Source for Doing Theology, with Special Reference to Christology," in Wilmore and Cone, eds., *Black Theology: A Documentary History, Volume 2: 1980–1992*, 273–289.

42. See Alice Walker, *In Search of Our Mothers' Gardens: Womanist Prose* (San Diego, CA: Harcourt Brace Jovanovich, 1983), xi–xii.

43. William Jones, *Is God a White Racist? A Preamble to Black Theology* (New York: Anchor, 1973).

44. Anthony Pinn, *Why Lord? Suffering and Evil in Black Theology* (New York: Continuum, 1995), 136.

45. Ibid.

46. Ibid.

47. Pinn distinguishes between weak and strong humanism and prefers the latter as most oppositional to Christian theism. Ibid., 1–19, 141–144.

48. Ibid., 142.

49. Ibid., 142–143.

50. Zahan, *The Religion, Spirituality and Thought of Traditional Africa*, 5. Note that the bracketed substitutions are replacing male-gendered language in Zahan's commentary. For example, I replace "man" with "human" and other such terminology to reflect gender inclusiveness.

51. Ibid., 6.

52. "God" here would not represent the African Supreme Deity but the Christian Creator Deity.

53. Pinn, *Why Lord?* 120–121. Blues verses cited by Pinn from Paul Oliver, *Blues Fell This Morning: The Meaning of the Blues* (New York: Cambridge University Press, 1990), 128.

54. Pinn, *Why Lord?* 121.

55. Ibid., 137.

56. See Ana María Bidegain, "Women and the Theology of Liberation," in *Through Her Eyes: Women's Theology from Latin America*, ed. Elsa Tamez (Maryknoll, NY: Orbis, 1989), 31; Pablo Richard, "Liberation Theology in Latin America in Dialogue with Theologians from Africa, Asia and the Minorities in the United States," *Voices from the Third World* 18, no. 2 (December 1995): 39–40; Diego Irarranzaval, "How Is Theology Done in Latin America," *Voices from the Third World* 18, no. 1 (June 1995): 69–70; Elsa Tamez, "Cultural Violence against Women in Latin America," *Voices from the Third World* 18, no. 2 (December 1995): 187–188. The list of sources could continue. However, the point is that, from reading the works of Latin American theologians, one is not informed about the provenience of racism and anti-Africanness in Latin America. I would argue that racism is so pernicious and insidious in Latin America that a systematic theological reflection on White supremacy and the Black religious experience in Latin America, similar to the one articulated by James Cone in the United States, is long overdue.

57. Lloyd Stennette, Mauro Batista, and Barry Chevannes, "The Situation of the Black Race in Latin America and the Caribbean," in Eagleson and Torres, eds., *The Challenge of Basic Christian Communities* 47. Also see Jeanne Beecher, "No Apartheid to Confront: A Conversation with Caetana Maria Damasceno," *Women in a Changing World* (December 1988): 18–19, for a similar Brazilian feminist perspective on racism and poverty.

58. Boff's 1984 article is included in a large volume on Latin American liberation theology from the 1950s to the 1980s. See Leonardo Boff, "Defense of His Book, *Church and Power*," in *Liberation Theology: A Documentary History*, ed. Alfred Hennelly (Maryknoll, NY: Orbis, 1995), 433.

59. Gustavo Gutiérrez, *A Theology of Liberation* (Maryknoll, NY: Orbis, 1988), xxii. First English translation in 1973.

60. My translation. See Quince Duncan et al., *Cultura Negra y Teología* (San Jose, Costa Rica: Editorial Departamento Ecuménico de Investigaciones, 1986).

61. Initially, African theology was the venue for the most conspicuous debate between these two camps. However, a new trajectory has emerged where theologians have begun to integrate these two approaches. See Simon Maimela, ed., *Culture, Religion, and Liberation: Proceedings of the EATWOT Pan-African Theological Conference,*

Harare, Zimbabwe, January 6–11, 1991 (Pretoria, South Africa: Penrose Book Printers, 1994); Emmanuel Martey, *African Theology: Inculturation and Liberation* (Maryknoll, NY: Orbis 1993).

62. "Response from Latin America," in Abraham and Muby-Beya, eds., *Spirituality of the Third World*, 135.

63. Stennette, Batista, and Chevannes, "The Situation of the Black Race in Latin America and the Caribbean," 52.

64. The Million Man March (October 16, 1995) and its generated literature attest to the persistent factor of African-derived religions in African North American religiosity. See Kim Martin Sadler, ed., *Atonement: The Million Man March* (Cleveland, OH: Pilgrim, 1996). The unpublished summary documents pertaining to the social and spiritual purpose of the march include tremendous insights from classical African religions via Maulana Karenga's cultural nationalist theory, *Kawaida*.

65. See Eboussi Boulaga's usage of this term in the citation in chapter 4, 186.

66. Barry Chevannes, "Our Caribbean Reality," in *Caribbean Theology: Preparing for the Challenges Ahead*, ed. Howard Gregory (Kingston, Jamaica: Canoe, 1995), 66.

67. Chevannes, "Some Notes on African Religious Survivals in the Caribbean," 19.

68. He presents an example of a man whom many believed died as a result of "Obeah." Although the medical doctors and presiding minister at the funeral confirmed that he died of leukemia, the community held fast to the belief that he died from "Obeah."

69. Chevannes, "Some Notes on African Religious Survivals in the Caribbean," 19.

70. Hebrews 11: 1. From *The New Revised Standard Version of the Holy Bible*.

71. Long, *Significations*.

72. Hebrews 11: 1–2. From *The New Revised Standard Version of the Holy Bible*.

73. Ashley Smith, "The Religious Significance of Black Power," in *Troubling the Waters*, ed. Idris Hamid (San Fernando, Trinidad: Rahaman, 1973), 44.

74. Erskine, *Decolonizing Theology*, 12.

75. Ibid.

76. Erskine describes both Revival and Rastafari as "cults."

77. Smith, *Conjuring Culture*, 115.

78. Ibid.

79. Boulaga, *Christianity without Fetishes*, 77. Cited by Young, *A Pan-African Theology*, 100.

80. Williams, *Caribbean Theology*, 2.

81. Ibid., 194–197.

82. Ibid., 203.

83. Ibid., 204.

84. Ibid., 205.

85. Ibid.

86. Since the publication of his book, Williams has actually expanded his discussion of the encounter between Christianity and African-derived religions. He authored "Gospel and Cultures," pamphlet 10 of a series sponsored by the World Council of Churches. Williams raises even more forthrightly the moral problems that attended and are still at work in the oppression and belittlement of African religion and culture by the missionary churches. Williams forwards insightful commentary on the tension between enculturation and acculturation in the Caribbean situation of cultural encounter via slavery and colonialism. See Lewin Williams, *The Caribbean: Encultura-*

tion, Acculturation and the Role of the Churches (Geneva, Switzerland: WCC Publications, 1996).

87. Chevannes, "Our Caribbean Reality," 65.

88. See David Asomaning, "Jung and the Outside World," *Journal of Religion and Health* 34 (Spring 1995): 78–79. Here Asomaning outlines what he calls a "hermeneutics of complexification."

89. James Houk, *Spirits, Blood, and Drums: The Orisha Religion in Trinidad* (Philadelphia: Temple University Press, 1995), 180. Houk concurs with Melville Herskovits, who maintained that reinterpretation is a necessary outcome of syncretism, but Houk seems to exaggerate or reconceive Herskovits's understanding of reinterpretation. Herskovits was the earliest scholar to develop a theory of syncretism in the social sciences.

90. Ibid., 55.

91. Alleyne, *Roots of Jamaican Culture*, 23.

92. Métraux, *Voodoo in Haiti*, 326.

93. My understanding of aesthetics is related to religious feeling and aesthetic performances as opposed to applied or technical aesthetics. This aesthetic analysis of Spiritual Baptist religion is inspired by Zora Neale Hurston's aesthetic theorizing about the sanctified church in North America during the early twentieth cenutury. Although previously cited, her comments are again relevant: "[T]he Sanctified Church is a protest against the high-brow tendency in the Negro Protestant congregations as the Negroes gain more education and wealth. It is understandable that they take on the religious attitudes of the white man which are as a rule so staid and restrained that it seems unbearably dull to the more primitive Negro who associates the rhythm of sound and motion with religion. In fact, the Negro has not been christianized as extensively as is generally believed. The great masses are still standing before their pagan altars and calling old gods by a new name." See Hurston, *The Sanctified Church*, 103.

94. Aiyejina and Gibbons, "Orisa (Orisha) Tradition in Trinidad," 42.

95. Alleyne, *Roots of Jamaican Culture*, 18.

96. I surmise that a theory of masquerading will be applicable in other Caribbean and American contexts as well but I will have to undertake a study of other contexts before making any conclusive statements.

97. Carol G. Braham et al., *The Random House Webster's College Dictionary* (New York: Random House, 1991), 834.

98. See Rosalind Hackett, "Revitalization in African Traditional Religion," in *African Traditional Religions in Contemporary Society*, ed. Jacob Olupona (St. Paul, MN: Paragon House, 1991).

99. Masqueraders are usually male. In many African cultures, females are excluded from masquerade societies and from even viewing them. The female-initiating Poro Society of the Mende in Sierra Leone is one exception.

100. Frank Willett, *African Art: An Introduction* (New York: Thames and Hudson, 1993), 180.

101. Benjamin Ray, *African Religions: Symbol, Ritual and Community*. Englewood Cliffs, NJ: Prentice Hall, 1976), 142–143.

102. Member of the *Egun* (Ancestor) society.

103. Ray, *African Religions*, 144.

104. Augustine Onyeneke, *The Dead among the Living: Masquerades in Igbo Society* (Nimo, Nigeria: Holy Ghost Congregation and Asele Institute, 1987).

105. Translation: If we did the rituals the spirit instructed us to do, people would

not call us Christian. Modda B. (pseudonym), cited from taped interview with Claudette Anderson, Golden Spring, St. Andrew, Jamaica, July 14, 2003. Claudette Anderson is a Jamaican doctoral student in the Institute of Liberal Arts at Emory University. She has done significant research on Jamaican folk medicine. Caribbean studies scholars have also examined Caribbean masking traditions and the concept of masking in their elaborations of cultural and literary theories. See especially, Maureen Warner-Lewis, *Kamau Brathwaite's Masks: Essays and Annotations* (Kingston: Institute of Caribbean Studies, 1992); George Lamming, *Season of Adventure* (London: Allison and Busby, 1979); George Lamming, *Enterprise of the Indies* (Port of Spain, Trinidad: The Trinidad and Tobago Institute of the West Indies, 1999); Nana Wilson-Tagoe, *Historical Thought and the Literary Representation in West Indian Literature* (Gainesville, FL: University Press of Florida, 1998), 182–222; Gerard Aching, *Masking and Power: Carnival and Popular Culture in the Caribberan* (Minneapolis: University of Minnesota Press, 2002).

106. Despite the previous quotation, it is worth reiterating that some Revival Zionists of today might not even be aware of how they masquerade as Christian and might be prone to deny it if confronted with this theory. Just as the ritual dissociation, which reportedly occurs during a masquerading ceremony, leaves the masquerader unaware of the ancestral possession of his body and personality, so also are Revival Zionists often unconscious of their masquerading traditions, which allow for the preservation and authoritative influence of African-derived traditions in their religion. Theophus Smith's previously cited commentary with regard to Black North American conjurational strategies is pertinent to this discussion. He writes: "Such legitimation strategies are rarely explicit and conscious, of course, and may even be forgotten or repressed if ever rendered transparent." See citation information in n. 77 of this chapter.

107. Recall the previous discussion of Boulaga's scholarship on 213.

108. Aiyejina and Gibbons, "Orisa (Orisha) Tradition in Trinidad," 41–42.

109. Zahan, *The Religion, Spirituality and Thought of Traditional Africa*, 47–48.

110. I choose to capitalize Word to stress the theological significance of ancestral wisdom to which Africans faithfully adhere. As Jesus is the Word of God for some Christians, and the Bible is the Word for other Christians, the Word (collective wisdom) of the Ancestors is the sine qua non of African religious life and practice.

111. Plantation chattel slavery was a death-dealing institution structured upon anti-African values, which forced enslaved Africans to confront the multidimensional experience of corporeal, cultural, spiritual, and psychological death as constructed and therefore tragic and premature rather than as a natural experience in the human life cycle.

112. Recall Eboussi Boulaga's insights on aesthetics and African religiosity as noted at the end of chapter 4.

113. See chapter 3, 200ff., where I discuss these practices more extensively.

114. Zahan, *Religion, Spirituality, and Thought of Traditional Africa*, 45.

115. See Barry Chevannes' discussion of "dual membership" in *Rastafari and Other African-Caribbean Worldviews*, 2–3.

116. Zahan, *Religion, Spirituality, and Thought of Traditional Africa*, 45.

117. Williams, *The Caribbean: Enculturation, Acculturation and the Role of the Churches*, 8.

118. Ibid., 7–8.

119. Carlos Cardoza, personal communication, Decatur, Georgia, November 14, 2001. Also see Carlos Cardoza, *Mission: An Essential Guide* (Nashville, TN: Abingdon, 2002).

120. This would not preclude the incorporation of Christology in African-centered, liberation-focused Caribbean theological reflection, especially given the significance of Christology in Rastafari. This is not to give validity, however, to the Christian Christ—Rastas would not claim him—but to affirm their Rasta Christ.

121. See the introduction to this volume, 9–10, and n. 19, where I define local awareness as an imperative in liberation theologies.

122. My understanding of the theologian's pretext is especially influenced by Carlos Mesters's discussion of the distinctions among pretext, context, and text in the hermeneutic circle of liberation theology. The *pretext* encompasses a person's or community's lived reality while the *text* is the actual Bible, and the *context* is the experience of living out one's faith in communion with others. See his *Defenseless Flower: A New Reading of the Bible* (Maryknoll, NY: Orbis, 1989).

123. Laurenti Magesa, *African Religion: The Moral Traditions of Abundant Life* (Maryknoll, NY: Orbis, 1997), 12.

124. Although, in this instance, I do not insert the qualifier "Eurocentric" before "Christianity," this was surely the only Christianity known to enslaved Africans in Jamaica and their descendants over any extensive period of time.

125. This is not to say that I do not stand by my interpretation of Revival Zion as a "Christian Myalist" African-derived religion. It is to say that the Revival Zion and Rastafari methods of appropriation and reinterpretation of Christian sources can be adopted by Blacks who are members of orthodox Christian denominations.

126. Williams, *The Caribbean: Enculturation, Acculturation and the Role of the Churches*, 7–8.

127. Nathaniel Samuel Murrell and Burchell K. Taylor, "Rastafari's Messianic Ideology and Caribbean Theology of Liberation," in Murrell, Spencer, and McFarlane, eds., *Chanting Down Babylon*, 395.

128. See n. 115 above.

129. Renee L. Hill, personal communication, New York, NY, November 10, 1998.

130. Christians usually interpret non-Christian spiritual power as demonic and evil.

131. Charles Long's essay "Primitive/Civilized: The Locus of a Problem" in his book *Significations*, 79–96, deconstructs this typology in the history of religions specifically and in Western intellectual traditions generally.

132. John Cobb, "Being a Transformationist in a Pluralistic World," *Christian Century* (August 1994): 750.

133. Theophus Smith offers an insightful extended analysis of Black religious practices in North America in the light of their African-derived pharmacological meanings. See *Conjuring Culture: Biblical Formations of Black America*, 5–6, 18, 90–100, 143–145, 216–226.

134. This is a common practice in Haiti and Trinidad. Also see Murphy, *Working the Spirit*, for descriptions of food preparation in African-Caribbean religious rituals.

135. Chevannes, *Rastafari: Roots and Ideology*, 34–35. Chevannes convincingly argues that the persistence of the taboo against salt in the Kumina, Revival Zion, and Rastafari religions is a symbol of African resistance to European culture.

136. I was personally escorted through some of these sacred places by Kumina practitioners during my research in St. Thomas in 1996.

137. Kenneth Bilby and Elliot Leib, "Kumina, the Howellite Church and the Emergence of Rastafarian Traditional Music in Jamaica," *Jamaica Journal* 19, no. 3 (1986): 22–28.

138. Rex Nettleford's comments on Rastafari support the point here made. According to Nettleford, "Rastafari can claim to be the only major indigenous Caribbean-creole phenomenon of its kind (apart from Garveyism). All other such 'total systems' that have served Jamaica and the wider Caribbean in its resistance-driven process of 'becoming' have been imported, whether they be Christianity, political nationalism, militant trade unionism, socialism . . . or latter-day market-forces liberalism. To argue from this that Rastafari cannot solve the wide-ranging problems of Jamaica and is therefore useless is to ignore the fact that none of the above importations, all of 'pedigreed stature,' has been able to do so either. The case for tolerant, open, and frank discourse on a belief system such as Rastafari here recommends itself." See his article "Discourse on Rastafarian Reality" in Murrell, Spencer, and McFarlane, eds., *Chanting Down Babylon*, 321.

139. Aldolpho Ham, "A Dialogue between the Theology of Liberation and the Caribbean Black Theology," in *Looking at the Theology of Liberation Together: An Ecumenical Reflection within the Caribbean: March 6–9, 1991*, ed. Burchell Taylor (Kingston: Jamaica Council of Churches, 1991), 43.

140. Sankeralli, ed., *At the Crossroads*.

141. JoAnne Terrell provides the most thorough and compelling examination of this subject in Black/womanist theological discourse. Her theological analysis argues for the sacramental value of sacrificed human life, not just the life of Jesus but the lives of Black people as well. See *Power in the Blood*.

142. Young borrows the term from Amilcar Cabral. See Africa Information Service, ed., *Return to the Source: Selected Speeches of Amilcar Cabral* (New York: Monthly Review, 1973), 49. Also see Young's examination of re-Africanization in *A Pan-African Theology*, 37, 139, 198.

143. See Jacob Olupona, "Major Issues in the Study of African Traditional Religion," in *African Traditional Religions in Contemporary Society*, ed. Jacob Olupona (St. Paul, MN: Paragon House, 1991), 25–35.

144. Chinweizu, *The West and the Rest of Us: White Predators, Black Slavers and the African Elite* (Lagos, Nigeria: Pero, 1987), xii.

145. These concepts are elaborated in Vernon Robbins's forthcoming book. See *The Invention of Christian Discourse* (Brussels, Belgium: DEO, forthcoming).

146. *Textual* refers to much more than literal scripts. It is used in its most comprehensive hermeneutical sense to include cultural materials, persons, experiences, institutions, and so on.

Bibliography

Abimbola, Kola. "Yoruba Diaspora." In *Encyclopedia of Diasporas: Immigrant and Refugee Cultures Around the World*, ed. Melvin Ember, Carol R. Ember, and Ian Skoggard. New York: Kluwer Academic/Plenum, forthcoming 2005.

Abimbola, Wande. *Ifa Will Mend Our Broken World*. Roxbury, MA: Aim, 1997.

Abraham, K. C., ed. *Third World Theologies: Commonalities and Divergences*. New York: Orbis, 1990.

Abraham, K. C., and Bernadette Mbuy-Beya, eds. *Spirituality of the Third World*. Maryknoll, NY: Orbis, 1994.

Aching, Gerard. *Masking and Power: Carnival and Popular Culture in the Caribbean*. Minneapolis: University of Minnesota Press, 2002.

Adams, Rachel. *Sideshow U.S.A.: Freaks and the American Cultural Imagination*. Chicago: University of Chicago Press, 2001.

Africa Information Service, ed. *Return to the Source: Selected Speeches of Amilcar Cabral*. New York: Monthly Review, 1973.

Aiyejina, Funso, and Rawle Gibbons, "Orisa (Orisha) Tradition in Trinidad." *Caribbean Quarterly* 45, no. 4 (December 1999): 35–50.

Alleyne, Mervyn. *Roots of Jamaican Culture*. London: Pluto, 1988.

Anzaldúa, Gloria. *Borderlands/La Frontera*. San Francisco: Spinsters/Aunt Lute, 1987.

Appiah, Anthony. *In My Father's House: Africa in the Philosophy of Culture*. Oxford: Oxford University Press, 1992.

Appiah-Kubi, Kofi, and Sergio Torres, eds. *African Theology en Route*. Maryknoll, NY: Orbis, 1979.

Aptheker, Herbert. *Negro Slave Revolts in the United States: 1526–1860*. New York: International, 1939.

Arens, W., and Ivan Karp. *Creativity of Power: Cosmology and Action in African Societies*. Washington, DC: Smithsonian Institution Press, 1989.

Aristide, Jean-Bertrand. *An Autobiography*. Trans. Linda M. Maloney. Maryknoll, NY: Orbis, 1993.

Armstrong, Douglas V. "Afro-Jamaican Plantation Life: An Archaeological Study of Drax Hall." *Jamaica Journal* 24, no. 1 (June 1991): 3–8.

Asomaning, David. "Jung and the Outside World." *Journal of Religion and Health* 34 (Spring 1995): 78–79.

Augustus, Earl Julian, et al., eds. *Issues in Caribbean Theology.* Port of Spain, Trinidad: Antilles Pastoral Institute, 1972.

Awolalu, J. Omosade. "Sin and Its Removal in African Traditional Religion." *Journal of the American Academy of Religion* 44, no.2 (1976): 275–287.

Banbury, R. Thomas. *Jamaica Superstitions; or, The Obeah Book: A Complete Treatise of the Absurdities Believed in by the People of the Island by the Rector (Native) of St. Peter's Church, Hope Bay, Portland.* Kingston, Jamaica: de Souza, 1895.

Barclay, Alexander. *A Practical View of the Present State of Slavery in the West Indies.* London: Smith, Elder, 1826.

Barrett, Leonard. "The Portrait of a Jamaican Healer: African Medical Lore in the Caribbean." *Caribbean Quarterly* 19, no. 3 (September 1973): 6–19.

————. *The Ras Tafari Movement in Kingston, Jamaica.* Rió Pedras, Puerto Rico: Institute of Caribbean Studies, University of Puerto Rico, 1969.

————. *Soul Force: African Heritage in Afro-American Religion.* London: Heinemann, 1976.

————. *The Sun and the Drum: African Roots in Jamaican Folk Tradition.* London: Heinemann, 1976.

Barth, Karl. "The Revelation of God as the Abolition of Religion." In *Church Dogmatics,* vol. 1, pt. 2, ed. G. W. Bromiley and T. F. Torrance, 280–361. Edinburgh: Clark, 1936–1940.

Bascom, William R. "The Yoruba in Cuba." *Nigeria* 37 (1951): 14–20.

Bastide, Roger. *African Civilisations in the New World.* New York: Harper and Row, 1971.

————. *The African Religions of Brazil: Toward a Sociology of the Interpenetration of Civilizations.* Baltimore, MD: Johns Hopkins University Press, 1983.

————. *Les Religions Africaines au Brasil.* Paris: Presses Universitaires de France, 1960.

Bastien, Rémy. *Religion and Politics in Haiti.* Washington, DC: Institute for Cross-Cultural Research, 1966.

Baxter, Ivy. *The Arts of an Island: The Development of Culture and of the Folk and Creative Arts in Jamaica 1494–1962.* Metuchen, NJ: Scarecrow, 1970.

Beckwith, Martha. *Black Roadways.* Chapel Hill: University of North Carolina Press, 1929.

————. *Christmas Mummings in Jamaica.* New York: American Folk-Lore Society, 1923.

Bee, Robert. *Patterns and Processes: An Introduction to Anthropological Strategies for the Study of Sociocultural Change.* New York: Macmillan, 1974.

Beecher, Jeanne. "No Apartheid to Confront: A Conversation with Caetana Maria Damasceno." *Women in a Changing World* (December 1988): 18–19.

Bell, Hesketh. *Obeah: Witchcraft in the West Indies.* London: Low, Marston, Searle and Rivington, 1889.

Bidegain, Ana María. "Women and the Theology of Liberation." In *Through Her Eyes: Women's Theology from Latin America,* ed. Elsa Tamez, 15–36. Maryknoll, NY: Orbis, 1989.

Bilby, Kenneth. "Gumbay, Myal, and the Great House: New Evidence of the Religious Background of Jonkonnu in Jamaica." *ACIJ Research Review: 25th Anniversary Edition* (1999/4): 47–70.

_____. "The Koromanti Dance of the Windward Maroons of Jamaica." *Nieuwe West Indische Gids* 55, nos. 1–2 (August 1981): 52–101.

Bilby, Kenneth, and Fu-Kiau Bunseki. "Kumina: A Kongo-based Tradition in the New World." Brussels: Les Cahiers du Cedaf, vol. 8 (1983): 1–114.

Bilby, Kenneth, and Elliot Leib. "Kumina, the Howellite Church and the Emergence of Rastafarian Traditional Music in Jamaica." *Jamaica Journal* 19, no. 3 (1986): 22–28.

Blassingame, John, ed. *Slave Testimony: Two Centuries of Letters, Speeches, Interviews, and Autobiographies.* Baton Rouge: Louisiana State University Press, 1977.

Blome, Richard. *A Description of the Island of Jamaica.* London: Milbourn, 1672, reprinted by J. B. for Newman, 1678.

Blyth, George. *Reminiscences of Missionary Life, with Suggestions to Churches and Missionaries.* Edinburgh: Oliphant, 1851.

Bockie, Simon. *Death and the Invisible Powers: The World of Kongo Belief.* Bloomington: Indiana University Press, 1993.

Bodin, Jean. *Method for Easy Comprehension of History.* Trans. Beatrice Reynolds. New York: Columbia University Press, 1945.

Boff, Leonardo. "Defense of His Book, *Church and Power.*" In *Liberation Theology: A Documentary History,* ed. Alfred Hennelly, 431–434. Maryknoll, NY: Orbis, 1995.

Boles, John. *The Great Revival: The Origins of the Southern Evangelical Mind, 1787–1805.* Lexington: University Press of Kentucky, 1972.

Botkin, B. A. *Lay My Burden Down: A Folk History of Slavery.* Chicago: University of Chicago Press, 1968.

Boulaga, F. Eboussi. *Christianity without Fetishes: An African Critique and Recapture of Christianity.* Maryknoll, NY: Orbis, 1984.

Braham, Carol G., et al. *The Random House Webster's College Dictionary.* New York: Random House, 1991.

Brandon, George. *Santería from Africa to the New World: The Dead Sell Memories.* Bloomington: Indiana University Press, 1993.

Brathwaite, Edward. *Folk Culture of the Slaves in Jamaica.* London: New Beacon, 1981.
_____. "Kumina: The Spirit of African Survival in Jamaica." *Jamaica Journal* 42 (1978): 44–63.

Bremer, Fredrika. *The Homes of the New World: Impressions of America.* Vol. 2. New York: Harper, 1853.

Brown, Karen. *Mama Lola: A Vodou Priestess in Brooklyn.* Berkeley: University of California Press, 1991.

Bryan, Patrick. "Spanish Jamaica." *Caribbean Quarterly* 38, nos. 2–3 (1992): 21–31.

Buchner, J. H. *The Moravians in Jamaica.* London: Longman, 1854.

Cabrera, Lydia. *El Monte.* Miami, FL: Rema, 1971.

Caldecott, Alfred. *The Church in the West Indies.* London: Frank Cass, 1898.

Campbell, Horace. *Rasta and Resistance: From Marcus Garvey to Walter Rodney.* Trenton, NJ: Africa World, 1987.

Cannon, Katie, et al. *Inheriting Our Mothers' Gardens: Feminist Theology in Third World Perspective.* Philadelphia: Westminster, 1988.

Cardoza, Carlos. *Mission: An Essential Guide.* Nashville, TN: Abingdon, 2002.

Carr, Andrew T. "A Rada Community in Trinidad." *Caribbean Quarterly* 3 (Spring 1953): 35–54.

Cassidy, F. *Jamaica Talk.* London: Macmillan, 1960.

Cassidy, Frederic, and R. B. Le Page. *Dictionary of Jamaican English.* Cambridge: Cambridge University Press, 1967.

Chancery of the Order of Distinction. *The Order of Distinction.* Kingston, Jamaica: Chancery of the Order of Distinction, 1988.

Chevannes, Barry. "Our Caribbean Reality." In *Caribbean Theology: Preparing for the Challenges Ahead,* ed. Howard Gregory, 65–71. Kingston, Jamaica: Canoe, 1995.

———. *Rastafari and Other African-Caribbean Worldviews.* New Brunswick, NJ: Rutgers University Press, 1994.

———. *Rastafari: Roots and Ideology.* Syracuse, NY: Syracuse University Press, 1994.

———. "The Repairer of the Breach: Reverend Claudius Henry and Jamaican Society." In *Ethnicity in the Americas,* ed. Frances Henry, 263–289. The Hague: Mouton, 1976.

———. "Some Notes on African Religious Survivals in the Caribbean." *Caribbean Journal of Religious Studies* 5, no. 2 (September 1993): 18–28.

Chinula, Donald M. "Jamaican Exocentrism: Its Implications for a Pan-African Theology of National Redemption." *Caribbean Journal of Religious Studies* 6, no. 1 (April 1985): 46–59.

Chinweizu. *The West and the Rest of Us: White Predators, Black Slavers and the African Elite.* Lagos, Nigeria: Pero, 1987.

Chung, Hyun Kyung. *Struggle to Be the Sun Again: Toward an Asian Feminist Theology.* Maryknoll, NY: Orbis, 1992.

Clarke, John. *Memorials of Baptist Missionaries in Jamaica.* London: Yates and Alexander, 1869.

Cobb, John. "Being a Transformationist in a Pluralistic World," *Christian Century* (August 1994): 750.

Coke, Thomas. *A History of the West Indies, Containing the Natural, Civil and Ecclesiastical History of Each Island.* Vol. 2. Liverpool, England: Nuttall, Fisher and Dixon, 1808–1811.

Colin, Gordon, ed. *Power/Knowledge: Selected Interviews and Other Writings, 1972–1977, by Michel Foucault.* New York: Pantheon, 1980.

Collins, Patricia Hill. *Fighting Words: Black Women and the Search for Justice.* Minneapolis: University of Minnesota Press, 1998.

Colloque international sur la notion de personne en Afrique noire. *La notion de personne en Afrique noire, Paris 11–17 octobre 1971.* París: Éditions du Centre national de la recherche scientifique, 1973.

Cone, James H. *Black Theology and Black Power.* Minneapolis: Seabury, 1969.

———. *A Black Theology of Liberation.* Maryknoll, NY: Orbis, 1990. First edition, J. B. Lippincott, 1970.

———. *For My People: Black Theology and the Black Church.* Maryknoll, NY: Orbis, 1984.

———. *God of the Oppressed.* San Francisco: Seabury, 1975.

———. "An Interpretation of the Debate among Black Theologians." In *Black Theology: A Documentary History, 1966–1979,* vol. 1, ed. Gayraud Wilmore and James Cone, 609–623. Maryknoll, NY: Orbis, 1979.

———. *Martin and Malcolm and America: A Dream or a Nightmare.* Maryknoll, NY: Orbis, 1991.

———. *The Spirituals and the Blues.* Seabury Press, 1972.

———. "The Vocation of a Theologian." *Union News* (Winter 1991): 3–4.

Conniff, Michael L., and Thomas J. Davis. *Africans in the Americas: A History of the Black Diaspora.* New York: St. Martin's, 1994.

Cooper, Thomas. *Facts Illustrative of the Condition of the Negro Slaves in Jamaica.* London: Hatchard, 1824.

Cox, Francis. *History of the Baptist Missionary Society from 1792–1842*. Vol. 2. London: Ward, 1842.

Crahan, Margaret, and Franklin Knight, eds. *Africa and the Caribbean: The Legacies of a Link*. Baltimore, MD: Johns Hopkins University Press, 1979.

Craton, Michael, and James Walvin. *A Jamaican Plantation: The History of Worthy Park, 1670–1870*. London: Allen, 1970.

Crummell, Alexander, and Wilson J. Moses, eds. *Destiny and Race: Selected Writings, 1840–1898*. Amherst: University of Massachusetts Press, 1992.

Curtin, Philip. *The Atlantic Slave Trade: A Census*. Madison: University of Wisconsin Press, 1969.

_____. *Two Jamaicas: The Role of Ideas in a Tropical Colony: 1830–1865*. Cambridge, MA: Harvard University Press, 1955.

Cuthrell-Curry, Mary. "African-derived Religion in the African-American Community in the United States." In *African Spirituality: Forms, Meanings and Expressions*, ed. Jacob Olupona, 450–466. New York: Crossroad, 2000.

Dallas, R. C. *The History of the Maroons*. Vol. 1. London: Cass, 1803.

Daly, Mary. *Beyond God the Father*. Boston: Beacon, 1970.

Dance, Daryl. *Folklore from Contemporary Jamaicans*. Knoxville: University of Tennessee Press, 1985.

Davidson, Basil. *Black Mother*. London: V. Gollancz, 1961.

Davis, J. Merle. *The Church in the New Jamaica*. New York: International Missionary Council, 1942.

de Gobineau, Arthur. *The Inequality of Races*. New York: Putnam, 1915.

De la Beche, H. T. *Notes on the Present Condition of the Negroes in Jamaica*. London: Cadell, 1825.

Delany, Martin. "Report of the Niger Valley Exploring Party." In *Search for a Place: Black Separatism and Africa, 1860*, ed. Howard Bell, 133–134. Ann Arbor: University of Michigan Press, 1969.

Depestre, Réné. "Problems of Identity for the Black Man in Caribbean Literatures." *Caribbean Quarterly* 19, no.3 (September 1973): 51–61.

Deren, Maya. *Divine Horsemen, the Living Gods of Haiti*. 1953. Reprint, Kingston, NY: McPherson, 1991.

Dickson, Kwesi. *Uncompleted Mission: Christianity and Exclusivism*. Maryknoll, NY: Orbis, 1991.

Diodorus. *Diodorus of Sicily*. Trans. C. H. Oldfather. Book 3, vol. 2. London: Heinemann, 1953.

Douglas, Kelly Brown. *The Black Christ*. Maryknoll, NY: Orbis, 1994.

_____. "Womanist Theology: What Is Its Relationship to Black Theology?" In *Black Theology: A Documentary History*. Vol. 2: *1980–1992*, ed. Gayraud S. Wilmore and James H. Cone, 290–299. Maryknoll, NY: Orbis, 1993.

Du Bois, W.E.B. *Souls of Black Folk*. New York: Bantam, 1989.

Duncan, Quince, et al. *Cultura Negra y Teologia*. San Jose, Costa Rica: Editorial Departamento Ecuménico de Investigaciones, 1986.

Dunn, Richard. *Sugar and Slaves: The Rise of the Planter Class in the English West Indies, 1624–1713*. Chapel Hill: University of North Carolina Press, 1972.

Eagleson, John, and Sergio Torres, eds. *The Challenge of Basic Christian Communities*. Maryknoll, NY: Orbis, 1981.

Earl, Riggins. *Dark Symbols, Obscure Signs: God, Self, and Community in the Slave Mind*. Maryknoll, NY: Orbis, 1993.

Edgerton, Robert. *Mau Mau: An African Crucible*. New York: Ballantine, 1989.

Edwards, Bryan. *The History, Civil and Commercial, of the British Colonies in the West Indies.* Vol. 2. New York: AMS Press, 1966, (1793).

Edwards, Emmanuel. *Black Supremacy in Righteousness of Salvation Jesus Negus Christ Emmanuel "I" Selassie "I" Jah Rastafari in Royal Majestiy Selassie "I" Jahovah Jah Rastafar "I."* Bull Bay, Jamaica: Ethiopia Africa Black International Congress, n.d.

Eliade, Mercea. *The Quest: History and Meaning in Religion.* Chicago: University of Chicago Press, 1969.

Ellis, Marc H., and Otto Maduro, eds. *The Future of Liberation Theology.* Maryknoll, NY: Orbis, 1989.

Eltis, David, and G. Ugo Nwokeji, eds. *The Trans-Atlantic Slave Trade: A Database on CD-ROM.* Cambridge, UK: Cambridge University Press, 1999.

Emerick, A. J. *Jamaican Mialism.* Woodstock, NY: n.p., 1916.

Erskine, Noel Leo. *Decolonizing Theology: A Caribbean Perspective.* Maryknoll, NY: Orbis, 1981.

Eze, Emmanuel Chukwudi, ed. *Race and the Enlightenment: A Reader.* Cambridge: Blackwell, 1997.

Fabella, Virginia, ed. *Asia's Struggle for Full Humanity.* Maryknoll, NY: Orbis, 1980.

———. "Third World Women Doing Theology: An Introduction to the Women's Document." *Voices from the Third World* 11, no. 1 (June 1998): 172–174.

Fabella, Virginia, and D. Martinez, eds. *The Oaxtepec Encounter: Third World Women Doing Theology.* Maryknoll, NY: Orbis, 1988.

Fabella, Virginia, and Mercy Oduyoye, eds. *With Passion and Compassion: Third World Women Doing Theology.* Maryknoll, NY: Orbis, 1986.

Fabella, Virginia, and Sun Ai Lee Park. *We Dare to Dream: Doing Theology as Asian Women.* Maryknoll, NY: Orbis, 1990.

Fabella, Virginia, and Sergio Torres, eds. *Doing Theology in a Divided World.* Maryknoll, NY: Orbis, 1985.

———. *The Emergent Gospel: Theology from the Underside of History.* Maryknoll, NY: Orbis, 1978.

———. *Irruption of the Third World: Challenge to Theology.* Maryknoll, NY: Orbis, 1983.

Farmer, Paul. *The Uses of Haiti.* Monroe, ME: Common Courage, 1994.

Field, M. J. *Religion and Medicine of the Ga People.* London: Oxford University Press, 1937.

Findlay, G. G., and W. W. Holdsworth. *The History of the Wesleyan Methodist Missionary Society.* Vol. 2. London: Epworth, 1921.

Fiorenza, Francis Schüssler. *Foundational Theology: Jesus and the Church.* New York: Crossroad, 1986.

Fr. Clark for Malthus, *The Present State of Jamaica.* London: 1683.

Fraser, Lionel M. *History of Trinidad, from 1781 to 1813.* Port of Spain: Government Printing Office, 1891–1896.

Frazer, George. *The Illustrated Golden Bough.* Abridged by Robert K. G. Temple. New York: Simon & Schuster, 1996.

Frazier, E. Franklin. *The Negro Church in America.* New York: Schocken, 1964.

Furley, Oliver W. "Moravian Missionaries and Slaves in the West Indies." *Caribbean Studies* 5 (July 1965): 3–16.

Gardner, William James. *A History of Jamaica from Its Discovery by Christopher Columbus to the Year 1872.* London: Fisher Unwin, 1909. First published in 1873.

Gebara, Ivone. *Mary, Mother of God, Mother of the Poor.* Maryknoll, NY: Orbis, 1989.

Gilkes, Cheryl Townsend. "The Role of Women in the Sanctified Church." *Journal of Religious Thought* 2, no. 1 (Spring 1986): 41–59.

Glazier, Stephen. *Marchin' the Pilgrims Home: Leadership and Decision-Making in an Afro-Caribbean Faith*. Westport, CT: Greenwood, 1984.

Glennie, Alexander. *Sermons Preached on Plantations to Congregations of Negroes*. 1844. Reprint, New York: Books for Libraries Press/Black Heritage Library, 1971.

Gloss, Linda, and Clay Gloss, eds. *Jump Up and Say! A Collection of Black Storytelling*. New York: Simon and Schuster, 1995.

Goldenberg, David. *The Curse of Ham: Race and Slavery in Early Judaism, Christianity, and Islam*. Princeton, NJ: Princeton University Press, 2003.

Gordon, Shirley. *God Almighty Make Me Free: Christianity in PreEmancipation Jamaica*. Bloomington: Indiana University Press, 1996.

Goveia, Elsa V. *Slave Society in the British Leeward Islands at the End of the Eighteenth Century*. New Haven, CT: Yale University Press, 1965.

Grant, Jacquelyn. *White Women's Christ and Black Women's Jesus: Feminist Christology and Womanist Response*. Atlanta, GA: Scholars, 1989.

———. "Womanist Theology: Black Women's Experience as a Source for Doing Theology, with Special Reference to Christology." In *Black Theology: A Documentary History*. Vol. 2: *1980–1992*, ed. Gayraud S. Wilmore and James H. Cone, 273–289. Maryknoll, NY: Orbis, 1993.

Guano, Emanuela. "Revival Zion: An Afro-Christian Religion in Jamaica." *Anthropos* 89, nos. 4–6 (1994): 517–528.

Gutiérrez, Gustavo. *A Theology of Liberation: History, Politics and Salvation*. Maryknoll, NY: Orbis, 1988. Originally published in English by Orbis, 1973.

Gyekye, Kwame. *An Essay on African Philosophical Thought: The Akan Conceptual Scheme*. Philadelphia: Temple University Press, 1995.

Hackett, Rosalind. "Revitalization in African Traditional Religion." In *African Traditional Religions in Contemporary Society*, ed. Jacob Olupona, 135–148. St. Paul, MN: Paragon House, 1991.

Hall, David. *Worlds of Wonder, Days of Judgment: Popular Religious Belief in Early New England*. Cambridge: Harvard University Press, 1990.

Hall, David, ed. *Lived Religion in America: Toward a History of Practice*. Princeton, NJ: Princeton University Press, 1997.

Hall, Douglas. *In Miserable Slavery: Thomas Thistlewood in Jamaica, 1750–86*. Barbados: University of the West Indies Press, 1999.

Ham, Adolpho. "A Dialogue between the Theology of Liberation and the Caribbean Black Theology." In *Looking at the Theology of Liberation Together: An Ecumenical Reflection within the Caribbean: March 6–9, 1991*, ed. Burchell Taylor, 35–46. Kingston: Jamaica Council of Churches, 1991.

Hamilton, Grace. "The History of Jamaican Revival Religion." Unpublished paper. Kingston: African-Caribbean Institute of Jamaica, 1959.

Harding, Vincent. *There Is a River: The Black Struggle for Freedom in America*. New York: Vintage, 1983.

Hark, Walter. *The Breaking of the Dawn; or, Moravian Work in Jamaica*. London: Strain, 1904.

Hart, Richard. *Slaves Who Abolished Slavery*. Kingston, Jamaica: Institute of Social and Economic Research, UWI, 1985.

Haskins, C. H. *The Renaissance of the 12th Century*. Cleveland, OH: World, 1970.

Hennelly, Alfred T., ed. *Liberation Theology: A Documentary History*. Maryknoll, NY: Orbis, 1995.

Herskovits, Melville. *Dahomey: An Ancient West African Kingdom.* Vol. 1. New York: J. J. Augustin, 1938.

———. *Dahomey: An Ancient West African Kingdom.* Vol. 2. Evanston, IL: Northwestern University Press, 1967.

———. *The Myth of the Negro Past.* 1941. Reprint, Boston: Beacon, 1990.

———. "Problem, Method and Theory in Afroamerican studies." *Afroamérica* 1 (1945): 5–24.

Heywood, Linda, ed. *Central Africans and Cultural Transformation in the American Diaspora.* Cambridge: Cambridge University Press, 2002.

Hill, Robert. "Leonard P. Howell and Millenarian Visions in Early Rastafari," *Jamaica Journal* 16, no. 1 (1983): 24–39.

Hogg, Donald. "The Convince Cult in Jamaica." *Papers in Caribbean Anthropology* 58, ed. S. Mintz. New Haven, CT: Yale University Publications in Anthropology, 1960.

Hood, Robert. *Begrimed and Black: Christian Traditions on Blacks and Blackness.* Minneapolis, MN: Fortress, 1994.

Hopkins, Dwight N., and George Cummings. *Cut Loose Your Stammering Tongue: Black Theology in the Slave Narratives.* Maryknoll, NY: Orbis, 1991.

Hopper, Jeffery. *Understanding Modern Theology I: Cultural Revolutions and New Worlds.* Philadelphia: Fortress, 1987.

Horton, Robin. *Patterns of Thought in Africa and the West.* Cambridge: Cambridge University Press, 1993.

Houk, James. *Spirits, Blood, and Drums: The Orisha Religion in Trinidad.* Philadelphia: Temple University Press, 1995.

Hurston, Zora Neale. *Jonah's Gourd Vine.* Thorndike, ME: G. K. Hall, 1998.

———. *The Sanctified Church.* Berkeley: Turtle Island Foundation, 1981.

———. *Tell My Horse.* Berkeley: Turtle Island for the Netzahualcoyotl Historical Society, 1983.

———. *Voodoo Gods: An Inquiry into Native Myths and Magic in Jamaica and Haiti.* London: Dent, 1939.

Hutton, Clinton, and Nathaniel Samuel Murrell. "Rastas' Psychology of Blackness, Resistance, and Somebodiness." In *Chanting Down Babylon: The Rastafari Reader,* ed. Nathaniel Samuel Murrell, William David Spencer, and Anthony Adrian McFarlane, 36–54. Philadelphia: Temple University Press, 1998.

Idowu, E. Bolaji. *African Traditional Religion.* London: Sem, 1973.

———. *Olodumare, God in Yoruba Belief.* London: Longmans, Green, 1962.

Inkori, J. E. *Forced Migration: The Impact of the Export Slave Trade on African Societies.* London: Hutchinson, 1982.

Irarranzaval, Diego. "How Is Theology Done in Latin America?" *Voices from the Third World.* 18, no. 1 (June 1995): 59–78.

Isasi-Diaz, Ada Maria. *En la Lucha (In the Struggle): A Hispanic Women's Liberation Theology.* Minneapolis, MN: Fortress, 1993.

James, C. L. R. *The Black Jacobins.* New York: Vintage, 1963.

Janzen, John, and Wyatt MacGaffey. *An Anthology of Kongo Religion: Primary Texts from Lower Zaire.* Lawrence: University of Kansas Press, 1974.

Jesse, C. "The Papal Bull of 1493 Appointing the First Vicar Apostolic in the New World." *Caribbean Quarterly* 11, nos. 3–4 (September–December 1965): 62–71.

Johnson, Clifton, H. *God Struck Me Dead: Voices of Ex-Slaves.* Cleveland: Pilgrim, 1993.

Jones, William. *Is God a White Racist? A Preamble to Black Theology*. New York: Anchor, 1973.

Jordan, Winthrop. *White over Black: American Attitudes toward the Negro, 1550–1812*. Baltimore, MD: Penguin, 1969.

Kamalu, Chukwunyere. *Foundations of African Thought: A Worldview Grounded in the African Heritage of Religion, Philosophy, Science and Art*. London: Karnak, 1990.

Karp, Ivan, and Lavine, Stephen D., eds. *Exhibiting Cultures: The Poetics and Politics of Museum Display*. Washington, DC: Smithsonian Institution Press, 1991.

Kaufman, Gordon D. *An Essay on Theological Method*. Atlanta, GA: Scholars, 1975.

Kelly, J. *Voyage to Jamaica and Narrative of 17 Years Residence in That Island*. Belfast, Ireland: Wilson, 1838.

Kerr, Madeline. *Personality and Conflict in Jamaica*. Liverpool, England: University Press, 1952.

Kitzinger, Sheila. "Protest and Mysticism: The Ras Tafari Cult of Jamaica." *Journal for the Scientific Study of Religions* 8 (Fall 1969): 247–255.

Knitter, Paul. *No Other Name? A Critical Survey of Christian Attitudes toward the World Religions*. Maryknoll, NY: Orbis, 1990.

The Koromantyn Slaves or West Indian Sketches. London: J. Hatchard and Son, Piccadilly, 1823.

Küng, Hans. *Christianity and the World Religions: Paths of Dialogue with Islam, Hinduism, and Buddhism*. New York: Collins and Doubleday, 1986.

———. "No World Peace without Religious Peace." In *Christianity and the World Religions: Paths of Dialogue with Islam, Hinduism, and Buddhism*, ed. Hans Küng et al., 440–443. New York: Collins and Doubleday, 1986.

Laguerre, Michel S. *Voodoo and Politics in Haiti*. New York: St. Martin's, 1989.

Lamb, David. *The Africans*. New York: Vintage, 1987.

Lamming, George. *Season of Adventure*. London: Allison and Busby, 1979.

——— ed., *Enterprise of the Indies*. Port of Spain, Trinidad: The Trinidad and Tobago Institute of the West Indies, 1999.

Latortue, Gerard R. "The European Lands." In *The United States and the Caribbean*, ed. Tad Szulc, 173–190. New York: American Assembly Service, 1971.

The Laws of Jamaica, Passed by the Assembly. London: Hills for Harper, 1683.

Leslie, Charles. *A New History of Jamaica: From the Earliest Accounts to the Taking of Porto Bello by Vice-Admiral Vernon*. London: Hodges, 1740.

Levine, Lawrence. *Black Culture, Black Consciousness: Afro-American Folk Thought from Slavery to Freedom*. Oxford: Oxford University Press, 1977.

Lewin, Olive. *Rock It Come Over: The Folk Music of Jamaica*. Barbados: University of the West Indies Press, 2000.

Lewis, Gordon. *Main Currents in Caribbean Thought: The Historical Evolution of Caribbean Society in Its Ideological Aspects, 1492–1900*. Baltimore, MD: Johns Hopkins University Press, 1983.

Lewis, Matthew. *Journal of a West Indian Proprietor, Kept during a Residence in the Island of Jamaica*. London: Murray, 1834.

Lewis, Rupert. "Marcus Garvey and the Early Rastafarians: Continuity and Discontinuity." In *Chanting Down Babylon: The Rastafari Reader*, ed. Nathaniel Samuel Murrell, William David Spencer, and Anthony Adrian McFarlane, 145–158. Philadelphia: Temple University Press, 1998.

Long, Charles. *Significations: Signs, Symbols, and Images in the Interpretation of Religion*. Philadelphia: Fortress, 1986.

Long, Edward. *The History of Jamaica*. London: F. Cass, 1970 (1774).

Long, Charles. *Significations: Signs, Symbols, and Images in the Interpretation of Religion*. Philadelphia: Fortress, 1986.

MacGaffey, Wyatt. *Art and Healing of the BaKongo Commented by Themselves: Minkisi from the Laman Collection*. Bloomington: Indiana University Press, 1991.

Magesa, Laurenti. *African Religion: The Moral Traditions of Abundant Life*. Maryknoll, NY: Orbis, 1997.

Maimela, Simon, ed. *Culture, Religion, and Liberation: Proceedings of the EATWOT Pan-African Theological Conference, Harare, Zimbabwe, January 6–11, 1991*. Pretoria, South Africa: Penrose Book Printers, 1994.

Malden, K. S. *Broken Bonds: The S.P.G. and the West Indian Slaves*. Aberdeen, Scotland: Aberdeen University Press, 1933.

Mannix, Daniel P., and Malcolm Cowley. *Black Cargoes: A History of the Atlantic Slave Trade, 1518–1865*. New York: Viking, 1965.

Marley, Robert. "Get Up, Stand Up." Burnin' Island Records, 1973.

———. "Survival." *Songs of Freedom*. Island Records, 1979.

———. "Time Will Tell." *Bob Marley, Songs of Freedom*. Island Records, 1992. Originally released on *Kaya*, 1978.

Marsden, Peter. *An Account of the Island of Jamaica*. Newcastle, England: Hodgson, 1788.

Martey, Emmanuel. *African Theology: Inculturation and Liberation*. Maryknoll, NY: Orbis, 1993.

Mason, John. *Black Gods: Orisa Studies in the New World*. Brooklyn, NY: Yoruba Theological Archministry, 1985.

Matthews, Donald. *Honoring the Ancestors: An African Cultural Interpretation of Black Religion and Literature*. New York: Oxford University Press, 1998.

Mays, Benjamin E. *The Negro's God*. Boston: Chapman and Grimes, 1938.

Mbiti, John S. *African Religions and Philosophy*. London: Heinemann, 1969.

———. *Introduction to African Religion*. London: Heinemann, 1975.

McLarty, Robert. "Jamaica Prepares for Invasion, 1779." *Caribbean Quarterly* 4, no. 1 (January 1955): 62–67.

Mesters, Carlos. *Defenseless Flower: A New Reading of the Bible*. Maryknoll, NY: Orbis, 1989.

Métraux, Alfred. *Voodoo in Haiti*. New York: Shocken, 1972.

Metuh, Emefie Ikenga. *God and Man in African Religion: A Case of the Igbo of Nigeria*. London: Chapman, 1981.

Mintz, Sidney W. *Caribbean Transformations*. 2d ed. New York: Columbia University Press, 1989.

Mintz, Sidney, ed. *Papers in Caribbean Anthropology*. New Haven, CT: Yale University Department of Anthropology, 1960. Yale University publications in Anthropology series.

Mintz, Sidney W., and Richard Price. *An Anthropological Approach to the Afro-American Past: A Caribbean Perspective*. Philadelphia: Institute for the Study of Human Issues, 1976.

———. *The Birth of African-American Culture: An Anthropological Perspective*. Boston: Beacon, 1976.

Mitchell, Henry H. *Black Belief: Folk Beliefs of Blacks in America and West Africa*. New York: Harper & Row, 1975.

Moore, Joseph. "Religion of Jamaican Negroes: A Study of Afro-American Acculturation." Ann Arbor: University Microfilm Publication 7053, Doctoral Dissertation Series, 1953.

Moses, Wilson. *The Golden Age of Black Nationalism, 1850–1925.* New York: Oxford University Press, 1978.

Mowatt, Judy. "Only a Woman." *Only a Woman.* Shanachie Records, 1988.

Mudimbe, V. Y. *The Idea of Africa.* Bloomington: Indiana University Press, 1994.

———. *The Invention of Africa.* Bloomington: Indiana University Press, 1988.

Muldoon, James. *The Expansion of Europe.* Philadelphia: University of Pennsylvania Press, 1977.

Mulrain, George. Introduction to *At the Crossroads: African Caribbean Religion and Christianity,* ed. Burton Sankeralli, 1–4. St. James, Trinidad: Caribbean Conference of Churches, 1994.

Murphy, Joseph. *Working the Spirit: Ceremonies of the African Diaspora.* Boston: Beacon, 1994.

Murrell, Nathaniel, et al. *Chanting Down Babylon: The Rastafari Reader.* Philadelphia: Temple University Press, 1998.

Murrell, Nathaniel Samuel, and Burchell K. Taylor. "Rastafari's Messianic Ideology and Caribbean Theology of Liberation." In *Chanting Down Babylon,* ed. Nathaniel Samuel Murrell, William David Spencer, and Anthony Adrian McFarlane, 390–411. Philadelphia: Temple University Press, 1998.

Mveng, Englebert. "Third World Theology—What Theology? What Third World? Evaluation by an African Delegate." In *Irruption of the Third World: Challenge to Theology,* ed. Virginia Fabella and Sergio Torres, 217–221. Maryknoll, NY: Orbis, 1983.

Nettleford, Rex. "Discourse on Rastafarian Reality." In *Chanting Down Babylon,* ed. Nathaniel Samuel Murrell, William David Spencer, and Anthony Adrian McFarlane, 311–325. Philadelphia: Temple University Press, 1998.

———. *Inward Stretch, Outward Reach: A Voice from the Caribbean.* London: Macmillan, 1993.

The New Revised Standard Version of the Holy Bible. New York: Oxford University Press, 1989.

Nwala, T. Uzodinma. *Igbo Philosophy.* Vol. 1. Lagos: Literamed, 1985.

Oduyoye, Mercy Amba. "Reflections from a Third World Woman's Perspective: Women's Experience and Liberation Theologies." In *Irruption of the Third World: Challenge to Theology,* ed. Virginia Fabella and Sergio Torres, 246–255. Maryknoll, NY: Orbis, 1983.

———. *Who Will Roll the Stone Away? The Ecumenical Decade of the Churches in Solidarity with Women.* Geneva: WCC Publications, 1990.

Oduyoye, Mercy Amba, and Roina Fa'atauva'a'. "The Struggle about Women's Theological Education." In *Feminist Theology from the Third World: A Reader,* ed. Ursula King, 170–175. Maryknoll, NY: Orbis, 1994.

Ogbonnaya, Okechukwu. *On Communitarian Divinity.* New York: Paragon House, 1994.

Oliver, Paul. *Blues Fell This Morning: The Meaning of the Blues.* New York: Cambridge University Press, 1990.

Olupona, Jacob. "Major Issues in the Study of African Traditional Religion." In *African Traditional Religions in Contemporary Society,* ed. Jacob Olupona, 25–33. St. Paul, MN: Paragon House, 1991.

Oluwole, Sophie B. *Witchcraft Reincarnation and the God-Head: Issues in African Philosophy.* Lagos: Excel, 1992.

O'Meara, P., and P. Martin, eds., *Africa*. Bloomington: Indiana University Press, 1986.

Onyeneke, Augustine. *The Dead among the Living: Masquerades in Igbo Society*. Nimo, Nigeria: Holy Ghost Congregation and Asele Institute, 1987.

Origen. *The Song of Songs: Commentary and Homilies*. Trans. R. P. Lawson. London: Longman, 1958.

Orsi, Robert. *Gods of the City: Religion and the American Urban Landscape*. Bloomington: Indiana University Press, 1999.

——. *The Madonna of 115th Street: Faith and Community in Italian Harlem, 1880–1950*. New Haven: Yale University Press, 1985.

——. *Thank You St. Jude: Women's Devotion to the Patron Saint of Hopeless Causes*. New Haven: Yale University Press, 1996.

Ottenberg, Simon, ed. *African Religious Groups and Beliefs: Papers in Honor of William R. Bascom*. Meerus, India: Archana, 1982.

Outlaw, Lucius. "Language and Consciousness: Toward a Hermeneutic of Black Culture." *Cultural Hermeneutics* 1 (1974): 403–413.

Parry, J. H., and P. M. Sherlock. *A Short History of the West Indies*. London: Macmillan, 1956.

Patterson, Orlando. "Slavery and Slave Revolts: A Socio-Historical Analysis of the First Maroon War, Jamaica, 1655–1740." *Social and Economic Studies* 19 (1970): 289–325.

——. *Slavery and Social Death: A Comparative Studiy*. Cambridge, MA: Harvard University Press, 1982.

——. *The Sociology of Slavery: An Analysis of the Origins, Development and Structure of Negro Slave Society in Jamaica*. Teaneck, NJ: Fairleigh Dickinson University Press, 1975.

Payne, Daniel. *History of the African Methodist Episcopal Church*. New York: Arno, 1969.

Payne, Ernest A. *Freedom in Jamaica: Some Chapters in the Story of the Baptist Missionary Society*. London: Carey, 1933.

Pescatello, Anna. *Old Roots in New Lands: Historical and Anthropological Perspectives on Black Experiences in the Americas*. Westport, CT: Greenwood, 1977.

Peterson, Thomas Virgil. *Ham and Japheth: The Mythic World of Whites in the Antebellum South*. Metuchen, NJ: Scarecrow, 1978.

Phillippo, James M. *Jamaica: Its Past and Present State*. Westport, CT: Negro University Press, 1970 (1843).

Pinn, Anthony. *Why Lord? Suffering and Evil in Black Theology*. New York: Continuum, 1995.

Pliny. *Natural History*. Trans. H. Rackham. Bk. VI, vol. 2. London: Heinemann, 1947.

Pobee, John S., and B. von Wartenberg Potter, eds. *New Eyes for Reading: Biblical and Theological Reflection by Women from the Third World*. Geneva: WCC, 1986.

Price, Richard, ed. *Maroon Societies: Rebel Slave Communities in the Americas*. 2d ed. Baltimore, MD: Johns Hopkins University Press, 1979.

Raboteau, Albert. *Slave Religion: The "Invisible Institution" in the Antebellum South*. New York: Oxford University Press, 1978.

Ramsay, James. *An Essay on the Treatment and Conversion of African Slaves in the British Sugar Colonies*. London: Phillips, 1784.

Ranger, Terence O. "Recent Development in the Study of African Religious and Cultural History and Their Relevance for the Historiography of the Diaspora." *Ufahamu* 4 (1973): 17–34.

Rattray, R. S. *Religion and Art in Ashanti*. Oxford: Clarendon, 1927.

Ray, Benjamin. *African Religions: Symbol, Ritual and Community.* Englewood Cliffs, NJ: Prentice Hall, 1976.

Religious Tract Society. *Missionary Records: West Indies.* London: Religous Tract Society, 1834–1838.

Richard, Pablo. "Liberation Theology in Latin America in Dialogue with Theologians from Africa, Asia and the Minorities in the United States." *Voice from the Third World* 18, no. 2 (December 1995): 38–45.

Ricoeur, Paul. *Freud and Philosophy: An Essay on Interpretation.* New Haven, CT: Yale University Press, 1970.

———. *Interpretation Theory: Discourse and the Surplus of Meaning.* Fort Worth: Texas Christian University Press, 1976.

Rodney, Walter. *How Europe Underdeveloped Africa.* Washington, DC: Howard University Press, 1982.

Rose, G. H. *A Letter on the Means and Importance of Converting the Slaves in the West Indies to Christianity.* London: Murray, 1823.

Rowe, Maureen. "The Woman in Rastafari." In Rex Nettleford, ed., *Caribbean Quarterly Mongraph: Rastafari,* 13–. Kingston, Jamaica Caribbean Quarterly, University of the West Indies, 1985.

Sadler, Kim Martin, ed. *Atonement: The Million Man March.* Cleveland, OH: Pilgrim, 1996.

Samuel, Peter. *The Wesleyan-Methodist Missions in Jamaica and Honduras.* London: Partridge and Oakley, 1850.

Sanders, Cheryl, ed. *Living the Intersection: Womanism and Afrocentrism in Theology.* Minneapolis, MN: Fortress, 1995.

Sankeralli, Burton, ed. *At the Crossroads: African Caribbean Religion and Christianity.* Trinidad and Tobago: Caribbean Conference of Churches, 1995.

Schuler, Monica. "Afro-American Slave Culture." In *Roots and Branches: Current Directions in Slave Studies,* ed. Michael Craton, 121–155. Toronto: Pergamon Press, 1979.

———. "Akan Slave Rebellions in the British Caribbean." *Savacou* 1 (June 1970): 8–31.

———. *"Alas, Alas, Kongo": A Social History of Indentured African Immigration into Jamaica, 1841–1865.* Baltimore, MD: Johns Hopkins University Press, 1980.

———. "The Experience of African Immigrants in 19th Century Jamaica." Unpublished manuscript, 1972.

———. "Myalism and the African Religious Tradition." In *Africa and the Caribbean: The Legacies of a Link,* ed. Margaret Crahan and Franklin Knight, 150–155. Baltimore: Johns Hopkins University Press, 1979.

———. "Myalism and the African Religious Tradition in Jamaica." In *Caribbean Slave Society and Economy: A Student Reader,* ed. Hilary Beckles and Verene Shepherd, 295–303. Kingston and London: Randle and Currey Publishers, 1991.

———. " 'Yerri, Yerri, Koongo': A Social History of Liberated African Immigration into Jamaica, 1941–1867." Ph.D. diss., University of Wisconsin, Madison, 1977.

Seaga, Edward. "Revival Cults in Jamaica." *Jamaica Journal* 3, no. 2 (June 1969): 1–12.

Segundo, Juan Luis. *The Liberation of Theology.* Maryknoll, NY: Orbis, 1991.

Sharpe, Eric. *Comparative Religion: A History.* La Salle, IL: Open Court, 1990.

Short, K. R. M. "Jamaican Christian Missions and the Great Slave Rebellion of 1831–32." *Journal of Ecclesiastical History* 27 (January 1976): 57–72.

Simpson, George. *Black Religions in the New World.* New York: Columbia University Press, 1978.

_____. "Culture Change and Reintegration Found in the Cults of West Kingston, Jamaica." *Proceedings of the American Philosophical Society* 99, no. 2 (April 15, 1955): 89–92.

_____. *Religious Cults in the Caribbean: Jamaica, Trinidad and Haiti.* Rio Piedras: Institute of Caribbean Studies, University of Puerto Rico, 1970.

Sloane, Hans. *A Voyage to the Islands Madera, Barbados, Nieves, St. Christophers and Jamaica.* Vol. 1. London: Printed by B. M. for the author, 1707–1725.

Smith, Ashley. *Real Roots and Potted Plants: Reflections on the Caribbean Church.* Mandeville, Jamaica; Eureka, 1984.

_____. "The Religious Significance of Black Power." In *Troubling the Waters*, ed. Idris Hamid, 83–107. San Fernando, Trinidad: Rahaman, 1973.

Smith, Jonathan Z. *Imagining Religion: From Babylon to Jonestown.* Chicago: University of Chicago Press, 1982.

Smith, Robert W. "Slavery and Christianity in the West Indies." *Church History* 19 (September 1950): 173–186.

Smith, Theophus. *Conjuring Culture: Biblical Formations of Black America.* New York: Oxford University Press, 1994.

Smith, Wilfred Cantwell. "Comparative Religion: Whither—and Why?" In *The History of Religions: Essays in Methodology*, ed. Mircea Eliade and Joseph Kitagawa, 37–38. Chicago: University of Chicago Press, 1959.

_____. *Towards a World Theology: Faith and the Comparative History of Religion.* Maryknoll, NY: Orbis, 1981.

Somé, Patrice Malidoma. *The Healing Wisdom of Africa: Finding Life Purpose Through Nature, Ritual and Community.* New York: Jeremy P. Tarcher/Putnam, 1998.

_____. *Of Water and the Spirit: Ritual Magic and Initiation in the Life of an Africa Shaman.* New York: Putnam, 1994.

Stennette, Lloyd, Mauro Batista, and Barry Chevannes. "The Situation of the Black Race in Latin America and the Caribbean." In *The Challenge of Basic Christian Communities*, ed. John Eagleson and Sergio Torres, 46–50. Maryknoll; NY: Orbis, 1981.

Stewart, Dianne M. "African-Derived Religions in Jamaica." In *Encyclopedia of African and African-American Religions*, ed. Stephen Glazier, 165–169. New York: Routledge, 2001.

_____. "Womanist Theology in the Caribbean Context: Critiquing Culture, Rethinking Doctrine and Expanding Boundaries." *Journal of Feminist Studies in Religion* 20, no. 1 (Spring 2004): 61–82.

Stewart, J. A. *A View of the Past and Present State of the Island of Jamaica.* Edinburgh: Oliver and Boyd, 1823.

Stuckey, Sterling. *Slave Culture: Nationalist Theory and the Foundations of Black America.* New York: Oxford University Press, 1987.

Tafari-Ama, Imani. "Rastawoman as Rebel: Case Studies in Jamaica." In *Chanting Down Babylon: The Rastafari Reader*, ed. Nathaniel S. Murrell et al. Philadelphia, PA: Temple University Press, 1998.

Tallant, Robert. *Voodoo in New Orleans.* New York: Collier, 1962.

Tamez, Elsa. "Cultural Violence against Women in Latin America." *Voices from the Third World* 18, no. 2 (December 1995): 177–191.

Tamez, Elsa, ed. *Through Her Eyes: Women's Theology from Latin America.* Maryknoll, NY: Orbis, 1989.

Tanna, Laura. *Jamaican Folk Tales and Oral Histories.* Kingston: Institute of Jamaica Publications, 1984.

Terrell, JoAnne. *Power in the Blood? The Cross in the African American Experience*. Maryknoll, NY: Orbis, 1998.

Thornton, John. "Religious and Ceremonial Life in the Kongo and Mbundu Areas, 1500–1700." In *Central Africans and Cultural Transformations in the American Diaspora*, ed. Linda Heywood, 71–90. Cambridge: Cambridge University Press, 2002.

Thompson, Alvin. "Race and Colour Prejudices and the Origin of the Transatlantic Slave Trade." *Caribbean Studies* 16, nos. 3–4 (1976–1977): 29–59.

Thompson, Robert Farris. *Flash of the Spirit: African and Afro-American Art and Philosophy*. New York: Random House, 1983.

Tillich, Paul. *Systematic Theology*. Vol. 1. Chicago: University of Chicago Press, 1951.

Turner, Mary. *Slaves and Missionaries: The Disintegration of Jamaican Slave Society, 1787–1834*. Urbana: University of Illinois Press, 1982.

Umeh, John Anenechukwu. *After God Is Dibia: Igbo Cosmology, Divination & Sacred Science in Nigeria*. London: Karnak House, 1997.

van Nieuwenhove, Jacques, and Berma Klein Goldewijk, eds. *Popular Religion, Liberation and Contextual Theology*. Trans. Irene Bouman-Smith. Kampen, Netherlands: Uitgeversmaatschappij J. H. Kok, 1991.

Van Wing, Joseph. *Études Bakongo: Sociologie, religion et magie*. Bruges: Desclée, De Brouwer, 1959.

von Herder, Johann Gottfried. *Ideas on the Philosophy of the History of Mankind*. Trans. T. Churchill. New York: Bergman, 1800.

Waddell, Hope. *Twenty-nine Years in the West Indies and Central Africa, 1829–1858*. London: F. Cass, 1970 (1863).

Walker, Alice. *Anything We Love Can Be Saved: A Writer's Activism*. New York: Random House, 1997.

——. *The Color Purple*. New York: Pocket, 1982.

——. *In Search of Our Mothers' Gardens: Womanist Prose*. San Diego, CA: Harcourt Brace Jovanovich, 1983.

Walker, Sheila S. *Ceremonial Spirit Possession in Africa and Afro-America: Forms, Meanings, and Functional Significance for Individuals and Social Groups*. Leiden: Brill, 1972.

Walvin, James. *The Black Presence in England: A Documentary History of the Negro in England, 1555–1860*. London: Orbach and Chambers, 1971.

Ward, Edward. *A Trip to Jamaica: With a True Character of the People of the Island*. London: J. How, 1700. First printed in 1698.

Warner-Lewis, Maureen. "The Ancestral Factor in Jamaica's African Religions." In *African Creative Expressions of the Divine*, ed. Kortright Davis and Elias Farajaje Jones, 63–80. Washington, DC: Howard University School of Divinity, 1991.

——. *Central Africa in the Caribbean: Transcending Time, Transforming Culture*. Barbados: University of the West Indies Press, 2003.

——. *E. Kamau Brathwaite's Masks: Essays and Annotations*. Kingston: Institute of Caribbean Studies, 1992.

——. "The Nkuyu: Spirit Messengers of the Kumina." Kingston, Jamaica: Savacou, 1977.

Washington, James. *Frustrated Fellowship: The Black Baptist Quest for Social Power*. Macon, GA: Mercer University Press, 1986.

Wedenoja, William. "The Origins of Revival, a Creole Religion in Jamaica." In *Culture and Christianity: The Dialectics of Transformation*, ed. George Saunders, 91–116. Westport, CT: Greenwood, 1988.

West, Cornell. *Prophesy Deliverance! An Afro-American Revolutionary Christianity*. Philadelphia: Westminster, 1982.

Whiteley, Henry. *Three Months in Jamaica in 1832: Comprising a Residence of Seven Weeks on a Sugar-Plantation*. London: Hatcliard, 1833.

Willett, Frank. *African Art: An Introduction*. New York: Thames and Hudson, 1993.

Williams, Cynric. *Tour through the Island of Jamaica*. London: Printed for Hunt and Clarke by C. H. Reynell, 1826.

Williams, Delores S. *Sisters in the Wilderness: The Challenge of Womanist God-Talk*. Maryknoll, NY: Orbis, 1993.

————. "Womanist Theology: Black Women's Voices." In *Black Theology: A Documentary History*. Vol. 2: *1980–1992*, ed. Gayraud S. Wilmore and James Cone, 265–272. Maryknoll, NY: Orbis, 1993.

Williams, Eric. *British Historians and the West Indies*. New York: Africana, 1972.

————. *Capitalism and Slavery*. Chapel Hill: University of North Carolina Press, 1944.

————. "Caribbean Slavery and the Capitalist Economy." In *Caribbean Slave Society and Economy: A Student Reader*, ed. Hilary Beckles and Verene Shepherd, 120–129. Kingston, Jamaica: Randle, 1991.

Williams, Joseph J. *Voodoos and Obeahs: Phases of West India Witchcraft*. New York: Dial, 1932.

Williams, Lewin. *The Caribbean: Enculturation, Acculturation and the Role of the Churches*. Geneva: WCC Publications, 1996.

————. *Caribbean Theology*. New York: Lang, 1994.

Wilmore, Gayraud S. *Black Religion and Black Radicalism: An Interpretation of the Religious History of Afro-American People*. Maryknoll, NY: Orbis, 1983.

Wilmore, Gayraud S., and James Cone, eds. *Black Theology: A Documentary History*. Vol. 1: *1966–1979*. Maryknoll, NY: Orbis, 1979.

Wilson-Tagoe, Nana. *Historical Thought and the Literary Representation in West Indian Literature*. Gainesville, FL: University Press of Florida, 1998.

Witvliet, Theo. *A Place in the Sun: An Introduction to Liberation Theology in the Third World*. Maryknoll, NY: Orbis, 1985.

————. *The Way of the Black Messiah*. Trans. John Bowden. Oak Park, IL: Meyerstone, 1987.

Young, Josiah U. *A Pan-African Theology: Providence and the Legacies of the Ancestors*. Trenton, NJ: Africa World, 1992.

————. "God's Path and Pan-Africa." In *Black Theology: A Documentary History*. Vol. 2: *1980–1992*, ed. Gayraud S. Wilmore and James Cone, 18–25. Maryknoll, NY: Orbis, 1993.

Zahan, Dominique. *The Religion, Spirituality, and Thought of Traditional Africa*. Chicago: University of Chicago Press, 1979.

Index

Italicized page numbers refer to maps and tables.

Abdimelech, 72
abeng, 91, 266n3
Abeokuta village, 141, 180
Abimbola, Wande, 268n21
abolitionist movement, 18, 23, 79, 98, 100
  anti-Africanness and, 74, 76
  Kumina and, 146
  missionary views on, 82–84, 263–64n48, 264–65nn54–55
  Native Baptists and, 103, 105
absenteeism, 18, 248n26
Abyssinia, 120–21, 134, 136, 275n134
Accompong, 59
acculturation, 225, 289–90n86
acephalous movement, 122
addictive habits, 96, 268n16
aesthetic meaning of masking, 184–87, 221–22, 285n149, 291n112
aesthetics, 218, 290n93
Africa, *xxvi*
African-American missionaries, 11, 34, 92, 101–2, 105, 128, 270n33
African Caribbean Institute of Jamaica (ACIJ), 176, 179, 282n106
African cross, 158, 162, 164, 168
African identity, 143–45, 147–48, 277nn19–20

African Other, 11, 25, 34, 69–70, 88, 266n76
Afro-Baptists. *See* Native Baptists
Afrocentricity, 198–200
"Afro-Christian" religion. *See* Revival Zion
Afrophobia, 43–44, 61, 255n99, 255n102
  African religious heritage as scapegoat and, 177, 179–80
  anthropological poverty and, 172
  Black anti-Africanness and, 185, 285n145
  Black Jamaican struggles for freedom and, 116–17, 127, 171
  Caribbean theology and, 189, 202, 205, 214, 228–29, 231
  Christianity and, 58, 101, 169
  colonialism and, 11, 58
  in European imagination, 69–76
  womanist theology and, 201
afterlife, 32–33, 60–61, 67, 83, 86, 92, 96, 125–26, 261n164, 265n55
agency
  African-derived religions and, 171–72
  Caribbean theology and, 203